THE ECONOMICS AND MANAGEMENT OF INVENTORIES

PART B
INVENTORY MANAGEMENT

MATHEMATICAL MODELS OF INVENTORIES

STUDIES IN PRODUCTION AND ENGINEERING ECONOMICS

Edited by Professor R.W. Grubbström, Department of Production Economics, Linköping Institute of Technology, S-581 82 Linköping, Sweden.

Vol. 1 Production Control and Information Systems for Component-Manufacturing Shops (Bertrand and Wortmann).

Vol. 2 The Economics and Management of Inventories. Proceedings of the First International Symposium on Inventories, Budapest, September 1—5, 1980. Part A: Inventories in the National Economy. Part B: Inventory Management; Mathematical Models of Inventories (Chikán, Editor).

In preparation
Towards a Theoretical Basis for Energy Economics (Grubbström).

Studies in Production and Engineering Economics, 2B

THE ECONOMICS AND MANAGEMENT OF INVENTORIES

Edited by
ATTILA CHIKÁN

Karl Marx University of Economics
Budapest, Hungary

PART B
INVENTORY MANAGEMENT

MATHEMATICAL MODELS OF INVENTORIES

ELSEVIER SCIENTIFIC PUBLISHING COMPANY
Amsterdam — Oxford — New York 1981

The distribution of this book is being handled by the following publishers

658.787
E19

for the USA and Canada
Elsevier North-Holland, Inc.
52 Vanderbilt Avenue
New York, New York 10017, USA

for the East European countries, Democratic People's Republic of Korea, People's Republic of China, People's Republic of Mongolia, Republic of Cuba, and Socialist Republic of Vietnam
Akadémiai Kiadó, The Publishing House of the Hungarian Academy of Sciences, Budapest, Hungary

for all remaining areas
Elsevier Scientific Publishing Company
Molenwerf 1,
1014 AG Amsterdam, The Netherlands

Library of Congress Cataloging in Publication Data

Main entry under title:
The Economics and Management of Inventories.

(Studies in production and engineering economics; 2A—B)
Papers presented at the First International Symposium on Inventories, held in Budapest, Sept. 1–5, 1980, and sponsored by the Hungarian Academy of Sciences.
Bibliography: p.
Includes index.
Contents: pt. A. Inventories in the national economy — pt. B. Inventory management, mathematical models of inventories.
1. Inventories — Congresses. 2. Inventory-control — Congresses. I. Chikán, Attila. II. International Symposium on Inventories (1st: 1980: Budapest, Hungary) III. Magyar Tudományos Akadémia. IV. Series.
HC79.I6E25   658.7'87   81-12479
ISBN 0-444-99720-2 (pt. A)   AACR2
ISBN 0-444-99719-9 (pt. B)

ISBN 0-444-99718-0 (set)
ISBN 0-444-41963-2 (series)

Joint edition published by
Elsevier Scientific Publishing Company, Amsterdam, The Netherlands and Akadémiai Kiadó, The Publishing House of the Hungarian Academy of Sciences, Budapest, Hungary.

Printed in Hungary

CONTENTS

INVENTORY MANAGEMENT

Proc. First Int. Symp. on Inventories
Budapest, Hungary 1980

PROBLEMS OF MANAGEMENT OF PRODUCTION STOCKS AT AGRICULTURAL ORGANIZATIONS IN THE BULGARIAN PEOPLE'S REPUBLIC

VASIL ANATSKOV

Karl Marx College of Economics, Sofia, Bulgaria

1. THE ESSENCE AND ROLE OF PRODUCTION STOCKS

Material values of the society contain stocks - as their internal part - created by people in the production process. Depending on the final purpose of utilization of goods material stocks of society can be divided into two groups:

a/ Stocks of means of production, utilized in the production activity. These are: output stocks /like finished goods and stocks on the way/, stocks of production /stocks stored in the warehouses of consumers and supplying organizations/, in-process inventories and national reserves.

b/ Stocks for final consumption to meet all the personal and collective needs of people. Stocks of consumer goods and another part of national reserves belong to this group.

This categorization is based on the fact that national product can be divided into two parts also: means of production and consumer goods.

In our paper we deal with the problems of the first group, i.e. the stocks of production.

11

This type of stocks are such means of production which can be found in the warehouses of both producer and consumer companies serving a continuous and scheduled production process but temporarily excluded from this process. Both objects of work and means of production belong to the group of production stocks. If one wants to set up a real, well-established plan, production stocks must be necessarily included. This is especially important in agriculture, since the influence of weather conditions on agricultural production is well known and meeting objectives of plan is therefore always exposed to danger for objective reasons. That is why the existence of stocks of production /such as feedstuff, seed-corn, etc./ is indispensable from the point of view of the real plans.

Stocks of production do not take part in the process of production itself, nevertheless they increase efficiency by these guaranteeing continuity and schedule keeping of production. That is why stocks are by all means needed regardless of replenishment time. The necessity of stocks of production is reasonable also for the fact that damages deriving from breaking the schedule can amount to high multiple of stock-holding costs. For instance any lack of horned cattles' feedstuff affects yields unfavourably and consequently damage will be higher than the stock-holding cost of the feedstuff. If harvesting of cereals and feedstuffs lasts for a long time because of the shortage of different spare parts of tractors and combines, there will be a much higher damage for the farms, than the cost would be expended on obtaining and holding of spare parts.

Means of production are part of production stocks as long as they are not involved in.. the production process, i.e. until there are no essential changes in their characteristic features. For instance, hulling, dehydration, sterilization do not change the main features of the grain and that is why during these processes it remains stock.

Because of the special character of agriculture using of biological means of production /plants and animals/ seasonal production and the gain of crop - stocks like grain, feedstuff, breeding stock, manure, chemicals etc. function as stock for a long time and their proportion in inventories of the agricultural plants amounts to 45-50%.

In consequence of great volume, role of machinery and high rate of specialization of agricultural production, role of stocks of production is continually growing. It is practical to hold stocks of means of production both at the consumers and in the warehouses of agricultural complexes as well.

To improve organization and stock control of agricultural production scientific resolution of the following problems is necessary:

- fixing of norms and structure of means of production at the consumer companies and in the warehouses of supplying organizations;
- perfection of the control mechanism of stocks of production;
- determination of concentration of stocks of means of production;
- establishment of warehouse bases needed for storing of means of production.

2. FIXING OF STOCK NORMS OF MEANS OF PRODUCTION

Optimization of the volume of agricultural stocks is of great importance, because they represent a considerable part /45-50%/ of the circulation funds. The aim of fixing the norms is to eliminate the excesses and shortages in favour of a good efficiency. Consequently scheduled production must be assured by holding a minimum level of stocks and in-process goods. The right optimization of the production volume is in close connection with the complex analysis of the norming methods, operative control and structure of stocks in production.

The most advanced methods of fixing stock norms are based on their mathematical optimization by using computers. Nevertheless these methods have not been spread widely in today's practice yet. Before their adoption a lot of organizational and personal problems must be solved. These would change the control of the existing organization and the agricultural material-technical supply.

Fixing of norms at the agricultural plants in the Bulgarian People's Republic is ruled by the "Instruction for Norming Circulation Funds", sanctioned by the Ministry of Finances, Ministry for Supply and National Reserves and the Bulgarian National Bank. According to this instruction stock-level of raw materials, ingredients, manures, chemicals, medicines, fuels and wrappers must be determined for each individual item, while others in their aggregates.

Individual norms in terms of time /days/ are given to materials representing a large proportion /80%/ in the cost of production.

14

In this case the average of item-level norms is used for all other /not individually handled/ items in the given group of products. Norms in terms of time are determined for the average stock, the safety stock and the technological /preparatory/ stock.

Current stock serves as basis of the norm of a given material, as it means the volume capable to assure a continuous production during the replenishment period. This is a changing quantity; it is on the maximum level at the time of arrival of delivery, while it is on the minimum level just before the next delivery. For this reason the norm in terms of time is equal to the half of the yearly average of replenishment time. The average replenishment time can be calculated by dividing the number of days of the planning period /year/ by the number of deliveries. The number of deliveries can be determined by the quotient of the yearly material demand and the average volume delivered.

The absolute level of the maximum current stock of every company is actually equal to the product of multiplication of the average daily use and the norms in terms of days for a certain material. This last value means the average lead-time in terms of days. /The maximum level is equal to the volume delivered, the minimum level is equal to zero. The average current stock is equal to the half of its maximum / The average daily use scheduled is dependent on the planned volume for use and the length of the planning period of the given material. Calculation can be completed by the help of the next formula:

$$Nkg = \frac{P}{T} \cdot Na \qquad\qquad /1/$$

where Nkg = maximum of the current stock in terms of natural
units

P = planned use of a given material determined by production programming and norms for use

T = the length of the planning period in terms of days
/1 year=360 days, or 12 month, 1 month = 30 days/

Na = average lead-time

Safety stock is to assure the scheduled production in
cases if there is a break in delivery or a change in demand of
the given material. This is a stock of fixed volume. It is
determined as a ratio of the norm of the given material's
current stock. Safety stock is planned in case of the transit
supply form, but in case of a warehouse supply is not important.

Depending on deliveries in the Bulgarian People's Republic
the next proportions are valid in calculation of norms of safety
stocks:

Number of yearly deliveries	Safety stock in terms of proportion of current stock /%/
26 -	25
6 - 25	50
0 - 5	75

Technological stocks are held in favour of the continuous
production in cases if additional time is needed to prepare a
given material for production. The norm of the technological

stock must be determined in terms of days on the basis of the technologies of the preparatory operations. /For instance, time for loading, dehydration, sterilization, etc./

In case of means of production - as they represent a changing volume of stocks - different norms can be determined, such as maximum, minimum and average ones.

The maximum norm equals to the sum of the norms of the maximum current stock, the safety and the technological stock. The minimum norm is equal to the sum of the safety norm and the technological norms. The average norm is equal to the sum of the half of the maximum current stock-norm and the safety and technological norms. In case of norms of different materials - for instance seed, feedstuffs, spare parts, etc. - their special characters must be taken into account.

For example, seed norms are calculated by types of stock separately for every item. The norms of the current stock are determined in terms of allowances in kind - in kg /D/[1] - on the basis of the planned need of the given type of product, taking into account the length of the planning period /T/ and the warehouse norm /N/, both in days. The time norm of cereals is calculated for the period lasting from gathering to sowing, while in case of purchased crops, period between the contractual term of delivery and sowing is essential. In case of wheat for instance stock holding lasts for about 85 days.

---

[1] The planned demand of a given type of wheat is calculated by the product of multiplication of two factors: the sowing area /in hectare/ and the volume of seed required for a unit of the area.

Calculations are to be performed by formula /1/. The safety norm of wheat is determined in proportion of the yearly demand. In Bulgaria this proportion amounts to 5% by the order on norming of circulating funds.

In case of feedstuffs current and safety norms are determined group by group: forage /maize, barley/, rough fodder /hay, straw/, sapful /grape,.../, etc.

The current norm of a given feedstuff can be calculated by the help of formula /2/:

$$N_k = \frac{\frac{P}{2}}{T} \cdot N_d \qquad\qquad /2/$$

where: $\frac{P}{2}$ = half of the yearly demand of a given feedstuff.

The yearly demand is calculated on the basis of the average of the given year's livestocks, and unit feedstuff demand.

T = length of the planning period /360 days/.

N_d = the time-norm of feedstuffs. This is different for each group of feedstuffs. In case of corn feedstuffs it amounts about 180 days.

Safety stock is given in the proportion of the yearly demand /P/. In Bulgaria this value is 8.3% in case of corn fodders, and in case of rough fodders and sapful it amounts to 15%.

3. PROBLEMS OF IMPROVEMENT OF PRODUCTION STOCKS' MANAGEMENT

The increased role of economic aspects in material-technical supply have brought about the necessity of changing a lot of rules in the sphere of inventory control in production, in connections between producers and consumers and in case of material responsibility related to suppliers' obligations. Consequently the Council of Ministers has issued an order on 28th December, 1979, that is the "Order on the specific regulation of economic organizations and their subordinate units engaged in material-technical supply". The most important subject in it is the problem of material stocks.

In favour of being able to assure the material stocks needed, the National Planning Committee and the Ministry for National Reserves and Supply sanction the norms of material groups and follow them with attention during the drawing up of the material balances. Moreover, there are obligatory minimum stock levels for the supplying, commercial organizations concerning the most important material groups, given by item in terms of natural units.

Income of the managers of the supplying, commercial organizations depends on the fulfilment of the material stock plan. If material stock level is lower than the minimum sanctioned and the volumes delivered are high above the contractual ones, the managers' salaries will be reduced by 20%. In the future managers will be penalized if their companies do not fulfil the delivery obligations.

Supplying, commercial organizations and their units work on the basis of financial independence, they are completely responsible for the optimum level and structure of material stocks. Consequently the minimum norms of material stocks are regulated by the help of economic means, and accumulation above norms is strictly limited.

Workers of agricultural plants are interested in the decrease of material consumption dependent on themselves, contri-
buting hereby to the decrease of the consumers' stock of production in an indirect way.

4.   CONCENTRATION LEVEL OF STOCKS OF PRODUCTION

Stockholding at the consumers - let it be an optimum-level
- delays circulation of material resources in national economy.
Accumulated in form of stocks materials at the producers can be
utilized with much less versatility than the same materials
stocked at commercial organizations.

Accumulation /concentration/ of stocks at the supplying,
commercial organizations decreases stocks at the producers, increases the circulation of materials and assures continuous
output with a minimum volume of stocks and costs. All the advantages of mass-production arise if stocks are concentrated at
only a few, but big specialized supplying, commercial organizations.

The right proportions in stock allocation have a great importance from the point of view of limiting the increase of
stocks and in the respect of decreasing national expenses
connected to reserves. In case of a given stock volume at a
higner rotation speed it is possible to meet the demand of more
producers. Consequently enlarging warehouse bases and stock
accumulation at the supplying commercial houses is the most
rational and advantageous way of decreasing consumers' stocks.

The new economic mechanism of control in material-technical
supply stimulates the right concentration by the help of eco-

nomic means and at the same time tries to improve choice and stop shortages.

Nevertheless, an unjustified degree of concentration of some produces /feedstuff, wheat, manure, etc./ has brought about difficulties in delivery, increase in transportation costs and spreading of subjective factors in distribution of materials in short supply. That is why concentration must be accomplished on scientific basis and differentiated by groups of materials and levels of control.

5. ESTABLISHING OF WAREHOUSES NEEDED FOR STORAGE OF STOCKS OF PRODUCTION

Appropriate warehouse bases of supplying, commercial organizations serve as a condition for concentration of stocks of production. The right decision on problem of size and allocation of warehouses makes it possible to concentrate stocks of materials and spare parts to be held there at a few supplying, commercial organizations, instead of at many companies. It also makes possible to be able to store stocks of optimum volume and structure in order to supply the agricultural plants of a given area.

Appropriate supply of machine systems and equipment, the automatization of warehouse working processes, loading, sorting seem to be the guarantee of the high efficiency of the warehouse service.

In a socialist economy where means of production are in social property and the workers' steadily growing demands are met from the planned national output, scientific inventory management can be fully realized.

Proc. First Int. Symp. on Inventories
Budapest, Hungary 1980

A FRAMEWORK FOR DISTRIBUTED COMPUTERIZED INVENTORY CONTROL SYSTEMS

JOHN ANDERSSON

Institute of Business Administration, Oslo, Norway

Introduction

Regarding the amount of published material - shelf metres of books and articles - Inventory Planning and Control is undeniably one of the areas within the Quantitative Theory of Business Administration which is most comprehensively dealt with. Yet as far as practical application is concerned there is a great deal to be desired. An essential cause of this discrepancy between theory and practice can be explained by bad performance on the operational level[1].

Many sophisticated EDP-systems, using advanced forecasting and planning techniques, have failed due to such trivial deficiencies as wrong on-hand quantities, unreliable physical inventory counts, and incorrect actions by the stockroom people.

Replacing a manual cardex file, in itself an online dialogue system, with a computerized weekly batch system has been disasterous in many a company. Retrospectively it would have been more reasonable to maintain manual control for the operational part of the inventory control system, and computerize the tactical part, for example forecasting, lot sizing, and

---

[1] Operational refers to Anthony's (1965) definition of management Control levels: strategic, administrative (tactical), operational. An operational system could be described as an "everyday routine" which a multitude of a company's employees are in touch with.

"Operational control is the process of assuring that specific tasks are carried out effectively and efficiently" (Anthony, 1965, p 16 f).

23

safety stock calculation. Moreover IC^2 has been subordinated to financial EDP-systems and regarded as of secondary importance.

With the advent of inexpensive hardware the challenge is in terms of designing versatile application software. A key issue is systems development methods leading end users and middle management to take genuine responsibility in the design phase. Up to now computerization has frequently implied a depressing inertia. Necessary alterations, caused by for example a new business situation, are postponed or considered unrealistic.

Objective of this paper

This paper deals with ICS in three different areas:

1. Production inventories (intended for manufacturing)
2. Maintenance inventories
3. Customer goods inventories(intended for sales)

Though great differences between the three areas regarding the tactical level, many operational control functions and features are in common.

One purpose is to make a list of necessary standard functions, based upon a so called conceptual database. A second purpose is to present some practical rules for distribution of data records and computerized functions. Additionally there will be some propositions how to achieve a very high degree of flexibility in comparison with today's computerized ICS.

Three areas of Inventory Control in practice

The IC literature includes a great number of methods to categorize inventories. For our purpose it is sufficient with a classification into the three realms: Production, Maintenance and Customer goods (Sales).

Traditionally the Customer goods inventories have been entirely predominant. The mathematical-statistic theory which was developed has also been extended to the Production area. As late as in the mid 1960's there occurred no less than, what a sociologist of science would call, a

---

[2] Inventory Control (System) = IC(S)

paradigm shift[3]. There arose a division between <u>dependent</u> and <u>independent</u> <u>demand</u>, a principle formulated by Orlicky in 1965. Wight (1968) described in a brilliant article the disasterous consequences of applying the statistical methods on inventories of the dependent demand type.

During the 1970's we have experienced the breakthrough and triumphal progress of MRP (Material Requirements Planning) into manufacturing companies. The professional organisation APICS can make a merit of this progress, together with the trio Plossl, Orlicky and Wight. The MRP concept seems to have been incorporated in academic studies throughout the world as well.

The discipline of Maintenance Management is not for the present attractive to so many scientists. Inventories play a most important role in Maintenance, offering a lot of unique problems, for example extremely low turnover rates, difficulties to identify part numbers, tracing "individuals" within one part number and replacement of one part number by another.

Sales of spare parts to customers - often a very profitable activity - might be regarded as a mixture between the Maintenance and the Customer goods areas.

Also the Customer goods area has been subject to recent development of theory. One very interesting issue is the so called <u>push system</u>[4]. The joint control of central stock(s) plus regional warehouses has virtually always been of the "<u>pull</u>" type. The regional warehouses have ordered independently, thereby causing uncontrollable oscillations and stockouts. The

---

[3]<u>Paradigm</u> is a concept introduced by Kuhn (1962) who demonstrated that science is subject to "revolutionary leaps". Between such revolutions there are periods of "normal science" during which scientists are solving problems within the prevailing paradigm.

[4]A fairly profound theoretical treatment of push inventory systems is given by Brown (1979). Sawchuk (1980) shows practical results in a divisionalized company.

key point with "<u>push</u>" is that the replenishment decisions are based upon information about total stock status and total requirements at all locations. Substantial tangible benefits have been reported.

The "troika" Production, Maintenance and Customer goods inventories have an important common denominator, namely the item file or <u>part master file</u>. Figure 1 shows a so called conceptual database: necessary sets of information and the connections between these sets.

The framework, or skeleton, shown in Figure 1 contains most of the sets of information which are mandatory for the <u>operational</u> parts of the "inventory troika". All other data fields being useful (say 100-400 fields) will easily be generated in accordance with methods described later in this paper.

The design of ICS as a problem of mapping

What we here call a <u>system</u> might be regarded as a map of the reality, the so called referent system, see for example Andersson (1974) Ch. 5. A distinction can be made between mapping in the <u>static</u> sense, i.e. the structure and state variables which are time invariant, and in the <u>dynamic</u> sense. Although, at a first glance, mapping of the operational level of an actual inventory referent system might look trivial, there are a multitude of situations in real life where the map is not consistent with the terrain. Not only system designers have to be conscious of such mapping errors, but the end users "on the floor" must be able to make the appropriate adjustments.

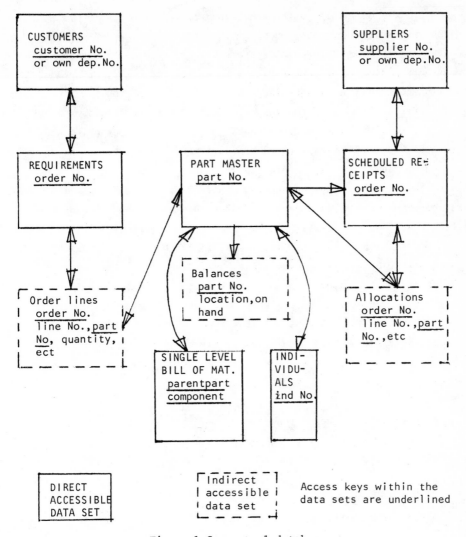

Figure 1. Conceptual database

The author wants to suggest that mapping accuracy might be measured
in three different dimensions:

1. Precision
2. Retrieval (or access) time
3. Timeliness

These three dimensions are jumbled together quite often.

27

Precision refers to those mapping errors which occur when an equilibrium is attained, i.e. when all data records are updated in a computerized ICS. Most financial systems have a very high precision, as accountants and auditors accept virtually no loss of money. Unfortunately, most financial reports are obtained several weeks or months too late.

Retrieval time is the response time to get the output on a VDU screen, or to obtain the requested data manually from paper printouts. Unfortunately much has been disputed on retrieval or access times in a narrow, technical sense, i.e. response in ≤ 2 seconds in 95 % of the cases. Another treacherous problem is online queries contra real time updating. In the first case you will receive data in less than 1 second but the information might be days, or even weeks, old.

The third dimension, timeliness, is for our operational level purposes a matter of paramount importance. There are virtually always some transactions in the pipeline even in real time updating systems! One example is comprehensive materials lists which may take ½-2 days to pick out the items. Another example is physical inventory counting. In designing an ICS and training users one must always be observant as to these delays. Maybe small, remote hand-terminals are a future solution. Existence of such terminals is reported from the USA[5].

Some vital standard functions of operational ICS

The author would like to suggest a list of functions, considered to be vital to all the three parties of the "inventory troika":
- the supply/demand report. Either displayed on VDUs or printed on paper, this report is the most important output of an ICS. The report offers a time-phased availability vector, and includes scheduled receipts, demands (allocations, gross requirements, etc) and projected on-hand
- reservation (allocation) item for item
- direct reservation of a whole order with the aid of a bill of material
- alterations and cancellations of reservations
- materials verifying which means an imaginary picking of all material lines of an order before release of the order to the stockroom

[5] Mentioned by G. Plossl in an inventory seminar in Oslo in the Fall of 1979.

- picking list. There are different methods, e.g. order picking or part number picking
- feedback of requisitions and picking lists. Variances of issued quantities are exception-reported
- goods receiving report. Variances of a delivery can be discovered at an early stage
- shortage flagging
- receiving of a shortage item. When a shortage-flagged item enters the receiving area, all the shortage lines are printed. Shortages can be shipped immediately, and need not pass through the stock
- printout of over-mature reservations
- input after physical counting. So called cycle counting is preferable, see Manufacturing Software Systems (1978). Variances shall not automatically lead to on-hand adjustments, but be subject to an investigation
- transaction file or audit trail which shows all transactions within a certain period
- replenishment signal. The replenishment rules may be very individual.

On optimal distribution of data processing

For especially multi-located organizations the inexpensive mini-computers offer an attractive solution. But what data should be distributed? Most companies are just beginning to look upon this problem systematically[6]. The author would like to suggest some variables to be incorporated in such a trade-off between central or local processing.

The condition for decentralizing a certain function, including the necessary data fields, is:

$$(C_1 + k_1) - (C_c + k_c) - n \cdot e < (p_c \cdot P_c - p_1 \cdot P_1) + (t_c \cdot T_c - t_1 \cdot T_1) + S \quad (1)$$

where

index c refers to the central computer, and index 1 to the local computers

n = number of assignments (e.g. transactions) of a certain function per year

C = annual hardware costs for processing and data storage

k = annual software costs

---

[6] See for example Woods (1977)

p = number of program breakdowns per year for the certain function

t = number of other breakdowns per year, caused by technical factors, other applications processed simultaneously, etc.

P = consequence cost per program breakdown

T = consequence cost per other breakdown

S = a subjective annual fee for getting better retrieval time in the local computer than in the central one (S could be < 0)

e = data transmission cost per assignment

Every term in formula (1) can be estimated. We would like to emphasize $t_c \cdot T_c - t_1 \cdot T_1$. If the local computer is not loaded with many applications $t_c \gg t_1$ and $T_c \gg T_1$ because the damage or annoyance is much larger when having a central computer breakdown with hundreds of VDUs affected, than in case of a local computer breakdown.

The solution is to achieve clusters of information so that any one of the functions is not dependent on both the central and the local computers. The local computer shall be kept clear of intricate batch processing and reserved for interactive processing as much as possible.

Changeable systems

Computer hardware has displayed an astounding development. You can buy 10 times more for every dollar today than five years ago, and this progress seems to go on for many years ahead. But COBOL which celebrates its 20th anniversary in 1980 is still flourishing! An exceedingly crucial issue, pertinent to both companies and governments, is to drastically enhance the productivity of the systems people.

A common method in the past two decades has been prefabrication. Development costs can be substantially reduced if they are shared between hundreds of user companies. In order to take care of most possible requirements, prefabricated systems get very large compared to any individual firm's needs. The individual firm must virtually always change its own routines or organisation. Sometimes this might be advantageous, sometimes not. But one still more severe drawback is the rigidity of computerized systems causing changes due to fluctuating business conditions difficult to make. Even petty alterations like expanding the job-order number from 5 digits to 7, is often considered to be impossible.

Only recently prefabrication is being replaced by more fruitful ways out: database managers, super-high level languages and application generators, see Figure 2.

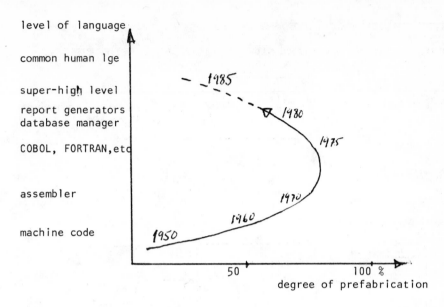

Figure 2. Progress of programming aids

One example of powerful super-high level languages is ADMINS 11.
One very interesting application generator for especially Production and
Inventory Management is Mitrol's MIMS. Both these ingenious tools have
their origin in scientific research at Massachusetts Institute of Technology.

Common requirements for super-high level languages and application
generators are:
- a report generator. The user must be able to design or change output
formats in minutes or hours without dependence on experts
- a field generator. A new data field can be added into an arbitrary record
with the help of a short instruction. Old fields can be changed or deleted
in a similar way
- a transaction generator. A new transaction can be added by declaring the
effects by means of a decision table or the like
- a file generator. A completely new file is added. Its records and connections with other files are declared.This challenging tool is sometimes
called a relation database.

Another aspect of flexibility is <u>portability</u>. Application software
must become more independent of hardware. In the future we guess, and hope,

it will be possible to create programs for any arbitrary computer brand and operating system, in accordance with the principle of Figure 3.

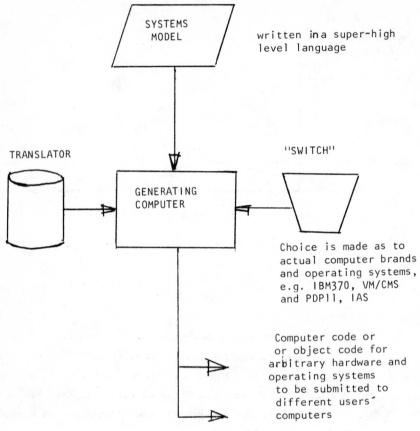

Figure 3. Generating systems for arbitrary computers

The systems modelling method has been introduced by Professor S.Persson. The method is based on the statement: Applying infinite computer power to a finite application problem will mean that the programming time tapers off to zero. The function of a computerized system, especially input, output and interactive processing, can be "simulated". The programming takes only minutes or one or two hours at most. The interior of the system is working 100-1000 times as expensive as usual, but due to tiny volumes it does not matter.

The systems analyser and designer can be in a vivid dialogue with the line managers and end users. Ambigous or abstract writings submitted to the decision makers could be curtailed. And the company has got a clear specification when bidding for proposals among hardware and software suppliers.

Because the model is written in a formal computer language it should not be impossible for a "translator" to transform the model into assembler, COBOL, PASCAL, etc.

Summary

There has been outlined a framework of the operational level of Inventory Control Systems for several areas, manufacturing, customer (sales), and maintenance inventories. Computer distribution with local minis is discussed, and a trade-off formula is suggested.

A so called conceptual database is the skeleton of the computer system. A number of standard functions are suggested. A modern inventory system must not be prefabricated to a high extent. Conversely, systems shall be designed by the users with the aid of super-high level languages and application generators. This seems to be the only way to achieve both user acceptance and rapid adjustments to fluctuating environment conditions.

References

Andersson J.(1974):Industriföretagets produktionsstyrning -om undersökning, syntes och förändring.(Production control in manufacturing companies - on inquiry,synthesis and change). Unprinted dissertation, Royal Institute of Technology, Stockholm.

Anthony R.N.(1965):Planning and control systems. A framework for analysis. Harvard Univ., Boston.

Brown I.J.E.(1979):The "push" system of inventory management. Preprint from '79 International physical distribution conference in Tokyo,June 4-7, 1979.

Bucci G., Streeter D.N.(1979):A methodology for the design of distributed information systems. Communications of the Association for Computing Machinery, vol 22, no. 4, April 1979.

Kuhn T.S.(1962):The structure of scientific revolutions.Univ. of Chicago Press, Chicago.

Manufacturing Software Systems (1978): MRP Software Review - the Standard system. Report, Williston, Vermont.

Orlicky J.(1975): Material requirements planning. McGraw Hill, N.Y.

Persson S.(1977): Systemskisser(The Systems modelling development method). Report, Swedish Association of Employers, Lidingö, Sweden.

Sawchuk P.A.(1980):Installing a "push"distribution system. Paper at APICS' seminar on Satellite inventory management in Atlanta, March 17-19 1980

Wight O.W.(1968):To order point or Not to order point. Production and Inventory Management, vol 9, no.3, 1968.

Woods L.D.(1977):Distributed processing in manufacturing.Datamation,October1977.

Proc. First Int. Symp. on Inventories
Budapest, Hungary 1980

USING CONTINGENCY APPROACH
IN THE ANALYSIS
OF COMPANY LEVEL INVENTORY SYSTEMS

KÁROLY BALATON

Karl Marx University of Economics, Budapest, Hungary

In order to realize effective inventory control within companies an adequate form of organization structure should be developed. The development of the structure of inventory control is a part of the company level organization development and because of this it cannot be done without taking into consideration the organization development of other fields of company activity. In consequence of this, when dealing with the development of organization structure of company level inventory control we have to start from the concept of organization development of companies as a whole.

The concept of company level organization development

Organization theory has long been characterized by searching for the one best way of organization and management. A clear example of this is Max Weber's teaching about the bureaucratic type organization. According to Weber the bureaucratic organization assures maximum level of efficiency.

Analyses of organization structure carried out in the 1960s have shown that there is no general way of organization

3*   35 which assures efficiency in every circumstances. That is, the structure of effective organization must be adapted to the context, within which the organization operates. Authors on contingency theory draw their attention to the environment, technology and size of organization as the main elements of context. The development of the methodology of organization analysis made it possible to investigate the relation between the elements of structure and context by using the means of mathematics and statistics. Empirically observed close connections between contextual and structural variables can make us feel that a certain contextual element (i.e. technology) determines mechanically the organization structure of the company. Really, these connections are the results of organization development carried out by the enterprise. Character and tightness of these connections are also influenced by the degree to what company recognizes the desired role of a contextual element in formulating the organization structure.

On the other hand, it must be admitted that within a certain state of context, or at a certain way of its changing, the company has not only one way of forming its organization structure. For example, when a company observes serious reduction in his sales turnover, the possible answers might be the following:

- development of new products,

- improvement of the quality of existing products,

- reduction of costs, etc.

It is obvious that adequate structures to the above mentioned strategies must be different from each other.

This example also shows that forming the organization structure serious attention should be devoted to the objectives and strategies of the company. In our view strategy has an intermediate role between the elements of context and structure.

Among the factors to be analyzed in connection with organization development we also mean the efficiency of organization. Under the term efficiency we mean the overall measure of company activity, financial and non-financial characteristics also. Efficiency qualifies also the organization development activity of a company. Connections existing between context, strategy and structure in an effective organization must be estimated differently as the same connections in a non-effective organization.

In our view, factors affecting organization structure are not taken as variables automatically determining the organization but as variables which have to be analyzed and taken into consideration by managers in the development of organization structure. Taking them into consideration might help the organization to work effectively in a certain environment.

Factors affecting the organization structure of company level inventory control

Inventory control is taken as one of the subsystems of the company. Our analysis is especially related to industrial enterprises. In the taxonomic model of an industrial enterprise besides inventory control we distinguish the following subsystems:[1]

- financing

- research and development

- production

- staffing

- marketing

The above mentioned subsystems are related to different parts of the environment of the company, and have to realize different objectives. According to these differences the factors affecting the structure of the subsystems are also different from each other.

Factors to be analyzed in forming the organization structure of inventory control can be grouped as follows:

- environment outside the company

- environment inside the company

- strategy of the enterprise

- type of company level organization

Effect of environment outside the company on the structure of inventory control

Environment outside the company means the elements on both input and output side. Elements of input environment

---

[1] Chikán et al. (1978): Készletek a gazdaságban (Inventories in the Economy). Közgazdasági és Jogi Kiadó, Budapest.

affect especially the inventory control of materials, energies and parts of goods bought from outside, while the elements of output environment relate to finished goods.

Among the elements of the outside environment we underline the need for analysing the following factors.

a.) The effect of product distribution and price control

One part of the effect appears through the channels of product distribution. In our recent economic management system the distribution of products can be organized through different channels. It might be a direct shipping from producer to consumer, shipping through commercial organizations of production means, through wholesale and retail organizations or through foreign trade companies. According to the channel a company uses, the activities of inventory control (e.g. frequency of ordering) are different.

The effect of price control appears through the price category a certain product belongs to. When prices are not fixed by the state then quantity of buying affects prices and so the frequency of buying.

Inventory control is also affected by the laws relating to the distribution of products. For example, contracts should be made or not, what conditions can be stated in contracts, etc.

b.) The effect of the character of the market on
    inventory control

Among the characteristics of market first we deal
with the effect of the equilibrium state of the market. It is
well known that demand and supply are only rarely in equilibrium, the characteristic feature of market is overdemand or
oversupply.[2] Under condition of overdemand,
which is general in our national economy, companies hold
reserves in stocks especially on the input side. Activities
and organizations are developed mainly in connection with input side inventories. Inventory control organizations on the
input side are forced to adapt passively to the behaviour of
suppliers.

Another factor to be investigated is the structure of
market. Under the structure of market we mean the number of
organizations taking part in the market of certain goods. Its
effect can be observed in the frequency of shipping, in lot-
size and in the way of organizing the shipping of goods.

Among the characteristics of market we have to
mention the frequency of changes. In case of a stable market it
is possible to use standard procedures and written rules,
while the changing character of market needs roles with less
formal regulation and processes with higher level of flexibility.

---

[2]Kornai (1971): Anti-Equilibrium. Közgazdasági és Jogi Kiadó,
    Budapest.

The effect of environment inside the company

Under the term environment inside the company we
mean the above mentioned subsystems of an industrial enterprise. Inventory control has connections in many ways with the
other subsystems. Among   these connections - from the point of
view of forming the structure of inventory control - we underline the following.

a.) The effect of production and production control

Connection between inventory control and production
can be observed most directly in case of inventories within
the production process. The organization of production process
in space and in time determines the need for semi-finished
goods and for goods in working processes. The effect on inventory control is different in case of a company of horizontal
or vertical structure of production. When vertical structure
of production is concerned, inventory control of semi-finished
goods assures the undisturbance of production processes between
different organizations of production. In case of horizontal
structure of production inventory control of semi-finished
goods can be organized within the organization of production.

From the point of view of the organization of
material supply the relation between the horizon of production
plans and programs and of the time lag from ordering until the
arrival of goods is rather important. When this time lag is
shorter or equal with the horizon of production programs, it is
possible to organize material supply on the basis of counted

needs of production, while in other cases inventory control based on stock norms becomes more feasible.

b.) Effect of the accuracy of technological preparation

Accuracy of technological preparation is closely connected with seriality of production. Higher level of mass production is usually followed by detailed, accurate technological preparation. Raising seriality of production makes it possible to use more developed methods for counting the inventory needs of production. Parallel with this, roles and activities in inventory control can be more specialized and standardized.

c.) Effect of the heterogeneity of production profile and variety of products

Increasing heterogeneity of production profile and growing variety of product within a certain profile increase the number of goods to be stored. Growing number of items in the inventory system increases the complexity of activities and the amount of information to be processed. All these events make it necessary to develop techniques applied in inventory system (e.g. using ABC-analysis).

Effect of corporate strategy on inventory control

The organization structure of inventory control has not only to be coordinated with effects coming from inside and outside of the company, but has to be able to meet the needs of the corporate strategy.

Objectives of the inventory system can be derived from the corporate strategy. E.g. If a company plans to enter a new market, the inventory system has to assure storing and shipping of goods meeting the needs of new consumers in quality and quantity, ordering of materials for production, etc. These objectives will change if the corporate strategy aims e.g. reduction of costs.

As the corporate strategy changes the organization of inventory control should also follow these changes.

Effect of the type of company level of organization on inventory control

The organization of inventory control cannot be separated from the overall organization development activity of the company. Basic principles of structuring the organization affect directly the organization of inventory system as well.

According to this there are alterations in the organization of inventory control in a linear type or in a functional type organization. When the organization structure is centralized or decentralized this affects the placing of activities, authorities and units of inventory control within the organization. Division of organization after markets or products will also cause changes in the structure of inventory control.

Connections outlined in this lecture draw our attention to the need for analysing and developing the structure of inventory control within its context, taking into account the effects of the company as a system and of its environment. Such approach to the development of the structure of inventory control might help us to create a system which is capable of effective working.

Proc. First Int. Symp. on Inventories
Budapest, Hungary 1980

INVENTORY CONTROL —
A LOGISTICS APPROACH

JÓZSEF BERÁCS

Karl Marx University of Economics, Budapest, Hungary

In my paper I give an analysis of some aspects of the
connections between inventory control and logistics.
The main points are as follows:

1. The inventory situation of the national economy,
   the unfavourable structure of inventories.

2. The appearance of logistics /as a functional activity
   of companies/ and its main characteristics.

3. The relations between inventory control and logistics.

4. Some results of a company level research concerning
   the subject.

1. The Inventory Situation of National Economy, the Unfavourable Structure of Inventories

During the last decade both economic control and management
and scientific research have been interested very much in
inventory problems.

It is an unanimous opinion of studies analysing the
situation, which are made from different purposes and by
different authors, that the present inventory structure is
unambiguously unfavourable.

One of the characteristics of inventory structure in Hungary is that - like in other socialist countries - a bigger proportion of inventories is hold on the "input side" /that is in materials/ of companies and relatively small stocks can be found on the "output side" of producers and manufacturers and at trade companies.

This structure has hardly changed over the past twenty years - as other readers emphasised too - although its unfavourable consequences much rather appear.

Measures taken by central economic control and management have resulted only in small changes in this respect. This situation plays also a great part in the statement of various researchers, that the inventory problem cannot be discussed in itself. Such an important question as for example the change of the inventory structure cannot be considered apart from the general state of economy. Relation between demand and supply and frequency of shortages are the most important among characteristic parameters describing this state.

To achieve progress substantial changes are needed in two fields:

First - the central economic control and management has to establish such an environment for the companies which helps to change the criticized inventory structure.

Second   -   the methods and view of company management have
             to be developed in such a direction which results
             in a better inventory maintenance through the
             improvement of connections between the enterprises.

Joined with the latter field I want to speak about logistics,
as a new endeavour, conscious use of which may help also in
changing the unfavourable inventory structure mentioned.

2. The appearance of logistics /as a functional activity
of companies/ and its main characteristics

Relatively large number of publications have dealt with
logistics or with its spheres in the past 1o-2o years.
Logistics /which is on the one hand a specific approach,
on the other hand a system of means/ helps in solving the
problems of supply. Its aim is to improve service and reduce
costs by better flow of goods from producer to user. It
includes those parts of connections between companies
respectively of company activities, which are related to
the flow of goods. It contains delivery, store keeping,
material handling, inventory control, packaging and a part
of information connections. Logistics deals also with the
flow of goods inside the company, but we do not discuss this
problem.

The appearance of logistics may be attributed to two reasons:

First: The <u>sharpening of market competition</u>, the increasing rate of development of international economic relations made it necessary from the side of the practice of the enterprises to investigate the processes of material flow between seller and buyer as a complex problem. That is, activities which affect each other or effect material flow directly, should be managed together.

Second: Spreading of the system theory and system approach urges the reevaluation of management and organization. In this way we can get to the flow of goods through the distribution of natural processes.

Regarding this process as a system, we may formulate subsystems, which were nominated previously elements of logistics /delivery, inventory control, etc./.

Starting from the system approach we can regard the flow of goods between seller and buyer as a <u>quasi-system</u>, which connects the suitable logistics systems of two companies having conflicting interests with each other.   That is, sales side of the seller and purchasing side of the buyer, as the illustration shows.

The figure drafts only the typical processes.   That is why I did not mark e.g. return flow of goods from the buyer to the seller, because it is not typical in the system, and it generally refers to something operating trouble.

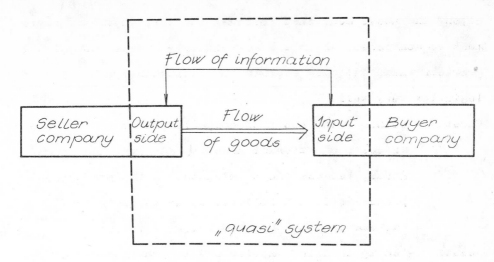

Fig.1. The "quasi" logistics system

This "quasi" system we can regard in a wider sense
as a logistics system from which both companies aim to
manage its own part on the basis of the same principle.
Aim of the system is realization of a smooth material
flow with relatively low costs.

This aim can be expressed by the idea of seller's service
level, which can be described with different parameters
or nonnumerical characteristics. One often uses for this
the rate of meeting demands by seller for a definite time
/for example 8o percent of demand will be met in 1o days/.

It may be a parameter for example the reliability of the
seller or readiness to meet   extra requests, etc.

Parameters describing service level show also the power
relations between seller and buyer, and the relations between
demand and supply too.

Beyond the above mentioned reasons, two very important facts must be mentioned, which are not entirely independent of the previous ones, but they explain the coming into limelight of logistics very well:

First   - Within total costs of companies there is an increase in costs of material handling and distribution of goods, because the development of the production processes is not followed by an adequate rationalization of circulation processes.

Second   - An up to date computerized information system speeds up the administrative task, following the flow of goods, and gives opportunity for such analysing which cannot be made by manual work.

3. The Relations Between Inventory Control and Logistics

On the basis of the above mentioned, inventory control is a subsystem of logistics system, and so their connection is determined by this relation. Theory of inventory control has been developed for a long time. But it is a fairly general opinion that practical implementations are far beyond it.

I think, however, that this lag can be decreased through counting inventory control as an element of the logistics system. It means first of all coordination of aims. Namely the more general aims of logistics system can be better adjusted to the aims of company policy, because they are on a more aggregated level and they are derived from market demands.

50

An example:

Let be the aim of inventory subsystem the minimization of costs. Suppose that this aim is followed by the whole of logistics system. Then optimums determined in inventory subsystem are only suboptimums in respect of the whole system, which will necessarily change, if we investigate it in connection with another element of the logistics system. For example: on the basis of the changes in delivery costs or in relations of sales, inventories /and so the inventory costs/ can be changed due to logistics reasons. But the more factors we want to take into account, the less is the chance for determining optimum with analytical models.

Cost minimization is substituted for profit maximization, which might happen at increasing costs too, if the increase in income is larger. But growing of income depends on market success an important element of which is the service level. It is a paying business for the enterprises, if their logistics costs are increasing, but by this means they can give more to their buyers.

The market recompensates this increasing cost on long term. The result of this connection is the phenomenon mentioned earlier, that the proportion of logistics costs shows an increasing trend within the total cost of enterprises. Unfortunately this is not a characteristic feature of our companies, and its unfavourable results appear at the deterioration of our market-potentials in foreign trade. There are certain central measures taken on the basis of which enterprises developing for example the material handling are

4*

in a more favourable situation. In spite of the fact that the
mechanization of material handling is an important task in
our country - which helps in solving labour shortage - the
rate of increase of expenditures on material handling machines
is smaller than the rate of other so-called productive investments.

Service level is qualified by the activities of seller to
accept and supply the orders. As it is well known, our
producing companies do more of their buyings under relatively
long length of delivery with random receiving times.
According to this, inventories accumulate at buyers as I
mentioned. Supposing one seller and some buyers, this
situation is unambiguously unfavourable. There is a need for
more co-ordinated operation of the "quasi" system of logistics.
For sake of making steps by sellers to increase the proportion
of sales from inventory on hand, some extra expenditures are
needed. This excess expenditure /which may be the cost of
store-room building, cost of higher inventories, mechanization
of material handling, etc./ is not demanded either by the
inside market, or by the regulation system.

Joinings exist, main task of which is the development of
logistics system, but these have no sufficient importance.
For example there is an association founded by foreign
trade companies, which uses its capital for the development
of packaging, warehousing, etc. activities of industrial
companies. Their target is to develop marketability and
service level.

Products, with wide assortment and short life-cycle, have distinguished importance from the point of view of inventory control. It is easy to verify mathematically too, that increasing assortment involves bigger increases in inventories than is of turnover. There are some articles /for example articles of fashion/ which have short life-cycle. It is very important here to forecast demand.

It seems to be a tendency that the growing number of assortment elements involves shorter life-time of particular goods. Both of them cause increases in inventories supposing the same level of service. To a certain extent this can be compensated by rapid deliveries, use of computers, or by the application of market research.

4. Some findings of a company level research concerning this subject

In the framework of the research work we analysed the connections between a commercial company performing both wholesale and retail activity and five producing companies. The commercial company purchases from about 1oo producers, and 4o percent of its actual buying is represented by the five companies mentioned. 3o percent of the sales of these five producers goes to the commercial company concerned, which is the largest buyer of the producers except one.

During the last year, market potential of goods deteriorated, due to decreases in export. Producers tried to compensate their difficulties in sales by modifying the structure of products, and by searching for new partners in some markets. To a certain extent it was successful, and due to this production hardly decreased compared to the level of the year before. Production of goods has seasonal fluctuations and inventory consequences of this are taken by commercial companies. Holding inventories of finished goods is not a characteristic feature of producers. Actually output inventories are equal to the technical needs of shipping.

Inventories held by producers decreased seriously, partly due to conscious actions and partly due to difficulties in supply. The general thesis which says that sharpening of market competition and exporting of goods increase the need for stocks of finished goods, seems to be invalid. Effect derived from restricting economic growth was stronger, that is instable demand draws lower level of inventories because of the growing risk of having stocks unsold.

Service level of sellers remained unchanged in the logistics system, and what is more, a part of sellers tried to change the system of conditions in that direction which is favourable for them. This might be observed in the effort of suppliers to increase the length of supply in order to ease their own problems. Besides this they tried to terminate their obligations to pay penalty after shippings later than stated in contracts. Deliveries are scheduled for a month, but actually more than a half of it is delivered in the last third of the month. Because of this a part of shippings usually remain for the next month. As a

54

conclusion we can state that at present it is not characteristic that producing companies solve their difficulties in
sales by increasing service level of logistics system.

References

1. Feliné Nagy Márta /1979/: Az anyagmozgatás helyzete az
                 iparban /Material Handling in the Industry/.
                 Ipargazdaság, 1979, 1o.
2. Heskett, J.L./1977/: Logistics - essential to strategy.
                 Harvard Business Review 1977/6.
3. Pfohl,H.C./1972/: Marketing-Logistik /Marketing-Logistics/.
                 Distribution-Verlag GmbH, Mainz 1972.

Proc. First Int. Symp. on Inventories
Budapest, Hungary 1980

GUIDELINES FOR LOT-SIZING SELECTION IN MULTI-ECHELON REQUIREMENTS PLANNING SYSTEMS

JOSEPH D. BLACKBURN and **ROBERT A. MILLEN**

Vanderbilt University, Nashville, TENN, USA

1. Introduction

Material requirements planning (MRP) systems were developed over a decade ago to meet the needs of manufacturers for better inventory control in complex assembly processes. A distinctive feature of these processes, which renders traditional inventory control techniques inappropriate, is that the demands (and resulting production schedules) for all components from raw materials through finished goods, are directly dependent on the schedule of requirements for higher level assemblies. This concept, termed dependent demand, is exploited by MRP systems to coordinate the inventory ordering policies for all the components of the manufacturing process, since shortage of a single item can halt the assembly process, resulting in sharply diminished productivity.

MRP systems were made possible by the emergence of the computer as a fast, economical information processor. Although the growth in acceptance of these systems has paralleled that of computers, the requirements planning systems in use today are, unfortunately, little more than data processors. In terms of the decision-rules employed for inventory control and production scheduling, these systems are unsophisticated, using ordering policies that myopically focus on a

[1] This research was supported in part by a grant from the Vanderbilt University Research Council.

single component at a time and that neglect the existing interdependencies among decisions at different levels of the assembly process.

Our research has been directed toward this need for better coordination of the ordering decisions at the different stages of the production process. In this paper we summarize this research and provide guidelines by which production planners can select or modify heuristic decision rules to achieve coordination and lower system operating costs.

The findings reported here are based on an analysis of the multi-stage lot-sizing problem for assembly processes. In this problem the objective is to minimize the sum of set-up charges and inventory holding costs across all stages in a single end item assembly process managed on a periodic review basis. The set-up, or ordering, cost is fixed and incurred whenever an order is placed, whereas the holding cost is assumed to be proportional to the end-of-period inventory. Demand by time period for the end product is assumed to be known with certainty over the planning horizon and must be satisfied from on-hand inventory. No demand for components at any intermediate stage exists except that generated by demand for the final product.

As shown in Figure 1, each part (or stage) in an assembly process is the input to at most one successor part, but may be assembled from multiple predecessors.

End Product Demand

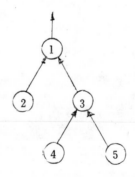

Assembly Structure Example

Figure 1

All lead times are assumed to be constant and, without loss of generality, equal to zero. In addition, there are no constraints on capacity at any stage.

A number of authors have developed optimum-seeking algorithms for the multi-level lot-sizing problem (see Blackburn and Millen (1980b) for a summary of this literature). However, these algorithms are largely unused in operating MRP systems due to their computational requirements, coupled with the need for a centralized production planning function.

Our initial studies of this problem found that most of the research on the development of heuristic procedures lacked a sound theoretical foundation, even for single-level assembly processes. Consequently, our first studies focused on the single-level lot-sizing problem under both static and dynamic (or rolling-schedule) operating conditions. These results are presented in the next section. Following this, an analysis of the multi-echelon problem is given.

2. Analysis of Single-Level Lot-Sizing Heuristics

2.1 The Static Problem

For a finite horizon, deterministic demand problem, it is well-known that the algorithm proposed by Wagner-Whitin (1958) provides an optimal solution for the single-stage problem. However, this algorithm is not extensively used in practice, primarily due to its computational requirements. As alternatives, a number of computationally -simpler heuristics have been proposed, yet these have not been accompanied by well-established cost performance guidelines by which production planners can select among the available heuristics. Studies of the comparative effectiveness of heuristics have been conducted (see Blackburn and Millen (1979a) for a literature summary), but these research efforts consisted of empirical tests performed on a small sample of problems and were unable to pinpoint causes of differences in cost performance among the heuristics.

The objective of our study was to isolate factors which could better explain any deviation from optimality by two of the better-known heuristics, namely the

Part-Period-Cost-Balancing (see Gorham, (1970)) and the Silver-Meal (1973) methods. Insights were gained by investigating the problem analytically, as well as empirically. Initially, an analysis of the implied objective functions of the heuristics, as compared to that of the Wagner-Whitin algorithm, was carried out under simplified conditions of an infinite horizon and constant demand per period. These conditions were assumed to insure that end-of-horizon and demand variability effects, whose presence tends to confuse the issue in most of the empirical tests, were eliminated.

As reported in Blackburn and Millen (1979a), the analytical study resulted in two main findings. First, the Silver-Meal (SM) heuristic is identical to the Wagner-Whitin (WW) method in the infinite horizon, constant demand case. Thus any differences between the two algorithms would be due to either horizon effects or demand variability. Second, it was found that the Part-Period (PP) method deviates from the decisions produced by WW under certain combinations of cost parameters and, moreover, that the bias is always toward larger orders than those of WW. The PP deviations can be explained in terms of a ratio called the lot-sizing index, $S/h\overline{D}$, where S is the cost of a set-up (or order), h is the per unit inventory holding cost per time period, and $\overline{D}$ is the average demand per period. Over certain ranges of $S/h\overline{D}$, the order interval under PP will exceed that specified under WW by one period, resulting in diminished cost performance.

To test the validity of these analytical findings under conditions of a finite horizon and variable demand, an extensive set of experimental tests were conducted (see Blackburn and Millen, 1979b). These empirical tests showed that the $S/h\overline{D}$ ratio has significant explanatory powers with respect to deviations from optimality by both the PP and SM heuristics.

2.2 The Dynamic, or Rolling-Schedule, Problem

Further analysis of the single-level experimental results indicated that the decisions of both the heuristics and the WW algorithm were influenced by the length of the planning horizon. In a previous study, Baker (1977) had demonstrated the horizon sensitivity of WW. However, the myopic nature of the PP and SM heuristics suggests that the effect of the horizon on the immediate decisions of these methods should be less pronounced than with Wagner-Whitin.

These observations led to the conjecture that the superior cost performance of the WW algorithm in a static situation might not hold in a dynamic, or rolling schedule, setting. That is, as in most applications, a firm faces a problem of indefinite length and, at any point in time, decisions are determined for some fixed planning horizon of, say, n periods, but only the imminent decisions are implemented. When the time arrives for the next order to be placed, a horizon of n periods is again "rolled out" and only the initial decisions are implemented.

To illustrate the difficulties that can occur when WW is used in this commonly-occurring rolling schedule environment, it is useful to consider again the simplified analytical problem of the preceding section--that is, infinite horizon and constant demand per period. Consider a problem with the following parameters:

Set-up cost, S   = 2450
Holding cost, h =   1
Demand, $\bar{D}$ = 100 units per period

In the infinite horizon problem, the order interval for both the WW and SM algorithms would be 7 periods (as computed by $(2S/h\bar{D})^{1/2}$). However, if a 10-period planning horizon were used in a rolling schedule setting, the solutions produced by the two algorithms would be markedly different. By optimizing over the planning horizon, WW would schedule orders of 5 periods each and roll forward 5 periods at a time. The SM heuristic would place orders of 700 and 300 for the 10-period problem, rolling forward 7 periods at a time. Thus, over the infinite horizon an optimal sequence of orders every 7 periods would be generated by Silver-Meal, and Wagner-Whitin would clearly deviate from the optimal solution.

One advantage of the WW algorithm which the preceding example fails to disclose is that it can better exploit demand variability in its decisions than the SM or PP heuristics. Consequently, a series of experiments were conducted to investigate the impact of the variance of the demand distribution, the length of the forecast window and the cost parameters on the cost effectiveness of the WW and SM lot-sizing methods in a rolling schedule implementation. A detailed description of this study is reported in Blackburn and Millen (1980a). The major finding is that for short forecast horizons, SM does outperform WW in a rolling schedule setting, even under conditions of demand uncertainty. As in the single-level static experiments, the explanatory variable appears to be the $S/h\overline{D}$ ratio, expressed as an average order interval $T = (2S/h\overline{D})^{1/2}$. For planning horizons up to about 2T order intervals, Silver-Meal tends to provide cost performance superior to that of Wagner-Whitin. However, WW dominates for all longer horizons.

These single-level lot-sizing studies show that, contrary to conventional wisdom, Wagner-Whitin is not optimal under all conditions in the standard dynamic setting and that the $S/h\overline{D}$ ratio is an important factor to consider in heuristic selection under static and dynamic conditions.

3. The Multi-Stage Assembly Process

In most MRP systems the production plan is generated by beginning with the end product and sequentially applying a single-level lot-sizing heuristic (such as Part-Period) down through the product structure. There are potential problems with this approach. From the single-level research reported in Section 2, we know that some of these heuristics have flaws which degrade their performance even at a single level. Moreover, this suboptimal approach of one echelon at a time, while computationally simple, can yield substantial cost inefficiencies.

In order to gain insights into the fundamental relationships between decisions at different levels of the assembly process, an analytical study was conducted on the lot-sizing problem, again under simplified conditions of an infinite horizon and constant demand per period. Assume that the components of the assembly structure are numbered from 1 to M, with the end product labeled 1 and such that if

62

component i is a successor of component j then $i < j$.

$P(j)$ = single successor of component j;

$C(j)$ = the set of predecessors of component j;

S_j = set-up cost for component j; and

h_j = per period holding cost per unit of component j.

Under the additional assumption that the number of orders from P(j) combined at stage j is a constant, k_j, the multi-stage lot-sizing problem reduces to finding a set of order intervals $(n_1,...,n_m)$ which minimizes

$$\sum_{j=1}^{M}\left(\frac{S_j}{n_j} + \frac{h_j \overline{D} n_{p(j)} (k_j-1)}{2}\right) \qquad (1)$$

subject to:

$$n_j = k_j n_{p(j)} \qquad (2)$$

$$n_j k_j \geq 1 \text{ and integer} \qquad (3)$$

where $n_1 = k_1$ and $n_{p(1)} = 1$.

Clarification of the interdependencies among stages of the assembly process can be achieved by rewriting (1) in terms of the echelon stock inventory concept introduced by Clark and Scarf (1960). Defining the echelon inventory at stage j to be all units held at stage j and its successors and the per unit echelon inventory holding cost, e_j, as $h_j - \sum_{i \in C(j)} h_i$, expression (1) can be rewritten as

$$\sum_{j=1}^{M}\left(\frac{S_j}{n_j} + \frac{e_j \overline{D} n_j}{2}\right) \qquad (4)$$

The echelon stock holding cost is essentially a holding cost based on the value added at stage j.

Close examination of (4) reveals some of the serious suboptimization problems that accompany the sequential application of a single-stage lot-sizing method in an assembly structure. Application of the Wagner-Whitin method to the product structure shown in Figure 1 would first find an optimal value of n_1 which minimizes $\left(\frac{S_1}{n_1} + \frac{e_1 \overline{D} n_1}{2}\right)$ and the resulting demand pattern of $n_1 \overline{D}$ units every n_1 periods would then be "passed down" to stages 2 and 3 and similar, single-stage problems would be solved on down through the product structure. Other single-stage heuristics would approach this problem in a similarly myopic fashion.

A better approach to this problem is suggested by rewriting expression (4), for the product structure shown in Figure 1, as

$$\frac{S_1 + S_2/k_2 + S_3/k_3 + S_4/k_3k_4 + S_5/k_3k_5}{n_1} + \frac{\overline{Dn_1}}{2} (e_1 + e_2k_2 + e_3k_3 + e_4k_3k_4 + e_5k_3k_5).$$

With estimates of $k_2, \ldots, k_5$, this expression could be used to make lot-sizing decisions at stage 1 with an adjusted set-up cost of

$$S_1 + S_2/k_2 + S_3/k_3 + S_4/k_3k_4 + S_5/k_3k_5$$

and a modified echelon holding cost of $e_1 + e_2 + e_3k_3 + e_4k_3k_4 + e_5k_3k_5$. Essentially, these adjusted costs serve to coordinate the lot-sizing decisions at stage 1 with the order intervals at all predecessor stages, for k_j is an estimate of the average number of orders from stage $P(j)$ to be combined into a single order at stage j.

In our analytical study of the simplified lot-sizing problem, several methods for computing estimates of the k_j were developed. The resulting cost modifications can be used by a single-level lot-sizing heuristic, such as Wagner-Whitin or Silver-Meal, in a multi-stage problem with no increase in computational effort and, at the same time, offer the potential of improved cost performance through better coordination of the lot-sizing decisions. These cost modifications were then tested experimentally under more realistic conditions of a finite horizon and variable demand (see Blackburn and Millen (1980b) for complete details). A description of the two cost modifications procedures which proved most effective in our empirical tests is reported here.

One cost modification procedure, the continuous approximation (CA), is based on a differential calculus approach to the solution of (4). Under this method, the estimates of the k_j are determined in the sequence of j=M, M-1,...,1 by solving

$$k_j = \max \left\{ \left(\frac{\hat{S}_j}{S_{P(j)}} \cdot \frac{e_{P(j)}}{\hat{e}_j} \right)^{1/2}, 1 \right\}$$

where

$$\hat{S}_j = S_j + \sum_{i \varepsilon C(j)} \frac{\hat{S}_i}{k_i} \quad \text{and} \quad \hat{e}_j = e_j + \sum_{i \varepsilon C(j)} k_i \hat{e}_i \qquad (5)$$

The resulting values of $\hat{S}_j$ and $\hat{e}_j$ are the modified set-up and holding costs, respectively, to be used for lot-sizing at stage j in the multi-echelon process.

Another effective procedure is based on integer approximations (IA) of the k_j values. These estimates are determined by solving for the smallest integer value of k_j such that

$$k_j(k_j + 1) \geq \frac{\hat{S}_j}{S_{P(j)}} \cdot \frac{e_{P(j)}}{\hat{e}_j}$$

where $\hat{S}j$ and $\hat{e}_j$ are defined as in (5). The order of calculation is again up the product hierarchy from stage M to stage 1.

The experimental results (expressed as an average percentage deviation from the cost of an optimal solution) are displayed below for the product structure of Figure 1. These results are based on a horizon of twelve periods, demands randomly generated from a uniform distribution over (0,200), and ten replications for each of the forty cost combinations employed.

Wagner-Whitin Algorithms			Silver-Meal Heuristics		
Unmodified	CA	IA	Unmodified	CA	IA
6.86%	0.44%	0.66%	14.66%	8.31%	8.67%

As indicated, the k-adjusted cost modifications greatly enhance the performance of the single-level lot-sizing algorithms in a multi-level setting. For the conditions studied, the Wagner-Whitin modified heuristics provide extremely good results with computation times about two orders of magnitude faster than that required for the optimal solution.

In research currently in progress, we are investigating the effectiveness of the cost-modified heuristics in a multi-level, rolling schedule setting. Future research efforts are planned which consider additional practical aspects of the requirements planning problem, such as capacity constraints at different levels of the product structure and processes with multiple end products.

References

1. Baker, K. (1977): "An Experimental Study of the Effectiveness of Rolling Schedules in Production Planning," Decision Sciences, vol. 8, no. 1, p. 19.

2. Blackburn, J.D. and Millen, R.A. (1979a): "Selecting a Lot-Sizing Method for a Single-Level Assembly Process: Part I - Analytical Results," Production and Inventory Management, vol. 20, no. 3, p. 42.

3. Blackburn, J.D. and Millen, R.A. (1979b): "Selecting a Lot-Sizing Method for a Single-Level Assembly Process: Part II - Empirical Results," Production and Inventory Management, vol. 20, no. 4, p. 41.

4. Blackburn, J.D. and Millen, R.A. (1980a): "Heuristic Lot-Sizing Performance in a Rolling-Schedule Environment," Working Paper 79-102, Owen Graduate School of Management, Vanderbilt University (to appear in Decision Sciences).

5. Blackburn, J.D. and Millen, R.A. (1980b): "Improved Heuristics for Multi-Echelon Requirement Planning Systems," Working Paper 79-101, Owen Graduate School of Management, Vanderbilt University.

6. Clark, A.J. and Scarf, H. (1960): "Optimal Policies for a Multi-Echelon Inventory Problem," Management Science, vol. 6, no. 4.

7. Gorham, T. (1970): "Dynamic Order Quantities," Production and Inventory Management, vol. 11, no. 2.

8. Silver, E.A. and Meal, H.C. (1973): "A Heuristic for Selecting Lot Size Quantities for the Case of a Deterministic Time-Varying Demand Rate and Discrete Opportunities for Replemishment," Production and Inventory Management, vol. 14, no. 2.

9. Wagner, H.M. and Whitin, T. (1958): "Dynamic Version of the Economic Lot Size Model," Management Science, vol. 5, no. 1.

Proc. First Int. Symp. on Inventories
Budapest, Hungary 1980

METHODS FOR LONG-TERM PLANNING OF STOCKS OF SEMI-FINISHED GOODS WITHIN AN EXTENDED MASS PRODUCTION PROCESS

GISELA BRITT

Wilhelm Pieck University, Rostock, GDR

For the sake of rapid reimbursement of circulating material assets with simultaneous increase of continuity of production /1/, a more comprehensive planning of circulating assets is to be involved in the annual production plans of companies. Important decisions are made for reasonable utilization of circulating funds of semi-finished products in accordance with long-term planning and the organization of production processes. At this stage of planning the main factor influencing the utilization of funds is the average demand for semi-finished products of a certain version of plan / $\overline{PFU}_{UFE}$ /, depending on the volume of production and on the intensity of circulating assets for semi-finished products / f_{UFE} /. Traditional methods for the estimation of circulating assets are still limited to the calculation of circulating assets after having made technological plans.

Planning of circulating assets needed by the plants means first of all the estimation of financial means, which is carried out within the process of annual planning. Financial planning needs previously determined technological process with maximal possible, exact forecast of effects influencing these

5*

processes. Due to the low level of planning of circulating
assets within the whole planning process of the company, these
assets play a passive role in the organization of production
and can be modified in the long run in harmony with the planning of production processes.

Integration of plans for circulating assets into the long-
term industrial planning provides that planning be based on
exact data, already known at the time of planning. /Or, if it
is not known, it can be determined./ Calculation methods of
estimating demand for semi-finished products are based on linear
or partly linear cost functions and on an even production
schedule from starting to finishing the product in question.

According to Fischer /2/ the following equation is to be
used to determine the average stock of semi-finished products:

$$\overline{PFU}_{UFE} = kzk \cdot p \cdot K_E \qquad\qquad /1/$$

and

$$\overline{f_{UFE}} = kzk \cdot p \cdot \frac{K_E}{WP}$$

where the cost coefficient of products of linear cost consumption is 0.5.

In most of the machine factories several series are simultaneously processed, the cost consumption of which is nonlinear, and their production period and schedule are varying. In
this case the necessary circulating assets for semi-finished
products can be forecasted only by addition of the values shown
in the cost curve envisaged for semi-finished product
stocks. Not all types of circulating assets can be estimated
on the basis of the producing costs of individual products. For

example, the growth of costs of sophisticated products depending on processing and organization is only known when the technological process is determined in all details, and the earli-
est possible term is in the annual planning period. As a consequence of investigations, it turned out that from the point
of view of planning average stocks of semi-finished products,
the total growth of costs in the whole production of the plant,
deriving from cost curves of individual products, is of primary
importance. Until unevenness of cost curves of individual products and variability in their production processes as well as
inter-cyclic parallelism are equalized, so that total cost
growth will be linear, the simplified method of equation /1/
is to be applied at calculating average stock demand of semi-
finished products. Thus, at the plant investigated in Fig. 1,
products of different labour intensity and of varying production programs are produced, where the schedule of production as
well as inter-cyclic parallelism are varying, and the growth of
costs is not typical by products.

The fact that the aggregate curves of all products of the
plant are linear is important for the estimation of average
stock of semi-finished products, thus the following values can
be calculated:

$$\overline{PFU}_{UFE} = kzk \cdot p \cdot K_E \qquad\qquad /2/$$
$$= 0.5 \cdot p \cdot K_E$$

If the total cost curve of the plant within the period investigated is progressive or degressive, the average value of
cost growth is $\gtrless 0.5$ and consequently the average demand for

circulating assets is higher or lower than stated in equation /2/.

When we are planning circulating assets in the long run, it is to be determined that in accordance with planning and organization of production how strong is the influence of variability of total cost growth on the average need for circulating assets. From this aspect, i.e. from the point of view of forecasting, average demand for circulating assets, and the specific demand for semi-finished products $\overline{f_{UFE}}$, a coefficient of unevenness in organization $\overline{k_{ug}}$ has been developed, where

$$\overline{k_{ug}} = \frac{\sum\limits_{i=1}^{p} AD_i}{\overline{AV}} \qquad /3/$$

For plants with linear total cost growth the average coefficient of unevenness is 1 for the entire investigation period, though time-depending measurements for $\overline{k_{ug}}$ - as shown in Fig. 1 - show considerable fluctuation.

In other cases the average stock level of semi-finished products may be calculated with the application of the following equation /see Fig. 2/ extended from equation /2/:

$$\overline{PFU}_{UFE} = 0.5 \cdot \overline{k_{ug}} \cdot \overline{K_E} \qquad /4/$$

It is verified here that product $0.5 \cdot \overline{k_{ug}}$ equals with the average cost growth of all the products mentioned in equation /2/ as well as with the total cost growth of the plants, so that

$$\overline{PFU}_{UFE} = \overline{kzk} \cdot \overline{p} \cdot \overline{K_E} \qquad /5/$$

70

A further simplification might be applied for the estimation of the specific input of semi-finished products $\overline{f_{UFE}}$ where planning in connection with the cost factor was completed by the planning of time factor , as well, so that

$$\overline{f_{UFE}} = \frac{1}{2} \cdot \overline{k_{ug}} \cdot \frac{\overline{A_E} \cdot \overline{p}}{\overline{AV} \cdot 360} \cdot \overline{KS} \qquad /6/$$

and

$$= \overline{kzk} \cdot \frac{\overline{A_E} \cdot \overline{p}}{\overline{AV} \cdot 360} \cdot \overline{KS}$$

The demonstrated method of long-term forecast of circulating asset intensity $\overline{f_{UFE}}$ has been applied in several large-scale plants manufacturing products of long production period. The results achieved prove with sufficient accuracy the expedience of the developed simple method for estimating average stock of semi-finished products in connection with production processes.

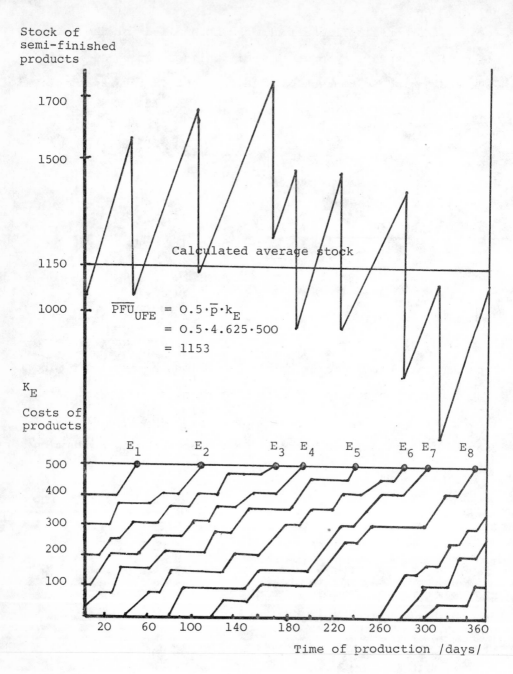

Stock of semi-finished products

1700

1500

1150

1000

Calculated average stock

$$\overline{PFU}_{UFE} = 0.5 \cdot \overline{p} \cdot k_E$$
$$= 0.5 \cdot 4.625 \cdot 500$$
$$= 1153$$

K_E

Costs of products

E_1 E_2 E_3 E_4 E_5 E_6 E_7 E_8

500

400

300

200

100

20   60   100   140   180   220   260   300   360

Time of production /days/

Fig. 1

Plant of unified production program, different production periods of goods and uneven schedule of production from starting to finishing of products. Growth of total costs of the plant is linear

$$\overline{PFU}_{UFE} = 0.5 \cdot \overline{k_{ug}} \cdot \overline{p} \cdot \overline{K}_E$$

$$\overline{PFU}_{UFE} = 0.5 \cdot 1.1829 \cdot 3.5 \cdot 120 = 248.41$$

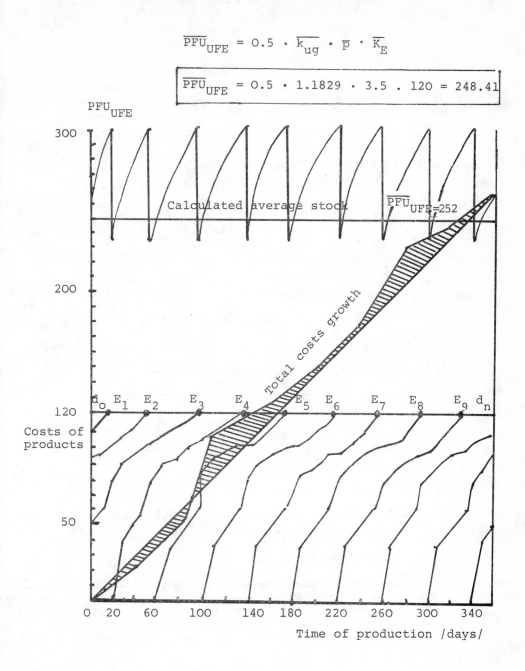

Fig. 2

Plant with unified production program, typical cost growth, even production periods and schedule <u>Total cost growth is non-linear</u>

73

SYMBOLS

$\overline{PFU}_{UFE}$ average stock of semi-finished products required
for a given period

kzk   cost growth coefficient of products expressing
cost-flow and organization of production

$\overline{kzk}$ average cost growth of all products within a
given period

p   quantity of finished products for the same
period

$\overline{f}_{UFE}$ annual average intensity of circulating funds
of semi-finished products /relation between the
annual average circulating funds for semi-finished
products,and total production - WP/

$\overline{KS}$ average estimation of costs /total production
cost per production value of M 100/

K_E cost of one product

$\overline{KE}$ average cost of total production within a given
period

$\overline{k}_{ug}$ average coefficient of unevenness within the
investigated period

AD_i average labour intensity per day in the course
of production of finished products E_i

$\overline{AV}$ daily average labour input for production

REFERENCES

1. Britt, Gisela and Britt, Karl-Heinz /1978/: Zur Ermittlung
   von Vorgaben für die technisch-ökonomische Aufgaben-
   stellung von Erzeugnisentwicklungen - Dissertation B.
   Wilhelm-Pieck-Universität Rostock, Sektion Soziali-
   stische Betriebswirtschaft /Investigation of limits for
   technical-economical specifications for designing
   products/.

2. Fischer, K. /1972/: Betriebsanalyse in der volkseigenen
   Industrie, Berlin: Verlag Die Wirtschaft /Analysis
   of enterprises in the nationally owned industry/.

3. Nick, H. /1974/: Intensivierung und wissenschaftlich-
   technischer Fortschritt. Berlin: Dietz Verlag
   /Intensifying and scientific-technical progress/.

Proc. First Int. Symp. on Inventories
Budapest, Hungary 1980

EFFICIENCY
AND EFFICIENCY MEASUREMENT
IN MATERIALS MANAGEMENT

ROLF ESCHENBACH

Vienna University of Economics, Vienna, Austria

Materials management is a business function dealing partly
with business input. Which parts of business input are concerned and which functions are fulfilled is still an inter-
nationally controversial question.[1] For our purposes -
efficiency and efficiency measurement - the term of materials
management will be defined as follows:

Subjects of materials management are:

- Raw materials and supplies,

- Capital goods,

- Services.

Materials management functions in a company are:

- Procurement market research,

- Value analysis,

- Materials planning,

- Acquisition (purchase, lease, barter, own
  production),

---

[1] comp. Grochla (Elements) p.14

- Follow-up,

- Inbound shipment,

- Receiving quantity check,

- Receiving quality control,

- Auditing,

- Storing,

- Utilization of goods and services not needed.

The concept of logistics further includes: Inplant transportation, production control, and outbound shipment. The term procurement also comprises immaterial goods, capital, people, and information.

In many companies, materials management contributes more to success than most of the other business functions involved. Buyers in important industries are the companies' biggest spenders disposing of more than 5o per cent of the gross profits on sales. Additional success in materials management often can be achieved through minor investments, i.e. without loss of flexibility, that is without additional risk taking. There is hardly any other business function where the employment of energy, intelligence, and organization will make itself well paid within such a short period of time.[2]

[2] comp. Eschenbach (Know-how) p.1837 ff
comp. Eschenbach (Purchasing Efficiency) p.91 ff

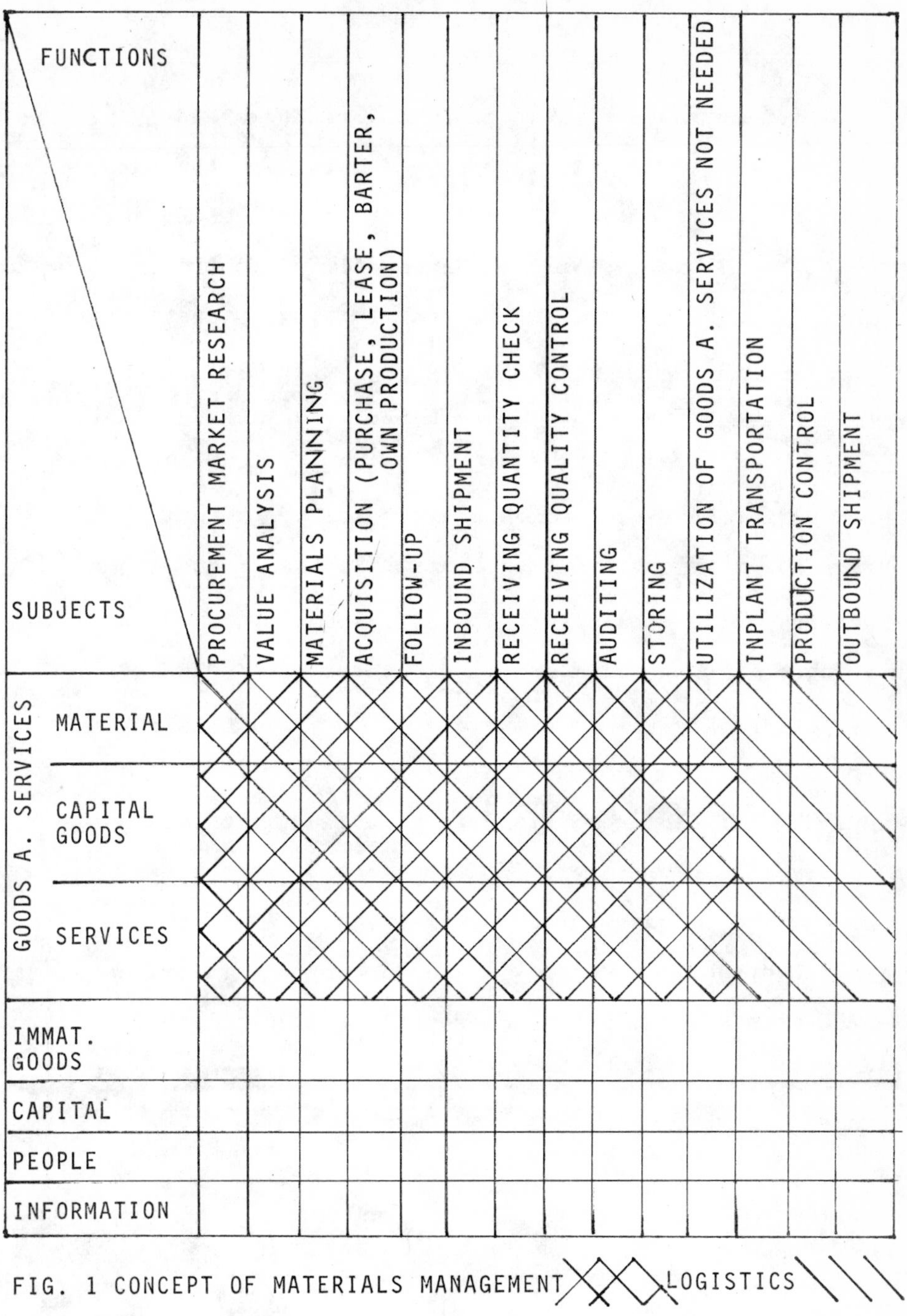

FUNCTIONS

SUBJECTS

GOODS A. SERVICES		PROCUREMENT MARKET RESEARCH	VALUE ANALYSIS	MATERIALS PLANNING	ACQUISITION (PURCHASE, LEASE, BARTER, OWN PRODUCTION)	FOLLOW-UP	INBOUND SHIPMENT	RECEIVING QUANTITY CHECK	RECEIVING QUALITY CONTROL	AUDITING	STORING	UTILIZATION OF GOODS A. SERVICES NOT NEEDED	INPLANT TRANSPORTATION	PRODUCTION CONTROL	OUTBOUND SHIPMENT
	MATERIAL														
	CAPITAL GOODS														
	SERVICES														
IMMAT. GOODS															
CAPITAL															
PEOPLE															
INFORMATION															

FIG. 1 CONCEPT OF MATERIALS MANAGEMENT ⟨XX⟩ LOGISTICS ⟨///⟩

3

The worldwide lack of numerous raw materials and energy
resources on the one hand and the increasing international
competition for outlets for industrial products and services
on the other force enterprises to fully utilize the materials management potential. However, most companies do not
know to what extent materials management can contribute
to their success and to what extent it actually does.
Systematic planning or even control of this potential do
not exist. Numerous companies think it impracticable to plan
and control success in the field of materials management
though performance evaluation and control are a matter of
course for many business functions. Neither production nor
marketing people feel themselves discriminated if they are
integrated into the firm's overall control system. Given
this fact and the possible chances of success, efficiency
control in materials management has long been neglected to
a considerable degree. Systematic guidelines are lacking
in theory and in practice. If management by objectives is
to be applied, management cannot leave such an important
activity outside the company's closed control system. Also
considerations regarding the direction of capital investment at a possibly supra-company level call for methods and
standards of materials efficiency measurement.
Various groups are interested in measuring the achievements
of materials management:

- The company's management,
- Materials personnel,
- Under certain circumstances also public
  institutions.

All three groups need criteria for directing resources to
the different activities within a company. Both planned and
measured achievements are important factors in determining
the allocation of capital and manpower. To find such allocation criteria is thus one of the most important targets
of efficiency measurement in materials management.

We are still at the beginning of investigations into
materials efficiency measurement. However, there seem to
exist certain lines of development to be taken up in
future discussions. The practical requirements of materials
management controlling evolving in various companies determine the direction of this development.

There are three ways of measuring efficiency:

- By absolute and relative index numbers,
- By measuring the quality of materials manage-
  ment tools,
- By measuring the achievement of objectives.

Absolute index numbers, for instance on inventories or the
level of purchase prices, do not tell much about the efficiency of a company's materials department. The fact that
they are still determined by companies does not make them
more useful. In any case, success or failure cannot be
measured by this method. Better suited are proportional
numbers if actually interconnected data are related to
each other. Most of these index numbers, however, are un-
suited for inter-firm comparisons - but it is these com-

parisons that are requested again and again - because the individual circumstances are too different in the various companies even among companies within an industry. Proportional numbers, on the other hand, can be used to a limited extent for the periodic comparison of one and the same firm. On account of the numerous internal changes regarding the company's setup and processes hardly more than two or three years can be compared.

First though incomplete empirical investigations into one industrial sector of the Federal Republic of Germany indicate certain correlations between the quality of the materials management tools used and the purchasing efficiency: The higher the organizational level (e.g. independent purchasing department, materials handbook, exact definition of tasks and responsibilities) and the more extensive the materials management know-how (e.g. supplier evaluation, value analysis) are, the lower were purchasing prices and the better procurement conditions under comparable circumstances.[3] These correlations have to be studied more thoroughly with the aim of quantifying them to a larger degree and making them universally valid at least for some industries or company size categories.

The most promising efficiency measurement in materials management seems to be to measure the achievement of

[3] comp. Eschenbach (Purchasing Efficiency) p.91 ff

82

objectives. This, however, is based on the assumption
that there are quantified and scheduled objectives set
in materials management. Objectives setting of this kind
almost does not exist in today's business practice. Examples
would be:

- Financial targets (e.g. costs, liquidity),
- Performance targets (e.g. deliverability,
  warranties, quality),
- Schedule targets.

Target planning and target attainment control can clarify
the contribution of materials management to the company's
total financial result. They help to integrate materials
management controlling into the overall control system
of the company. Since the development of the future-oriented
accounting (controlling) processes is underway on an international scale, it seems to be a highly favourable time
for integrating materials management into this project.

Every type of efficiency measurement requires that all
materials functions in enterprises can be assigned to
particular positions and that the position holders have
the necessary authority to fulfill their task.[4] In
particular small companies violate these basic rules.
Thus it seems to be necessary in the future to concentrate on the special problems of materials management

[4] comp. Tanew (Elements) p.25 ff

in small and medium-sized companies to maintain their
competitiveness in a sound national economy.

Literature

Eschenbach, R.: (know how) Das materialwirtschaftliche
know how - Ergebnisse einer empirischen Untersuchung
und Empfehlungen zur Verbesserung des Einkaufserfolges -
(Know-how) Materials Management Know-how - Results of
an Empirical Investigation and Recommendations for Enhancing Efficiency in Purchasing - Brauwelt 118 (1978)
p.1837 - 184o

Eschenbach, R.: (Einkaufserfolge) Einkaufserfolge und Ein-
kaufsverhalten - Ergebnisse einer empirischen Untersuchung
und Empfehlungen zur Verbesserung des Einkaufserfolges -
(Purchasing Efficiency) Purchasing Efficiency and Purchasing
Behaviour - Results of an Empirical Investigation and Recommendations for Enhancing Efficiency in Purchasing -
Brauwelt 119 (1979) p.91-94

Grochla, E.:(Grundlagen) Grundlagen der Materialwirtschaft,
(Elements) Elements of Materials Management,
Wiesbaden 1973

Tanew, G.: (Grundlagen) Grundlagen der Planung und Er-
folgskontrolle in der Materialwirtschaft,
(Elements) Elements of Planning and Efficiency Control
in Materials Management,
Dissertation, Vienna 1978

Proc. First Int. Symp. on Inventories
Budapest, Hungary 1980

THE CHANGING ROLE
OF INVENTORIES IN THE ENTERPRISE.
AN EXAMPLE FOR THE ADAPTATION
OF THE MANAGEMENT

KATALIN FARKAS

Institute of Economics, Hungarian Academy of Sciences, Budapest, Hungary

My paper is dealing with the question, inspired by the works and thoughts of Professor János Kornai,[1] what an effect has the shortage of certain materials as a steady and re-producing state on the forms and structure of relative slacks, which exist together with the shortages. I will answer the above, rather general, question only regarding one grade of the economic hierarchy /the enterprise/ and one kind of slacks /the inventories/.

My assumptions come from the detailed investigation of a case, describe certain characteristics of the adaptive process under shortages and can be regarded as a verbal-empirical test of Professor Kornai's theory on the shortage.

I will study a single adaptive action of a big Hungarian enterprise, which demonstrates the forms of adaptation which are characteristic for a resource-constrained economy. The question is: how and why got on the agenda of management the inventories, what action it stimulated and with what a result?

1. The enterprise, its resources and its market situation

1.1. The Pamutnyomóipari Vállalat /Cotton-printing enterprise/ has been founded in 1963, during the administrative-reorganizing action of the government. It has a significant

---

[1]First of all by his most recent book: Economics of Shortage. North-Holland Publ. Co., Amsterdam 1980.

place both in the textile and in the cotton production
with its 9 plants and its garments trade. /Just to illustrate its dimensions: it has 18,400 employees, and its
gross value of production is 5.3 billion Ft-s, 194 million m^2 of clothes./
The enterprise is vertical; its plants represent the whole
production cycle from spinning to printing and garments
trade had been added in the last years.

1.2. Let us look now at the history of the firm from the point
of view of resources, which resource constrained its
working most over various periods.

In the first period after its foundation, the possibilities of development /investment/ were extremely scarce.
The net revenue of the firm was almost totally centralized,
the remaining resource has hardly assured maintenance.

The 1971-75 period brought essential change for the whole
branch of industry. The so-called reconstruction of the
textile industry in accordance with a government resolution became a preferential credit target, and this meant
relatively abundant investment possibilities /capital/.

When the enterprise was founded it had at its disposal
relatively abundant /and in international comparison
relatively cheap/ labour force. Neither the firm's nor
the central economic management did foresee that this
situation will radically change, they considered it as
given and so it did not get on the management's agenda.
At the end of the sixties, the labour force had become a
bottleneck, more and more machinery stopped because of
the shortage of labour, and it became very quickly one of
the most important questions on the agenda of the firm
and of the branch. This gave one of the reasons for the
reconstruction program of the government.

Let us mention here also the stocks /or inventories/ as
forms of resources. The inventories /materials, unfinished
and semi-finished goods and the output stocks/ up till
1976 did not interfere with the working of the firm so

much as they would get in the center of the managerial
attention. Somehow the inventories always played part in
the incentive system of the firm, but never as a central
element.

1.3. It is an important characteristic of the firm that it
imports most of its basic materials and exports more than
the half of its outputs, roughly in equal proportions
on the socialist and capitalist market.

From the point of view of adaptation and inventories this
means both advantages and disadvantages. Most of the cotton
used /60 %/ come from the Soviet Union. The Soviet partner
delivers the cotton ordered for a whole year during a very
short period, so it has to be stored up till using it.
This disadvantage is also acknowledged by the Hungarian
National Bank in the financing system.

As in Hungary there is no production of textile machinery
the firm has to import the machines and the spare parts as
well. This is a disadvantage from the point of view of its
adaptive ability because of two reasons. First, there is a
long procedure of getting permission, and second the long
time of delivery of the socialist partners; the orders are
accepted by them two years in advance. And it is also in
vain that the capitalist firm would be willing to deliver
spare parts in two weeks; according to the regulation and
control of Hungarian foreign trade the firm has to order
the spare parts from the capitalist market one year in
advance. It is no wonder that compared to use there are
the biggest stocks accumulated in spare parts.

The mark of the resource-constrained /or shortage/ economy
can be found on the organization of the firm as well: all
the essential functions /such as buying, selling and
programming of production/ are totally centralized. Within
the competence of the plants lie only the administration
of labour force, the technology and the management of some
materials. The possibility of wage-increase in the plants
is determined by the incentive system of the firm con-

nected with the fulfilment of the plan and the new form
of this incentive system is strongly connected with the
change in stocks.

2. The system and practice of the management of inventories within the firm

As all the economic processes, the management of inventories
also has two aspects: it is taking place both in the financial
and in the real sphere of the firm. This duality appears in
the organization of the firm too: the inventories are dealt
with by the financial and production administration.

2.1. The Hungarian National Bank finances the inventories by
various kinds of credit. The targets concerning the
financing of inventories are given to the management of
the firm and the plants by the financial department of
the firm. This target comes from the level of working
capital acknowledged by the National Bank. Concerning
this level the firm often initiates bargaining with the
Bank; with the expression used by the management they
"ask for a correction". At the headquarters of the firm
they set up the targets for reduction of the inventories
by analyzing the data of the previous year. This is
broken down for the plants, and the responsible person
/generally the financial manager or the engineer-in-
charge of the plant/ is given.

2.2. The tasks of the real sphere concerning the inventories
are dealt with by the sales department /purchasing textile
materials, sales/, the purchasing department /purchasing
and storing a part of non-textile materials/ and the
purchasing department of the plants /purchasing and
storing the other part of non-textile materials/.

I. The textile stocks fall within the authority of the
sales department and are managed centrally. In the
centrally managed stock group there is a part of
non-textile stocks /mainly chemicals and the spare
parts for imported machinery/ - this is the authority
of the central purchasing department.

II. Another group of inventories   is purchased
     centrally, but stored at the plants. This is de-
     termined partly by rationality and partly by neces-
     sity. It is rational that the materials used in all
     the plants are purchased centrally and that they
     can get a discount as they purchase big quantities.
     It is a necessity because suppliers are unwilling to
     deal with the plants and deliver in small quantities.
     The special structure and functioning of the market
     presses the enterprise to act as a single purchaser
     and to organize the distribution within the firm.

     The practice of management in this group is the
     following: the orders of the plants /more exactly the
     claims/ are passed over to the purchasing department
     at the headquarters /previously approved by the
     financial manager of the plant/, they are summed up
     or in certain cases regrouped or revised, and the
     purchase is carried out. The materials go to the
     stores of the plants and the purchasing department
     of the plant dispose of them.

III. The third group of inventories is both purchased and
     stored by the plants. The most important in this group
     are the dyestuffs. The financial managers of the
     plants consider whether it is necessary and how much
     is necessary to buy from a certain material. This is
     the group of inventories in which there are targets
     given to the financial manager of the plant to reduce
     the stocks.

     For being able to evaluate the importance of the above
     groups let us look at some proportions concerning
     the inventories: the purchasing department of the
     firm purchases about 60 % of the non-textile materials.
     The non-textile materials amount to 25 % of the total
     of the inventories of the whole firm. These propor-
     tions show that the importance of the totally central-
     ized textile stocks is much higher, and that the small
     part of inventories is managed by those who use them.

3. Economic incentives

The targets concerning the management of inventories are of course connected with direct economic incentives. The bonuses condition of the financial manager and the purchasing departments of the plants is determined by the headquarters of the firm, and they have to work out a plan with the necessary measures. There is a similar condition for the purchasing department at the headquarters concerning the centrally stored stocks. Nevertheless this is in general only one of the bonuses conditions and only a part of the bonuses depends on it. In a series of interviews it turned out that among the direct bonuses conditions of the managers the inventories played a bigger role only in the last 3-4 years. This is so in spite of the fact that the enterprise was criticized soon after its foundation because of the system of management concerning inventories which essentially is the same also today.

It may be assumed that in this steadiness we have found an example of how immense a role has the routine, "the norm", the beaten path in the economy.

Obviously the routine is only one of the reasons why this rather obscure system lasts. There is a practical /or technical/ reason as well: an organization which deals with more than 100,000 kinds of materials may not be totally centralized, as no center is able to control in such details directly. Another substantial reason is that there has not been such a significant change in the functioning and structure of the market since 1968, which would have caused a change in the organization of the enterprise which adapts to the possibilities of purchasing and sales.

4. Markets, structure of inventories, rotation period

4.1. We can draw the conclusion that the long-term position of the firm on the market and the power relations on the market are unchanged also from the relatively steady

structure of its inventories /See Table 1./ This phenomenon exists on national economic level as well; Ervin
Fábri[2] similarly relates the market situation to the
structure of inventories.

Table 1

The structure of inventories at the end of the year
/PNYV/

	1970	1971	1972	1973	1974	1975
Materials	64.8	60.6	59.9	60.6	54.4	55.5
Unfinished and semi-finished		22.9	26.2	22.3	26.2	26.0
	35.2					
Output		16.5	13.9	17.1	19.4	18.5
Total	100.0	100.0	100.0	100.0	100.0	100.0

Source: Balance-sheets of the enterprise.

Note: The data are not comparable from 1976 on because
of the change in financing the cotton stocks.

4.2. It is characteristic also of the enterprise the predominance of materials and the relatively low rate of
outputs in the inventories. The opinions got at the
enterprise and the national economic analyses together
support that neither this enterprise is an exception:
its management and organization is impressed by the
"seller's market" as the national economy. The above
proportions are reproduced while the value of inventories
increased more than twofold.

Let us see, what is the reason of the higher than the
national output stocks proportion at our enterprise!
We cannot think that it expresses a higher sensitivity
to the market situation.

[2]Chikán, A. - Fábri, E. - Nagy, M.: Készletek a gazdaságban
/Reserves in the Inventories/. Közgazdasági és Jogi Könyvkiadó,
Budapest 1978.

A rather big part of the output stocks /6-9 % of the total value of inventories/ are exported goods under forwarding formalities, which for the buyer has not paid yet.

Regarding the output stocks on hand neither this enterprise differs from the national economic average.

The enterprise produces almost exclusively to order. Thus the managers generally hold the view that in the ideal case the enterprise may work with an output stock which covers the needs for one day. That means, they consider the output stock /the existence of it, and especially the growing output stock/ as a sign of friction in production or as an organizational fault, definitely as a "bad" thing.

This apprehension has another reason as well: under the given technological discipline, workshop discipline and quality distribution, from the goods ordered by capitalist firms they start to manufacture 10-12 % more than the order. /This is the so-called "overproduction" or "production for security"./

There is a habit or "norm" in the textile markets: the buyer insists on giving the exact disposition, so that the goods coming from the "overproduction" are not sellable at regular prices only with allowances.

4.3. The _rotation period_ also demonstrates very well the role of inventories in the management of the firm. The longer the rotation period the bigger sum has to be allocated to finance the inventories. And when credits - especially short-term credits - play a part in the financing process, the enterprise has to take into account the rather high interests. The rotation period of inventories is demonstrated in   Figure 1.

The steep growth of the rotation period gives reason why the inventories got in the center of the attention of the management. The question was how it was possible to reduce the quantity of stocks. The growth took place in such a structure of inventories in which the materials are predominant.

Figure 1

The rotation period of inventories at the enterprise, days
/inventories, total/

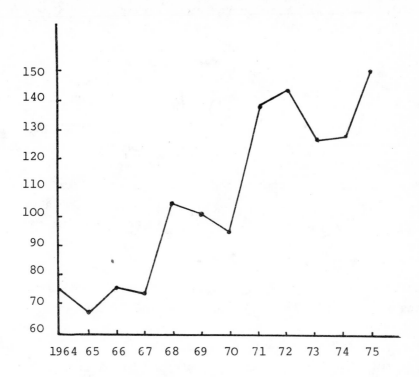

The sudden increases generally did not come from the changes in the market, but from the institutional changes of the actors of the market. The first jump /1968/ comes from the change in the organization and methods of foreign trade. The goods sold remain the property of the firm up till the price comes in. The second jump /1971/ comes from the closing down of the Cotton Wholesaler Enterprise and from the materials stored at the producing firms.

There are of course market actions as well especially in the last years: the enterprise tries to use the advantageous possibilities with tactical purchasing. /The National Bank supports these actions with preferential credits./

As we have seen in this section, as a result of direct economic incentives the situation of the firm regarding the inventories has not improved, rather deteriorated because of the longer rotation period and the higher interests. The enterprise was constantly insolvent. The attention of the management turned more and more to the inventories. On the 1st of January 1976 the new incentive system of the firm came into operation.

5. The incentive system since 1976

To see the changes brought with the new system we have to know something about the old one. The previous /working since 1972/ incentive system of the firm was based on the indicator called "calculated gross profit of the plant". This means the difference between the price of a good and its variable costs. The target for the plant prescribed in the plan was the production of a quantity of gross profit and the wage increase of the plant was related to the fulfilment of this target.

The new incentive system on national economic level /in 1976/ and the high level of inventories compared to the production /and the fact that this was not possible to change by direct measures/ made the management of the firm to place a new - value added type - indicator in the center of its incentive system, the so-called "basic indicator of the plant". It was unchanged that the wage increase at the plants depends on the fulfilment of this new indicator. With this step the protective role of the firm for its plants melted further, the charges on resources appeared in the target of the plants.

The construction of the basic indicator is the following: it starts from the calculated gross profit of the plant, this is diminished by the amortization, the charges on fixed and working assets, and may be diminished or increased by the so-called corrections. The corrections drive the plants directly to execute certain tasks, but as they are built in the indicator indirectly affects the economic interests of the whole collective of the plant. There are two kinds of correction: the first urges the improvement of quality, the allowances and the penalties diminish the gross profit with a corrective

94

multiplier; the other type of correction applies to the inventories. It had a radical effect as proved by the emphasis
given it in the plants.

The correction concerning inventories may both increase and
diminish the value of the basis indicator. The basis indicator can be increased by   25 % of the reduction of
inventories compared to the basis, and   50 % of the value
of growth of the inventories must be deducted from it. The
sanctions are not symmetric, the drive against growth in
the inventories is much stonger. It can be seen that the
primary aim was to stop the further expansion of the inventories.

The aim was reached beyond expectation: in 1976 the firm was
able to hold down the level of inventories on the level
acknowledged by the National Bank, what did not occur in
the previous years. This made possible to pay back a part
of their credits, and this diminished the interests. The
liquidity position of the firm improved so much that in June
of 1977 the Bank declared that its management is "balanced
and outstanding" and offered a so-called liquidity credit
contract. This means that the firm can ask for 50 million Fts
credit three times in a quarter without special application
and without offering an explanation.

The effect of the new incentive system can be demonstrated
by the fact that the correction coming from the reduction
of inventories increased the value of the basic indicator
by 3.5 - 7.5 %.

It is interesting that the output stocks reduced the more.
This raises the question how is it possible that the group
of inventories theoretically least convertible, meeting the
most detailed demands can be mobilized most easily? Obviously
we have to look for explanation also in this case in the
resource-constrained economic system, in the market which is
functioning generally with an excess demand.

We cannot disregard that the special and normal market
phenomena are mixing: the fact that on the textile market

the goods manufactured not to order may be sold only with allowances increases the demand. The action of the firm went together with a short textile boom in 1976.

But in the second year after the introduction of the new incentive system came out the problems of it; first of all in the conflict among the plants and the growing claims for correction of the plants /for one reason or for other a certain amount of inventories should not burden their inventories/. This makes impossible the functioning of the system if the above conflicts and claims reach a limit. It may occur that the drive for reduction of inventories causes smaller or bigger shocks in the production, and that its multiplying effects make other problems important. This indicator brings the problem of all basis-type incentives: the result reached will be part of the next-year plan and in consequence of this starts the well-known mechanism of bargaining over the plan.

There is another element in the incentive system of the firm which affects the output stocks besides the smooth production: this is the <u>bonuses condition according to deliveries.</u> The bonuses condition of the management of the plant is that the deliveries should take place at least 85 % according to the production program. We can see also from this that if the stock of orders equals the capacities, the output stock can be regarded as a friction in production or sales, and must be reduced by all means.

The history of the control within the firm concerning inventories stands for itself. Though the adaptive action described is very simple, it seems that we found a typical example of the adaptation processes of the Hungarian economic system. On the basis of this example we may formulate some assumptions:

1/ It is characteristic that the stimulus leading to adaptation is long /in our case at least two years/, and rather strong /liquidity problems/. The action of adaptation took place as a result of strong intervention /alteration of the incentive system/ and it gave rise to a reaction with

not expected intensity. Generally speaking with this speciality
the process carries the possibility and danger of adaptation
full of shocks, campaigns and putting out fire.

2/ For the management of the firm the functioning different from they got used to, different from "normal" /in
our case the expansion of inventories and the liquidity
problems/ shows which question became important, what should
be on the agenda of the firm.

3/ The structure of inventories is special, generally
characterized by the predominance of materials and the
relatively high level of inventories. The whole economic
system works with higher reserves for security because
of the shortage of materials, the uncertain purchasing
possibilities, in other words, because of the resource
constraint. The other factor for predominance of materials
is that materials are more convertible than the inventories
stored at a higher level of readiness /unfinished goods,
semi-finished goods, units/.

This trend is enforced also by that if the production is
vertical and the materials needed are on hand, then less
cooperation and inter-firm relation is needed.

Maybe the reason for the higher level of inventories
on national economic level which is described by the literature
as wasting is just the shortage.

We can formulate the conjecture that just this level of inventories is suitable for the working of the system, this is
normal.

4/ The standard literature on models of inventories
and processes concerning the inventories, or rather the
models based on stock signals draw conclusion on the production
strategy to be followed from the inventory process, so that
the output stocks are the clear-cut signal of boom or depression.
My assumption on the other hand is that in a system working
with the above characteristics not the output stocks are those
which stimulate the production and signal the market situation.

Its role is taken over - in a modified way - by the stock of
orders. This is investigated also by János Kornai and András
Simonovits[3] and by Zsuzsa Kapitány.[4] The rule of reaction
in this case would be the inverse of the rule of adaptation
to output stocks: the growth in the stock of orders would
cause growth in the production and its reduction would cause
decrease in production. It is obvious that this rule does not
prevail in its pure form, so that the response is not simply
growth or reduction of the production but the change in its
structure. The possibility for this is given by the orders
which in a resource-constrained economy usually cover the
whole capacity. For this possibility to change the structure
of production is needed the special situation in which the
markets for the products of the firm are not homogeneous;there
are essential differences between them.

[3] Rendelésjelzésen alapuló szabályozás egy Neumann gazdaságban. Szigma, 1975/4.

[4] Simulation analysis of economies stochastically controlled
by stock- and order-signals. Studies, No. 19. Hungarian
Academy of Sciences, Institute of Economics, Budapest 1980.

Proc. First Int. Symp. on Inventories
Budapest, Hungary 1980

LOTSIZING
IN AN AUTOMATED WAREHOUSE*

THOMAS J. HODGSON[1] and TIMOTHY J. LOWE[2]

[1] *University of Florida, Gainesville, FL, USA*
[2] *Purdue University, West Lafayette, IN, USA*

1.   INTRODUCTION

In any automatic warehousing system utilizing computer-controlled stacker cranes for high volume material handling, a class of decision problems can be identified. The function of the system is the automatic control of the storage and retrieval of items in a warehouse. As described in [3], and [5], incoming items are assigned to pallets, perhaps several items to a pallet, and a minicomputer assigns the pallet to a location in the storage racks. The material handling is done by automatic stacker cranes. When a request for an item in storage is received, the stacker crane retrieves the pallet. Once the material is removed from the pallet, the pallet may be stored for future use or returned to the storage location if it still contains items. Decision problems associated with automatic warehousing systems are classified in [5] as design and scheduling. Design questions involve such things as the number of stacker cranes used, physical dimensions of storage bays, number of storage bays, and physical dimensions of the warehouse. Scheduling questions involve pallet assignment (assigning items to pallets), storage assignment (assigning loaded pallets to storage locations), and interleaving (sequencing rules for storage and retrieve requests).

*Research partially supported by Office of Naval Research.

7*

Several recent papers [3], [5], [7] have addressed the storage assignment problem. In [5] storage assignment rules are compared under the assumption of no interleaving. In [3], the analysis is extended to interleaving. Heskett [4] proposed that inventory items should be assigned to storage locations according to the cube order index (COI). The COI is the ratio of the space required per item and the order frequency of the item. An application of the COI rule can be found in [7]. It has been shown [2], that if a certain "factoring assumption" holds, the COI rule will minimize total material handling cost (or time).

In a production setting, the amount of product warehouse space needed for an item is traditionally determined on the basis of inventory and production cost considerations. If a company uses economic order quantity analysis to determine lot sizes, production quantity decisions resulting from this analysis will determine the warehouse space allocated to each product. Thus, lot size decisions and warehouse allocation decisions are treated independently, the former providing information (space needed) to the latter.

This paper concerns treating these two decision problems as one. That is, to analyze the problem of determining order quantities and warehouse space allocation in order to minimize total production, inventory carrying, and material handling cost. In a sense we are expanding the definition of "scheduling" in [3] and [5] to include the simultaneous determination of lot sizes and storage locations.

In a recent paper, Wilson [11] addressed the problem, but treated the allocation problem as a discrete problem. He assumed a finite number of locations in the warehouse and treated the space allocation problem as an assignment problem. Treating the problem in this fashion, a problem with a large number of warehouse locations becomes difficult to solve. We treat the space allocation problem as a continuous layout problem [2]. This is the approach taken in [3], [5], [9] and [10].

Consider a production vector $(Q_1, Q_2, \ldots, Q_n)$, where Q_i represents the production lot size of product i. The total yearly production, inventory carrying, and material handling cost can be expressed as:

$$T(Q_1, \ldots, Q_n) = \sum_{i=1}^{n} P_i(Q_i) + \sum_{i=1}^{n} I_i(Q_i) + M(Q_1, \ldots, Q_n), \qquad (1)$$

where $P_i(Q_i)$ represents the yearly production cost of product i (as a function of Q_i), $I_i(Q_i)$ represents the yearly inventory carrying cost of product i and $M(Q_1, \ldots, Q_n)$ represents the minimum yearly material handling cost. That is, given the production vector, M represents the material handling cost which results from an optimal (cost minimizing) storage scheme. We have treated the production and inventory costs as separable by product. However, the material handling cost is not separable since the material handling cost for product i depends on all Q_j.

The main advantage of treating the problem as formulated in (1) is that the problem size is drastically reduced over the formulation by Wilson. In Wilson's formulation if there are m storage locations, then the number of variables is m x n. Under the formulation in (1), the number of variables is n.

2. ASSUMPTIONS AND NOTATION

We assume that during each storage trip from the I/O point to the storage area or visa versa, the stacker crane carries only one item. The material handling system operates with no interleaving. The material handling cost for an individual trip to or from the storage area is a linear function of the time for the trip. Let t_i be the cost, per unit of crane travel time, for item i. The time for material loading or unloading is ignored. As noted in [5], these times are small compared to crane travel time. The system consists of a single crane and one storage rack (area). It is easiest to visualize the storage area as a plane oriented in the vertical direction (see Figure 1). The analysis is easily extendable to the case of a single crane serving a single two sided aisle, however this case unnecessarily complicates the analysis.

We assume that the production cost $P_i(Q_i)$ is of the classical form. That is, if D_i is the demand rate for item i and if C_i is the setup (or order cost) associated with each lot of item i, then $P_i(Q_1) = C_i D_i/Q_i$. Note that more complex production cost functions can be handled. Similarly, we could consider more complex inventory carrying cost functions, but assume that $I_i(Q_i) = k_i Q_i/2$, where the coefficient k_i reflects the cost of item i, cost of capital, etc. Let A_i represent the area necessary to store one unit of item i.

3.   ANALYSIS AND COMPUTATIONAL RESULTS

We assume that the warehouse input-output (I/O) point is located in a corner of the storage area, and that the crane can travel, simultaneously, in horizontal and vertical directions. Let (0, 0) be the coordinates of the location of the I/O point, and any point in the storage area has coordinates (x, y), x, y $\geq$ 0 (Figure 1). Let v_1 and v_2 be the horizontal and vertical speed, respectively, of the crane. If an item is stored at location (x, y), the time for the crane to travel between the I/O point and the location of the item is $\max\{x/v_1, y/v_2\}$, and the crane travel time for storage, and retrieval of this item is $4 \max\{x/v_1, y/v_2\}$, where the number 4 reflects two round trips between the I/O point and the item location.

To obtain insight, we formulate expression (1) for the single item case. For a fixed value of Q_1, it can be shown (see [2]) that the optimal storage layout for the single item is a region, of area $A_1 Q_1$, enclosed by a contour of the function $f(x, y) = \max\{x/v_1, y/v_2\}$. Let z be the functional value of a contour of f. The area, $q(z)$, of the optimal storage region can be expressed as a function of time by $q(z) = v_1 v_2 z^2$. Since the total area of the storage region must equal $A_1 Q_1$, set $A_1 Q_1 = v_1 v_2 z^2$. Thus, the value of the function f at the boundary of the storage region is $z = (A_1 Q_1/v_1 v_2)^{1/2}$.

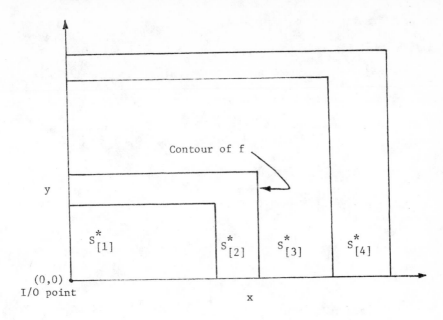

Figure 1. Warehouse Storage Regions

The average time for the crane to travel from (to) the I/O point to (from) the location of one unit of the item in the storage region is (see [2]),

$$(1/A_1 Q_1) \int_0^{(A_1 Q_1/v_1 v_2)^{1/2}} (2v_1 v_2 z)\, z\, dz \;=\; (2/3)(A_1 Q_1/v_1 v_2)^{1/2}.$$

Since for each item the crane makes 4 one-way trips between the location of the item and the I/O point, and D_1 items are "turned over" in the storage area per year, the minimum yearly material handling cost is $M(Q_1) = (8t_1 D_1/3)(A_1 Q_1/v_1 v_2)^{1/2}$, and thus

$$T(Q_1) = C_1 D_1/Q_1 + k_1 Q_1/2 + (8t_1 D_1/3)\,(A_1 Q_1/v_1 v_2)^{1/2} \qquad (2)$$

Although $C_1 D_1/Q_1$ and $k_1 Q_1/2$ are convex in Q_1, it is clear that $M(Q_1)$ is not convex. However, it is easy to show that there exists a single local minimum of $T(Q_1)$ over $Q_1 \geq 0$ and thus any of a variety of one dimensional search procedures (see [8]) will minimize $T(Q_1)$. In addition, $T(Q_1)$ is psuedo-convex on $\{Q_1 | Q_1 > 0\}$ since (2) can be written as $\phi(Q_1)/Q_1$, where $\phi(Q_1)$ is positive and convex on $\{Q_1 | Q_1 > 0\}$ (see [1]).

103

We now formulate the n item case relying on the notation and development in [2]. Let $L = \{(x, y) \mid x \geq 0, y \geq 0\}$, i.e., L denotes the set of points in the storage rack. As before, the travel time function to any point $(x, y) \varepsilon L$ is expressed by $f(x, y) = \max \{x/v_1, y/v_2\}$. Let $\{S_i, i = 1, \ldots, n\}$ be a collection of nonoverlapping subsets of L (a layout) such that the area of $S_i = A_i Q_i$, $i = 1, \ldots, n$. $H_n(L, A)$ denotes the collection of all such layouts. If item i is assigned storage region S_i, the average one way travel time between the I/O point and the location of an item i is

$$(1/A_i Q_i) \int_{S_i} f .$$

The yearly material handling cost for item i is

$$(4t_i D_i / A_i Q_i) \int_{S_i} f , \tag{3}$$

where (3) reflects 2 round trips for each item, D_i items per year, and a cost of t_i per unit time. For notational convenience, define $r_i \equiv 4t_i D_i / A_i Q_i$. Using (3),

$$M(Q_1, \ldots, Q_n) = \min_{(S_1, \ldots, S_n) \varepsilon H_n(L, A)} \left[\sum_{i=1}^{n} r_i \int_{S_i} f \right]. \tag{4}$$

The solution $\{S_i^*, i = 1, \ldots, n\}$, to the right hand side (rhs) of (4) can be found by [2]:

i) Ordering the items such that $r_{[i]} \geq r_{[i+1]}$, $i = 1, \ldots, n-1$. (5)

ii) Defining $S_{[1]}^*$ as the region of L closest to the I/O point, enclosed by a contour of f; defining $S_{[2]}^*$ as the region nesting about $S_{[1]}^*$ and enclosed by another (larger valued) contour of f, and so on (Figure 1).

Using ii), the definition of f, and integrating the rhs of (4):

$$M(Q_1, \ldots, Q_n) = 2/(3(v_1 v_2)^{1/2}) \sum_{i=1}^{n} r_{[i]} \left[\left(\sum_{j=1}^{i} A_{[j]} Q_{[j]} \right)^{3/2} - \left(\sum_{j=1}^{i-1} A_{[j]} Q_{[j]} \right)^{3/2} \right]. \quad (6)$$

When $i = 1$ in (6), define $\sum_{j=1}^{i-1} A_{[j]} Q_{[j]} \equiv 0$ and so for the single item case,

(6) agrees with our earlier analysis. Note that the ordering $[1], \ldots, [n]$

in (6) is <u>dependent</u> upon the values $Q_1, \ldots, Q_n$, so the functional form of

M is known only after $Q_1, \ldots, Q_n$ are known. Using (6) in (1), no apparent

conclusion can be made about the properties of $T(Q_1, \ldots, Q_n)$. Even though

$P_i(Q_i)$ and $I_i(Q_i)$ are convex, it is not clear that the rhs of (6) <u>even for a</u>

<u>fixed ordering of the items</u> has any desirable properties (such as psuedo-

convexity) which could be exploited in optimizing $T(Q_1, \ldots, Q_n)$. However,

for a fixed ordering of the items,

$$T = \sum_{i=1}^{n} \left[C_{[i]} D_{[i]} / Q_{[i]} + k_{[i]} Q_{[i]} / 2 \right] + M(Q_{[1]}, \ldots, Q_{[n]}) \quad (7)$$

is differentiable, and hence at any local minimum the gradient vanishes. We

exploit this property in the following algorithm.

Formally, at the kth iteration $Q^k \equiv \{Q_1^k, \ldots, Q_n^k\}$, let ρ^k be an ordering of

the items such that (5) holds and let T^k be the function defined by (7) with

the ordering induced by ρ^k. Let T^{k*} be the value of T^k at a local minimum

of T^k. Define as $Q^{k+1} \equiv \{Q_1^{k+1}, \ldots, Q_n^{k+1}\}$ the vector which attains T^{k*}.

Step 1   Choose an initial starting point $Q^1 > 0$. (A natural starting

         point is some fraction of the solution obtained by minimizing

         (7). Set $k = 1$ and determine ρ^k.

Step 2   Form T^k.

Step 3   Find a T^{k*} and Q^{k+1}.

Step 4   Determine ρ^{k+1}. If $\rho^{k+1} = \rho^k$, stop. Otherwise, set $k = k+1$

         and go to Step 2.

In the above algorithm, at some iterate Q^k, it may be that more than one ordering of the items satisfies (5). In this case we adopt the convention that ρ^k is <u>any</u> ordering of the items which satisfies (5). In Step 4, by $\rho^{k+1} = \rho^k$, we mean that if [i], i = 1, ..., n is the ordering of the items induced by ρ^k, then at Q^{k+1},

$$D_{[i]}t_{[i]}/A_{[i]}Q_{[i]}^{k+1} \geq D_{[i+1]}t_{[i+1]}/A_{[i+1]}Q_{[i+1]}^{k+1}, \quad i = 1, \ldots, n-1. \quad (8)$$

A property of the algorithm is that the objective function strictly decreases at each transition from Step 4 to Step 2 (reordering of items). The reason for this is that $\rho^{k+1} = \rho^k$ is a necessary condition for optimality. We formally state this result below and then motivate the proof. A detailed proof appears in [6].

<u>Theorem</u> If $\rho^k \neq \rho^{k+1}$, then $T^{k*} > T^{k+1*}$.

The proof of the theorem is based upon the fact that if $\rho^k \neq \rho^{k+1}$, there exists some $j \leq n-1$ where $r_{[j]} < r_{[j+1]}$. But then, upon interchanging the <u>ordering</u> of items [j] and [j+1] in the layout (without changing any of the item quantities) the material handling cost strictly decreases. One can continue to make these pairwise interchanges until (5) holds. Each such interchange strictly decreases the material handling cost. Since the item quantities do not change in the interchange procedure, the setup and holding costs do not change. Thus, it follows that T strictly decreases by the interchange procedure so that $T^{k*} > T^{k+1}$. With $T^{k+1} \geq T^{k+1*}$, the result follows.

A FORTRAN program implementing the algorithm has been written and tested on the AMDAHL 470 computer. In the algorithm, Newton's method [8] was used in Step 3. Fifty-eight problems with n = 5 were run with an average computation time of .02 seconds per problem. In these problems $A_i = 1$ for all i; C_i, D_i, k_i and t_i were randomly generated. Seventeen problems required at least one reordering of the items (transition from Step 4 to Step

106

2) prior to termination. In one problem (.03 seconds) the items were reordered four times and the total cost was reduced by one half (initial solution was evaluated at the EOQ values for the items). To test computation time sensitivity to n, problems of various dimensionality were run. Computation times appear in Table 1.

Table 1. Computation Time vs Number of Products

NUMBER OF PRODUCTS	COMPUTATION TIME CPU SECONDS
5	.02
10	.46
15	.83
20	1.42
25	2.18
35	4.48
50	8.96

REFERENCES

1. Avriel, Mordecai, Nonlinear Programming: Analysis and Methods, Prentice Hall, Inc., Englewood Cliffs, N.J., 1976.

2. Francis, Richard L., and White, John A., Facility Layout and Location: An Analytical Approach, Prentice Hall, Inc., Englewood Cliffs, N.J., 1974.

3. Graves, Steven C., Hausman, Warren H., and Schwarz, Leroy B., "Storage-Retrieval Interleaving in Automatic Warehousing Systems" Management Science, Vol. 23, No. 9 (May 1977), pp. 935-945.

4. Heskett, James L., "Cube-Per-Order Index-A Key to Warehouse Stock Location," Transportation and Distribution Management, Vol. 4 (August 1964), pp. 23-30.

5. Hausman, Warren H., Schwarz, Leroy B., and Graves, Steven C., "Optimal Storage Assignment in Automatic Warehousing Systems" Management Science, Vol. 22, No. 6 (February 1976) pp. 629-638.

6. Hodgson, T. J. and Lowe, T. J., "Production Lotsizing with Material Handling Cost Considerations, Research Report 79-7, Industrial and Systems Engineering Dept., University of Florida, Gainesville, FL, Dec., 1979.

7. Kallina, Carl and Lynn, Jeffrey, "Application of the Cube-Per-Order Index Rule for Stock Location in a Distribution Warehouse," Interfaces, Vol. 7 (November 1976) pp. 37-46.

8. Luenberger, David G., Introduction to Linear and Nonlinear Programming, Addison-Wesley Publishing Company, Reading, Massachusetts, 1973.

9. Papineau, Robert L., Francis, Richard L., and Bartholdi, John J., "A Minimax Facility Layout Problem Involving Distances Between and Within Facilities," AIIE Transactions, Vol. 7, No. 4 (1975), pp. 345-355.

10. Thorton, V. Darryl, Francis, Richard L., and Lowe, Timothy J., "Rectangular Layout Problems with Worst-Case Distance Measures," AIIE Transactions, Vol. 11, No. 1, (March 1979) pp. 2-11.

11. Wilson, Hoyt G., "Order Quantity, Product Popularity, and the Location of Stock in a Warehouse," AIIE Transactions, Vol. 9, No. 3 (September 1977), pp. 230-236.

Proc. First Int. Symp. on Inventories
Budapest, Hungary 1980

A COMPARISON OF MULTI-ECHELON INVENTORY CONTROL SYSTEMS

H. M. HORSMAN and F. WHARTON

University of Hull, Hull, UK

INTRODUCTION

In most published research on inventory control it is assumed that items are stocked at single locations which can be treated as independent and autonomous units. Manufacturing companies, however, are more likely to have distribution systems in which the same item is stocked at two or more levels - so-called multi-echelon systems. The question then arises as to whether each location should be allowed to operate as an autonomous unit or whether some form of centralised control is desirable.

With decentralised control, the timing and size of orders placed by depots on a central warehouse would be based only on local stock status and take no account of the needs of other locations or what stock was actually available at the central warehouse. Orders on the factory would be based on a knowledge of only central stock status and work already in progress. If centralised, replenishment orders on the factory would take account of total stock in the system and allocations to a particular depot would take account of stock status at other depots.

Clearly one advantage of decentralised control is that it is simple and self-regulating with no need for integrated communications and data processing systems. But the availability and cost of such information systems is changing rapidly with the development of microcomputers and the falling costs

109

of integrated data processing. Economic considerations must increasingly favour centralised control where it can be shown to significantly reduce stock investment.

We report here some results from a study of the steady state behaviour of a two-echelon distribution system in which a central factory and warehouse supply the needs of geographically dispersed regional depots. Computer simulation was used to investigate circumstances under which a form of centralised control would seem to be advantageous. In particular, the effects of demand, manufacturing lead time, number of depots and replenishment frequencies were explored.

The essential operating characteristics assumed are those of a typical light/medium engineering company distributing finished products to between eight and twenty-four regional depots.

ALLOCATION SYSTEMS

Most published research on multi-echelon systems concerns narrow aspects of simplified centralised control. Little application of developed theory has been reported.

Simpson (1959) has shown that if stock arriving at a central warehouse is to be distributed immediately with no further emergency replenishment, then it should be allocated between depots so as to equalise the probability that each depot runs out before the next allocation. This rule effectively minimises the residual stock in the system at the end of the warehouse replenishment cycle. Brenner (1969) has derived a similar result. A simpler allocation rule was used by Lampkin (1966) in that allocations were simply proportioned to depot demand. Cran (1966) has recommended that a proportion of safety stock be held back for topping up later, whilst Hadley and Whitin (1963) suggest that all stock allocations to depots should be delayed as long as possible. Detailed procedures for allocating stocks have been described by Brown (1977) in which a latest shipment data is calculated for

110

each item so that there is flexibility in making up transhipment loads.

Whilst the advantages of centralised control are often discussed qualitatively, as Hollier (1976) has stated in a review of published literature "the centralisation of control has received little attention by way of decision criteria indicating situations which warrant centralisation...an effective cost-benefit analysis of the two types of control system is almost non-existent."

The simulation model described below was used to compare the steady state behaviour of two systems. In the decentralised control system, orders of a fixed size were placed on the factory whenever warehouse stock (less back orders) and work in progress fell below a re-order level. Similarly, depot orders of fixed size were placed on the warehouse when depot stock plus stock on order fell below a re-order level. Near optimal values for warehouse and depot re-order levels were determined experimentally.

In the alternative centralised control system, the timing of orders on the factory was based on total stock in the system. Stock levels were reviewed weekly and a fair share of existing finished stock based on mean depot demand was notionally allocated to each depot. No stock was actually shipped until a depot reached its re-order level. The quantity shipped would be the current notional fair share less existing depot stock. In this way stock is reserved for other depots for as long as possible. In the absence of a further replenishment of warehouse stock, depots would be expected to run out at approximately the same time. The facility to impose maximum and minimum constraints on shipments was incorporated as a means of controlling depot replenishment frequency. Inter-depot transhipments were not allowed.

Thus the form of centralisation used was simple but incorporated several principles adovcated by previous authors, in particular, continuously revised fair share allocations of available stock with actual shipments delayed as long as possible.

111

THE BASIS FOR COMPARISON

We define total stock in the system to be work in progress in the factory and finished stocks in the warehouse and depots. For a given total mean
demand and manufacturing lead time, the mean level of work in progress is
independent of the control system.

Finished stock comprises working stock and residual stock. Working
stock is defined to be on average half the manufacturing batch quantity.
Thus working stocks are also independent of control for the same manufacturing batch quantity.

Residual stock, therefore, is the average finished stock in the system
when a new manufacturing batch quantity arrives in the central warehouse.
If warehouse and depot stock control were perfectly integrated residual stock
would comprise only depot safety stock. In practice, however, because of
the less than perfect (negative) correlation between warehouse and depot
stocks some residual stock other than depot safety stock is inevitable.

Thus for two systems giving the same customer service, if manufacturing
and delivery lead times are identical and if manufacturing batch quantities
are the same, differences in average total stock investment will be the
difference in average residual stock at the end of each manufacturing cycle.
It is residual stock,therefore, measured in weeks of supply, which is used
as the main crtierion in comparing the relative effectiveness of centralised
control.

In theory, the question of whether to centralise depends on the trade
off between saving in residual stock investment and the marginal cost of imposing a centralised control system.

THE MODEL

Whilst there are a wide variety of manufacturing and distribution configurations, we consider here a relaitvely simple but common configuration
in which a single factory and central warehouse supplies a number of regional

112

depots. The operating characteristics assumed are based on actual systems encountered in light and medium engineering industries. Attention is restricted in the main to high turnover items which contribute more significantly to stock replenishment and holding costs.

Total expected annual demand was allowed to range from 500 to 10,000 units per annum. Actual demand at between 4 and 24 depots was assumed to be independently Poisson distributed. It was at first assumed that mean demand would be the same at all depots although this assumption was relaxed in later experiments.

Depot stock levels were reviewed each week and could be replenished one week later. In effect, the distribution lead time was uniformly distributed between one and two weeks when stock was available. The mean depot replenishment cycle was varied. In the decentralised control system its length was determined by the order quantity whilst with the centralised control system it was controlled where necessary by using the minimum or maximum delivery quantity parameters.

Manufacturing batch quantities were fixed in each simulation and ranged from the equivalent of 4 weeks to 20 weeks of supply. The manufacturing lead time was assumed to be Normally distributed, typical parameters being a mean of 8 weeks and a standard deviation of 2 weeks.

The backlogging of depot orders was allowed but not customer orders. It was assumed that all systems were required to meet 95 per cent of customer demand. Near optimum control parameters were determined experimentally for each set of conditions. Each simulation comprised 2000 weeks of continuous operation under steady state conditions.

RESULTS

The steady state behaviour of the centralised and decentralised control systems were compared for wide ranging sets of parameters. We summarise here only the main effects observed.

Depot Replenishment Cycle

We comment first on the effect of depot replenishment frequency. In the experiments described the manufacturing batch quantity was the equivalent of 8 weeks total demand, manufacturing lead time was assumed to have a mean of 8 weeks and standard deviation of 2 weeks, mean total demand was 5000 units per annum and desired customer service was 95 per cent. The central warehouse supplied 8 depots.

In Fig.1 we illustrate the effect on residual stock of changing the average time between depot replenishments. Factory work in progress and average finished working stocks remain constant at 8 weeks and 4 weeks respectively throughout.

Under decentralised control, mean time between depot replenishments was increased by increasing the depot order quantities. As shown in Fig.1, residual stock increases with replenishment cycle. Clearly in the conditions simulated here, there is very little correlation over time between warehouse and depot stock levels. In effect, the system operates with the equivalent of two independent working stocks, one in the central warehouse and the other in the depots. Under these circumstances, it would not be entirely illogical, as has been claimed, to treat depot stocks as though they are independent and to determine an appropriate size for depot orders based on a trade-off between average investment in depot stock and material handling costs per order.

Also illustrated is the effect of centralised control. When factory orders are based on total stock and depots are allocated an unconstrained fair share of available stock there is a considerable reduction in residual stock. Warehouse and depot stocks are effectively integrated and the system operates with one working stock.

114

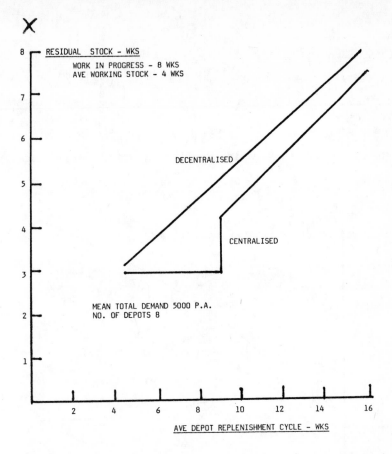

Fig.1: Residual stock and average depot replenishment cycle

The average time between replenishments was reduced by lowering the maximum allowable shipment to depots. This only served to increase the frequency (and presumably cost) of deliveries without significantly reducing minimum residual stock. When average replenishment cycle length was increased by raising the minimum allowance shipments, since it was no longer possible to integrate warehouse and depot replenishment cycles, the system's behaviour degenerated into that of a fixed order quantity system. There was some saving in residual stock arising from the fact the timing of factory orders was based on total stock in the system and not just warehouse stock thereby improving to some degree the correlation between warehouse and depot stock levels.

8*

Warehouse Replenishment Cycle

Centralised control would seem to be most effective when warehouse and depots share the same mean replenishment cycle, i.e. when fair share allocations are unconstrained. Illustrated in Fig.2 is the effect of increasing the mean warehouse/depot replenishment cycle in a configuration with 8 depots. Demand and lead time distributions were as assumed above.

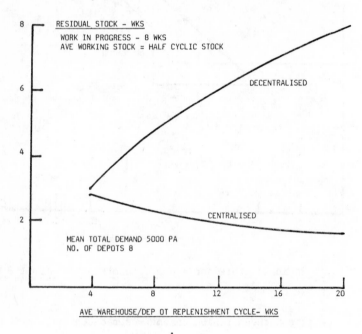

Fig.2: Residual stock and average warehouse/depot replenishment cycle

The advantage of centralised control increases with cycle length. Although the safety stock component of residual stock falls in both systems, the extra working stock requirement in the decentralised system has an overriding effect.

Demand and Lead Time Distribution

The two sources of variability in these simulations were customer demand and manufacturing lead time. It is these combined effects which cause the breakdown in correlation between warehouse and depot stocks in the decentralised system. In Fig.3 we illustrate the effect of changing the mean (and coefficient of variation) in demand and the variance in lead time for 8 depots and a mean warehouse/depot replenishment cycle of 8 weeks.

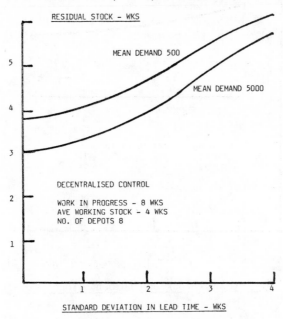

Fig.3: Residual stock, mean demand, lead time standard deviation

Reducing total mean demand increases the coefficient of variation in demand at the depots and consequently the variance in depot replenishment cycle time. Clearly for realistic variances in manufacturing lead time and depot replenishment cycles, the efficiency of decentralised control rapidly diminishes. It was found that introducing a variance in mean demand between depots further accelerated the process.

Number of Depots

It was expected that the decentralised system would be more efficient as the number of depots increased since, for the same total demand, the co-efficient of variation in demand at the central warehouse would decrease. As shown in Fig.4, however, the effect was not very significant over the range of depots considered, i.e., from 4 to 24 depots.

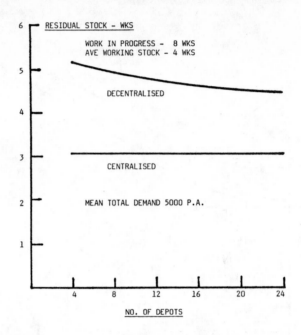

Fig.4: Residual stock and number of depots

An Actual Distribution System

The model was adapted to suit the particular characteristics of an actual production and distribution system in which control is at present decentralised. There were differences in production control but, more significantly, a proportion of finished stocks from the central warehouse was used to supply random export orders and direct customer orders as well as 8 depots (high cost, low turnover products) or 23 depots (low cost, high turnover items). The additional random demands on central stocks further enhanced the likely advantages of centralisation for all products.

CONCLUSIONS

Even under the relatively idealised operating conditions simulated here, centralised control can significantly reduce stock investment. Centralised control effectively integrates warehouse and depot working stocks.

With decentralised control, since residual stock increases with depot replenishment cycle, it is not unreasonable to apply classical inventory theory in determining appropriate depot order quantities. Using centralised control, however, the saving in stock investment is greatest when fair share allocations are unconstrained and warehouse and depot replenishment cycles coincide. Variable depot replenishment costs should therefore be taken into account in determining appropriate manufacturing quantities or cycle time. In practice the case for centralised control is likely to be stronger than is indicated here. In our experience companies operating independent control systems do not establish or adhere to optimal control parameters. The tendency is for depots to maintain higher safety stocks than was assumed above to compensate for unreliable supply from central warehouses. A common reason for poor service is the tendency for production controllers to be overly optimistic about manufacturing lead times. Decentralised control systems observed in practice are not as efficient as the basis for comparison used above.

Perhaps more important, however, is that we have here made rather conservative assumptions about demand and lead time distributions and based conclusions on steady state behaviour. In reality it is unlikely that such steady state conditions would exist for long. Manufacruring and delivery lead times are subject to unexpected disruptions and demand is unlikely to be as stationary and as regular as has been assumed in the simulations. Possibly the strongest arguments for centralised control concern its relative stability and efficiency in transient conditions.

References

Brenner J.L. (1969): Stock control in a many depot system, <u>Naval Research</u>
<u>Logistics Quarterly</u>, Vl6, 359.

Brown, R.G. (1977): <u>Materials Management Systems</u>, J.Wiley.

Cran, J.A. (1966): A two-level inventory control rule in a distribution system. <u>Proceedings of the 4th International Conference in</u>
<u>Operations Research</u>, Boston, J.Wiley, 864.

Hadley, G., Whitin, T.M., (1963): An inventory-transportation model with
N locations, Chap.5, <u>Multi-stage inventory models and</u>
<u>techniques</u>, Scarf, H.(ed.), Stanford, California.

Hollier, R.H., Vrat, P. (1976): A review of multi-echelon inventory control
research and applications, Technical Report, Department
of Engineering Production, University of Birmingham,
England.

Lampkin, W. (1966): A second look at Haussmanns inventory control model with
special reference to the central store/sub-store problem.
<u>Operations Research</u>, Vl4, 59.

Simpson, K.F. (1959): A theory of allocation of stocks to warehouses,
<u>Operations Research</u>, V7, 797.

Proc. First Int. Symp. on Inventories
Budapest, Hungary 1980

CENTRALIZATION OF MATERIAL STOCKS JUSTIFIED BY ECONOMIC REASONS. DECISION AIDS AND RESULTS IN THEIR APPLICATION

HARRY KLINGER, CLAUS-JÜRGEN PRZYBOROWSKI[1] and KLAUS WILHELM[2]

[1] Technical University, Dresden, GDR;
[2] Technical Institute, Zwickau, GDR

The planned transition of management and planning of industry and construction engineering to the basis of trusts was a further step on the way to better utilization of the advantages of socialist production relations in the German Democratic Republic. The establishment and development of trusts permit and require new dimensions in the detection of effectivity reserves in social production.

Such a notable possibility in the field of materials management is the intensive utilization of material stocks in trusts or in their factories by territorially distributed production and storage structures. Under these conditions the problem of centralization of stocks of materials is the spatial or dispositive concentration of stocks of various materials within the framework of existing or prospective delivery networks.

Centralization of material stocks results in:
- increase of disposibility, mobility and reaction ability of material stocks
- decrease of the absolute quantity of material stocks but guaranteeing material delivery according to demand and consumption

121

- decrease of purchase costs
- simplification of the firms' material requirement and supply
  planning, disposition and ordering
- influence on the rational organization of transport, transhipment and storing processes
- simplification of interfactory cooperation relations

Economic limits are set to the centralization of material
stocks by increasing transport distances and transport costs
for material delivery and the existing transport, transhipment and storing capacities.

This demands economically based determination of the percentage of centralization of stock-keeping.

At the Technical University of Dresden various methods were
developed in the sense of decision aids [1, 2] for centralization of storage from the aspect of economically based decision-
making.

The purpose of the present work is to introduce a further
development of the economico-mathematical model published in
[1] and [2] , in form of an approximation procedure.

1.   Description of the optimization task

1.1. The optimization problem

Basis for the determination of optimal centralization of material stocks is the quantification of the expenditures depending
on the degree of centralization of material stocks (Zg) , which
latter can approximately be described by

$$Zg \sim \frac{1}{m} \qquad (0 \le Zg \le 1) \qquad\qquad (1)$$

whereby m represents the storing locations for a certain

material /Fig. 1/.

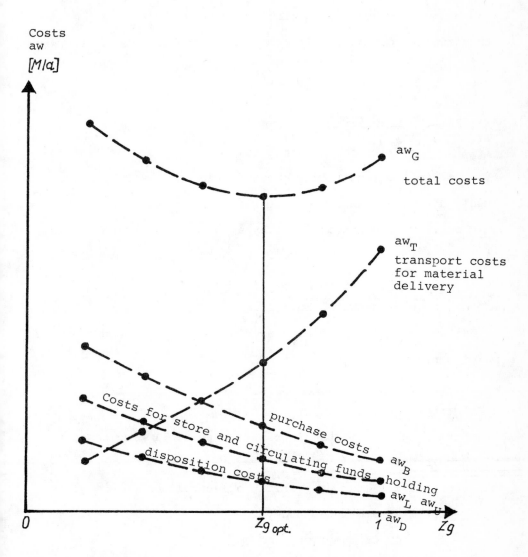

Fig. 1: Costs depending on the degree of centralization of

material stocks with regard to the discrete value

range of the degree of centralization

The determination of the optimal degree centralization comprises decisions on:
- number of storing places and their local distribution
- stock levels to be stored at the various storing places and
- consumption places to be provided with material where minimum costs are guaranteed in accordance with the given security degree of functioning of material stocks.

1.2. Storing conditions

A prerequisite for mathematical modelling is the description of storing conditions, shown in Figs 2.1. - 2.3. The supply of a given number of material consumption places V_k (k = 1 ... x) is accomplished by a number of storing places b_j (j = 1 ... m), being normally supplied by a number of specialized suppliers L_1 (l = 1).

Our assumptions are the following:
1. The number of storing places is at most equal to the number of consumption places.
2. A consumption place is always supplied by its respective storing place.

With regard to stock distribution the following cases are distinguished:

a/ decentralized storing /variant of actual condition/ with

j = 1 (1) m storing places

k = 1 (1) x consumption places

whereby m = x

x ≥ 2

b/ centralized storing

　　with　j = m = 1

　　　　k = 1 (1) x

　　whereby　x $\geq$ 2

c/ partially centralized storing

　　with　x > m

　　whereby　x $\geq$ 3

　　and　　m $\geq$ 2

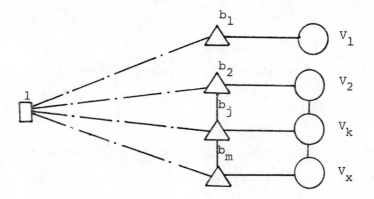

Fig. 2.1. Principle of decentralized storing

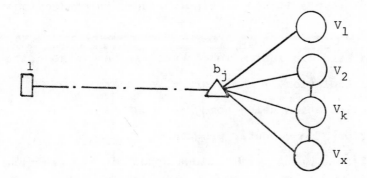

Fig. 2.2. Principle of centralized storing

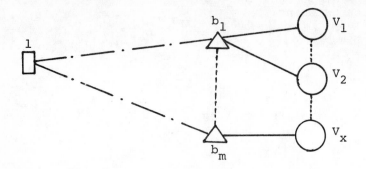

Fig. 2.3. Principle of partially centralized storing

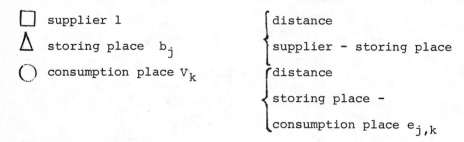

□ supplier 1

△ storing place b_j

◯ consumption place V_k

{ distance

supplier - storing place

{ distance

storing place -

consumption place $e_{j,k}$

2. Method of solution

As a basic method for solution we choose the comparison of variants, since the possible number of centralization variants is small, due to position factors of the inventory control system. The economico-mathematical model having been developed for this is shown in [2]. It is based on the evaluation of expenditures of established storing variants in connection with optimization.

For obtaining a solution we can use various methods:

a/   manual calculation of the storing variants

b/   manual calculation using nomograms

c/   application of a computer program

Despite these means restrictions appear in the practical work, which arise not so much from the method but from the registration of primary data necessary. This regards the evaluation of costs referring to materials, to their stocks and delivery and material consumption statistics, satisfying the requirements of the model.

That is why an approximation procedure was developed, providing sufficient accuracy for the determination of optimum centralization, the more it was proved that this procedure leads to the same result as the detailed model.

The approximation procedure is based on the following considerations:

1. Because of their dependence on the degree of centralization of material stocks and their essential role in influencing total costs, the following are the most important cost factors: the costs for stock holding (aw_L), circulating funds holding (aw_U) and transport costs for material delivery (aw_T). Purchasing costs (aw_B) have a great part in the total costs, but show indifferent behaviour regarding the degree of centralization of material stocks, so their value cannot be influenced by centralization of material stocks. Disposition costs (aw_D) have a small portion within total costs and are therefore negligible.

2. The change in stock level in case of centralization, compared with stock level in the decentralized case can be given as follows:

$$\overline{V}_Z \ (m_1 \ / \ m_o) = \overline{V}_d \ \frac{m_1}{m_o} \ \sqrt{\frac{m_o}{m_1}} \qquad (2)$$

where:

$\bar{V}_Z(m_1/m_o)$ -   mean material stock in case of centralization or partial centralization

$\bar{V}_d$ -   mean material stock for decentralized storing

m_o -   number of storing places for decentralized storing

m_1 -   number of storing places for centralized or partially centralized storing

    With regard to these considerations one has the following economico-mathematical model /approximation procedure/:

objective function: $\quad Z = aw_{Gi} \longrightarrow \min \quad (i=1 \ldots r) \quad (3)$

where

$$aw_{Gi} = aw_{Li} + aw_U + aw_{Ti}$$

cost equation: $\quad aw_{Gi} = \Big[[\bar{V}_i \, [U_L + pr \, (Z_{PFA} + p \cdot Z_{KD})]$

$$+ \sum_{j=1}^{m_i} \sum_{k=1}^{x_i} (e_{j,k} \cdot b_{j,k} \cdot U_T)] \Big] i \quad (4)$$

secondary conditions: $\quad F_{V_{j,i}} = F_{N_{j,i}}$

$$b_j = \sum_{k=1}^{x_j} b_{j,k}$$

determination of the stock per variant i /approximation/:

$$V_i = \bar{V}_{io} \, \frac{m_i}{m_{io}} \sqrt{\frac{m_{io}}{m_i}} \quad (5)$$

or

$$V_i = \bar{V}_{io} \cdot k_Z \quad \text{/table value/} \quad (6)$$

Legend:

i = index of the storing variants ($i = 1 \ldots r$)

aw_{Gi} = total costs of storing variant i   [M/a]

aw_{Li} = costs for stock holding of storing variant i   [M/a]

aw_{Ui} = costs for holding of circulating funds of

storing variant i   [M/a]

aw_{Ti} = transport costs for material supply of

storing variant i   [M/a]

j = index of the storing places ($j = 1 \ldots m$)

b_j = yearly material demand at storing place j   [ME/a]

U_L = specific storing costs   [M/ME.a]

pr = price of materials   [M/ME]

Z_{PFA} = yearly production assets rate   [%/a]

P = portion of circulating funds financed by

credits ($0 \overset{<}{=} p \overset{<}{=} 1$)

Z_{KD} = yearly interest rate of the credits of

circulation funds   [%/a]

$e_{j,k}$ = transport distance for material supply

from storing place j to consumption place k   [km]

U_T = specific transport costs of material supply   [M/ME.km]

$b_{j,k}$ = yearly material demand of consumption place

k, being supplied by storing place j   [ME/a]

$F_{V_{j,i}}$ = storing capacity available at storing place

j for variant i   [ME]

$F_{N_{j,i}}$ = necessary storing capacity at storing place

j for variant i   [ME]

$\overline{V}_{io}$ = mean material stock of the actual condition

storing variant (basis)$_{io}$ [ME]

9

m_i = number of storing places of variant i

m_{io} = number of storing places of the basic variant (io)

V_i = mean material stock of variant i   [ME]

For efficient determination of the stock level, a degression coefficient:

$$k_Z = \frac{m_i}{m_{io}} \sqrt{\frac{m_{io}}{m_i}} \tag{7}$$

is listed in a working table /Table 1/. The value of k_Z depends on the number of storing places by decentralized storing vs. the number of storing places for centralized or partially centralized storing.

Table 1. Degression coefficient of material stocks (k_Z) by centralized or partially centralized storing $(m_i$ vs. decentralized storing (m_{io})

m_{io} \ m_i	10	9	8	7	6	5	4	3	2	1
10	–	0,949	0,894	0,836	0,723	0,707	0,632	0,548	0,447	0,316
9		–	0,943	0,882	0,817	0,746	0,666	0,577	0,471	0,333
8			–	0,935	0,866	0,791	0,707	0,612	0,500	0,354
7				–	0,926	0,845	0,755	0,655	0,535	0,378
6					–	0,912	0,817	0,707	0,577	0,409
5						–	0,894	0,775	0,632	0,447
4							–	0,836	0,707	0,500
3								–	0,817	0,577
2									–	0,707
1										–

$$k_Z = \frac{m_i}{m_{io}} \sqrt{\frac{m_{io}}{m_i}} \qquad \text{where } m_{io} > m_i$$

APPLICATION RESULTS

Application of the economic-mathematical model resulted in
stock economies up to 30% and cost economies for stock holding
up to 20% in various fields for selected groups of materials.
In the fields investigated about 70% of material stocks is to
be held in centralized stores. But centralized stock holding
is not always justified by economic reasoning. Possibilities
and limitations for the centralization of material stocks
might result from specific conditions in an enterprise, e.g.
- consumption, storing and transport characteristics of the
  material, value of the material
- distance relations
- available capacities for storing, transport, and transhipment

There are the following tendencies of general validity for
the distribution of material stocks:
1. Value- and stock-intensive materials, i.e. materials, raising especially high demands for storing because of their
   high value and/or utility value properties are generally
   to be stored in a centralized way.
2. Consumption- and transport-intensive materials, i.e.
   materials having especially high demand for transport and
   transhipment because of their high quantities being consumed per consumption place or of their properties /state
   form, size, weight/ are generally to be stored in a decentralised way.

Up to now the investigations concerning centralization of
material stocks have been related to selected material groups

or positions. At present the problem is to accomplish investigations on centralization of material stocks in a wider scale.
This regards potential economic fields as well as the material
assortment to be stored. For this purpose the approximation
procedure introduced gives a working basis for well-founded
management decision making.

REFERENCES

[1] Altenburg, U., Helfer, Klinger, H., Köblitz and Wilhelm,
     K.: Optimale Zentralisierung der Materialvorräte in
     Betrieben mit territorial verteilten Leistungsorten
     /Optimal Centralization of Material Stocks in Enterprises
     with Territorially Distributed Store-rooms/, In: Wissen-
     schaftliche Zeitschrift der Technischen Universität
     Dresden /Scientific Journal of Technical University of
     Dresden/ 23 /1974/ 6, p. 1331.

[2] Klinger, H.: Möglichkeiten und Grenzen der Zentralisier-
     ung von Materialvorräten in Betrieben und Kombinaten
     /Possibilities and Limits of Centralization of Material
     Stocks in Enterprises and Trusts/,   In: Materialien
     des IX. Internationalen Symposiums für Materialwirtschaft
     /Papers   of the 9th International Symposium on Material
     Management/, DDR-Beitrag III/5, Prag 1975.

[3] Altenburg, U.: Zentralisierung von Materialvorräten in
     Baukombinaten oder nicht? /To Centralize Material Stocks
     in Construction Trusts,   or not?/, In: Bauplanung -
     Bautechnik 30, Berlin, VEB Verlag für Bauwesen /Planning
     and Technics of Construction/, /1976/3, pp. 112-114.

[4] Wilhelm, K. and Przyborowski, C.-J.: Vorratsökonomische
     Effekte bei der Zentralisierung der Lagerwirtschaft
     /Economic Effects of the Centralization of Inventory
     Systems/, In: Bauplanung - Bautechnik 34, Berlin, VEB
     Verlag für Bauwesen /Planning and Technics of Construc-
     tion/, /1980/5, p. 208.

Proc. First Int. Symp. on Inventories
Budapest, Hungary 1980

MATERIAL CONSUMPTION NORMS. THE BASIS FOR PLANNING DEMAND AND STOCKS

KARL KRUZSZ

P. Stuchky State University of Latvia, Riga, USSR

Material consumption norms, if they are technically and economically well established, play an important role in planning and control of material-technical supply.

As it is well known, demands for raw and other materials are determined by two factors: the material consumption norms per unit of production, and the planned volume of production. Determination of the absolute value of stock norms requires the figures of the average daily material consumption, which can be computed from the total material demands and the length of the plan period. Consequently, the reliability of the normative basis of planning is a decisive factor in the elaboration of a well-established material-technical supply plan.

This means that material consumption norms and a rational, economical material consumption have a great importance. Significance and actuality of this problem have been expressed also in decisions and resolutions of the Communist Party and the government of the Soviet Union.

The National Planning Board of the Soviet Union has issued an order to enforce the directives of the Party's XXVth Congress and the resolution of the Council of Ministers passed on

135

July 12th, 1979: "System of Progressive Technical-Economic Norms and Their Utilization in Planning". The enforcement of this resolution contributes to planning on higher and higher levels, i.e. if there are scientifically based technical-economic norms initiated in practice they result in well-founded proportionate plans and a more effective social production.

Everything mentioned above completely relates both to the normative base and the planning of material-technical supply.

In consequence of this order, ministries and other supreme authorities of the Soviet Union and Planning Boards of the Union Republics have been bound to improve organization and care for norms. In addition to this it seems to be a basic requirement to form a normative basis in the automatized systems of planning and control on the levels of national economy, branches of industry and companies.

Norming of material consumption means the planning of necessary material input of production. This activity includes determination, sanctioning of norms, allocating them to specific work places, organization of realization and control of these norms. The objective of norming is to provide production with technically and economically well-established norms determined per unit of production, and the basic task is to determine and maintain such norms.

We have to point out that the economical use of materials depends to a great extent on the technically well-established, progressive raw material, fuel, and energy consumption norms. As a matter of fact, these norms are the basis for technical-economic planning and for adequate organization of production.

Without knowing well-established material consumption norms per unit of production, it is impossible to organize the material-technical supply, to determine the costs of production and to economize with the materials. At the same time, it is well known that paralell with the increase of the volume of production, the savings obtained by the reduction of unit material consumption are also increasing, possibly at an even higher rate. A one-percent increase in material consumption equals a five-billion-rubles increase of the national income for the national economy as a whole.

As material consumption norms are the basis for the planning of production and consumption, they have to be employed generally at each level of the national economy, starting from the enterprises to the National Planning Board.

This principle is the basis of organization for determining material consumption norms in the whole national economy. The Department for Norms and Normatives of the National Planning Board of the Soviet Union is the highest authority in charge of all works in the national economy regarding material consumption norms. Coordination and management of methodological work in the field of material consumption norms is done by the Scientific Research Institute for Planning and Norming, an institute of the National Planning Board of the USSR.

Control and organization of norming is the task of the technical departments of the ministries and other authorities, and of the technical departments at the enterprises. Ministries /authorities/ and the subordinated scientific-research and technological organizations are in charge of the elaboration and introduction of the methods of norm determination generally and at the level of branches of the economy.

The consumption norm is a planned, maximal quantity of materials, which is required for a unit of production of determined quality under specified conditions. By the conditions of production the system of technological, organizational and constructional characteristics of production are meant, all those which affect the material consumption norms.

We have to emphasize that any change in the conditions of production should be followed by the revision of material consumption norms. Besides, all material consumption norms should be progressive, that is, more economical than the former ones. The progressive norms, based on the streamlined organization of technical conditions of production, contribute to the introduction of new technology and modern technological processes, which guarantee a more economical material consumption. Progressive norms should be dynamic, too, that means, they should tend towards technological and organizational development. Besides, norms should be real, in accordance with the actual conditions of production.

Industrial enterprises use a large assortment of basic materials. The analysis of the savings in materials needs such indicators which accurately show profitability of the structure of production, the level of development of technological processes, and the state of organization, as well. Such indicators are, for example, the norms of material demand, the annual production, the coefficient of material consumption, the coefficient of producing and processing. The use of norms computed by the help of the gross consumption coefficients /which include all material input, useful and wasted as well/ is to be extended.

The consumption of each specific material can be described by a given input structure. The material consumption norm generally involves the following factors: the net /useful/ material consumption and the technological and organizational wastage and refuses.

The above mentioned structure of material consumption norms and the analysis of the factors affecting their progressivity make it possible to elaborate some computing methods for the sake of a more rational and a more economical consumption of material resources, considering optimal actual conditions. The basic methods are the calculational and empirical methods.

One of the greatest tasks of determination of progressive material consumption norms is the perfection of methodology. This task can be successfully completed

- if we determine the task correctly,
- know the structure of the norm and all the factors affecting the decrease of the elements,
- introduce the modern methods of determination of norms,
- perfect the organization and the voucher system,
- organize the material accounting and the analysis of material consumption and norms.

Additionally, we should mention that perfection of norms is a complex task, including the solution of several other problems, e.g., organization of the elaboration, approbation, changing and revision of norms, the incorporation of individual methods in a system, further perfection of the organic voucher system, the organization of determination of norms, revealing all of the possibilities of economical material consumption.

Determination of progressive norms presupposes the simultaneous introduction of an organic system of methodological principles and normatives and the use of the standardized accounting system for norms for the national economy as a whole.

The standardized system is a theoretically standardized approach to determination of norms, an organic system of structuring material consumption norms, which makes it possible for the enterprises to simplify the calculation of norms and the computation of the aggregated figures of material resources and of the material-technical supply in the national planning system.

The first methodological experiments in the sixties in Lithuania provided the basis for further work. The experiences with their elaboration and the introduction of their methods have been applied for the elaboration of technical-material norms also on the branch level. It should be remarked that the method of determination of the material consumption norm for a given material, supposing the same technological process and the same organization of production, is the same in every branch of the economy. There are no differences in a machine factory or in an instrument factory in the consumption norm for the production of a given screw. There can be differences only in the norms of wastage and refuses, which should be taken into consideration when computing the norms. This regards different kinds of technological processes, like galvanization and colouring of metals, welding and soldering, caloric treatment and chemical processes.

General development of progressive norms leads to the conclusion that future methodological study-aids will be of inter-branch character, which means that national suggestions will be elaborated, and soon after also different industrial material consumption norms, too, together with the standardized, centrally determined accounting certifications needed. Further standardization of the methods is not to be oriented to the different groups of materials /e.g. metals, plastics, papers, etc./, but either to the technological processes of production or the types of the finished products, taking into consideration whether the material is to be cut lengthwise or crosswise, or it is casted, moulded, or pressed.

For the time being the procedure for determination and re-vising of norms is as follows: The ministries, other authorities and subordinated enterprises revise and approve material consumption norms yearly, setting out from targets determined by the National Planning Board /expressed as a certain per cent of the norms from the basic year/. In most cases these targets are aimed at the reduction of material consumption norms. In the following year organizational-technical plans are based on these targets.

The efficiency of norm-determination can be characterized by the results in reducing consumption norms. On the basis of the achieved results, the goals determined by the highest author-ities can be controlled.

At the same time, it is not possible to determine the real results in norm-control merely on the basis of savings as a percentage. This originates in the fact that in case of a given change /substitution/, increase in consumption of the other materials are not taken into consideration. For this reason, in our opinion the enterprise should make a plan not only for the percentage of reductions in consumption of basic materials, but for all other material resources required for the production of the final product. In other words, reduction of the required materials should be characterized by a complex indicator.

Considering the high development rate of sciences and technology, and the continuously increasing scale of production and demands for material resources, regulation of material consumption norms is possible only by the extensive use of mathematical methods and of modern computer technics. Material consumption can be planned only on the basis of well-established technical norms, which norms should be revised operatively in case of any changes in the conditions of the production.

However, for the time being, computers have been applied only to a limited extent for computation of aggregate group norms. In our opinion computers can solve much more difficult tasks, too.

For example, on the basis of information about parameters of parts, technological processes and quality requirements, computers could calculate optimal assortment of materials and their norms by operations and by finished good items.

This would promote the technically well-established determination of material consumption norms and the almost immediate supervision of changes in production conditions and their effects.

Consequently it is necessary to think over the organization scheme of material consumption norming together with aggregating, storing, analysing and revising by the help of computing techniques on every level beginning with companies up to the National Planning Board. Norms must become real means of planning, they should enforce the balance principle and effective material consumption.

Proc. First Int. Symp. on Inventories
Budapest, Hungary 1980

INTER-COMPANY RELATIONS
FROM THE POINT OF VIEW
OF INVENTORY CONTROL

HENRIK MÄRCZ

Metalloglobus Company, Budapest, Hungary

Inventory control and inter-company relations - having close causal connections - are day-to-day problems both on company and national economy levels.

It is a well-known fact that in our economy user stocks are higher than the level acceptable by international standards and proportion of growth of stock levels to the increase of production is nearly three times more than it is in most industrial countries.

Another problem is the inappropriate allocation of inventories, namely that

- 70% of stocks are at users,
- 15% of stocks are at producers,
- 15% of stocks are at the special firms trading with
  production means /TPM firms/.

In the following we are to discuss some questions, which seem to be important reasons leading to this situation - from the points of view of these special trading /TPM/ firms.

Merchant capital - in its classical form - has been developed from industrial /production/ capital in order to utilize the well-known economic advantages. The distribution

10

of stocks given above shows that on the national economy level circulating funds of industry /production/ have not been forwarded to trading funds, have made a move within the production sphere and became funds for holding materials to be used. On national economy level this process has only explanations /that is creating safe conditions for production at users/, but it is without any economic advantages - on the contrary, it is explicitly disadvantageous. Among the most important reasons for this false distribution of stocks one can find the disordered inter-company relations and the lack of trust among producers, merchants and users.

Before the introduction /in 1968/ of the new decentralized economic management system in Hungary fluctuations of production and consumption had to be smoothed by administrative means, by centrally controlled distribution organizations. Since 1968 it has been the task of commercial companies, of the so-called TPM firms.

Establishment of these special firms and the trading methods introduced by them have not involved relevant changes either in the volume of stocks or in their disproportionate distribution. Flow of circulating funds has not become a spontaneous process and under these circumstances these TPM companies waited for realization of redistribution of circulating funds and - after that - for the decrease of users' stocks again from the application of administrative means.

But it is in contrast with the principles of our economic management system and also with the aims of independent company activity to redistribute funds of firms by decisions of author-

ities. Accumulating funds within companies can only be restricted by the system of income taxes placed on profits.

Today it is evident that redistribution of circulating
funds will not be carried out by central means. Mobilization
of financial means is only possible by bilateral agreements of
TPM firms and users carried out on the basis of mutual trusts
and interests. These processes are also enforced by top level
proposals.

Mutual trust is a decisive factor at every field and it
is rather valid for the relations between consumers and FTPM-s.
The highest possible level of this trust is reached when users
believe in prompt service of TPM firms for most of the products
and at every time. Unfortunately the proportion of prompt
services is not higher than 5 to 15 percent   in the practice
of TPM firms. This is a low level even if accepting the hypothesis that the trading firms mentioned have only about 50% of
circulating funds and stocks needed on the basis of economic
calculations.

Increasing the ratio of prompt shipments instead of
trade based on longer term contracts is also the purpose of
TPM companies. The reason for this is a more simple administrative activity, higher differential price to be counted,
higher level of service and in case of market competition the
more favourable conditions for these companies. TPM firms -
due to complete misexplanation of their function - are the
weakest elements of connections after contracts. When a
producer is to decide on his preference in fulfilling his
contracts he counts TPM firms in the third place: first he
delivers to export and second time directly to users. It is

10*

the argument of producers that TPM firms must have stocks piled up, and can suffer delays better. As a consequence of this reasoning 5 to 8 percent of actual deliveries always are in delay.

A much more astonishing and even more negative practice is the final user's behaviour not to accept deliveries of TPM firms in terms contracted. Finding different causes, e.g. the task of TPM firms is to pile up stocks, they are not willing to accept shipments at due term if they are not in direct need of the specific product. In the activity of TPM firms, pursuing a strict inventory control, this is a disturbing factor - it forces them to locate high percentage of circulating funds in stocks of products not having been accepted by buyers. These stocks piled up may not be sold after prompt service until final decision of buyers. In this case active role of stocks at TPM firms is rather questionable. We can formulate the statement that structure of stocks at a TPM firm is first of all a consequence of contracting discipline of buyers.

Since the Hungarian National Bank plays an important role in financing stockholding of most TPM firms, and since there is a strong aspiration from the central organs /including the Bank/ to stimulate /or sometimes force/ companies to keep their inventory investment low, it is not rare that TPM firms are forced to sell out mobile stocks. Within such circum-stances one can sell fast only those goods which are needed. Articles mentioned are usually bought and piled up for prompt service due to intensive demand for them but under the given conditions it is quite general that these stocks are to be sold without realizing benefits of prompt service.

148

Prompt service is one of the highest level services of TPM firms - to increase its percentage is also an interest of the national economy. But when low level discipline in keeping shipping contracts is the everyday practice, the increase in percentage of prompt service cannot be realized.

It is our plan for the near future to increase discipline of keeping contracts, that is, not to accept modification or cancellation after due terms without penalty. In the short run this behaviour will cause difficulties at users but in the long run it materializes in a more adequate inventory control and better use of stocks of TPM firms. Enforcing of the keeping of contracts has been the aim of a recent directive of the National Board for Materials and Prices, too. The essence of this directive is that central regulations for prices and price differentials are valid for delivery terms of 30 days /i.e. seller must specify the month for which delivery is scheduled/. In case of accepting longer terms /or, better to say, intervals/ suppliers have to give discount from the price and when they accept shorter terms they may count extra price differentials. This directive caused vivid reactions among suppliers and buyers. Most of the TPM firms /including our firm, the METALLOGLOBUS/ tried to offer regularly scheduled deliveries for users.

Demanding regularly scheduled delivery means responsibilities not only for suppliers but also for buyers. In case of a miscalculation of terms they are to take the consequence of it. If it is explicitly stated in supplier's proposals for contract the need for regularly scheduled delivery is drawn back immediately. After the withdrawal mentioned users lose their right for demanding regularly scheduled delivery and their interest in it is not obvious.

For example in August 1979 METALLOGLOBUS made a written offer to nearly 500 buyers of non-ferrous metal to make contracts for regularly scheduled delivery for one year's run in 1980. Responses returning showed that only 19 buyers need regularly scheduled delivery. It is interesting that buyers accepting our offer were mostly buyers of small quantities representing only a very small proportion of demand raised for our products.

Besides regular deliveries TPM firms try to improve the supply - simultaneously with decreasing relative stock levels and changing disproportionate distribution of inventories - by making bilateral agreements with users. One of the possible ways to realize it is creating partnership contract between a TPM firm and his reliable buyer. After this agreement, TPM firm makes purchasing, and holds stocks at his own storerooms located on the plant of consumers and from there he supplies users with different kind of goods needed for production in the form of prompt service. TPM firms pay renting fee and average transporting cost for store-rooms operated on the plant of users and run them by their own employees. Stock levels sufficient and necessary for an undisturbed production process are determined jointly and they pursue joint inventory policy. TPM firm and user finance together the circulating fund necessary for keeping stocks. To create such funds at signing contract the TPM firm buys former stocks of the user. It is the obligation of the user to give over a certain percentage of his funds freed up by not keeping stocks of the given items to the TPM firm - after a special agreement. Remaining proportion of funds freed up is at the disposal of the users without any obligations.

Circulating funds necessary for turnover and inventory control are mainly financed by TPM firms functioning as a gesture of partnership contract. Administration and accounting of turnover is by inside rules of the TPM firms. Central regulations /e.g. taxation/ related to the whole activity are based on regulations of TPM firms. Trade margins are counted after normal regulations of TPM firms. Total value of summarized trade margins is the common result of the joint activity. Revenue after taking into account the costs of stock piling activity are divided between the firms concerned after the proportion of funds provided by them.

Partnership contract established on the rules mentioned above has the following main characteristics:
- It assures the most favourable prompt service for users at the place of their location without their own holding of stocks.
- It frees a certain proportion of circulating funds allocated before and at the same time assures a more favourable structure of inventories.
- The user shares on the result of efficient inventory control and trading activity having been provided with a more favourable service at lower price than before.

In the framework of the contract as a first step the
user and the TPM firm estimates level of stocks necessary for
an undisturbed production based on turnover per year and
delivery lead times. Usually this level is lower than the sum
of former stocks held separately by consumer and the TPM firm.
TPM firm buys all the stocks of the user releasing so circulating funds of the consumer.

Supply of production means on the basis of joint financial
funds shows that there is a common interest between consumer
and trader when they are searching for better ways of supply.
On the basis of mutual interests industrial capital can be
moved on towards commercial capital to a more favourable extent, and as a consequence of this process the structure of
national inventories can show up a positive change. The
question might be raised why this form is not spreading in a
fast spontaneous process if it is based by mutual interests
from every side. The reason for this problem is somewhere in
the companies' lack of flexibility.

It is also an unanswered question that under this new
type of conditions and in this modified environment the whole
process of supply should be perfected or not. Whether it is
possible to change this rigid structure of inventories by a
few up-to-date methods. Whether it is possible to make changes
within the existing structure of firms or there is a need for
complete restructuring of trading firms. Production means
functioning as goods for sale take part in economic processes
as an independent commodity. One of the basic characteristics
of it is that contrary to trading with goods for final con-

sumption, in the trade of production means obligations are not overwhelming but strategies formulated on a complex way in plans create the needs. As a consequence of the above-mentioned reasons plan information in the trade of production means is much more reliable than in other fields of trade, which creates a good reason and solid background for partnership contracts.

Proc. First Int. Symp. on Inventories
Budapest, Hungary 1980

ROLE OF COMPUTERS
IN INVENTORY MANAGEMENT.
THE RETAILING CASE

LUCIANO MARCHI

University of Pisa, Pisa, Italy

Before discussing the role of computers in inventory management, we shall briefly specify the "general form" of any business data processing system.

Any "business data processing system" or "information system" is composed of inputs, processing operations, data bases, and outputs. Inputs into the system consist of transactions data, data base adjustments, inquiries, and outputs of other systems. These inputs are frequently collected from "source documents" and converted to machine-sensible data by a data preparation process such as keypunching, key-to-tape, etc.. Other input data (especially inquiries) may be generated by on-line terminals. Additional data is supplied from the records contained in the data bases of the system itself. Data is then processed in order to update the data bases and to furnish the outputs of the information system in the form of control listings, reports, documents, responses to inquiries (in written form or displays), and inputs to other systems.

A general "system flowchart" of an information system is particularly useful for summarizing inputs, outputs, and data bases required by a particular computer application, from the viewpoint of the users and their needs of information /O'Brien, 1975, pp. 289-290/.

Let now consider the problem on the side of the retailing, defining first a general model of that activity for data processing purposes.

We have a merchandise flow starting with vendors who supply inventory items. These items converge at the firm where a receiving function is performed. After that function is carried out, the items are moved into appropriate warehouse inventories. The items then go through patterns of convergence and divergence within the firm until they ultimately diverge to consumers through a selling function.

In conjunction with the merchandise flow network we can identify five decision and information subsystems which must be integrated for effective system management. These include the purchasing subsystem, the logistics subsystem, the inventory stock status subsystem, and the inventory planning and control subsystem /Hopeman, 1969, pp. 8-11/. They are described briefly below.

The purchasing subsystem is designed to handle analytical decisions in areas such as price determination, vendor selection, value analysis, and so forth. In addition, this subsystem performs the information processes associated with the purchasing function.

The logistics subsystem is conceived to coordinate the transportation function from vendors to the firm. It also coordinates the merchandise handling function within the firm.

The marketing subsystem is designed to take decisions in the area of product assortment, selling price, and promotion, and also to perform related information processes.

The inventory stock status subsystem essentially performs a function consisting in the gathering and disseminating of information.

The inventory planning and control subsystem, finally, is

the analytical center of the stock flow network. Among other functions, it is responsible for: determining forecasts of inventory requirements, selecting the appropriate quantity of items to stock and to order, determining when orders should be placed, and maintaining appropriate levels of inventory turnover.

Once the general network of the decision and information flows is designed, specific inputs, outputs, and processing functions must be established for any subsystem. Moreover, it is necessary to define some objectives to serve as system evaluation. In our case, a temptative definition of the general objective of inventory management as a whole is: to minimize the amount of money invested in inventory and required to cover "carrying costs", furnishing in the meantime a merchandise assortment that will meet consumer's needs, avoiding also out-of-stock conditions.

Without going into the details of each information subsystem, a specific analysis is made for the inventory planning and control subsystem in conjunction with the inventory stock status subsystem. Special attention is devoted to the activities of forecasting sales, choosing appropriate levels of safety stock, determining reorder points and economic order quantities.

Inputs into the inventory information system consist of sales transactions data, as well as data describing items received by the receiving department of the firm. Inputs also include "miscellaneous inventory transactions" such as adjustments for lost or damaged or returned items.

The data base of the system consists of an "inventory master file" which is checked for items availability, reorder points, economic order quantities, etc.. It is updated to reflect changes in inventory especially caused by sales and receipt of new items.

Outputs of the inventory information system include <u>inventory</u> <u>listings</u> of each transaction which allow control totals and other types of data processing controls to be accomplished. The purpose of such controls is to guard against errors or fraud in the input or processing of the data and to provide an "audit trail" to facilitate the auditing of the system.

Data describing miscellaneous sales transactions is a major system output and becomes the primary input into the marketing system. Information concerning out-of-stock items, reorder points, and economic order quantities is sent to the purchasing subsystem.

A final major category of outputs consists of <u>inventory</u> <u>and sales analysis reports</u> for management by product, by product line, by sale territory, etc.. These reports help management to determine: (1) whether the items being reordered and their amounts require adjustment, (2)whether any item is becoming obsolete, (3) unusual variations in inventory activity, and (4) the items which account for the majority of the sales of the firm /O'Brien, 1975, pp. 298-299/.

With regard to the processing functions, we may distinguish some principal procedures or programs:

- <u>Initialization procedures</u>. In the field of sales forecasting, for istance, there is the determination of the trend and cyclical components of sales on the base of historical data. The normal frequency of initialization is annual.

- <u>Planning and optimization procedures</u>. The principal ones are the procedures for the determination of the optimum economic quantity and reorder point. Normally the economic order quantities are revised on annual base, and the reorder points every month or less referring to the variability of demand and delivery periods.

- <u>Control reporting procedures</u>. Examples of control

reporting procedures are those producing stock status reports
describing the items in inventory (opening balance, receipts,
issues, adjustments, quantity on hand, quantity on order,
average unit cost, last cost, minimum and maximum balance,
etc.), signaling particularly the occurrence of certain limit
conditions.

Other control reporting procedures are those of inventory
or sales analysis. These procedures are designed either (1) to
describe the current sales with respect to the average inventory
for determining the stock turnover, or (2) to express the
percentage of each item value to the total value of inventory
(items reported in decreasing percentage value as to the Abc
listing), or (3) to compare the current sales with those
accomplished in the preceeding year in order to express the
percentage change, and so forth.

Let now detail the analysis to the principal activities of
the inventory planning and control system, starting with
"sales forecasting".

Annual sales forecasts may be made by estimating a
"reasonable" change from the sales of the preceeding year or
by using more complicated statistical forecasting techniques
(such as multiple regression analysis based on the main elements
that influence the sales: population, income, general price
level, and so forth).

In our experience, most computer applications in the field of
sales forecasting consist of historical data extrapolation,
based on exponential smoothing, and corrected as to consider
trend and cyclical fluctuations.

Sometimes, additional computations are necessary to consider
the probability of any level of sales. For fast moving items
the Gaussian distribution or normal curve is generally used;
on the contrary, for low moving items the Poisson distribution

seems more adequate.

Running the procedure on the computer it is particularly important to store a great mass of historical data in order to determine trend and cyclical components of sales.

In conjunction with sales forecasting, planning and control of inventory levels are of outstanding importance. We must say that many retailers simply order sufficient stock to begin the month (or any other specified selling period) with an inventory that exceeds estimated monthly sales by some "basic amount". However, it is necessary to consider other factors such as time needed before a new order can be received, "safety stock" related to a certain probability of not running out of stock, and so forth. Furthermore, different approaches are necessary for staple, perishable, and fashion items.

For staple items, whose demand is not subject to wide fluctuations in preference, a systematic method of reordering merchandise is based on the following data: (1) the reorder period /RP/ which is the time interval that normally elapses between orders, (2) the review period, that refers to the frequency of inventory checking to determine stock levels, (3) the delivery period /DP/, which is the time interval that elapses between the time an order is placed and the time the merchandise is delivered, (4) the expected rate of sales /s/ for a basic period of time /day, or week, or month/, (5) the safety stock /SS/ necessary to face deviations from expected sales, that is to prevent an out-of-stock condition if actual sales exceed expected sales or an order is delayed, (6) the amount of stock actually on hand /HS/, (7) the amount of stock actually on order not yet received /OS/.

The amount of merchandise to be ordered, at every reorder point of time, should meet the expected sales during the combined delivery and reorder periods, plus an additional safety stock that prevents out-of stock conditions depending on delayed orders or increased demand.

Reversely, it is necessary to assure that the stock existing on hand in inventory and on order at any review point of time is not exceeding the safety stock plus the expected rate of sales for the combined delivery and reorder periods. In symbol: max (HS + OS) = (DP + RP)s + SS.

The safety stock, in particular, depends on the level of service to be offered to consumers, and may be determined by observing the sales fluctuations that have accurred in the past. Assumed that the rate of sales can be forecast with reasonable accuracy (and adopting the Poisson distribution to describe variations in retail sales), for a chance of not running out-of-stock of approximately 99%, 95%, and 80%, the safety stock is equal respectively to $2.3\sqrt{x}$, $1.6\sqrt{x}, \sqrt{x}$, where $x = (DP + RP)s$.

According to the preceeding hypotesis, a general stocking rule is that the level of safety stock needed on fast-moving merchandise is usually lower than the safety stock required on slow-moving items /Marquardt et al., 1979, pp. 267-270/.

Instead of ordering a variable quantity of merchandise at any reorder point of time, most retailers utilize a system of ordering a fixed quantity of merchandise when the stock reaches a reorder point in units.

Fixed order points (in units) and order quantities may be arbitrarily set by management. However, the computer can be programmed to utilize mathematical techniques to calculate reorder point and economic order quantity.

The optimum reorder point in units can be easily calculated with respect to the preceeding assumptions. If an order is placed when the inventory reaches that level, it should arrive just when the inventory reaches the level of safety stock.

Therefore, it is necessary to place the order when the level of available stock is equal to the delivery period for the expected rate of sales plus the safety stock:(DP)s + SS.

At that time, the quantity of merchandise to order, that is the economic order quantity /$\hat{OQ}$/, can be obtained on the computer given the following data: (1) the cost-price per unit of merchandise /CP/, (2) the inventory carrying cost per unit as a percent of the unit cost-price /cc/, (3) the ordering cost, that is the fixed cost of placing an order /OC/, and (4) the annual sales in units /S/.

Assuming that OQ/2 is the average quantity of items in inventory, the total anuual inventory cost /TIC/ would be: TIC = (CP)cc x OQ/2 + OC x S/OQ.

By use of calculus, we can determine the optimum order quantity /$\hat{OQ}$/ in terms of all the other variables. Thus, differentiating TIC with respect to OQ, equating the expression to zero, and solving for OQ, we have:

$$\hat{OQ} = \sqrt{2(OC \times S) / (CP)cc}.$$

Indeed this would be a general model for a retailer. In precisely this same sense, a computer can be programmed to determine optimum order quantity by processing the above mentioned data (cost-price per unit of merchandise, inventory carrying cost, ordering cost, and annual sales in units). Moreover, it is possible to modify the computer program taking into account "quantity discounts", "joint ordering", and so forth (in order to approach the "perfect" OQ), doing with the program anything that can be done with the general model developed by calculus.

Determined the economic order quantity for any items, it is also possible to estimate the most favourable level of stock turnover. In fact, assuming that the average amount of inventory is equal to OQ/2, the rate of stock turnover can be easily obtained by dividing the annual sales for that average measure of inventory.

Beside the staple items, it is useful to consider the particular categories of fashion, and perishable items.

Fashion items, such as clothing and home furnishings, present the most complex inventory problems because they are usually offered in many different styles, colours, sizes, materials, and so forth. Their major characteristics are: (1) a short product life span, (2) relatively unpredictable sales level, as the purchases of the consumers depend essentially on impulse basis or on subjective evaluation of the item and its close substitutes, (3) broad assortment, needed to create favourable store image /Marquardt et al., 1979, pp. 270-271/.

The solution normally adopted for the problem of fashion items is that of holding, in addition to the safety stock, a supplementary stock for the basic merchandise assortment demanded by consumers, the so-called "basic assortment reserve".

Another category of merchandise that should receive a particular treatment is that grouping perishable items (such as fresh fruits and Christmas gift boxes) and those items that are likely to become obsolete because of time (such as newpapers).

The major characteristic of perishable items is their "shelf life", as they must be sorted out in a short time. A possible approach to solve the problem is that of "marginal analysis", based on the following data: (1) the selling price /SP/, (2) the cost-price /CP/, (3) the iventory carrying cost /CC/, and (4) the reduced selling price /RP/, that can be obtained if perishable items cannot be sold before they lose quality or become obsolete.

The first step of the procedure is that of determining the frequency distribution of sales, that is the probability associated with every level of sales. This can be easily done by checking the data base of the system (to measure how many times each level of sales occurred in past). The probability are then cumulated.

The procedure will finally determine the quantity for which the cumulative probability is equal to the mimimum probability of selling at least an additional unit in order to justify the stocking of that unit. The latter is determined using the following formula:

$$p = \left[(CP + CC) - RP\right] / (SP - RP).$$

With regard to the recent developments in computer hardware, a particular consideration has to be given to the point-of-sale terminals that provide one-time capture and recording of data as soon as it becomes available throughout the retail organization. Eliminating copying data, point-of-sale terminals eliminate transcription errors, and speed the flow of information to management.

In many cases, however, the failure to make the best use of computers lies in an excessive concern with hardware, before an adequate analysis of objectives, inputs, outputs, and processing operations is made. The success of any information system depends not only on the effciency with which data is processed, but also on whether the system provides the information needed by management.

In the latter sense, the computerized information system should do most of the data selection and filtering, as to provide the information needed (displayed and perceived) at the required level of detail.

The critical deficiency under which most managers operate is not the lack of relevant information but the overabundance of irrelevant information /Ackoff, 1967/. The problem is often that of receiving much more data then it is possible to absorb and spending a great deal of time separating the relevant from the irrelevant.

As a consequence, the inventory information system should furnish much more on demand reports rather than broadcasting general-purpose reports that serve everyone and no one. It should also more widely utilize the exception principle, in order to determine by means of standards (control limits) when to present a certain type of information as output.

Selctivity can also be increased by the way in which information is displayed. Techniques for increasing perception include the use of standard report formats, graphical displays, and various schemes for drawing attention to the most critical variables /Emery, 1969, p. 99/.

Beside the selectivity, it is also necessary to increase the flexibility, accuracy, and tempestivity of the information system, in order to maximize the effectiveness with which the individual, organizational, and social objectives should be satisfied.

In fact, the information requirements change with the changing character of the environment and of the processes used within the organization, as well as with the changing insights of the users in the light of subsequent experience and knowledge.

The information system must therefore be capable of responding to changed processes and user's needs, particularly via the organizational arrangements that link computer analysts to users in a continuing dialogue and by appropriate forms of continuing evaluation /Banbury, 1979/.

References

ACKOFF, RUSSEL., "Management Misinformation Systems", The Institute
of Management Sciences, Vol. 14, December, 1967.

BANBURY, JOHN, Information, Decision-Making and Control, and the
Process of Systems Analysis, Pisa, Crest Course, 1979.

BERTINI, UMBERTO, Il sistema d'azienda. Schema di analisi /The Analysis
of Business Systems. An introduction/, Pisa, University Press, 1977.

CAVALIERI, ENRICO, Sulle relazioni tra modelli economico-aziendali e
matematico-statistici /The Theory of Business Administration and
the use of Mathematical Models/, Chieti, University Press, 1974.

EMERY, JAMES C., Organizational Planning and Control Systems. Theory
and Technology, London, The MacMillan Co., 1969.

HOPEMAN, RICHARD J., Systems Analysis and Operations Management,
Columbus, O., Charles E. Merrill Publishing Co., 1969.

MARCHI, LUCIANO, Il sistema informativo aziendale. Elaborazione
elettronica delle informazioni e pianificazione dei processi
informativi /Business Information Systems: Analysis and Design/,
Pisa, University Press, 1980.

MARQUARDT, RAIMOND A., MAKENS, JAMES C., and ROE, ROBERT G., Retail
Management. Satisfaction of Consumer Needs, Hinsdale, Ill.,
The Dryden Press, 1979.

O'BRIEN, JAMES A., Computers in Business Management. An Introduction,
Homewood, Ill., Richard D. Irwin, Inc., 1975.

Proc. First Int. Symp. on Inventories
Budapest, Hungary 1980

CONTROL OF MULTI-LOCATION INVENTORY SYSTEM

ENDRE MEGYERI

Karl Marx University of Economics, Budapest, Hungary

The paper deals with a computer-based operative inventory control system. The flow of goods within the system is shown in Figure 1.

In the system $b = 1, 2, \ldots, k$ types of products are to be distributed among $p = 1, 2, \ldots, n$ numbers of consumer warehouses, having storage capacity of Z_p each.

Output of materials from stores per time unit /in days/ is a random variable, controlled by the consumers themselves, who are outside of the system.

Materials enter the system at a railway junction, far from users, in quantities q and are to be immediately forwarded in unchanged lots to the place of consumption, where they arrive after a lead time λ.

Input per time unit /in days/ from product b is a random variable. It is one of the tasks of control to realize such a distribution of input, which makes it possible to meet consumers' demand.

Distribution among consumers is organized centrally by "consumer input dispositions".

167

Input to the system shows a quasi-seasonal distribution during a one-year period and it might happen that - together with preliminary deliveries - it exceeds the demand per year /see Figure 2/. Because of this it is possible to have such level of stocks which - in the short run - exceeds storing capacity of consumers. Surplus stocks are stored in <u>rented warehouses</u>. It is possible to use number g /g = 1,2,....,m/ rented warehouses, each having a storing capacity of Z_g. Control of using rented warehouses is also organized centrally in the system.

In periods when input is less than consumption, user's stocks are decreasing, and this process might and must be balanced by using stocks from rented warehouses. The process is controlled by "<u>consumer dispositions for transshipments</u>".

<u>Item structure</u> of materials entering the system is not obviously equal with consumers' demand. This alteration, within technically possible limits, raises the question of reasonable <u>substitution</u>. Possibility and need for substitutions are taken into consideration in the control of the distribution system and are also analysed in the control of dispositions and stock levels.

Operative control of input and output /consumption/ of the system is organized from outside. Control within the system can only manipulate with storing to consumers to rented warehouses and by transshipments. Dependent variables of control are the stock levels in warehouses.

The <u>control system</u> was formulated on the basis of the following considerations: In consumer warehouses the basis for management is the so-called <u>two-bin inventory control system</u>. In this system two parameters have to be decided in advance: reorder point /s/ and ordering quantity /q/. The basic rule for control is to place an order quantity /q/ at stock level /s/ /see Figure 3/.

In our model reorder level is supposed to be equal with safety stock plus stocks under delivery, and order quantity is equal with the quantity of an input. /The latter is equal with the quantity of a wagon./ Input quantity units are at the same time the norms of actual stock level. Adding safety stock level to the latter gives the level of maximum stock under conditions of normal replenishment.

Under normal conditions the system is to be operated on the following rule: If stocks decrease to the level of reorder point or below, a disposition is to be placed for the arrival of the next wagon. Decision is made on the basis of inventory situation of the consumers: If there is a danger of shortage, then actions should be taken in order to increase stocks. These situations are called <u>states of potential shortages</u> and the need for decision is called <u>impulse of consumer decision</u>. But the system concerned has five such characteristics which make it impossible to apply such a simple inventory mechanism alone.

<u>First</u>: It should be taken into consideration that incoming orders /dispositions/ from various warehouses might exceed the volume of input to the system. Then the question is raised: In what order should "waiting" orders /dispositions/ be met? The problem is solved by using priorities. We can use priorities defined in two different ways.

FIGURE 1

THE SCHEME OF PRODUCT FLOW IN THE SYSTEM

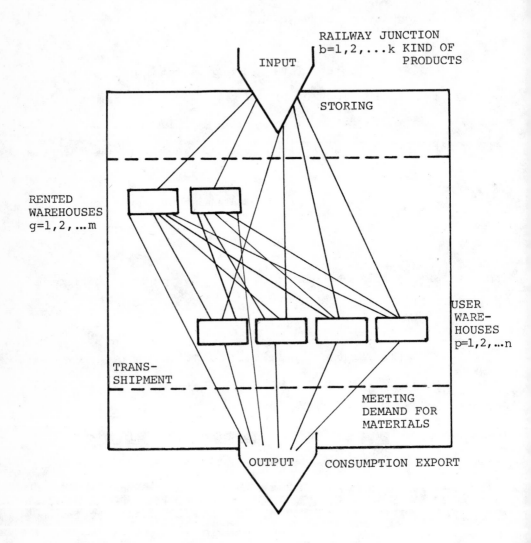

FIGURE 2

INPUT AND CONSUMPTION PROCESS OF A CERTAIN ITEM

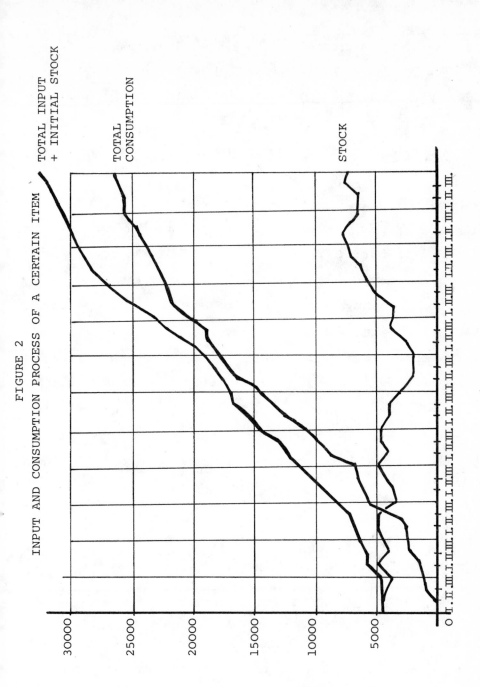

TOTAL INPUT
+ INITIAL STOCK

TOTAL
CONSUMPTION

STOCK

The first is created in the system of programming as a quotient of reorder point and actual stock. For example, safety stock level as a reorder point is divided by the volume of actual stock. It is obvious that in a case when actual stock level is less than safety level, the priority index $/P_1/$ is larger than one. The larger the value of priority index, the higher the danger of shortage. When distributing incoming materials, priority is given to the warehouse having the highest value of priority index.

In the second case, priority is given by the management, "outside" of the system; in case of equal priority indices which warehouses are to be preferred.

Second: Input of materials to the railway junction might exceed the possible level of volume of dispositions placed by the rule of two-bin system. Even in the case when wagons are to be forwarded without delay after customs and transferring. That means a need for decision to be created also by the input of materials. This is called input impulse.

To solve the problem of surplus input is possible by widening the sphere of reorder /signal/ stock levels, and priority indices. Secondary signal stock level is the sum of safety stock volume and input unit, representing also current stocks. Secondary priority index $/P_2/$ is formed by dividing the above mentioned signal stock level by the value of actual stock. Placing priority in this phase of activity, when actual stock is between safety level and maximum stock level and which is called phase of equilibrium is similar to that of the former case.

172

FIGURE 3

TWO-BIN INVENTORY CONTROL SYSTEM

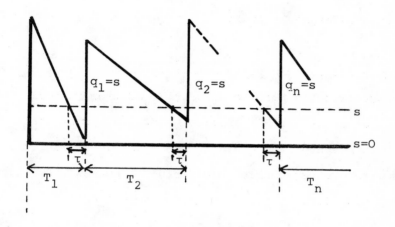

FIGURE 4

States of the system

I	State of potential shortages	$P_1 > 1$
II	Equilibrium state	$P_1 \leq 1$
		$P_2 \geq 1$
III	State of saturation	$P_2 < 1$
		$P_3 \geq 1$
IV	State of over-saturation	$P_3 < 1$
		$P_4 > 1$

$$P = \frac{\text{signal stock}}{\text{actual stock}}$$

Third: While consumption is nearly uniform, input to the system /from import/ follows a quasi-seasonal distribution within a year. Incoming materials have to be distributed in every case, although it causes quasi-seasonal stocks, the level of which is much higher than the sum of safety stock and current stock volume.

In this class of system activity - called phase of saturation - interests in placing priorities will be changed. While stocks needed for normal functioning of the system are to be secured for each of the consumers, terminal accumulation of stocks might be reasonable in certain warehouses. Because of this in this class of functioning of the system both priority indices - by the use of signal stock levels - and management rankings are changed. New signal stock level proposed is the quotient of the maximum volume of stock capable for storing in consumer warehouses item by item and the value of current stock level, with possible corrections.

Fourth: At intervals when input to the system is high, stocks may reach such a level that consumer warehouses are saturated or there is a need for a rented warehouse or materials are to be stored in warehouses, the owner of which is not a consumer of goods concerned. This phase of functioning is called over-saturation. /Classes of system functioning are shown in Figure 4./

In principle, it would be possible to direct materials to rented warehouses only in that case when consumer warehouses are filled up. A reason against this behaviour is the limited capacity of rented warehouses to accept wagons, and the fact that overloading causes high extra costs. It is reasonable to distribute incoming materials uniformly among as many warehouses as possible, taking also into account their capacity to accept wagons. This makes it necessary to start using rented warehouses before consumer storage capacities are fully exhausted. In the proposed system this problem is solved by rotating consumer and rented warehouse dispositions, also in accordance with the capacity of rented warehouses to accept wagons. Controlling this combined storage - consumer and rented warehouses - new signal stock levels are priority indices used; among them are the ones related to rented warehouses. For sake of creating consumer priorities maximum possible levels of storing item by item are used as signal stock levels. For deciding on signal stock levels for rented warehouses the main points of view are the following: distance of shipment, costs of storage, and capability to accept wagons.

Transshipments from rented warehouses to the ones owned by consumers are also connected to certain conditions. First of all, a disposition to change the place of storage is to be placed when stock level at consumer warehouses decreases below the level of minimal signing stock level, that is, below the safety stock level, and there is no input. To start transshipments placed before that time might be reasonable in consequence of certain interests. Such interests are: higher level of safety, reduction of costs of using rented warehouses and uniform loading of input capacity. Because of this we created a regulation system working on the following principle: At intervals when input expected is less than anticipated consumption, transshipment is started when consumer's stock level is getting close to the sum of the safety stock and current stock, namely when the level of stocks reaches a newer signal stock level from above.

Fifth: As item structure of imported materials can only be influenced within certain limits and there is a possibility for substitutions between materials, the problem of substitution is to be taken into account when formulating inventory control. The question is raised as follows: If there is shortage in certain goods and its stock level decreases below the safety level, what kind of rule can regulate the replacement of the needed quantity by stocks, input or transshipment of other goods.

Two possible courses of substitution are built into the control system: combined and unique substitution. In the former case substitution is realized by using up two more kinds of products - which together will have the properties of the original one. In case of unique substitution of missing stock of a product creating narrow capacity is supplemented from stocks of a given substituting product or with its input and transshipment.

Control of substitution is organized in such a way that priorities may be placed between forms of substitution and substituting goods, that is, combined substitution may be preferred to unique substitution, substitution with goods on stock to goods from input, the latter one to transshipment, etc.

The basic principle of storing and transshipment may be called principle of balanced filling up. This principle works

as follows: Next unit of disposition is always directed to
that warehouse the supply level of which is the smallest.

Control of dispositions can shortly be characterized by
the following: According to the program of stock actualization
the actual stock levels of warehouses are counted before each
disposition. These stocks are related to signal stock levels
and the actual phase of system functioning is determined. Then
we choose priorities belonging to that phase, give necessary
dispositions for storing in, transshipment and substitution.
After that actualization of stock levels is performed. This
process goes on until there is consumer or input impulse in the
system. The whole process is performed by programmed automatic
decisions. /Functioning of the system in phase I and phase II
is shown in Figure 5./

Although the proposed system can be operated according to
programmed decisions automatically, in each phase of functioning in certain cases it might be advisable to intervene individually or to think about reasonability of individual intervention. Because of this the system was built on the principle
of management by exceptions. We have defined two groups of exceptional interventions: qualified and non-qualified situations. To make qualified interventions or the need to decide
on such an action come from the state of functioning of the
system concerned. Characteristics of critical states are determined in advance and they are built into the automatic
system of control. Using these criteria, the proposed inventory
control system determines automatically the cases when exceptional interventions are to be balanced, analyses them and

FIGURE 5
States I and II
DECISION AND ACTION TABLE FOR STORING

IS $P_1 > 1$?	Y	Y	N	N	N
IS $P_2 > 1$?	-	-	Y	Y	N
IS THERE INPUT?	Y	N	Y	N	Y
TAKE WAREHOUSES HAVING PRIORITY!	X	X	X	X	-
GIVE STORING ORDER	X	-	X	-	-
DECREASE INPUT	X	-	X	-	-
INCREASE STOCKS IN WAREHOUSE HAVING PRIORITY	X	-	X	-	-
CORRECT THE INDEX OF PRIORITY	X	-	X	-	-
TURN BACK TO THE BEGINNING OF THE TABLE	X	-	X	-	-
LOOK AFTER POSSIBILITIES OF TRANSSHIPMENT	-	X	-	X	-
TURN OVER TO STATE III	-	-	-	-	X

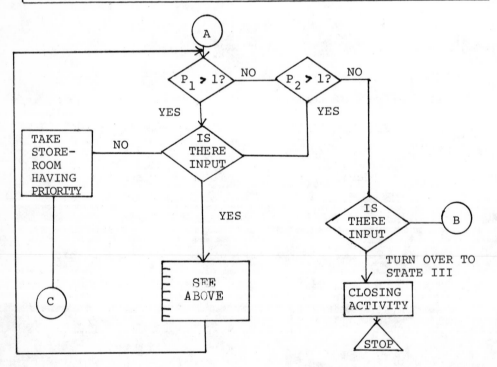

FIGURE 6

DECISION TABLE FOR THE SYMBOLS OF MANAGEMENT BY EXCEPTIONS

	1	2	3	4	5	6
$P_1 > 1$?					N	N
- FOR EVERY ITEM AND WAREHOUSE?	Y	N	N	N	-	-
- FOR CERTAIN ITEMS IN EVERY WAREHOUSE?	-	Y	N	N	-	-
- FOR CERTAIN WAREHOUSES AND FOR ALL OF THE PRODUCTS?	-	-	Y	N	-	-
- BY ACCIDENT FOR CERTAIN ITEMS AND WAREHOUSES?	-	-	-	Y	-	-
IS THERE INPUT?	N	N	N	N	-	-
IS THERE ANY STOCK IN RENTED WAREHOUSES?	N	N	N	N	Y	Y
IS THERE A POSSIBILITY FOR SUBSTITUTION?	N	N	N	N	-	-
$P_5 < 1$?						
- IN ALL WAREHOUSES RENTED?	-	-	-	-	Y	N
- IN ANY OF THE WAREHOUSES RENTED?	-	-	-	-	-	Y
MAKE REPORT ON TURNOVER AND STOCKS!	X	X	X	X	X	X
GIVE SIGNS ABOUT THE STATE OF EXCEPTION TO						
- PRODUCT MANAGER!	X	X	X	⊗	X	⊗
- TO THE HEAD OF SALES DEPARTMENT!	X	X	⊗	X	X	X
- TO THE HEAD OF PURCHASING DEPT.!	X	⊗	X	-	X	-
- TO THE HEADS OF FELLOW-DEPTS.!	X	X	-	-	X	-
- TO THE MARKETING DIRECTOR!	⊗	X	-	-	⊗	-
- TO THE ECONOMIC DIRECTOR!	⊗	-	-	-	⊗	-
- TO THE TECHNICAL DIRECTOR!	⊗	-	-	-	-	-
- TO THE GENERAL DIRECTOR!	⊗	-	-	-	-	-

⊗ = possible level of actual supervision and decision!

provides information on inventory status /reports and prognoses/ to different levels of management. Cases needing exceptional intervention can be divided into two groups: cases threatening with shortage or with overfilling. Within these groups sub-states can be defined, depending on the grade of potential shortage or overfilling.

Our proposal is summarized in a decision table. In the table possible levels of management entitled to intervene are also signed. Authority to decide follows hierarchy of management, and information supply is organized horizontally, too. /See Figure 6./

Unqualified exceptional interventions are made when there is information on other kinds of disturbances in the system and this information is not built into the automatic system of control. /E.g., one of the warehouses is unable to accept input terminally; or there is a need for giving individual storage disposition to one of the consumers in connection with materials which are not usually used by him./

Information subsystem of the proposed inventory control system can be implemented in three phases:

a/ information and decision system of automatic control;

b/ information subsystem for the system of analyses and estimation;

c/ management information system.

Information and decision system of automatic control contains information necessary for program-module of dispositions.

Input information:

1. data on normatives

    a/ signal stock levels

    b/ planned consumption per day in the period concerned

    c/ unit volumes of input

2. data on turnover of goods

    a/ input at the railway junction

    b/ input at different warehouses

    c/ transshipment

    d/ output of goods

3. data on stocks

    a/ initial stock level

    b/ stocks under shipment

    c/ stocks in consumer warehouses

    d/ stocks in rented warehouses

Output information:

1. input dispositions

2. dispositions about transshipments

3. data on stocks /closing stock levels/

    a/ stocks under shipment

    b/ consumer stocks

    c/ stocks in rented warehouses.

Proc. First Int. Symp. on Inventories
Budapest, Hungary 1980

APPROACH TO DATA PROCESSING
IN RATING INVENTORY
IN SUPPLY ENTERPRISES

VASIL MIKOVSKY

Ministry of Supply and Material Reserves, Sofia, Bulgaria

Safety stock, as far as the present methodology is concerned, is described in the sense of a stock created in order to guarantee a regular supply in case of supply distur- bance in the rhythm of consumption. Also, safety stock has to ensure the supply of consumers without considering the ways of supply directly from the store or in transit, i.e. it is concentrated in the warehouses of the supply enterprise. The only exception is when the items are consumed only by one final consumer /a plant/. No doubt, transition to such a forma- tion and regulation of safety stock would require an additional set of organizational actions.

The methodology outlined here differs from the one in practice, according to which safety stock is determined on the basis of the amount of the current supply and on the fluctua- tions of the amounts of supplies. The present methodology states that the safety stock should be determined on the basis of indicated deficits by months. The surplus of resources above the needs per month of a particular item of supply is defined as a negative deficit. The reverse is treated as a

positive one /this is a real deficit/. /See Figure 1 which
concerns the fluctuation of the level of stock of an item for
a one-year period./

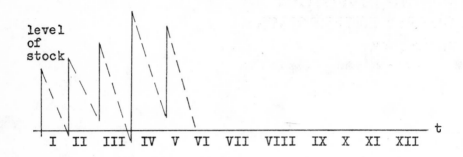

Figure 1

We would like to stress that under the conditions of the
system of supply in action, determining safety stock on the
basis of the deficit is more reasonable, because deliveries
are not planned according to their amount and dates due, but
according to the quantities by items for a given period of
time, most often a quarter of the year. Under these circumstances, the deficits are a more reliable basis of determining
safety stock than the number and amount of deliveries.

The problem described here supposes determining safety
stock in case when receipts and consumption of items are relatively regular, i.e. there exists not more than one quartile,
during the three months of which there are no deliveries, and
not more than one, during the three months of which there is
no consumption.

Safety stock is determined on the basis of changes of
the deficit by months for the accountancy period and consump-

tion data of the planned period. The deficit at the end of the given month is estimated as a difference between the sum of the resources needed from the beginning of the accountancy period till the end of the corresponding month and the sum of the amounts of supply for the same period of time /including the availability of resources at the beginning of the same period/. Safety stock is determined on the basis of the deficit estimated in natural units /tons, kilograms, meters, square meters, etc./ and in relative values /days/. Table 1 gives an example of determining the monthly deficit for an annual period of time.

Table 1   Determining the deficit

Indicators	Initial stock	Months											
		1	2	3	4	5	6	7	8	9	1o	11	12
Consumption in tons		45	45	45	6o	6o	6o	9o	9o	9o	45	45	45
Supplies in tons	1o	2o	45	6o	9o	45	9o	o	9o	16o	2o	5o	5o
Deficit in tons		15	15	o	-3o	-15	-45	45	45	25	o	-5	-1o

The amount of supplies and the dates of delivery are of a random character and also there are random deviations in planned demand. That is why the deficit is a random variable whose stochastic statistical characteristics can be determined.

According to Table 1 the annual average deficit is equal to 18.3 tons and the standard deviation is equal to 26.44 tons.

In order to verify the existence of non-typical random deviations the sum or the difference of the average deficit and the standard deviation is multiplied by 3 and compared to each monthly deficit. If the monthly deficit is greater than the above-stated sum or smaller than the above-stated difference, it is eliminated from the final evaluation of the average deficit and the standard deviation. It depends greatly on the specific characteristics of the delivery process and the characteristics of the statistical data whether the critical meaning of the test would be greater or smaller than 3. In the given example there are non-typical random deviations. While determining safety stock the coefficient of significance for different items is evaluated. It varies between 1 and 3 /although in some case it may be even greater than 3/ depending on the importance and the specific characteristics of the delivery of certain items. It is related to the probability of not admitting any deficit. If the coefficient of significance equals 2, then the probability of not having a deficit is greater than or equal to 75%; in case it equals 3, the same probability is equal to or greater than 88.9%, whatever the probability distribution of the deficit /see Table 2/.

Table 2   Coefficients of significance and the corresponding probabilities of not admitting a deficit

Coefficient	1.2	2	3	4	5	6	7	8	9	1o
Probability	3o.6	75.o	88.9	93.8	96.7	97.2	98.o	98.4	98.8	99

The amount of safety stock in natural units for the accounting period is determined by multiplying the coefficient of significance by the standard deviation. So far as the above-stated example is concerned, the safety stock at a 75% probability will equal 52.88%. Its relative value /in days/ is evaluated by dividing the above-stated amount by the daily consumption, i.e. 52.88 : 2 = 26 days. A more detailed determination of safety stock is demonstrated by a mathematical description of the method.

Keeping in view the features of supply in our country with a relatively regular supply and consumption, safety stock is not supposed to be allowed to exceed 60 days. Therefore, it is stated as a rule that the amount of items contracted will be supplied during the three-month period. Cases, in which items contracted for a given quartile are supplied in the next quartile, are excluded in practice.

Safety stock in natural units for the planned period is determined by multiplying safety stock in days for the accounted period by average daily consumption for the planned period.

Safety stock, evaluated thus by items in days and in natural units, together with statistic data and indicators about receipts and consumption by items are elaborated for analysis. While evaluating the safety stock, the following condition must be accounted for: Magnitude of safety stock may decrease but not increase, i.e. there may be some increase, but further investigation, explanation and enquirement are needed.

In order computers to be used, mathematical description of the method is necessary. The following symbols are used:

B - safety stock

R_t - consumption during month t belonging to the accounting period

Q_i^t - a specific delivery during month t /t=1,2,...,12; i=1,2,...,n_t/

n_t - number of deliveries during month t /t=1,2,...,12/

$Q_t = \sum\limits_{i=1}^{n_t} Q_i^t$ - amount, delivered during month t

S_{t-1} - residual value at the end of the preceding month

β_t - deficit during month t

R_t^n - consumption during month t of the planned period

β_ϕ - average value of the deficit

$\mathbb{G}_\beta$ - standard deviation of the deficit

ϕU - critical value, used in estimating positive non-typical deviations

$\phi U'$ - critical value, used in estimating negative non-typical deviations

$Q_t + S_{t-1}$ - monthly resources

The values of Q_t, S_{t-1}, R_t and B are interconnected in the following way: $Q_t + S_{t-1} = R_t + B + \xi$.

The value of the safety stock is determined on the basis of the deficits β_t, which are evaluated in the following way:

$$\beta_t = \sum\limits_{s=1}^{t} (R_s - Q_s)$$

188

Using ΦU and $\Phi U'$ non-typical deviations of monthly deficits are verified.

In order to estimate the critical values ΦU and $\Phi U'$, the statistical characteristics β_Φ and σ_β are to be estimated according to the following formulas:

$$\beta_\phi = \frac{\sum_{t=1}^{12} \beta_t}{12} \; ; \qquad \sigma_\beta = \sqrt{\frac{\sum_{t=1}^{12} (\beta_t - \beta_\phi)^2}{12}}$$

The probability, according to which ΦU and $\Phi U'$ are estimated is evaluated on the basis of an analysis of experimental statistical data at a probability distribution, according to the following formula:

$$P_a \, (\beta_t \le \beta_\phi + a \, \sigma_\beta) = \frac{a^2 - 1}{a^2} \; ; \qquad a = \sqrt{\frac{1}{1 - a}} \; ;$$

"a" is the critical coefficient by which non-typical deviations are estimated. ΦU and $\Phi U'$ are estimated according to the formulas:

$$\Phi U = \beta_\phi + a \, \sigma_\beta \qquad \text{and} \qquad \Phi U' = \beta_\phi - a \, \sigma_\beta$$

If any of the following inequalities $\beta_t > \Phi U$ and $\beta_t < \Phi U'$ is satisfied, the corresponding deficit β_t is not taken into account while estimating the final values of β_ϕ and σ_β.

Safety stock is estimated by means of σ_β and the coefficient of confidence k, which is pointed out on the basis of a given by an expert probability P_k which stays for not having a deficit. P_k and k are interrelated in the following way:

$$P_k \ (\beta_t \le \beta_\phi + k \ \sigma_\beta) \ge 1 - \frac{1}{k^2} \ ; \qquad k = \sqrt{\frac{1}{1 - P_k}} \ ;$$

the absolute value of   B for the accounting period is equal to:

$$B = k \ \sigma_\beta$$

The relative value in days is estimated by dividing the computed amount in natural units by the average daily consumption for the accounting period:

$$B_o = \frac{k \ \sigma_\beta \ 360}{12 \atop \underset{t=1}{\Sigma} \ R_t}$$

The absolute value of the safety stock for the planned period is equal to:

$$B = B_o \ \frac{\overset{12}{\underset{t=1}{\Sigma}} \ R_t^n}{360}$$

The average cycle stock is estimated on the basis of the quantity delivered to the warehouses of the supply enterprises. We will clarify this problem by using Table 1. Suppose that only 3oo of the delivered 72o tons have passed through the warehouses. There are 15 deliveries in the warehouses of the supply enterprises and two of them have been done on consecutive days.

190

Deliveries done on consecutive days are united in a single delivery. We get 14 deliveries. Deliveries handled by different suppliers or executed by different kinds of transportation on the same day or on consecutive days are treated in the same way.

Non-typical deliveries follow a similar way of investigation and elimination by report with elimination of the deficits of safety stock. It is admitted that non-typical deliveries do not exist after the above-mentioned operation is conducted.

Under this assumption, the value of an average delivery is estimated by dividing 3oo by 14. It is equal to 21 tons.

The maximum stock quantity in days is evaluated by dividing the average delivery by the daily consumption of the accounting period, i.e. 11 days.

The average stock is equal to the half of the maximum stock quantity /5 days in the given example/. The caution rate is equal to the sum of the maximum stock quantity and safety stock and the lead time stock /38 days in the given example/.

The minimum stock quantity in this case is equal to the safety stock, i.e. 28 days.

The above-stated stock indicators, estimated on the basis of data about average daily consumption for the planned period are evaluated in natural units and are applied to the system of stock management.

The mathematical description of the method of determining the average cycle stock in the warehouses of supply enterprises at a relative steadiness of deliveries and consumption can be done by using the following symbols:

Q_{ci} - total receipts of a given material /item/ during the same day /or consecutive days/ in the warehouses for the accounting period;

Q_ϕ - average value of the receipts for the accounting period;

n - number of receipts in warehouses during the accounting period;

n' - number of the days, during which we have untypical receipts /number of non-typical receipts/ during the accounting period;

σ_Q - standard deviation of Q_{ci};

$I_{\phi r}$ - average cycle stock;

I_{maxT} - maximum stock quantity;

I_{min} - minimum stock quantity;

I_H - caution rate of the stock.

Determination and elimination of non-typical deliveries are done by using the coefficient c which is determined on the basis of a previously set probability P_c for the sake of determining non-typical deliveries.

Statistical characteristics are determined as follows:

$$Q_\phi = \frac{\sum\limits_{i=1}^{n} Q_{ci}}{n} \; ; \qquad \sigma_Q = \sqrt{\frac{\sum\limits_{i=1}^{n} (Q_{ci} - Q_\phi)^2}{n}}$$

$$C = \sqrt{\frac{1}{1 - P_c}}$$

The limits of the typical area are determined as follows:

$$Q_{ul} = Q_\phi + c\,\sigma_Q \; ; \qquad Q_{11} = Q_\phi - c\,\sigma_Q$$

If there is a single receipt above the upper limit Q_{ul} or lower than the lower limit Q_{11}, it is treated as a non-typical one. After the reasons of its presence are analysed, it may be excluded from further compilation, when Q_ϕ and σ_Q are evaluated. Under these circumstances n is decreased by n'. Non-typical cases can be removed without being analysed, or a sample survey can be conducted when a great number of items is studied. The automatized system projected on the basis of the present methodology eliminates non-typical cases without analysing them.

After conducting the above-stated procedures, the maximum stock quantity is evaluated /in days/:

$$I_{maxT} = \frac{360\ Q_\phi}{\displaystyle\sum_{t=1}^{12} Q_t} = 11\ \text{days} \qquad /I_{\phi T} = \frac{I_{maxT}}{2} = 5\ \text{days}/$$

The stated way of evaluating the average cycle stock differs from the one currently in use /i.e. using the average interval between the deliveries/. This is done in order to assure the compactivity of the safety stock and the average cycle stock as well as to approach reality better.

The given example states that the lead time stock is equal to one day. The rate of the stock is equal to the sum of the average cycle stock, the lead-time stock, and the safety stock:

$$I_H = I_{\phi T} + B + 1 = 5 + 26 + 1 = 32\ \text{days}$$

Maximum stock quantity is evaluated according to the following formula:

$$I_{max} = I_{maxT} + B + 1 = 11 + 26 + 1 = 38 \text{ days}$$

The minimum stock quantity is equal to the safety stock:

$$I_{min} = B = 26 \text{ days}$$

This methodology was tested at the General Center of Information Management in 1976. We think it is a reliable one.

Proc. First Int. Symp. on Inventories
Budapest, Hungary 1980

LEGAL REGULATIONS FOR THE IMPLEMENTATION OF EFFICIENT INVENTORY CONTROL AT COMBINES AND ENTERPRISES

CHRISTINE NEUHÄUSER

Karl Marx University of Leipzig, Leipzig, GDR

This paper deals with legal regulation of inventory control and store-room management in the GDR. First it is necessary to study briefly the relationship between inventory control and store-room management and their politico-economic significance. Then the legal aspects of management, by which efficient state-level regulation of inventory control and store-room management are to be implemented, both in combines and in other enterprises, will be considered. The point is to illustrate, from the theoretical point of view of democratic centralism, the co-ordination of the legal aspects of management at different levels of administration.

Inventory control and store-room management mean essential preconditions for the continuous realization of the economic processes of production. They serve to provide the population with consumer goods, and to provide the economy with means of production in appropriate quantity and quality, and at the correct time.

Both state institutions and combines, enterprises have to realize inventory control and store-room management according

13*

to the principle of democratic centralism, using various legal measures based on corresponding rules. We are to discuss, how and by which legal aspects of management the central regulation inventory control and store-room management are carried out by the state authorities.

The state influences inventory control within the framework of planning by the issue of state plan-related reference numbers based on legal rules. Such state plan-related reference numbers are issued by the State Planning Board and the Ministries in accordance with the Ministry for Materials Management. The State Planning Board and the Ministry for Materials Management are bodies of the Government of the GDR. The State Planning Board lays the foundations for decisions on fundamental questions of social development and controls the process of planning. The Ministry for Materials Management is especially responsible for the co-ordination and control of material-technical supply in the national economy as a whole, and for assuring high level of efficiency in the use of the materials. The state reference numbers given by the State Planning Board and the Ministries refer to:

- minimum stocks for selected products
- quantity of materials in circulation
- standards of supply and consumption for selected and politico-economically important energy sources, raw materials, materials and components.

The standards of supply consumption and stocks shall be discussed in detail. The Ministry for Materials Management fixes such standards for natural resources, raw materials, etc. in a given nomenclature. The elaboration of selected standards of stocks is going on in the following way:

Ministries responsible for working out the need and consumption of materials, equipment, and consumer goods, receive coordinated standard values from the Ministry for Materials Management at the beginning of the year preceding the plan year. These standard values are co-ordinated with supply and consumption. On this basis they have to elaborate the proposals for state standards of stocks. The state standard proposals are forwarded to state authorities /usually to the Ministries/ responsible for the branches of producers, consumers and traders, and then they are subdivided among combines and firms. Working out drafts of plans, combines and enterprises have to consider the state standard proposals. To what extent state standard proposals become real measures, these state authorities learn when the drafts of plans are defended by the combines and enterprises. After co-ordination with these authorities, the state standard proposals have to be presented for confirmation to the Ministry for Materials Management by the Ministries responsible for the elaboration of demand and consumption of materials, equipment, and consumer goods. By that phase the elaboration of state standards is finished.

The confirmed state standards for stocks together with the national economic plan are forwarded by the State Planning Board to the responsible state authorities as state planning reference numbers.[1] They are distributed to combines and firms.

[1]These state planning reference numbers are called state planning orders in the GDR.

The state standards for stocks are binding on all institutions, combines and enterprises and form the foundation for the implementation of the plan as well as for the approval of inventory control. They define the quantitative level of stocks for the branches of management and for selected sources of energy, raw materials, etc. They are expressed as the number of days the stocks may be held.

Such state influence on inventory control is reasonable and necessary in case of economically significant energy sources, raw materials, etc. There is an overall state interest in the appropriate stocks at different branches. The aim is to form stocks which are reasonable from the point of view of the whole economy. Since it is often difficult to synchronize demand and supply of these raw materials and other kinds of materials, combines and enterprises are not able to decide on the level of stocks which are necessary from the point of view of the national economy. Therefore they have to get binding instructions for keeping appropriate inventories. Concerning other raw materials and materials classified as less significant, combines and enterprises are able to plan their own inventories. This is supervised by the approval of the plan by the responsible authority.

In the GDR it is a dominating opinion that state standards for stocks also represent a legal category besides their inherent economic contents. They are legally relevant, because they are binding rules as state planning reference numbers. This legal binding is necessary for securing the fulfilment of the plan. So far the state standards for stocks are legal aspects of management, and they are defined as state planning decisions. State planning decisions include legally binding decision regarding tasks, methods of solution and conditions for realisation. As targets and measures they form the foundation for the shaping of optimum plans, for effective decisions on implementation of these plans and for the approval of their results. Planning decisions form a basic legal category of planning law.

It is a clear consequence of all these that we know to how deal on the one side with the requirements set by the state standards for stocks on the activity of combines and enterprises and, on the other side with those ways by which they have to influence their inventory control, and stocks.

Drafting of plans of combines and enterprises is regulated by the state planning reference numbers, and also the implementation of plans is secured. This obliges the combines and enterprises to transform the state planning reference numbers into their own planning of stocks through the elaboration of business standards for stocks. Additionally, legal rules oblige combines and enterprises also to elaborate standards for stocks of raw materials and other materials in those cases when no state standards for stocks are given.

Business standards for stocks are of great significance for inventory planning at combines and firms. They have the following functions:
- to transform the aims of the central state level planning of stocks into the firm's inventory planning;
- to guarantee material and financial planning of the amount of

stocks and the inclusion of the stocks into the planning of
demands for material;
- to serve as a basis for the formation of binding state minimum stocks and for the formation of state standards for
stocks of producers and consumers.

Because of their legal nature, state standards for stocks
of enterprises are business planning reference numbers and
thus they are business planning decisions. They determine, on
a technical and economic base, the average level of stocks for
one product /individual standards for stocks/ or for a group
of products /group standards for stocks/. In case of material
planning they are expressed, regarding time, as the number of
days stocks may be held, and regarding quantity, as natural
units. In case of financial planning they are described
according to value. The business standards for stocks are
elaborated by the appropriate departments of combines and
enterprises and are confirmed by the general manager of the
combines or by the top manager of the enterprise. Thus
planning decisions of firms are decisions taken on their own
responsibility about a specific target, defined in terms of
figures, which is given to the branches of enterprises as a
binding standard for their contribution to the fulfilment of
the firm's plan. They are binding rules for these branches.
State planning decisions form their basis.

Business standards for stocks do not represent inflexible
figures to combines and enterprises. The aims covered by the
standards for stocks are essentially determined by the development of conditions of production including transport,

circulation and storage. Because of this, it is necessary to revise the standards for stocks of firms every year and to adapt them to the new conditions. It is the task of combines and enterprises, by means of standards for stocks, to recognize material reserves and to accelerate their utilization. This is done as follows. By the optimization of stocks necessary for production, it is determined for instance what amount, and for how long, raw materials and other materials have to be stored for continuous production. Organization of production according to scientific-technological knowledge will influence the results. The aim of business standards for stocks based on the procedure described is always to reach the same or even a higher volume of production with less inventories.

Business standards for stocks as an aspect of management influence the recognition of reserves and their rational utilization. This meets the demand expressed by the state planning reference numbers to increase the rate of circulation of the materials, to increase stocks only in order to meet the requirements of the process of production in combines and enterprises, and thus to influence the effectiveness of inventory control.

Often it is difficult in practice to adhere to the optimum level of stocks at combines and firms. A lot of factors can cause deviations. These may be deficiencies in their own activities, for instance production that does not meet the plan, or improper distribution of materials, false information as to dement for the product. But deficiencies can also result from other factors, for instance from very long delivery times for materials needed, belated or too early deliveries by the partner, or cancellation of contracts for delivery, etc. Combines and enterprises have the duty to abolish deficiencies in their own fields. They have the duty not to break contracts and this is enforced by imposing fines. Business standards for stocks form the basis for the contents of delivery contracts ensuring the supply of materials for production. They determine the content of agreements as to how often the deliveries shall be made and how much shall be delivered at each time. By fixing the times and quantities of deliveries in the contracts a planned and effective storage of stock and production are secured, because deliveries fixed by these agreements make it possible to realize the planned volume of stocks.

Contracts for supply are concluded by combines and enterprises on their own responsibility. The extent to which the contents of the activities of combines and enterprises have to be confirmed is determined by the state and business planning reference numbers. Contracts represent binding decisions for the parties involved. These contracts are aspects of management regarding the responsibility of the combines and enterprises for the formation of their own inventories.

Beyond the contracts, the "regulation of inventory control" is an essential legal aspect of the management of combines and enterprises in order to carry out and control the processes of inventory control, transport and circulation. They serve the uniform regulation of continuously repeating

processes in the fields of inventories. Because of their legal
nature they are decisions for individual enterprises.

Decisions made by the general manager of a combine or by the
top manager of an enterprise are based on and are within the
framework of legal rules: they include binding legal decisions
for the branches of enterprises.

The contracts of the "regulations of inventory control" form
the organizational principles for the inventory operations and
the delimitation of the tasks of departments and branches which
are involved in inventory control. The following points belong
to the "regulations of inventory control": The structure and
organization of inventory control; tasks, rights and duties of
the store-room management; the arrangement of the arrival of
goods and the activities of storage; book-keeping and
statistics in store-room management; industrial safety and
safety against burning, etc. At the same time such instructions
in the "regulations of inventory control" must be based on a
planned rationalization in the field of inventories.

Proc. First Int. Symp. on Inventories
Budapest, Hungary 1980

PRODUCTION SMOOTHING.
STOCK LEVEL MIDDLE-TERM PLANNING
OF PRECONSTRUCTION ELEMENTS

BYRON PAPATHANASSIOU

*Technical Chamber of Greece, Branch of Central Macedonia,
Thessaloniki, Greece*

1. The production smoothing problem

The object of this paper is to deeply investigate the problem of production smoothing and the proper stock level in the middle term planning of the production of preconstructive elements.

In order to satisfy the fluctuating demand, the production planning policy could be:

a/ keeping steady the production level so that the stock level can cover the demand fluctuation

b/ adapting the production level to every demand, so that in cases of a proper forecast a steady safety stock is permanently preserved

c/ planning a system which can give a medium solution between the policies a/ and b/.

The first policy offers the advantage of keeping a steady manpower and a complete production smoothing. The disadvantage is, however, the necessity of keeping an important amount of initial stocks to cover supplementary needs and, consequently, a serious cost of stocks.

205

The second policy gives exactly the advantage of keeping a low level of stocks which corresponds to a low cost of stocks, while the cost of production presents fluctuations as per the demand. The disadvantage of this policy is the substantial inability of its application and its keeping.

The third policy might be the easiest one to be applied and needs the fixing not only of how much, but also in what way the production will be changed, e.g. hiring or firing of manpower, overtime work, employment of sub-contractors, etc., or a combination of all the above.

Objective purpose, of course, remains the cost minimizing. For the achievement of this aim, one has to consider:

a/ the estimated demands of the future periods of the planning horizon

b/ the conditions which determine the original state of the production unit /e.g. manpower, stock level, etc./

c/ the mathematical relations and the restrictions which represent the operation of the production system and the cost /e.g. relationship between the number of employees, and the production rate, cost functions, etc./

d/ the parameters for each time period which are correspondingly needed.

The mathematical expressions, the restrictions and the parameters are possibly different from period to period within the planning horizon, but generally are considered as fixed elements for the production smoothing.

For the determination of the variables, decision is usually made by the application of decision rules which may be simple rules of experiences, or simple estimation methods, or, ultimately, optimization models by using computer data processing.

2. Stock level

It has been proved that the auto-determination of the stock level or even its determination on the basis of experience is inadequate because it leads either to shortage, or, on the contrary, to a stock superabundance, that is a useless engagement of capital.

The basic aim of stock control is the proper securing of stocks at the proper place and in the proper time with a minimum cost. More specifically, an object of planning and control is the most effective management, which is achieved by a deep mathematical investigation of the temporal and quantitative handling of stock.

3. The object of this paper

The present study is examining the problem which is faced by a construction company, which applies a close preconstruction system and looks forward to a production smoothing with a complete satisfaction of demand, using always the relevant manpower.

In the course of the problem's study, the form of relations and parameters which must be considered for scientific planning of production smoothing will be deeply investigated. Consequently our problem may be determined as follows: If production planning is referring to a total period of time T which is divided into equal sub-periods t, and there are forecasts of requirements z_t to cover a demand of product units in every sub-period, it is requested that the production level P_t /in production units/ and the manpower B_t /in a number of production units/ for the period t /1,...,T/ must be determined, provided that the available capacity in machinery, equipment, etc. is limited.

3.1. The mathematical model

P_t = production of the period T /where t=1,...,T/   /tn/

x_t = production at the proper time of work period t   /tn/

y_t = production at overtime work of period t   /tn/

z_t = the distribution level during period t   /tn/

a_o = stock level at the beginning of period t   /tn/

A = the maximum possible stock level   4,000 /tn/

k_1 = production cost per unit in regular time $/\frac{m.u.}{tn}/$ *

k_2 = production cost per unit in overtime work $/\frac{m.u.}{tn}/$

k_3 = sale's profit per unit $/\frac{m.u.}{tn}/$

k_4 = firing cost per work unit $/\frac{m.u.}{tn}/$

k_5 = cost per work unit $/\frac{m.u.}{tn}/$

As production unit the metric ton /tn/ of preconstructive concrete elements is taken.

The restrictions of the problem are determined by the following side-conditions.

1. The production x_t in regular work time cannot exceed a maximum level of production X_t.

* Author's note: m.u. stands for monetary unit.

This level X_t is determined by the available capacity in machinery equipment and other factors

$$x_t \leq X_t$$

2. The manpower B_t gives also a fluctuate decision variable as a function of the production x_t, that is

$$x_t \leq c_1 B_1 - c_o \qquad /1/$$

where c_1 and c_o form positive parameters and also c_1 presents the possibility of production by one group and c_o is the waste personnel's performance.

3. Correspondingly also we have:

$$y_t \leq Y_t \qquad /2/$$

4. The manpower level in every period obeys the following relationship:

$$B_t - B_{t-1} - D_t + F_t = 0$$

$$D_t \leq \frac{B_o}{2} \cdot D_t - x_{D_t} \leq \frac{B_o}{2} \qquad /3/$$

D_t indicates the number of the hired employees and F_t the number of fired workers in each period t, B_{t-1} the level of personnel during the immediate previous period and B_o the initial level of work force, x_{D_t} = employments which will not be performed.

For reasons of a smooth operation it is not worthwhile to employ new groups of workers more than the half of the original ones.

5. The overall of sales z_t of every period cannot be higher than the forecasted demand.

It is expressed by the relation:

$$z_t \leq Z_t \qquad\qquad /4/$$

6. The production P is defined by the relation:

$$P_t = x_t + y_t$$

7. The relation of the sizes a_o, P_t, z_t should be:

$$a_o + \sum_{t=1}^{T} (P_t - z_t) \leq A \qquad\qquad /5/$$

which means that the stock level of period t is equal to the level of the initial stock /the one which existed at the beginning of the first period or at the start of the time period T/ plus the sum of differences of production and sales which derived in various periods from the beginning to the considered period t and cannot exceed the level A, by all means.

The objective function of which maximizing is required must include all variables which appear in the above relations and represent or result expenses or income /e.g. sales/.

Each variable is actually multiplied by a proper factor to express the total cost or profit. Thus, the objective function is formed:

$$\max. K = \sum_{t=1}^{T} (-k_1 \, x_t - k_2 \, y_t + k_3 \, z_t - k_4 \, F_t + x_5 \, X_{D_t}) \quad /6/$$

where K is the total cost or profit of business during the period T.

Relations 1, 2, 3, 4 specify the requested mathematical model.

This model expresses mathematically the problem of production smoothing in middle term planning of preconstructive elements, while the solution of the model, that is determination of conditions for the different variables, gives the optimum program.

Below, an example for the better understanding of the whole matter is given.

An example of a three-month production of preconstructive elements will be used.

For instance, in a preconstructive element production unit the regular and overtime work amounts to the period t /e.g. months/ /where t=1,...,3/ in 2000 tn, 1000 tn, 2000 tn, for every sub-period.

Every work group's capacity in each sub-period reaches 20 t, which means that the total production will be the production of each group multiplied by the number of groups.

The original number of work groups at the beginning of the period is $B_o = 60$. The forecasts of possibility for sales

for every sub-period are 2000 tn, 2500 tn, 1400 tn. Initial
stock level is 3000 tn.

The cost factors per unit are:

k_1 = 400 (m.u./tn)

k_2 = 500 (m.u./tn)

k_3 = 15000 (m.u./tn)

k_4 = 10000 (m.u./tn)

k_5 = 1000 (m.u./tn)

The use of the above mentioned conditions in the model,
by help of a computer /DIEL ALFATRONIC/ and a SIMPLEX program,
gives the following results:

$x_1 = x_9 =$ 0	$x_{22} =$	650
x_{10} = 2,000	$x_{23} =$	300
x_{11} = 2,500	$x_{24} =$	650
x_{12} = 1,400	$x_{25} =$	0
$x_{13} = x_{15} =$ 0	$x_{26} =$	0
x_{16} = 1,350	$x_{27} =$	0
x_{17} = 700	$x_{28} =$	90
x_{18} = 1,350	$x_{29} =$	30
x_{19} = -5	$x_{30} =$	30
x_{20} = -5	$x_{31} =$ 5,000	
x_{21} = -5	$x_{32} =$ 7,500	
	$x_{33} =$ 8,900	

max.K = 88650,000 m.u.

Production at regular period X_t: 1350 tn, 700 tn, 1350 tn.

Production at overtime work y_t: 650 tn, 300 tn, 650 tn.

Manpower /work group/ B_t: 90, 120, 150

Forecasts /demands/ Z_t: 2000 tn, 2500 tn, 1400 tn.

These results show that in the three periods we will have a total production 500 tn and a total demand 5900 tn, which means that 900 tn will be taken from the original stock a_o.

It also shows that in the first, second and third period, 30 work groups must be employed in each of them, so that the original number of 60 groups will arrive at 150.

Naturally, from the objective function the number

$$1000 \cdot \frac{3\,B_o}{2} \cdot 1000 \cdot 90 = 90,000 \text{ m.u.}$$

must be subtracted.

References

1. Brown Z. /1959/. Statistical Forecasting for Inventory Control. McGraw-Hill Book Company, New York, Toronto, London, p. 232.

2. Eilon S. /1977/: The production smoothing problem. The Production Engineer, p. 123.

3. Ferry Douglas /1972/: Cost Planning of Buildings. Crosby Lockwood, London, p. 258.

4. Kamper P. /1972/: Steuerung der Lagerbestände /Stock Control/ f+h "fördern und heben". Vol.15, p. 831.

5. Mc Neill Th., Clark D. /1966/: Cost Estimating and Contract Pricing. American Elsevier Publishing Company Inc., New York, p. 258.

6. Psoinos D. /1976/ /Greek/: Management of Production Systems, Stocks Scheduling and Control /University lectures/.

7. Silver E. /1967/: A Tutorial on Production Smoothing and
   Work Force Balancing. Operations Research,
   Vol. 15, No.6, p. 941.

8. Sobel Mathew /1969/: Smoothing Start-up and Shut-down Costs
   in Sequential Productions. Operations
   Research, Vol. 17,   p. 133.

9. Thome R. /1977/: Produktionskybernetik /Production
   Cybernetics/. Erich Schmidt Verlag, p. 174.

10. Waldmann K.-H. /1980/: On the Optimality of /z,Z/ Order
    Policies in Adaptive Inventory Control.
    Zeitschrift für Operations Research /ZOR/,
    Vol. 24, p. 61.

Proc. First Int. Symp. on Inventories
Budapest, Hungary 1980

FUNCTION ORIENTED DISTRIBUTION OF DATA PROCESSING FOR MATERIAL MANAGEMENT

BÉLA POMPÉRY

Association for the Development of Computer Technology in the Chemical Industry, Budapest, Hungary

Data processing in Hungary has a past of 20 years. Already the first data processing applications involved material accounting, because of the important role of materials in production. The share of material inputs is relatively high in our country; they generally amount to over 50 percent of the value of production.

STAGES IN THE DEVELOPMENT OF DATA PROCESSING

It is well known from an American author[1] that the completion of an information system can take 20 years and there are 6 stages in this process. /TABLE 1./

- The first phase is the acquirement of the methods of data processing and only some separate programs are to be finished. /In Hungary, we frequently began with the material accounting./

- In the second phase stand-alone sub-systems are developed and used routinely in off-line processing. /These

[1] Nolan, R.L.: Managing the crises in data processing, Harvard Business Review 57.2. 1979.

TABLE 1

Establishment of an Information System

PHASES	1.	2.	3.	4.	5.	6.
CHARACTERISTICS	STARTING	SPREADING	CONTROL	INTEGRATION	DECENTRALIZATION	ADVANCED
ACTIVITIES	1-2 PROGRAMS	STAND-ALONE SUBSYSTEMS	HIGHER LEVEL SUBSYSTEMS	INFORMATION SYSTEM		
DATA SYSTEMS	PURPOSE-ORIENTED	SUBSYSTEM ORIENTED	PROJECT ORIENTED	DATA BANK	DECENTRALIZED	
ORGANIZATION OF SYSTEM	1.	ADDITIVE	2.	3.	4.	CORRECTED
ORG. METHOD	BATCH DATA PROCESSING		FREQUENT PROCESSING	DATA PROCESSING AND INQUIRING		DISTRIBUTED FUNCTIONS
TERMS /YEAR/	4 - 6	Ø	5	3	5	2
LEVEL OF OPERATIVITY	Ø					

COSTS

20!

processes in our country frequently involved material management./

- In the third phase the stand-alone sub-systems are combined into a higher level system, and the results of the data processing are made available for the management.
- In the fourth phase the data systems are integrated, and a data bank is established.
- The fifth phase is the beginning of a considerable decentralization, distribution of functions, when data processing networks operate.
- The sixth stage is the perfection of the processes, the realization of the advanced system.

The six phases mean that the data processing systems should be reorganized after the second, third and fourth phases, that is the systems become obsolete in 5-6 years and a reorganization should be effectuated by the means of hardware and software.

CENTRE OF INTEREST: OPERATIVITY

In Hungary many enterprises have reached the first three phases, and now we are working on the fourth /integration/ and fifth /distribution/ phases. Consequently, there are sufficient and reliable systems at our disposal for a reliable preparation of decision making for the top management. But these systems often cannot promote the operative management sufficiently. Reports are not yet up to date.

Consequently, the management is interested in data processing operativity. At the enterprises, where a computerized

materials management reporting system exists as an output of
the electronic data processing, the improvement of the systems
should be aimed at the perfection of operativity. In the last
years different systems have been projected and tested in order
to enhance operativity. Operativity actually can be based on
two basic alternatives:

- the ownership of a computer with sufficient processing
  capacities, or
- data processing, distributed among several computers.

The first could be applied by enterprises located in one
spot. In this case the input and output data can be handled
easily, since processing depends not on geographical distance,
but only on the capacity of the computer.

In the other cases operativity could be hardly reached by
only one computer. I should like to demonstrate some of these
cases.

ALLOCATION AND RE-ALLOCATION BETWEEN THE ENTERPRISES AND THE
TRUST CENTER

In our country there are trusts and combines[x], where the
materials management is decentralized exclusively. The enterprise is responsible for the orders, storage, and consumption
of materials. There are some materials purchased in vast
amounts, for example, in our industry such as sulphur, pyrite,
phosphate, and the steel tubes in the oil industry. There are
about 50 materials used by more than one enterprise of the
trust or of the combine.

[x] By combine we mean a vertically integrated plant.

218

The annual or quarterly agreements are contracted by the trust or combine in the name of the enterprises. The operative orders are issued by the combine. This is especially important when the arrival of a train or ship, loaded with these materials, is announced. On the basis of the order registers, the trust manages the distribution of materials, giving instructions for the transport.

This method requires a well established management system for the handling of the daily turnover and stock information. In our case several million forints have been saved by such a system.

SHORTAGE GOODS AND EXCESS STOCKS

In the last years several associations have been founded to increase productivity. The members are independent enterprises, associated for a given aim. The associations are established mainly according to territorial principle. An important aim is to exchange stocks, mainly the so-called "shortage goods". Another aim is to minimize stocks of materials consumed by many of the members. The cooperation is supported by a data processing system. Each of the member enterprises decides about the kind of products which it wants to include in the cooperation. It is conceivable, for example, that there are 25,000 products in the storehouses of a given enterprise. From these, 2,000 are used by other enterprises, too. In this case the enterprise is obliged to provide information about the 2,000 articles for the association.

On the average, there are 20 members in each association. Each association has a data processing system, where the information on the products, consumed by each member, are accumulated. This method proved to be useful especially for the exchange of shortage goods.

DISTRIBUTED FUNCTIONS

First, I would like to analyze the efficiency of the computer /TABLE 2/. These are:

- plans, reports, statistics, accounts - required periodically
- eventually necessary plans, evaluations, which could be processed efficiently with a /large/ computer.

Operative tasks could be performed by small computers as well. In material-management withdrawals from stocks could refer to:

- articles
- groups of articles
- internal orders of materials
- transport contracts.

The problem is the distribution of these functions among the small computers available. The storages, capacities and performances of small computers are different /TABLE 3/. The technical parameters of the computer and its other qualities are also important for us. With the help of such an evaluation decision can be made on how to satisfy the operative demands:

- with data entry machines /group 1/ verified basic data can be transmitted to the computer centre;

- with microcomputers /group 2/ several different listings
  could be performed, cumulated, aggregated, collected and
  inquiried;
- minicomputers are suitable for the solution of almost
  every kind of task which formerly could have been solved
  only by large computers.

The abilities of the small computers, their costs, and the
terms of delivery are the limiting factors for the operativity
that can be reached.

Let us suppose that operativity is to be ensured on
- workshop
- factory
- central level /TABLE 4/.

a. In the first case correct data sources can be employed at
   best.
b. In the second case operative data output can be performed
   /for example material stocks/.
c. In the third case correct data are provided by the workshops, and the direct information is registered in the
   factories, where these operative data are needed.
d. In the fourth case there are several alternatives, for
   example: the operative data output and the inquiring of
   data are decentralized in the workshops or in the factory,
   where there are data input and data storage possibilities
   as well as operative evaluations.

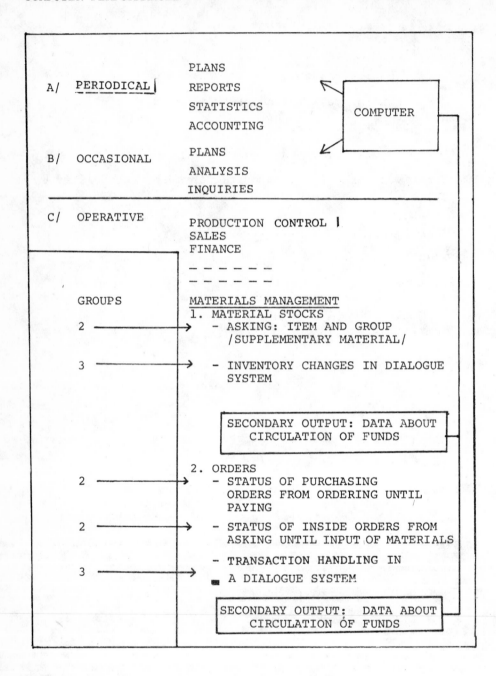

TABLE 3

SMALL COMPUTERS

FUNCTIONS, PROPERTIES	CLASSES								
	1. DATA PREPARATION			2. MICRO-COMPUTERS			3. MINI-COMPUTER		
	A	B	C	D	E	F	G	H	I
I. TECHNICAL CHARACTER-ISTICS									
TERMINALS									
STORAGE CAPACITY									
CONTROL									
PROGRAM ABILITY									
TELEPROCESSING									
ETC.									
II. PROPERTIES									
DATA PREPARATION	X	X	X	X	X	X	X	X	X
DATA PRESENTATION									
FIELD DISPLAY	X	X							
RECORD DISPLAY		X	X	X	X	X	X	X	X
HARD COPY			X		X	X	X	X	X
PRINTING			X			X	X		
DATA CHECK									
FORMAL		X	X	X	X	X	X	X	X
LOGICAL			X		X	X	X	X	X
HANDLING OF BASIC DATA			X		X	X	X	X	X
HANDLING OF ACTUAL DATA									
CUMULATION					X	X	X	X	X
SUMMING					X	X	X	X	X
STORING					X	X	X	X	X
DATA INQUIRIES									
SEQUENTIAL			X	X	X	X	X	X	X
DIRECT					X	X	X	X	X
ACTUAL DATA IN DIALOGUE									
SYSTEM								X	X
ETC.									
III. PRICE, TERMS OF									
SHIPMENT, USAGE,									
ETC.									

223

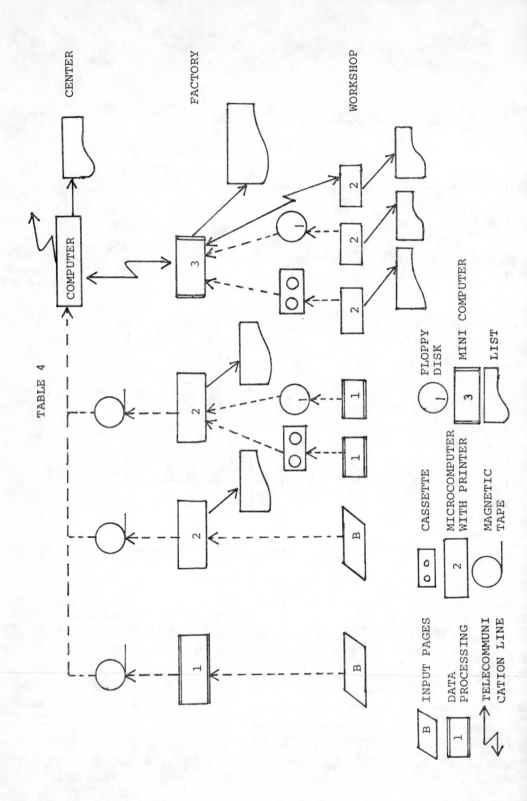

TABLE 4

CENTER

FACTORY

WORKSHOP

COMPUTER

3

2 2 2

2 2

B 1 B

CASSETTE

MICROCOMPUTER
WITH PRINTER

MAGNETIC
TAPE

FLOPPY
DISK

MINI COMPUTER

LIST

INPUT PAGES

DATA
PROCESSING

TELECOMMUNI
CATION LINE

224

TABLE 5

DATA PROCESSING

C/ OPERATIVE

DATA POINT

A	TTACHED
R	ESOURCE
C	OMPUTER

IBM 5100 SERIES
HP 3000 SERIES

CHANGES
- FIXED DATA
- ACTUAL DATA

A/ PERIODICAL
B/ OCCASIONAL

TRANSPORTING

FINANCE

STORE-ROOM

TRANSMITTER

PURCHASING

PRODUCTION

SALES

COMPU-TER

| MAINTENANCE | LABOUR FORCE | ACCOUNTING | PLANNING |
| SERVICE WORKSHOPS | FIXED CAPITAL | STATISTICS | ANALYSIS |

In the case when there is an on-line connection among the computers by cables, then the data processed in the centre could be printed in the factory and in the workshops, too. A few pages of data list are transmitted by cables generally. This level has already been reached in our branch of industry. For example, TABLE 4 presents the organization of data processing in the TAURUS company. The data processed in the computer centre are printed up to 50 pages locally. The required information is transmitted by cables.

I feel it necessary to show briefly an advanced solution /TABLE 5/:

- operative data processing is distributed for departments /computers from group 3/,
- the small computers are interconnected, so operative inquiries and evaluations can be realized by the departments,
- the data are transmitted to the centre, too, where regular computations take place,
- in the centre some other data processing tasks are solved.

Unfortunately, we have not reached the phase of building such a system yet. We have the hardware facilities but the software development and the implementation of these systems is planned for the next five years.

Proc. First Int. Symp. on Inventories
Budapest, Hungary 1980

ECONOMIC INVENTORY MANAGEMENT BASED ON DEMAND PLANS

THOMAS REICHMANN

University of Dortmund, Dortmund, FRG

I. Introduction

During recent years the interest taken by business administration in economic inventory management has shown a marked increase. This is due not
least to the fact that the proportion of storage costs in overall costs has
been increasing. Together with the costs for inter-company transport, this
now accounts for more than 25% of overall costs in some companies. This high
proportion of costs suggests not only that new inventory and transport
techniques should be looked for on the technical sector but also that cost-
saving planning and optimization methods should be looked for, on the
commercial sector.   Prime interest is attached not to mathematically
elaborate inventory models which are based predominantly on a deterministic
demand but to those approaches to a solution which approximate commercial
practice as far as possible. In this development simulation models play
an important role. The possibilities detailed below of drawing up sales
forecasts (demand plans) with the help of multivariate time series analysis
in the form of   correlation and regression function, forecasts which can
serve as a basis for ascertaining material requirements, have hitherto been
largely ignored in connection with material management.

II. Planning the internal demand directed by production specifications and/ or planning directed by inventory issues as a prerequisite of economic inventory management

Economic inventory management is determined by the level of costs caused by it. These are the costs involved in the company's inventory volume, handling costs and costs of storage capacity. The inventory level is determined by the quantity of incoming stock and essentially by the rhythm of demand for goods issued. This demand may be based on production specifications or on inventory issues.

The problem of demand planning specified by production has been fully dealt with in literature.[1] Based on production program schedules stipulating the type, quality and quantity of products to be produced per time unit, the corresponding material requirements can be determined by means of pre-scriptions or parts lists.

Inventory management directed by inventory issues is characterized by certain reordering policies, e.g. the reorder point system ((S,q)-policy), the scheduling period system ((t,S)-policy) or the Min-Max policy ((s,S)-policy).[2] All systems are characterized by the fact that an order for replenishment is placed as soon as the inventory level drops below a fixed value or after according to fixed periodic pattern.

---

1 See e.g. Trux, Walter R., Data processing for purchasing and stock control, London 1971, S. 257 - 281; Grupp, Bruno, Materialwirtschaft mit
  EDV, Grafenau 1975, S. 91 - 108; Grochla, Erwin, Grundlagen der Materialwirtschaft, 3. Aufl., Wiesbaden 1978, S. 42 - 46.
2 See Reichmann, Thomas, Wirtschaftliche Vorratshaltung, eine gemeinsame
  Aufgabe für Einkauf, Materialwirtschaft und Betriebsleitung. In: Zeitschrift für Betriebswirtschaft, 48. Jg. (1978), S. 565 - 578; Naddor,
  Eliezer, Inventory Systems, New York/London/Sydney 1966, S. 138 - 142,
  246 - 252, 292 - 299; Teresine, Richard J., Materials Management and
  Inventory Systems, New York/Amsterdam 1976, S. 71 - 122.

The necessary reorder level is then determined in the case of the (s,q)-policy for instance, by the average internal demand ascertained in the past, expressed by the average demand per day, to be multiplied by the leadtime, that is the time delay between the placing of the replenishment order and its actual addition to stock. This method is used under economic aspects in industrial enterprises for auxiliary materials and supplies and for incedentals, because the administrative expenses involved in production specificated ascertainment of materials needed would be excessively high. Both types of disposition methods, that based on production specificated and that directed by inventory issues can result in considerable miscalculations. Demand planning based on production specifications deduces the material requirements from the prospective production schedule, specifying the products to be made within a specific planning period according to type and quantity.[3] The precision of disposition methods based on production specifications can thus never exceed that of the production schedules on which plans are based and which may, however, display considerable inaccuracies. Whenever there are no customer orders for the total planning interval, hypotheses have to be made as to the probable sales for corresponding production orders within the planning period. In the case of companies with a demand position strong enough, the uncertainty as to the composition and temporal distribution within the sales programme and the production programme derived from it may well lead to their placing orders for only a percentage (e.g. 25%, 60% or 100%) of their demand for a certain material with their suppliers on account of the breakdown of the parts list, with the consequence that the first supplier bears the risk of having to

3 See Grochla, Erwin, Grundlagen der Materialwirtschaft, 3. Aufl., S. 42;
   Trux, Walter R., Data processing for purchasing and stock control,
   S. 311 - 316.

supply in addition or not to supply fixed quantities depending on cyclical, structural or purely seasonal demand.

If this demand position does not exist, there will be a considerable planning risk concerning inventory management, despite an elaborate breakdown of parts lists or similar disposition methods based on production specifications.

Disposition directed by inventory issues, taking for granted that future demand will tend to develop in the same way as in the past, is also problematical.[4] When analysing past demand, four types of demand can be differentiated:

a) continuous demand (with sporadic fluctuations)

b) increasing or decreasing demand as a function of sales demand

c) seasonal demand

d) demand characterized by a single increase and decrease (product life
   cycle).

Stochastic demand forecasting methods serve to establish the patterns of this (secondary and tertiary) demand, e.g. the moving average technique or the exponential smoothing technique (single and double smoothing).[5] If the past records time series for a demand which does not correspond to types a) - d), this may be due to determining factors which cannot simply be covered by mathematical and statistical methods such as moving average or exponential smoothing. In case of apparently irregular demand or not fully known demand for the planning period, a start must be made on a systematic analysis of the determining factors governing the demand for products to

---

4   See RKW-Schrift, Rationelle Vorratshaltung, Berlin - Köln 1975, S. 115;
    Grochla, Erwin, Grundlagen der Materialwirtschaft, 3. Aufl., S. 58.
5   See Brown, Robert G., Statistical Forecasting for Inventory Control,
    New York/Toronto/London 1959; Zeigermann, Jürgen R., Elektronische Da-
    tenverarbeitung in der Materialwirtschaft, Stuttgart 1970, S. 57 - 89;
    Lewis, Colin D., Demand Analysis and Inventory Control, Westmead (Eng-
    land) 1975, S. 83 - 90.

be manufactured and sold, both for the disposition based on production specifications and for that directed by inventory issues, in order to provide a corresponding forecast of sales and production quantities and thus of the consequent material requirements.

III. Demand planning based on factors influencing demand on the market

Informations as to the future development of demand can be gathered from past patterns of the connection between demand to be forecasted and the factors determining it.[6] Thereby it has to be attended, however, that on the one hand economic facts are generally dependent not on one but on several influencing factors, and on the other hand that these influencing factors may change in the future. This means that the demand of an enterprise must not be computed from past data (e.g. depending on time) but that fore-casting methods are necessary which will correctly reflect interrelations, recognized in the past, between the object of the forecast and its influenc-ing factors even if these latter change in the course of time. For this purpose it is necessary to find out in a first step the actually determining factors on demand from the multiplicity of internal and external influencing factors. Correlation analysis possibly with the help of Bravais-Pearson's coefficient of correlation are appropriate means of finding an answer to this question:[7]

$$r = \frac{\Sigma \ (dx \cdot dy)}{\sqrt{\Sigma \ (dx)^2 \cdot (dy)^2}}$$

6 See e.g. Kreuz, Werner, Dynamische Absatzprognoseverfahren, Zürich/ Frank-furt/M./Thun 1979.
7 See Reichmann, Thomas, Lachnit, Laurenz, Unternehmensführung mit Hilfe eines absatzorientierten Frühwarnsystems. In: Zeitschrift für Betriebs-wirtschaft (Sonderheft), 49. Jg. (1979), S. 107 - 119; Hunziker, Alois, Scheerer, Fritz, Statistik. Instrument der Betriebsführung, 5. Aufl., Stuttgart 1975, S. 141; Förster, Erhard, Rönz, Bernd, Methoden der Korre-lations- und Regressionsanalyse, Berlin 1979, S. 241 - 252.

With the help of electronic data processing, interrelations can in this way
be checked quickly and reliably and relevant influencing factors determined,
even if there is a relatively high number of influencing factors concerned.

Certain influencing factors act at the same time as the sales trend. Other
factors are anticipated in time or have a time lag. In order to clarify
these temporal interdependencies, the correlations between the time series
of the dependent variable, demand, and the various independent variables
have to be calculated on different time bases. From the correlation
coefficient series of an influential factor it can then be seen whether
the connection is simultaneous, anticipated in time, or whether there is a
time lag. Influencing factors anticipated in time are, of course, better
suited to demand forecasting with regard to their economic effects.

Table 1: Coefficients of correlation

Periods	Coefficients of correlation
t-2	0.80
t-1	0.90
t	0.75
t+1	0.70

The pattern existing between demand and influencing factors determining
demand can then be determined for example by means of simultaneous-multiple
or stepwise-multiple regression analysis.[8]

The following example of a demand analysis by means of stepwise-multiple
regression analysis for radio recorders offered by an enterprise in the
electronics industry is designed to clarify the method: The correlation

8 See Reichmann, Thomas, Lachnit, Laurenz, Unternehmensführung, S. 107 -
   119 , hier S. 110 - 113; Schuchard - Ficher, Christiane u.a., Multivariate Analysemethoden, Berlin/Heidelberg/New York 1980, S. 49 - 104.

analysis is said to have shown that the number of types on offer, the advertising expenditure (in TDM), expenditure on entertainment electronics per head of the population and the average market price of the item have a decisive effect on the demand for radio recorders. The forecast for the planning period can then be derived by means of regression functions.

Table 2 : Regression Functions

Variables	Parameter a	Parameter b	Value of variable x	Forecast demand y'_u (unit)
Nº of units on offer	1,400	1,600	3	6,200
advert. expenditure in TDM	1,350	200	20	5,350
Exp. on entertainment electronics	3,600	220	10	5,800
Ø market price	1,400	14	325	5,950

$$\frac{\sum_{u=1}^{w} y'_u}{w} = \frac{23,300}{4} = 5,825 \text{ number of units}$$

In addition to the forecast values it is advisable to prepare a calculation of the average deviation from the forecast. This covers the average deviation between realized value and forecast value which, ascertained from the past, gives an idea of the future range of deviation.

It is of great significance for cost and sensitivity analysis as it shows the upper and lower limits to which the planning of disposable and used capacity and of employment is to be adjusted.[9]

9 See Reichmann, Thomas, Lachnit, Laurenz, Unternehmensführung, S. 107 - 119, hier S. 114 - 119.

Table 3: Deviation from Forecast Value

Actual volume		Forecast volume		Absolute volume deviation	
Quarters	Units	Quarters	Units	Quarters	Units
4/77	6,356	4/77	5,825	4/77	531
1/78	6,300	1/78	6,070	1/78	230
2/78	3,600	2/78	3,626	2/78	26
3/78	5,100	3/78	4,238	3/78	862
4/78	6,000	4/78	5,764	4/78	236
1/79	3,900	1/79	4,542	1/79	642
2/79	4,500	2/79	5,154	2/79	654
Total			35,219		3,181
Average			5,031		454
Percentage of average deviation		$\frac{454}{5,031} \cdot 100 = 9 \%$			

For the numerical example used here the deviation from the forecast volume
is 9%, i.e. the demand for radio recorders (5,825) may vary between 5,563
and 6,087.

IV. Determination of optimum inventories taking demand plans into account

If the sales program in its quantitative composition and temporal distribution has been ascertained with the help of correlation and regression
analysis shown in section III and if the probable deviations from the forecast value have been determined, these factors from the basis for inventory
management. With reference to the example of radio recorders the material
requirements can then be ascertained on the basis of a breakdown of the
parts lists, the quantity to be firmly ordered at a fixed time being

- 8 -

234

determined by the lower forecast value of 5,563 units and the quantity for flexible subsequent disposition by the upper forecast value of 6,087 units. An orientation of the inventory to the probable range of deviation in material requirements will usually lead to reduced stocktaking costs. This applies in the short term to inventory costs; in the medium term this also applies, through possibilities for more precise calculation of inventory requirements, to the costs of inventory capacity, and possibly to handling costs.

With a view to material disposition directed by inventory issues, e.g. auxiliary materials and supplies, an ordering policy oriented towards the expected sales development will generally also bring about considerable cost savings in the inventory sector. If the sales forecast for a certain product class, e.g. radio and television sets, indicates an overall cyclical or structural decline, the quantities already scheduled for order can be quickly replaced by new quantities before a slower inventory reduction indicates that stocks and consequently inventory costs are too high.

In figure 1, the simplified assumption has been made for the inventory quantity $\bar{y}$ that the number of orders per planning period cannot be varied. If the number of orders is freely variable, number and quantity of optimum orders are to be re-ascertained, possibly with the help of dynamic order quantity calculation.[10]

Under varying market conditions optimum stockpiling can be achieved only by connection of multivariate sales forecast and inventory planning. The probability that these methods will be used will increase to that extent to which the data processing capacity available to companies increases, providing thereby free capacities for time series analysis.

10 See Gahse, Sigfrid, Optimale Bestellmengen, IBM Form 81533-1, Sindel-
    fingen 1968; Steiner, Jürgen, Optimale Bestellmengen bei variablem
    Bedarfsverlauf, Wiesbaden 1975.

Figure 1: (t,S)-policy with multivariate sales forecast

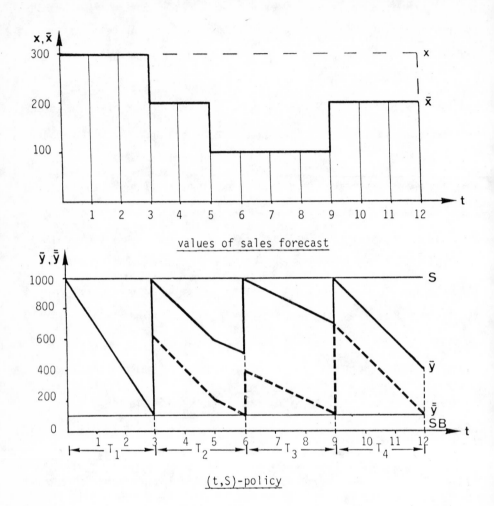

values of sales forecast

(t,S)-policy

Reference List:

Brown, R.G. (1959): Statistical Forecasting for Inventory Control, McGraw Hill, New York/Toronto/London 1959.

Förster, E., Rönz, B. (1979): Methoden der Korrelations- und Regressions- analyse (Methods of Correlation and Regression Analysis), Verlag Die Wirtschaft, Berlin 1979, 324 pages.

Gahse, S. (1968): Optimale Bestellmengen (Optimum Order Quantity), IBM, Form-Nr. 81533-1, Sindelfingen 1968, 10 pages.

Grochla, E. (1978): Grundlagen der Materialwirtschaft (Fundamental Materials Management), 3. ed., Betriebswirtschaftlicher Verlag Dr. Th. Gabler, Wiesbaden 1978, 272 pages.

Grupp, B. (1975): Materialwirtschaft mit EDV (Materials Management and Electronic Data Processing), Lexika-Verlag, Grafenau 1975, 216 pages.

Hunziker, A., Scheerer, F. (1975): Statistik. Instrument der Betriebsführung (Statistics. Instrument of Business Administration), 5. ed., C.E. Poeschel Verlag, Stuttgart 1975, 480 pages.

Lachnit, L. (1979): Systemorientierte Jahresabschlußanalyse. Weiterentwicklung der externen Jahresabschlußanalyse mit Kennzahlensystemen, EDV und mathematisch-statistischen Methoden (Financial Statement Analysis), Betriebswirtschaftlicher Verlag Dr. Th. Gabler, Wiesbaden 1979, 439 pages.

Lewis, C.D. (1975): Demand Analysis and Inventory Control, Saxon House/Lexington Books, Westmead (England)/Lexington, Mass. USA, 1975, 234 pages.

Naddor, E. (1966): Inventory Systems, John Wiley & Sons, Inc., New York/London/Sydney, 1966, 341 pages.

Reichmann, Th. (1978): Wirtschaftliche Vorratshaltung, eine gemeinsame Aufgabe für Einkauf, Materialwirtschaft und Betriebsleitung (Economic Inventory Management, A Cooperative Problem of Purchase, Materials Management and Business Administration). In: Zeitschrift für Betriebswirtschaft, 48. Jahrgang (1978), S. 565 - 578, Betriebswirtschaftlicher Verlag Dr. Th. Gabler, Wiesbaden 1979.

Reichmann, Th., Lachnit, L. (1979): Unternehmensführung mit Hilfe eines absatzorientierten Frühwarnsystems (Business Administration Using Early-warning Systems Based On Sales Forecasting). In: Zeitschrift für Betriebswirtschaft (Sonderheft), 49. Jahrgang (1979), S. 107 - 119, Betriebswirtschaftlicher Verlag Dr. Th. Gabler, Wiesbaden 1979.

RKW-Schrift (1975): Rationelle Vorratshaltung (Efficient Inventory Management), Beuth Verlag, Berlin-Köln 1975, 192 pages.

Schuchard-Ficher, C. (1980): Multivariate Analysemethoden (Methods of Multivariate Analysis), Springer-Verlag, Berlin/Heidelberg/New York 1980, 346 pages.

Steiner, J. (1975): Optimale Bestellmengen bei variablem Bedarfsverlauf (Optimal Lot-Size with Varying Demand), Betriebswirtschaftlicher Verlag Dr. Th. Gabler, Wiesbaden 1975, 255 pages.

Tersine, R.J. (1976): Materials Management and Inventory Systems, North-Holland Publishing Company, New York/Amsterdam 1976, 420 pages.

Trux, W.R. (1971): Data processing for purchasing and stock control, McGraw Hill, London 1971, 368 pages.

Zeigermann, J.R. (1970): Elektronische Datenverarbeitung in der Materialwirtschaft (Electronic Data Processing for Materials Management), Forkel-Verlag, Stuttgart 1970, 222 pages.

Proc. First Int. Symp. on Inventories
Budapest, Hungary 1980

ZONE DEFENSE
IMPROVES STOCKROOM RECORD ACCURACY

WILLIAM A. SANDRAS, JR.[1] and STEVEN F. BOLANDER[2]

[1] *Hewlett-Packard, Ft. Collins, COL, USA*
[2] *Colorado State University, COL, USA*

Your parts storeroom is staffed with good people; it is locked and has an established cycle count team - yet you are still plagued with stock record inaccuracies. What more can you do short of a sophisticated, automated, or on-line system? Zones provide a method for you to inexpensively and substantially improve record accuracy, neatness, job enrichment and morale.

The Stockroom Dilemma

You have just been promoted as the new manager of a large stock stockroom. The stockroom is locked, has an established cycle count team and makes 75,000 transactions on 30,000 active stock numbers each month. The cycle count team is perpetually taking a physical inventory of different stock items. When you accepted the managerial position, you accepted the challenge and recognized the need to substantially improve the inventory record accuracy level of the stockroom. You agreed to do this in the next twelve months while maintaining the current level of expenditures.

What will you do? Your stockroom is already locked so that excuse for inaccuracy is gone. You have an excellent cycle count team and so that step has been accomplished. The people you have working for you are at least as good as can be expected for the entry level positions they occupy. Still, inaccuracies usually stem from carelessness. "Accuracy awareness" campaigns have been pushed but resulted in only temporary relief of the problem. Whenever possible, specific errors are called to the attention of the responsible individuals; however, unless an error is detected quickly, it is usually difficult to precisely determine who caused the mistake. Furthermore, current cost restraints restrict the usage of on-line CRT terminals and automated picking systems. What do you do? A <u>Zone Defense</u> may be the answer.

The Zone Defense

As stockroom manager you are held responsible for overall stockroom accuracy. To help you manage more effectively, sub-divide the stockroom into more manageable sections (zones) and place an individual in charge of each zone. Expect from them the same zone accuracy that your boss expect from you for the entire stockroom. The person in charge for each zone becomes responsible for <u>all</u> activities in the zone and its resulting inventory record accuracy. These zone activities include verification of incoming material counts, storage and issue of material, cycle counting, troubleshooting, error correction and necessary paper work.

At the Hewlett-Packard plant in Colorado Springs, inventory record accuracy had always been a significant problem. All of the traditional stockroom techniques had been tried with some success. But the results were just not good enough. The zone defense approach proved to be the answer.

The warehouse, located in a separate facility, was divided into two areas: small parts and bulk items. The zone defense approach was first applied to the small parts area. The area was subdivided into smaller manageable zones and a stockroom employee was trained and placed in charge of each zone. That zone person had complete authority to carry out all transactions appropriate to the zone. The concept worked so well that nine months later the bulk area was also zoned. Similar successes were once again achieved. A problem area was turned into a show case for other Hewlett-Packard plants, now adopting the system with similar success.

Zone Defense Results

So what can you expect from this idea? At Hewlett-Packard the zone defense approach produced the following results:

Employee morale increased significantly. Initially, stockroom personnel exhibited a certain amount of hesitation in departing from the traditional organization where no one, except the stockroom manager, was directly accountable for record accuracy. The old comfortable system, which minimized personal responsibility for stockroom accuracy, was replaced

241

with a system that exposed and measured individual accuracy. However, within a few months, the zone personnel became justifiably proud of their record accuracy improvements and gladly pointed out their achievements. Evidence of the morale increase was seen in the neatness of each zone area. Those who are familiar with stockrooms are well aware of their usual unkept appearance - but not so with zones. The zones were clean, with parts put away as if an inspection by company executives was due. In addition, Hewlett-Packard found other employees requesting transfers to the stockroom. Prior to the zone defense approach, these requests were very rare, due to the poor attitude regarding stockroom work. But now, the pride of stockroom personnel soared as they received positive feedback on their results. This feedback (Figures 1-4) re-placed the former feedback that was received only when things went wrong. Each employee could now do measurable and meaningful work.

Zones provided management with an effective tool to isolate problem areas. For example, in Figure 4 it can be seen that Zone D began experiencing record inaccuracies in the 22nd week. Noticing the obvious trend and investigating the zone, the stockroom manager found poor employee performance to be the problem. By calling this to the employee's attention, and working with him, the problem was corrected and the zone accuracy trend was reversed in the 25th week. Before zone defensing, it was much more difficult to isolate the cause, thus limiting specific and timely corrective action.

Year-end audits became a matter of inconvenience rather than a period of grave concern. The stockroom manager knew the level of control and accuracy that had been achieved before the audit took place, and the auditors were pleased by the ability to measure and display control throughout the year. Even if you have an established cycle count team, zones will allow you to significantly improve your inventory record accuracy. Using the zone concept, inventory is cycle counted, not by an outside cycle count team, but rather by those responsible for the zone. Zone personnel cycle count their own inventory and correct their own errors. Naturally, supervisors may wish to become involved in some recounts or adjustments. This gives the supervisor a chance to understand the problem, counsel the employee, and obtain valuable first-hand information for performance appraisal.

HP found the zone concept helpful in meeting affirmative action and EEO objectives. Prior to implementation of the zone concept, personnel in the bulk parts area were on a higher pay curve than personnel in the small parts area. This pay differential was due to the requirements for more strenuous work and the requirement for knowledge of fork lift operation in the bulk parts area. Personnel in the bulk parts area were mostly men, and personnel in the small parts area were mostly women. This had a negative impact on meeting EEO and affirmative action goals. When zones were implemented, the pay grade of the small parts area was upgraded to equal that of the

bulk parts area. The extra part numbers and associated responsibility in the small parts zones balanced the physical and fork
lift work responsibility of the bulk part zones. And, as
might be expected, the equalization of pay brought more men into
the small parts area and in turn opened up opportunities in the
bulk area for women.

HP realized a 5-15% space savings in the bulk areas of the
stockroom facility. Following the implementation of zones,
each zone person had the built-in incentive to consolidate his
material in as few places as possible to minimize personal
effort and improve efficiency and accuracy.

If you are correctly staffed today, the implementation of zones
should not cause you to increase your staff. In fact, as your
people become familiar with the new procedures and expectations,
a slight reduction in work force may be possible. For example,
eighteen months after the implementation of zones, HP found
their work force to be 14% smaller than it would have been,
had zones not been implemented. This was primarily due to the
increased output associated with each zone. Of course, these
output increases should be recognized by the organization
through their appropriate reward structure, but only if
accuracy is maintained.

Zone defense worked. HP found that stockroom employees exceeded their accuracy goals (measurement discussed in next
section) and achieved the overall accuracy goal within 12

months. Figure 1 shows the composite record of all zones in the stockroom. The zone approach started in March of 1973, reached the 80% goal in October of 1973. It dropped below 80% the next month, but went over the goal the following month and has remained well above that goal ever since. For example, Figure 2 shows the most recent weekly average accuracy record. During this time period, the accuracy record never fell below 90%.

Some zones reached the goal more rapidly than others. For example, Figure 3 shows the results from Zone G, one of the more spectacular zones. From the implementation of the zone approach, it took Zone G nine weeks to achieve its accuracy goal. While all zones did not improve this rapidly, one can expect significant record accuracy improvement in both the short and long run.

The current opinion of the zone approach was recently expressed by HP's (Colorado Springs Division) current stockroom manager. She said: "I feel that the biggest contribution made by the zone concept is confidence in our onhand balances. These are now vital numbers with purchasing and production control."

Accuracy Measurement and Standards

In retrospect, a goal of 80% seems rather low, but to those involved at the time, it seemed like an insurmountable objective. Now, however, HP consistently achieves accuracy levels in the high 90's, using a measurement criteria more strict than found in most companies.

245

FIGURE 1: Composite Average of all Stockroom Zones

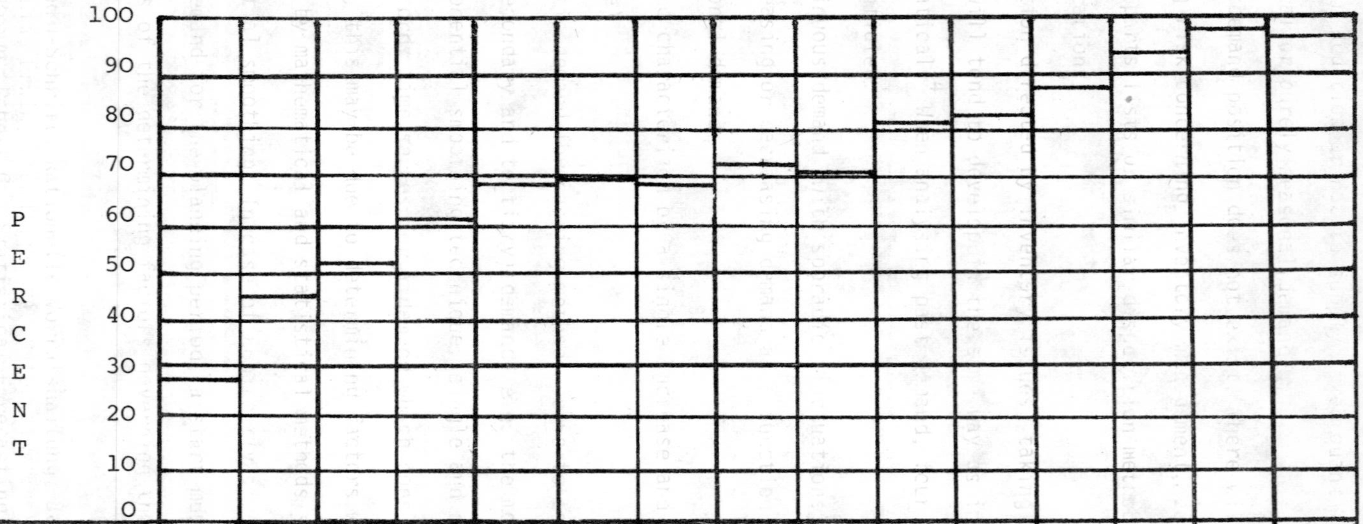

Month	1973 Mar	A	M	J	J	A	S	O	N	D	1974 J	F	M	A	M
No. Inv.	8296	10175	11821	11427	10656	8811	9166	9705	10073	11198	10541	8681	7333	7737	8318
No. in Sort Tol.	1659	4782	7447	8227	8312	8960	7150	7958	7957	9182	8749	7639	6966	7505	7985
Percent in Sort Tol.	28	47	63	72	78	79	78	82	79	82	83	88	95	97	96

Zone defense improves stockroom record accuracy

FIGURE 2: Composite Average of all Stockroom Zones
/Most recent data/

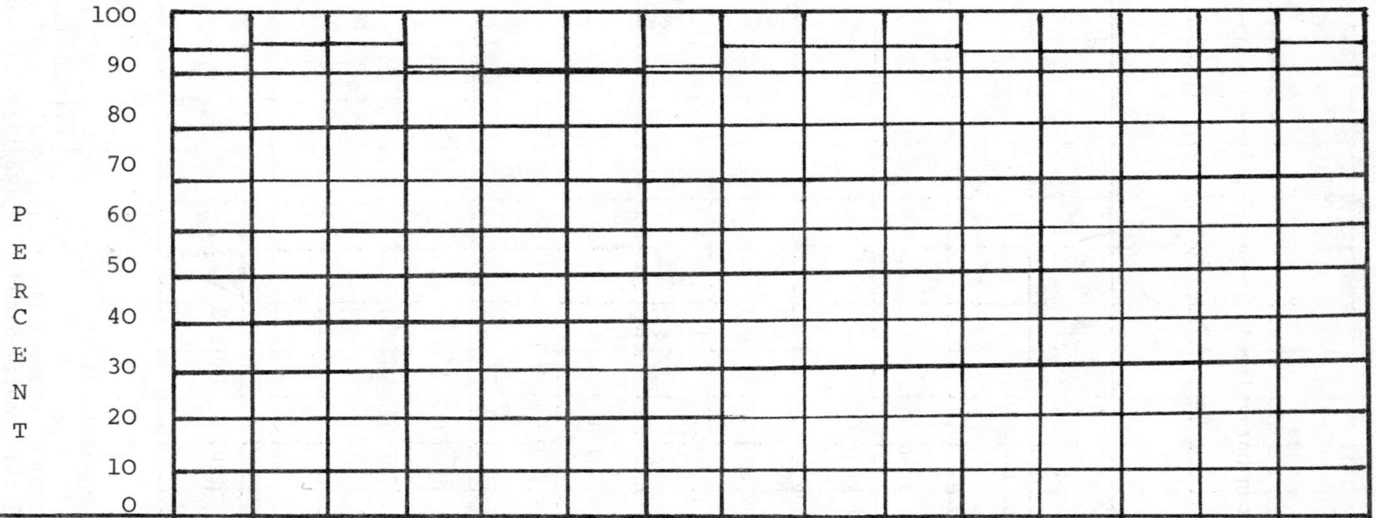

Week	1976 43	44	45	46	47	48	49	50	51	52	1977 1	2	3	4	5
No. Inv.	8085	7642	7709	8130	8463	7789	8760	8465	7743	7622	5085	5364	6199	7449	7657
No. in Sort Tol.	7594	7243	7315	7370	7650	7014	7943	8016	7341	7211	4771	5060	5839	7002	7198
Percent in Sort Tol.	94	95	95	91	90	90	91	95	95	95	94	94	94	94	95

Production and inventory management - Second Quarter, 1978

247

FIGURE 3: Composite Average of Zone G /At implementation/

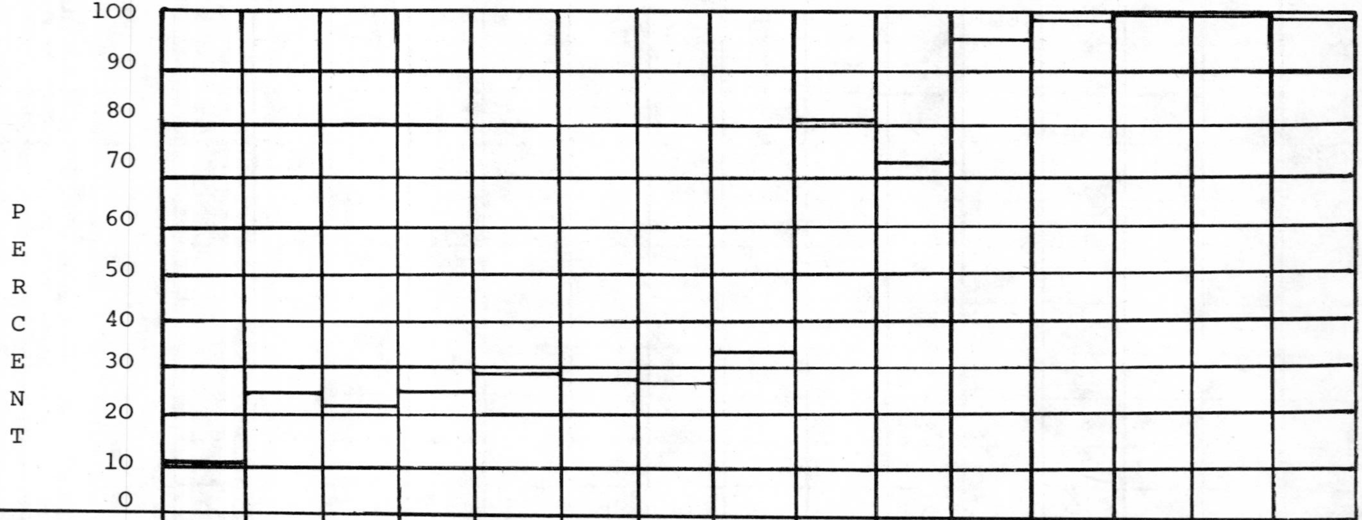

Week	1973 26	27	28	29	30	31	32	33	34	35	36	37	38	39	40
No. Inv.	9	8	9	8	41	40	48	59	79	97	451	440	744	1097	734
No. in Sort Tol.	1	2	2	2	12	11	13	20	64	72	431	424	728	1085	724
Percent in Sort Tol.	11	25	22	25	29	28	27	34	81	74	96	98	99	99	98

Zone defense improves stockroom record accuracy

FIGURE 4: Composite Average of Zone C /Showing correction phase/

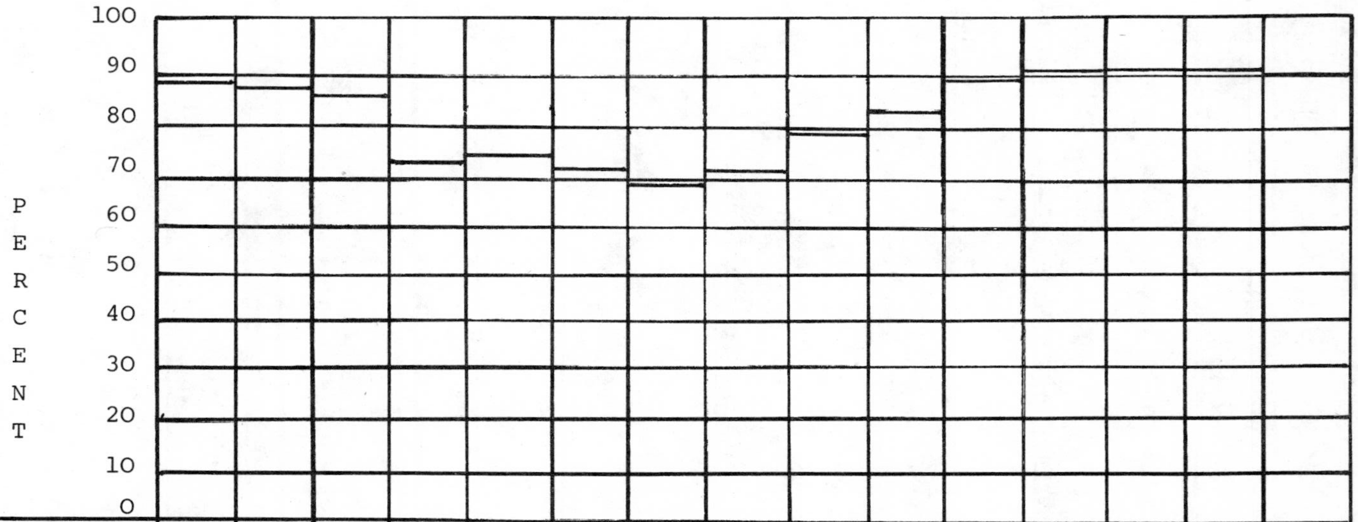

Week	1976 19	20	21	22	23	24	25	26	27	28	29	30	31	32	33
No. Inv.	904	847	710	384	269	299	340	437	617	838	1264	1348	1292	1165	883
No. in Sort Tol.	801	748	609	284	203	213	230	315	474	705	1118	1218	1168	1048	789
Percent in Sort Tol.	89	88	86	74	75	71	68	72	77	84	88	90	90	90	89

Production and inventory management - Second Quarter, 1978

249

In measuring accuracy, HP considers all adjustments to inventory - not just cycle count transactions. If an error is discovered, and an inventory count and adjustment is made to correct the situation, this adjustment is reflected in the accuracy level of the part, even though a cycle count may not be needed on the part for some time. In fact, the count that was performed to correct the error now becomes valid as a cycle count.

In addition, the measurement of tolerance also differs in HP. In many companies, A level parts can typically be off by $\pm 1\%$ and still be considered in tolerance; B items off $\pm 2\%$ and C items off $\pm 3\%$, resulting in a tolerance chart, shown in Graph 1.

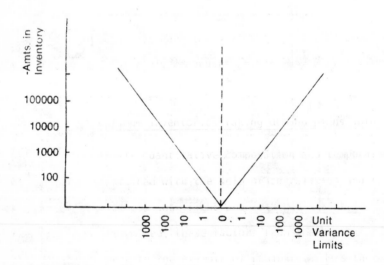

Graph 1. Tolerance levels using Standard Approach ($\pm 1\%$)

As can be seen in Graph 1, to maximize inventory accuracy, the best time to count is when the inventory quantity is high. The tolerance formula is more forgiving at the high end than at the low end.

HP uses a formula that is more consistent at both the high and low ends so that personnel would be encouraged to cycle count when it was more effective, i.e. when fewer parts are on hand, not when inventory is at a maximum. As a result, HP considers a part to be out of tolerance when the deviation exceeds the square root of the on-hand balance (down to a deviation of ± 5 units) or whenever the deviation exceeds $50.00. This formula is applied equally to A, B, and C level items and results in a tolerance chart typical of that shown in Graph 2.

While the graph is not perfectly vertical, it is more forgiving at the low end and much less forgiving at the high end than the approach shown in Graph 1.

In addition, so that employees do not have to be concerned with the formula during counting, and to provide a record of performance, each zone receives a weekly report containing a list of those counts that were both in and out of tolerance.

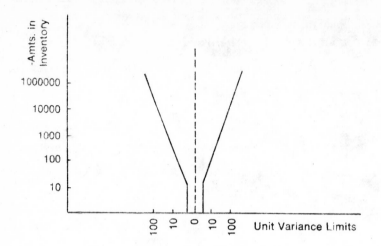

Graph 2. Tolerance levels using Square Roots

Implementing Zone Defenses

Specific details of how you should implement the zone concept
will depend upon individual company structure, personnel, and
policy. However, some observations may be helpful:

- The fewer people in each zone the better - in fact, one per
zone may be best. A "floater" will be necessary to cover
for illness and temporary overloads.
- While it is important to have workloads balanced in each
zone, don't be overly exact in balancing. Some people work
faster than others, and if you put the fast workers in the
busy zones, you can pay them accordingly. Secondly, zone workloads can be adjusted as you become familiar with the concept
and the resulting workload in each zone. Furthermore, employees in smaller zones could prove their capabilities by im-

proving their own accuracy and by helping other zones during peak times. Demonstration of this growth potential would result in their being transferred to a larger zone or their own zone being expanded. The incentive - higher pay for the increased contribution.

- Give each zone complete responsibility for all inventory of a given stock number - including the parts in the bin and the bin overflow. There should be no ability to "pass the buck" to another person or zone.

- If possible, have all part numbers of a given zone in a relatively contiguous area. For items that are exclusively bulk stock (as opposed to items that fit in a bin), this may necessitate a physical reorganization to put all pallets of a given stock number within the racks assigned to a given zone. At first impression, it would appear that more pallet space would be required to accommodate bulk zones, however, the shelfinitiated stock consolidation done by each zone manager at HP more than offset the extra spaces needed for zones.

- Each zone should have complete responsibility for all activity within that zone, including incoming counts, put away and issue of material cycle counting, troubleshooting, error correction, and associated paper work. You may elect to have supervisors do cycle-recounts or inventory adjustments exceeding a certain dollar value, for audit purposes. Note that the zone concept abolishes the cycle count team and places the cycle counting activity within the zone.

- Be certain that adequate work stations are provided for each zone. Their transactions will represent a significant volume of dollars for your business and work stations conductive to accuracy are essential.

- Each zone should receive reports, listing the part numbers for which they are responsible, their inventory value, a list or audit trail reflecting the daily transactions made, a status of cycle count activity, and a report showing the percent of _in_ tolerance cycle counts as compared to the goal.

- Place accuracy charts for each zone or group of zones in a prominent place with the goal and current level of accuracy clearly displayed. At HP, a four-week average was used for the display to highlight improvements (or problems) while preventing random errors from obliterating over all trends.

Proc. First Int. Symp. on Inventories
Budapest, Hungary 1980

PRACTICAL APPROACH
TO THE ABC ANALYSIS.
ITS EXTENSION AND APPLICATION

JÓZSEF SÁRAI

State Corporation for Product Management, Budapest, Hungary

During the last decade the use of computers has become
general in Hungarian enterprises. One of the main spheres of
their application is the ABC analysis. Within this sphere, its
application has been extended to decision-making as well,
besides material recording and accounting. The ABC analysis
has become a generally applied method.

The most general field of the application of the ABC
method is the concentration analysis of stocks. Application of
this method in this sphere is based on the discovery that every
item of stock has a different weight in consumption. Therefore,
when applying the ABC method, the value of the material
consumption in a given period is a suitable way of classification.

In our present practice, analyses generally end up with
an analysis based on the value of the consumption. In the
interest of progress in this field the following two further
possibilities must be taken into consideration.

1. The extension of the ABC method to stock-cumulation

Besides ranging and grouping on the basis of the value of
material consumption, it is worth analysing the items on the

basis of the yearly chronological standard values too. Comparison of these groups and the items of every group with the groups and items formed on the basis of the consumption value can provide useful information and make an interesting contribution to assessing a company's activities. An analysis of the standards has great importance from the financial point of view. Such an analysis can reveal the most important items from the point of view of capital investment.

There is an interesting variation of this extended analysis according to the basis of consumption range whereby items are ranged on the basis of consumption data, but relative numbers /or cumulated ratio/ must be formed on the basis of chronological standards too. When evaluating the results, it must not be forgotten that stock-cumulation also reflects the range based on consumption values. In practice, the concentration of the standard stock values does not reach the concentration of consumption values. Partly this is natural since it refers to the higher turnover rate of the most important raw materials. But there can be hidden a real danger. I mean the company may hold relatively little stock from the most important raw materials and at the same time it may have excesses or immobile stocks of high value and wide variety from the less important items.

2. Refinement /precision/ of the ABC analysis

A refinement of this method must in any case be achieved in the interest of a genuine assessment of the stock-position. Categorization only on the basis of the consumption value seems rather mechanical and using this as the only basis of the differentiated inventory control   may conceal serious errors. That is why categorization based on the consumption value must be modified depending on the concrete conditions of inventory control. Aspects of re-categorization can differ with certain companies. Here I deal with the aspects of general validity, and with one possible method of taking them into consideration.

Besides the consumption value as one aspect of the final ABC grouping, the following factors are to be examined:

- conditions of supply
- conditions of consumption
- storing conditions
- the link between goods /complementarity and possibility for substitution/.

Depending on their place along a certain scale of an adequate measure concerning every aspect, items can be put into "A", "B", and "C" groups similarly as on the basis of the consumption value. "Numbers" by different aspects and the subjective weights attributed to them can determine the categorization of a certain item.   Let us now turn to a discussion of these aspects.

Range by consumption value is given by the primary analysis. Grouping on the basis of this can happen in different ways. At the end of the computer analysis every item can be grouped. In the case of the other possible aspects grouping cannot be such an unambiguous numerical peculiarity which could determine the place of a certain item. Therefore, the criteria for categorization must be given aspect by aspect. It is to be noted that aspects mentioned in my paper and the requirement system have been based on specific Hungarian circumstances. This is especial-ly so in the case of conditions of supply. These criteria can differ among given companies too.

The first additional aspect concerns the conditions of supply. Criteria of belonging to group "A":

- a long lead time /this means one year or more/
- no possibility of scheduling
- there is an obligatory minimum order and this quantity is much more than the whole annual demand of the company
- there is a low reliability degree /from 50 to 75%/ of fulfilment of the orders in time.

Criteria of group "B":

- there is a 90-360-day long lead time
- there can be a quarterly scheduling /if order is placed a year ahead/
- the minimum quantity of order must not be more than the yearly demand
- the reliability degree of fulfilment in time is from 75 to 90%.

Criteria of group "C":

- the longest cycle of lead time is 90 days
- there is not an obligatory minimum quantity to be ordered, or it is not important
- there is a 90-100% reliability degree of fulfilment orders on time.

The second additional aspect is the conditions of consump-tion. In this respect there is a close link between the group-

ing of an item and the characteristic features of supply. If
there is a problem concerning supply, the type /character/ of
consumption becomes a more important aspect.

Criteria of group "A":

- there is a consumption of accidental character

- demand cannot be planned in advance

Criteria of group "B":

- there is a periodical demand

- planning of the demand and its volume is uncertain

Criteria of group "C":

- materials for continuous consumption belong to this group

- there is a demand of deterministic character

The third additional aspect is the storing conditions.

Criteria of group "A":

- items requiring specific treatment and storing

- there is a bottleneck in warehouse capacity

Criterion of group "B":

- there is limited capacity of storing

Criterion of group "C":

- there are no special criteria or warehouse limits.

The final aspect is the possibility of substitution.

Criteria of a given item belonging to group "A":

- this is specific material, there is no possibility for
  substitution

- it complements others

- it is a very important complement

Criteria of group "B":

- substitution is possible, but not economical

- using it as complement is limited /technically/.

Criteria of group "C":

- there is a variety of materials applied as complements

- they cannot be used to substitute for others.

Items must be classified in "A", "B" and "C" groups one by one, according to the criteria mentioned above. Classification is rather subjective, but it is avoidable if criteria given can be enumerated. In the case of many items, the use of computer is a basic requirement.

Depending on the group, every item becomes coded, aspect by aspect. The value of the point is

3 if it belongs to group "A"

2 if it belongs to group "B"

1 if it belongs to group "C".

It is the task of the management of the company to give the weights attributed to a given aspect. /It is practical if the sum of the weights is 1./

To get the final range, it is necessary to form a weighted average /sum of the results of multiplication of points and weights concerning every aspect/. This average will necessarily amount to minimum 1 and maximum 3.

Final categorization can happen according to these averages, for instance:

Group "A" from 2.51 to 3.00

"B" from 2.01 to 2.50

"C" from 1.00 to 2.00

Such a detailed analysis can much better meet the demand than in case of a differentiated inventory control where stress must be laid upon the most profitable items.

The method described here is advantageous because experts must think over these problems /aspects/ related to the items one by one before using the computer, and thus decision-making can be promoted in such an indirect way too.

Application of this method requires computer-technics, especially in case of many items. If there are less /200-500/ items manual technics can be also used with success. In 1977-1978 at the Hungarian Works for Plastic Processing there has been a successful application of this method in computing inventory norms.

Proc. First Int. Symp. on Inventories
Budapest, Hungary 1980

INVENTORY CONTROL OF SPARE PARTS IN SUPPLYING ORGANIZATIONS

ZDZISŁAW SARJUSZ WOLSKI

Research Institute of Raw Materials, Warsaw, Poland

1. Introduction

The last 25 years of this century are characterized by a particularly strong intensification of mechanization and automation of various fields of human activity. It concerns production, transport services, as well as widely understood consumption. We apply highly advanced technological equipment, machines and vehicles requiring proper exploitation. Maintaining them ready for use demands fulfilling many conditions, the most important of which is having spare parts /starting from simple ones to whole sets/ in the needed place or time. The production of modern goods does not guarantee the satisfaction of certain social needs. It results in a significant role of an effective and reliable system of supplying the national economy with spare parts. The shortage of one major part may make the manufacture and maintenance of even a very good car impossible. We may even say that since a damaged vehicle cannot fulfill its function, the missing part has the value of the car. Without it, the car changes into a useless though nicely varnished piece of junk.

2. Spare parts supplying system in national economy

Owners and users of various vehicles, machines and aggregates are scattered all over the country. That necessitates that the supplying and storage systems of spare parts for any kind of machines have a multi-level structure. We may come across the solution involving a main warehouse and several auxiliary warehouses or even hundreds of warehouses within service stations or shops.

Those solutions are rational as far as the quantity of stored parts in the whole supplying system is concerned. The concentration of stored goods makes their use more flexible in case of their relatively small total number. Facing the stochastic character of worn out spare parts and thus the stochastic nature of demand, the theorem of the additivity of variance used for making reserve stock is suitable here.

The above outlined general rules of the flow of material, however, do not result in detailed solutions of the supply system and the tasks of its particular organizations. Moreover, it should be stressed here that "up to now, no comprehensive theory of multi-level systems has been developed. This would in any case be very difficult, because of the diversity of variations in these systems."[1]

---

[1] W.R. Trux: Data processing for purchasing and stock control. McGraw-Hill, London, 1977, p. 254.

3. Functions and tasks connected with inventory control

We differentiate two scales of activity connected with stock control, i.e. medium- and short-term scales. The main warehouse /its computing centre/ should be an organization responsible for the implementation of planning functions on a medium scale. A two-year period is the time limit for this activity.

The scheduling of needs of the whole organization of supply within the period of the planned approaching year is the main purpose in this activity.

On the basis of this plan the orders for particular spare parts will be placed and implemented by producers or foreign trade enterprises /import deliveries/.

The working out of a yearly plan of needs covers the following tasks:

a/ specification of yearly demand for a variety of goods

b/ rating the stocks

c/ comparing needs with deliveries

d/ working out a quarterly delivery schedule.

The major purpose of the activity on a medium scale is to ensure indispensable home and import deliveries to satisfy expected needs for a given year.

The real inventory control in a supply system will be done on a short-term scale.

It is suggested that these activities would be carried out by auxiliary warehouses /or by their computing centres/. The units will implement the following tasks:

a/ short-term demand forecasting

b/ determining the norms of spare parts, constituting control norms

c/ regulating spare-parts deliveries.

The more exact presentation of these problems is given below.

4. Proposed solutions of inventory control

Short-term demand forecasting is the major task for auxiliary warehouses. What we mean here is the forecast of a demand expected value and standard deviation for particular spare parts, as known from service stations and retail trade.

Forecast periods and control rules should depend on the group /ABC method/ within which a given spare part was classified. The proposed forecasting periods are as follows:

- group A: 4 weeks,

- group B: 12 weeks,

- group C: 1 year.

Demand forecasting for spare parts of groups A and B should be based on the models of exponential smoothing which have been comprehensively developed in various works.[2]

It is worth mentioning that there are models which take into account linear trends and periodic fluctuations.

---

[2] R.G. Brown: Statistical Forecasting for Inventory Control. McGraw-Hill, New York, 1959; C.C. Holt et al.: Planning Production, Inventories and Work Force. Prentice-Hall, Inc., Englewood Cliffs, New York, 1960; C.D. Lewis: Scientific Inventory Control. London, Butterworths, 1970.

The evaluation of the nature of forecast errors is an essential aspect in forecasting /including short-term forecasting/. One of the possible procedures is the sequential testing of the stability hypothesis of a model within a time period while applying a sign of errors test /i.e. deviation of real demand values from forecast values/ and a mean error of prediction test. In case of simple forecast models, other solutions are possible. An example of this may be seen in the following model:[3]

$$\hat{y}_t = \alpha y_t + (1 - \alpha)\hat{y}_{t-1}$$

for a parameter of the Trigg[4] signal absolute value, i.e.

$$\alpha = |ST_t|$$

where:

$$ST_t = \frac{c_t}{d_t}$$

$$c_t = \delta (y_t - \hat{y}_t) + (1 - \delta)c_{t-1}$$

$$d_t = \delta |y_t - \hat{y}_t| + (1 - \delta)d_{t-1}$$

[3] Meaning of the symbols:

$\hat{y}_t$ — average calculated after period t

$\hat{y}_{t-1}$ — former average /calculated after period t-1/

y_t — real demand value observed in period t

α — exponential smoothing parameter

[4] D.W. Trigg, A.G. Leach: Exponential Smoothing with an Adaptive Response Rate. Opl. Res. Q. Vol. 18, No.1, March 1967.

Positive results have also been obtained in the following linear model when accepting the Trigg signal absolute value parameter:

$$\hat{Y}_{t+T} = a_{0,t} + a_{1,t} \cdot T$$

$$a_{0t} = 2 S_t^{[1]}(y) - S_t^{[2]}(y)$$

$$a_{1,t} = S_t^{[2]}(y) - S_{t-1}^{[2]}(y)$$

where $S_t^{[i]}(y)$ are single- and double-smoothed averages, respectively, thus:

$$S_t^{[1]}(y) = S_{t-1}^{[1]}(y) + \alpha \left[y_t - S_{t-1}^{[1]}(y) \right]$$

$$S_t^{[2]}(y) = S_{t-1}^{[2]}(y) + \alpha \left[S_t^{[1]}(y) - S_{t-1}^{[2]}(y) \right]$$

Various attempts have proved that the above model is characterized by a great ability to adapt to changes observed in a forecast time period. In view of its usage in the economy, this is a very important model.

Next to the forecast of an expected value of the demand, cyclical evaluation of its standard deviation is necessary. Allow me the following simplification:

$$\sigma_t = 1.25 \ d_t$$

$$d_t = \delta \left| y_t - \hat{y}_t \right| + (1 - \delta) \ d_{t-1}$$

Forecast for yearly demand for spare parts belonging to group C is proposed as based on a classical model of a development tendency /regression equation/. This simplified approach is justified by the size of the discussed group, low prices and, usually, small gabarits for spare parts. Since the model is well known, we shall not discuss it in detail.

The selection of an <u>inventory control</u> model in an auxiliary warehouse is the next problem. May we suggest, for spare parts belonging to groups A and B, a model being a combination of two classical control models, i.e. re-order level policy and re-order cycle policy models. This model is described as combined re-order level and re-order cycle policy.[5]

Control criterion, however, is formulated as follows: spare parts inventory control in an auxiliary warehouse should be done in such a way that the probability of a spare-parts shortage occurring is no greater than a predetermined number p, described as risk coefficient. We accept as a rule the ordering of deliveries from the main warehouse to a given auxiliary warehouse in the following cycles /i.e. in planned ordering places/:

- for group A spare parts: 4 weeks
- for group B spare parts: 12 weeks

The level of stock to be maintained in an auxiliary warehouse is described as follows:

$$PS = \hat{y} \, (OC + OR) + k \cdot \sigma_y \sqrt{OC + OR}$$

<hr>

[5] C.D. Lewis presented it in his work: Scientific Inventory Control. London, Butterworths 1970, pp. 9-10.

where:

$\hat{y}$ - demand forecast for a given spare part

OC   - delivery ordering cycle   /i.e. 4 or 12 weeks/

OR   - implementation period of complementary orders

k   - value resulting from the accepted risk coefficient p, shortage of spare parts

σ_y - standard deviation of the demand.

Comparing the state of inventory in warehouse $/s_m/$ and on its way $/s_d/$ with norm PS, which may call for re-ordering delivery /Z/ from the main warehouse, will be done in the agreed cycles. It may look as follows:

$$Z = \begin{cases} PS - (s_m + s_d) & \text{if: } s_m + s_d < PS \\ 0 & \text{if: } s_m + s_d \geq PS \end{cases}$$

Moreover, there will be a re-order level /PA/, signalling the necessity of placing an additional order, apart from those scheduled, when the whole inventory in a warehouse and that on the way are below this level.

The re-order level may look as follows:

$$PA = y \cdot OR + k \cdot \sigma_y \sqrt{OR}$$

The size of an additional order /z/ will result from the following relation:

$$Z = \begin{cases} PS - (s_m + s_d) & \text{if: } s_m + s_d \leq PA \\ 0 & \text{if: } s_m + s_d > PA \end{cases}$$

270

Value k results from arbitrarily accepted coefficient p, the shortage of stock, and is read on a cumulative normal distribution function table.

Inventory control of spare parts belonging to group C is to follow much simpler rules. They constitute the modification of a re-order level policy model. Thus, to place one order for yearly needs resulting from the demand forecast is accepted as a rule. Moreover, there is a re-order level which signals the necessity of placing an additional order.

It is sound practice to divide the spare parts of group C into four subgroups each of which would be ordered in different quarters of a year, helping to create a regular schedule for the whole year.

5. Conclusions

Practical implementation of the presented principles and inventory control models in auxiliary warehouses has numerous and various conditions.

Technical problems here top the list.

Assuming frequent processing of large sets of information while also using occasionally many complicated and time-absorbing models /e.g. forecasting models/ the regularity of inventory control depends on the full utilization of a variety of computers. We mean central computers /e.g. R-32 type/, minicomputers, terminals, data recording devices, an indispensable network for data teletransmission, and so on.

Proper inventory control depends on credible, current and detailed information being at the disposal of a computing centre of the auxiliary warehouse.

The information mainly concerns the number of spare parts sold in retail trade or at service stations /while repairing a car/, existing stock and possible delivery. POS /Point of Sale Systems/ is very useful here since it allows the collection of data directly on working posts, to control data, to introduce data into a mini-computer, to emit-tabulogram which reflects the current situation.

It should be stressed that ensuring proper storing and conveying of information about spare parts demand on time is one of the main conditions of effective inventory control.

Proc. First Int. Symp. on Inventories
Budapest, Hungary 1980

OPTIMAL PLANNING OF INVENTORIES.
A METHOD FOR THE IMPROVEMENT
OF LIQUIDITY
AND EFFICIENCY OF ENTERPRISES

ERICH SOOM

St. Gallen College, St. Gallen, Switzerland

1. THE IMPORTANCE OF INVENTORIES

The capital required for balancing time fluctuations in payments is in close connection with inventory on hand, which is part of the current assets. These assets are composed of commodities, which are to be transformed within a short period for their realization as final products. This period is essentially a time function of the storage of raw materials, semi-finished products and finished products, and, in addition, it depends on the quantity of the products and on the required activities in the process of production. The longer this period, and the greater the quantity of the required products and the production activities, the greater the capital required for stocks financing. As inventories are generally short-term assets, they can be financed by short-term outside capital, e.g. credit.

Inventories of enterprises frequently grow to considerable proportions   as it is presented in the following tables:

18

Table 1

liquid assets	58 million Fr	8.6 %	
buyers	224 " "	33.1 %	
other assets	38 " "	5.7 %	
material stocks	357 " "	52.7 %	30.4 %
total current assets	677 million Fr	100.0 %	57.5
total assets of enterprises	1176 million Fr		100 %

Table 2

<u>Optimal entries</u> /in 1000 F/

<u>Balance sheet</u>

Assets		Liabilities	
liquid assets	15,200	short-term outside capital	20,000
material stocks	45,800	long-term outside capital	8,000
equipment	4,000	own capital	37,000
	65,000		65,000

<u>Profit and Loss Account</u>

SPENDING		INCOMES	
material costs	100,000	sales	140,000
operational costs	5,060		
other costs	25,940		
profits	9,000		
	140,000		140,000

rentability of turnover	6.43 %	quick ratio	0.76
rentability of total capital	13.85 %	current ratio	1.55

274

In connection with this, great importance can be attributed to the relative liquidity and to the absolute liquidity,
which is the difference between the total current assets and
the short-term outside capital.

Profitability means the proportion of the profits to the
total capital employed. A distinction must be taken between
profitability of the own capital and of the outside capital.
The first is the proportion of the net profits to the own
capital and the second is the proportion of the net profits to
the gross capital. In addition, the so-called turnover rentability is very important: the proportion of the profit to the
production of the enterprise. The calculation of liquidity is
derived from the balance sheet and rentability can be calculated from the profit and loss account. The value of stocks in
the balance sheet actually means the engagement of assets for
a fixed date, while the profit and loss account consists of
costs of the engagement of assets for a given period. To this
belong the gross costs of warehousing and the interest of
capital, tied up in stocks. Subsequently we call these costs
as economic costs.

2. THE TYPES OF STOCKS

According to Figure 1 material stocks can be divided
into two groups:

- commodities in the process of manufacturing

- commodities in stores

Stocks amount to about 53 percent of the current assets and
30 percent of the gross capital. Of course, this proportion is

not true for each enterprise, because it depends on the character of the enterprise whether it is a producer or a trading company; on the grade of the make or buy; on the structure of the assortment, on the number of stages in storage and production, on the conditions of the market and on many other influencing factors.

Each of these factors affects the liquidity and profitability of the enterprise. Liquidity means the ability of the enterprise to fulfil its duties in time, in order to secure the undisturbed production process.

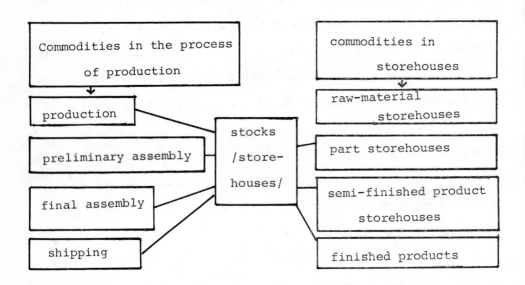

Fig. 1

In the first group the unit value of the commodity is gradually increasing in the process of production, in the second group the unit value of the commodity is generally unchanged.

The share of the different kind of stocks depends to a great extent on the type of the company /trading, servicing or producing enterprise/, on the structure of the process of production /one-stage or multiple stage process/, on the branches the production belongs to, on the character of the products, etc.

Our starting point for the calculation of costs of the engagement of assets and of the economic costs is a process of mass production type, with production to stock. In each stage of production for each cycle of order the formation of value is as it can be seen in Figure 2.

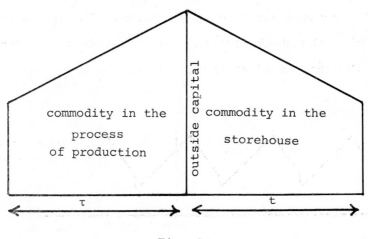

Fig. 2

On the left side of the figure we show the product in the process of production. Let us suppose that materials had been purchased before the beginning of the manufacturing process and so that at the beginning $\tau|$ of the manufacturing process a certain value of materials is at our disposal. During the effective manufacturing process a gradual increase takes place in the value, until the product reaches the final storage. For the sake of simplicity, we suppose that the increase in value of a given product is linear, which is not quite so in practice, but it seems to be acceptable as an approaching solution.

The right side of Figure 2 shows the products in storehouses. For the sake of simplicity let us suppose that the quantity of commodities in the storehouse is used up uniformly in time.

As there are many such cycles in time, Figure 3 shows the formation of stocks in time. This shows the gross /cumulated/ value of the engaged assets on a given day. The area under the diagram of the stock formation can be used for the computation of the charges of storage.

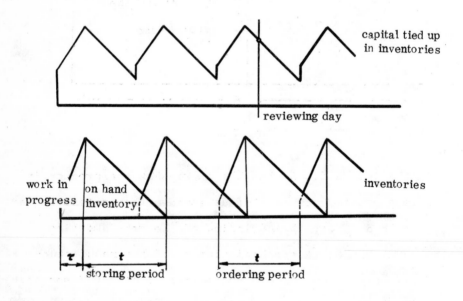

Fig. 3

3. THE POSSIBILITY OF MODIFICATIONS OF STOCKS

In order to improve the liquidity and profitability, both the costs of tied up capital and the economic costs should be reduced. Generally, there is no reason for the reduction of the engaged assets by such measures like for example the halving of order lots or by reduction of the safety stocks, independently from the reduction of the economic costs. The following measures result in the simultaneous reduction of the capital tied up and of costs:

- the reduction in the number of the storage and production stages
- norming
- the regulation of influencing factors
- the use of suitable control methods
- the regulation and control of physical inventories.

3.1 Reduction in the number of stages of storage and of production

A reduction in the number of stages of storage can be achieved mainly by in-process inventories, constructional and technological methods, and reduction of stages of production. So we can decrease the number of in-process stores, if parts and structural elements are transported directly from one stage of production to the other.

3.2 Norms and standardization

Introduction of standardization to the production process and the use of norms in individual phases would result in a considerable reduction in the number of products in the storehouse. At the same time, there is a saving in the required storage area. Additionally, the greater series result in more economical production, and consequently in a further saving in storage facilities.

3.3 Regulation of the influencing factors

Considering the stochastic consumption of materials, parts and components, there are 5 important factors:

- the structure of consumption
- the planning of consumption
- the readiness to deliver
- replenishment time
- cost factors

3.4 The selection of suitable control methods

The quantity of products in the manufacturing process and in stores depends considerably on the chosen control model. A difference should be made between static and dynamic models. In the first case the so-called control parameters, as the order lot and the intervals of ordering and replenishment are determined for a long term on the basis of cost optimalization. So there is no possibility for the automatic adjustment to the short-term changes of demands.

The most important in this group is the Andler model and its variants. This group of models is worth applying when there are no extreme fluctuations and significant trend or seasonal effects in consumption. In the dynamic models at least one of the control factors - order lots, the reorder period, or both - are adjusted automatically to the consumption and production conditions.

From now on we consciously deal only with static models but the conclusions in tendency and in content can be applied for the dynamic ones, too.

Supposing an original Andler model the starting point is the optimalization of costs. An order is to be placed for a q_0 quantity, which is the point of equilibrium between the costs of holding stocks and the costs of purchase. The components of the equation for the total costs are as follows:

V is the yearly quantity of consumption, k_3 is the cost of purchase for each order, EP is the unit price of purchase of the product in francs and p is the percentage of the holding cost.

The formula for the optimal quantity of orders is:

$$q_0 = \sqrt{\frac{200 \cdot V \cdot k_3}{p \cdot EP}}$$

This formula is adequate to the well-known Andler formula. The different variants of the Andler formula can result in the reduction in both the costs of storage and the total costs. These models are of common knowledge /for example see E. Naddor/, so we do not analyse the various variants, we investigate only their effect on the costs.

1. Version   The consideration of shortages

If we took into consideration deliberately the shortages at the end of the order interval calculating the costs, a saving would result in both the stocks and in the total costs. The less the required readiness for delivering, the greater the savings.

Example: A decrease in the readiness for delivering from 100 percent to 95 percent results in a decrease by 2.5 percent in the total costs and by 7.4 percent in the stock holding costs.

2. Version   Placement of collective orders

By collective order we mean orders for different products of the same group of products placed at the same time. As a consequence the order costs decrease which result in decreasing stocks and decreasing total costs. This method can be applied basically for placing orders of purchase. Savings considerably depend on the number of products in the collective order and on the specific purchase costs of products, and on their proportion to the fixed purchase costs.

Example: It is observable that a collective order for only 2-3 products results in savings in the storage area and in the costs up to by 15-25 percent.

3. Version   Part-shipments

An order is placed for the optimal lot but the shipment takes place only for determined parts of the order. In the case of part-shipments, on the one hand the additional administrative tasks /purchase, handling/ result in additional purchase costs, but on the other hand the costs of storage are reduced.

Example: Supposing in shipments four parts and a 20 percent share for the formerly mentioned purchase costs, there is a reduction in the costs of holding stocks and in the total costs

by 36.8 percent, compared with the former period, when no
part-shipment took place.

4. Version   Manufacturing time is taken into consideration

In the classical theory of stock control, above all in
the original Andler model, cost optimalization involves only
the cost of purchase and the stock holding costs, that is only
the costs of the products in the storehouses are taken into
consideration. Consequently this model does not concern the
costs related to the products in the manufacturing process.

Inclusion of the costs of products in the manufacturing
process to the optimalization, the decrease in the lots results in decreasing level of stocks in the process of manufacturing and in the storehouses.

Example: If we reduce the length of the manufacturing period
for a given component /taking into consideration the time
between the productive operations, too,/ by 30 percent and at
the same time we reduce the costs of production by 15 percent,
consequently the costs of tied up capital and the total cost
will be reduced /involving the products in the manufacturing
process, too/ by 17.1 percent, contrary to the fact that the
costs of the products in the storehouse increase by 2.7 percent
because of the cost equilibrium, considered by the optimalization.

5. Version   Positioning

Positioning means the realization of overlapping manufacturing processes. This method can be applied mainly for

orders between workshops. Additional administrative works and sequential operations for each position increase order cost, but there can be substantial savings in stocks.

Example: Employing the method of positioning in addition to the supposed conditions of the former example, the result would be a further decrease by 12 percent in the holding costs.

6. Version   Price reduction /Rabatt/

In case of the simultaneous purchase of many products it is common to have reduced prices which are granted on a certain quantity of purchase. The same is true for the production, too, because reaching a certain series in the mass production a completely new manufacturing process can be applied, which results in decreasing costs per unit of production. Therefore the profit is the difference between the purchase costs computed for the original and for the reduced price, taking into consideration the yearly consumption.

4. THE RELATION OF STOCKS TO THE LIQUIDITY

As we formerly mentioned under point 1, there is a close connection between the level of stocks and the indicators of effectivity and liquidity. At last we demonstrate the influence of optimalization and   selection of the method of production on the liquidity and profitability. According to the principle of cost optimalization - independently from the actually considered cost components - every anomaly from the optimal lot of order results in extra costs. Naturally the increasing costs result in a reduced profitability supposing the other conditions unchanged. The maximum profitability is reached at the optimal order lot. For example theoretically by halving the optimal lots the engaged capital is halved, too, but the consequence is an exaggerated increase in liquidity and at the same time a decreasing profitability. A simultaneous perfection of liquidity and profitability is possible in the case we employ the methods mentioned under 3.4. With one exception these versions ensure a simultaneous reduction in the costs of capital tied up and in economic costs. It is very important to mention that this effect could be reached without extra costs in other fields of activity of the enterprise. Consequently these are real savings.

BIBLIOGRAPHY

E. Soom: Optimale Lagerwirtschaftung in Industrie

/Optimal stock control in the industry/

Handel und Gewerbe, Paul Haupt Verlag, Bern 1976

- Integrierte Produktionsplanung und Steuerung

/Integrated planning and control of production/

Hallwag Verlag, Bern 1974

- Einführung in Operations Research

/Introduction to Operations Research/

Heft Nr.92 der Blauen Tr-Reihe, 2. Auflage

Hallwag Verlag, Bern 1974

E. Naddor: Lagerhaltungssysteme /Inventory systems/

Verlag Harry Deutsch, Frankfurt a.M. - Zürich, 1966

Proc. First Int. Symp. on Inventories
Budapest, Hungary 1980

UTILIZATION OF COMPUTER TECHNICS IN INVENTORY CONTROL

GUSTAV TOMEK

Regional Computer Centre of Colleges, Prague, Czechoslovakia

1. INTRODUCTION

At present effective inventory control is impossible without the application of modern computer technics. It can be stressed that without the application of computers in this field, we cannot speak about rational and systematic management.

Computer technics applied in this field represent a qualitative increase in the level of management, especially from the following points of view:

- it ensures information with necessary data readiness, and shows the necessary latest real state of things, provided that input data and their maintenance are performed suitably,

- it enables information processing in a multioptional way, i.e. information sorted, summarized and grouped according to various criteria and views,

- it enables the utilization of different exact methods, such as mathematical-statistical methods for partial calculation, e.g. optimization of different kinds,

- it enables us to pay attention to the wide variety of data to follow the maximum number of items in their detailed structure, providing, of course, that attention paid and organized differentially, is fully effective,

- it enables the realization of systems approach to inventory control which means that this sphere is a subsystem within the framework of higher subsystems, such as management of material and technical supply as a whole, operative management of production, etc. up to the integrated system of management of the whole enterprise.

From this point of view, real contribution is possible especially when an integrated system is built on the basis of uniform system of input data.

2. DEFICIENCIES IN THE UTILIZATION OF COMPUTERS IN THE SPHERE OF MATERIAL AND TECHNICAL SUPPLY

a/ The planning of material and technical supply

This sphere can be considered either from the standpoint of conceptional /technical-economic/ or of operative planning. As far as long-term /technical-economic/ planning is concerned, calculations of material consumption for main production branches are usually made. This means that calculations do not cover the whole of material consumption.

Therefore it is a question, whether this sphere of planning is suitable for applying a computer when the sphere of operative management has not been solved. Aggregated or estimated consumption norms are used and therefore the accuracy of calculations is not adequate to the possibilities of computer technics. Installation of computers in this sphere is important, especially when we use mathematical methods in the estimation of consumption, in structural analysis, etc.

Operative plans should provide instructions for ordering materials, on the basis of balance equations. Calculations are not always made for each of the items in the material supply system. Usually only a part of items of production assortment is considered. Computer reports are issued in form of summarized needs to cover orders according to delivery terms, etc.

When production with long running time is concerned, work in progress is usually not taken into consideration and summarization is made only for some parts of production. Calculations of material consumption are usually oriented exclusively to standardized materials.

b/ Operative field of material and technical supply

Enterprises are oriented first of all to stock records, to records on the turnover of individual items, and to presenting prescribed statistical reports. Apart from statistical reports on inventory turnover of selected groups of materials, data of inter-divisional relations are worked up. As for the scope of these works, the same what has been said in a/ remains valid, namely that work is oriented to the fundamental materials.

Series of existing processings cannot be judged as inventory control systems, due to the lack of two basic presumptions:
- planning of consumption or at least using of qualified methods of estimation,
- comparison of real state with fixed directive level of stocks /stock norms, minimum, maximum/.

The transition from mechanization to automation without new qualitative changes means that data processing is of mere statistical character, informs about certain states, especially in the operative field. They show as a rule only the situation of last month but not a long-term trend of state and turnover of goods which could enable further analyses, the application of mathematic-statistical method of consumption estimation, etc.

3. CHARACTERISTICS OF PRESUMPTIONS AND PRINCIPLES OF COMPLEX UTILIZATION OF AUTOMATION IN INVENTORY CONTROL

The application of computer technics in inventory control should respect the following principles of complex automation:

- Methodological and technical solution of processing the data of individual jobs must lead to the creation of an automated system, i.e. to a perfect automated system of enterprise management.
- Planning of material and technical supply must be solved as an integral part of operative planning as a whole, i.e. operative planning of sale, production and supply, from quarterly plans to short-term plans. Similarly, material supply must be processed as a complex subsystem, containing spheres of purchase, input and output of materials, the spheres of analyses, statistics, fixing of stock norms, control of inventory level and consumption, etc.
- Inventory control system must also comprehend historical surveys of consumption, purchase and inventory turnover, which serve as basic documents for calculating consumption

requirements, stock norms and for their comparison with
the real events.

- It is necessary to apply differentiated approach to inventory control of individual items, which must be perceptible
in width and periodicity of individual computer reports.

It will be suitable to indicate the highlights of solution
to some questions.

a/ <u>From the integrated solution to automated system of enterprise management</u>

The concept of integrated system of automatic management
originates from uniform system of input information, which represents first of all material consumption norms, performance
and tool norms, product and material price lists, directives of
production flow /directives of production operative planning/.
Input information such as summary of norms, calculations, etc.
is derived from these data. Functioning of the system is
based on the control sphere, understood as system of partial
norms, which is very important in certain types of production,
where standardization of technical preparation of production is
ensured by modularity and heredity of structures. Partial
norms ensure that each statement /data-information/ is registered in computer memory only once, no matter how many times the
respective component is used in different products. This fact
saves memory capacity and simplifies amendments.

On the basis of input data system further systems are made:

conceptual planning, as a system of long-term and yearly
planning,

- system of operative planning,
- system of operative functioning, subordinated first of all
  to the operative filling of production.

b/ Subsystem of supplying

Automation of the supplying system is to be worked partly
as a component of the mentioned system of planning and partly
as a component of filling system. A plan is the basic means for
the management of the economy and therefore it is also a basic
means for inventory control. The basis for ensuring material
is first of all the operative plan of material and technical
supply for each quarter of a year /according to terms of or-
dering/ originating from integral unity of planning sale,
production and supply. The basis is operative plan of sale,
from which operative production plan is generated. This operative production plan together with partial norms of material
consumption is a basis for the calculation of material consumption. In connection with these facts, the way of determining
consumption for individual sorts is to be fixed precisely.
Above all, it is necessary to divide standardized and non-
standardized materials, the latter then should be structured
to materials in stock /calculated on the basis of keeping the
necessary level of stock/ and materials "on request".

Own filling must, apart from current state of stock, give
information about long-term development of inventories and
follow inventory norms including plus-minus deviations in
comparison with real state of stocks.

The concept of automated system of management requires that individual projects of automation be in connection with the functioning of the whole system.

As an example, the filling of the supply department cannot, according to the system concept, represent only the classic filling within the frame of stock control but integrated filling of purchasing activities as they link for instance:

- filling of purchasing /i.e. filling of issued orders and order confirmations/
- filling of input including information about execution of orders
- filling of all kinds of outputs
- filling of stock status, non-moving items
- comparison of stock status with stock norm
- series of further analyses, such as fulfilling of material consumption norms, price analyses, turnover analyses, material demand factor of production, etc.
- prescribed statistical statements, etc.

c/   Differentiated approach to management

Differentiation enables the selection of different strategy for individual items, e.g. differentiation of delivery strategy, determination of inventory level ensuring proper delivery, kinds of signing the shortage of materials, way of organizing issues and, from the point of view of electronic data processing, in different periodicity of generating computer reports. It means practically the sorting of individual material items according to the method of ABC analysis, and eventually differentiation according to kinds and characteristic features of consumption development /season, trend, one-shot, etc./. Differentiated data processing will result in, first of all, periodicity of computer report signing deviations from stock norms and in computer reports characterizing lack of, or low level of turnover of items, even for periods selected differently, further in aggregation of data for different management levels, from supervisors to top level enterprise management, to individual purchasing clerks and workers in warehouses.

4. CONCLUSION

It remains to add some experiences about the progress of works aiming automation of supply in enterprises. Undoubtedly the best way proved to be the rationalization of supply management through the electronic data processing of operative planning. A very important step in data processing is the calculation of consumption. A number of enterprises do not realize further calculations, because they require complex filling and perfect signing of stock filling, which is mostly included in the next stage of automation. Definitely, the utilization of these partial calculations leads to a closer connection between the expert worker and the computer. That is why direct issuing of orders by computer are not realized in practice.

MATHEMATICAL MODELS
OF INVENTORIES

Proc. First Int. Symp. on Inventories
Budapest, Hungary 1980

ANALYSIS
OF A SYSTEM OF INVENTORY MODELS*

E. BARANCSI,[1] G. BÁNKI,[2] R. BORLÓI,[3] A. CHIKÁN,[4]
P. KELLE,[5] T. KULCSÁR[6] and GY. MESZÉNA[4]

[1] Socialist Enterprise Research Project, Hungarian Academy of Sciences, Budapest, Hungary
[2] Hungarian Association for Telecommunication, Budapest, Hungary
[3] Ministry of Labour, Budapest, Hungary
[4] Karl Marx University of Economics, Budapest, Hungary
[5] Institute for Computer Science and Automation, Hungarian Academy of Sciences, Budapest, Hungary
[6] Institute of Computer Research, Budapest, Hungary

I. Introduction

Inventory modelling is one of the most developed fields of operations research. Publications on inventory models could fill a small library and in the models one can find the most advanced and sophisticated methods, but practical applications of inventory models are far from the desired level.

We have analyzed the reasons of the discrepancy between theory and practice of inventory models and found some factors hindering the implementation. In some cases the organisation level of economic system does not make possible to create a comprehensive model. Sometimes decision makers are averse to apply models even in cases when conditions for modelling are given. Other managers would like to apply models even if conditions, circumstances are not appropriate. In most cases computers at companies are used for registration and are not oriented to decision making purposes, so they can not help in implementing models. We must also tell that a great proportion

*The material presented in this paper is based upon a research being within the frames of a special project supported by the Hungarian Academy of Sciences.

of models were created because of the mathematical interest of the problem without even considering the possibility of application.

On the other side some factors do help the application of inventory models. The inventory subsystem of a company can be structured well and modelled relatively easily because it is fairly closed, its input-output connections can be well defined, its objectives can be clearly determined and inventory decisions are mostly periodic rutin decisions, Top management is interested in inventories for they have very important influence on short-term adaptation of the company. A developed data processing system which is used for registration can provide a good statistical background for implementation of models.

II. Objectives of research

Our research has been oriented to the existing inventory models, in order to analyse them and build such a computerized model system which is available to managers for practical use considering the facts mentioned above. We have set the following objectives to our research:

1.) Through mathematical and economic analysis of models we want to learn some aspects of modelling inventories: What economic (management) situations are treated in the existing models and what kind of new models can be or should be built to these situations?

Which are those important factors and situations of inventory management which do not appear in models, why is that and how can these be involved into models?

What mathematical tools are actually used in the models
and how can this range be expanded considering the present
stage of mathematical theory?

What kind of groupings and generalizations can be given on
the basis of existing models?

2.) To promote applications we decided to build models into a
computerized inventory control system. So we wanted
- to analyse the existing models from points of view of
  computer programming;
- to establish a computerized model-library;
- to work out a model selection procedure which makes it
  possible that managers can get information about
  potentially applicable models without trying to force
  them to learn mathematics.

III. Methods of research

According to our estimation more than a thousand models
can be found in the international literature. We decided to
work on an appropriate sample first and then we proceed to extend that sample. So far we had collected and studied more
than 330 models.[1]

---

[1] The sample can be characterized by the following bibliographical data: Forty percents of models in the sample
originate from eleven books, fifty percents are from twelve
journals and the rest comes from research reports and from
other sources. As for the time-distribution: there are 7
models before 1960, 1961-65: 66 models. 1966-70: 112 models
and 1971-75: 99 models and 51 models from 1976.

We have put down a <u>verbal description</u> of each model (on 1-3 typewritten pages). All descriptions have the very same structure, namely beside the identification part they consist of the following parts: conditions, objective function, algorithm of the model and other notes.

We have composed a <u>code-system</u> which appropriately describes the characteristics of models. The code-system has been created on the basis of our priority knowledge of models. Obviously, we had to be extremely careful in selecting the features of models which would appear in the code-system, and also their ways of representation. Our code-system includes forty-five codes and each of them has two- to ten possible values from two. Every code corresponds to a property of models.

Some codes seemed to be far more important than other ones. These codes represent the main characteristics of models and usually have great influence on the other codes. These <u>main codes</u> (characteristics) are the followings: number of products, number of stores, input character, output character, dynamics, objective mechanism, reviewing period, handling of shortage, lead time.

With the identification number of the model, the forty-five code-values and the bibliographical specification, we have a <u>vector with fifty-seven characters</u> which describes a model. These vectors have been computerized and each of them is a record in our data set.

Having the fifty-seven characters record of all models on the computer we first needed a <u>program-system</u> which makes the model-system available for the users. The program-system has two basic functions:

- it must be able to print models meeting any given specifications (what is sort of a librarian function, which is necessary for both scientific and practical applications);
- it must be suitable for statistical evaluation of the model-system.

Having created this program, we started the evaluation procedure. At first we made the classical statistical examinations: printed some lists, namely frequency matrix, relative frequency matrix, contingency tables, conditional frequency matrix, conditional contingency tables.

It was a very important and multi-step problem to decide what variables (codes) are to be used for the contingency tables and what conditions are to be defined for calculating conditional frequencies and contingencies. Paralelly with this work we made preparations for using multi-variable statistical methods (i.e. factor- and cluster-analysis), and had experimental analysis.

That is the current status of our research, which is of course only a station in the process of our work, which is a multi-step procedure with many feedbacks, including the involvement and analysis of new models, the continuous improvement of capabilities of the computer program, the extention of analysis of existing models - and of course, the investigation of applicability of our system in practice, which will be discussed later.

IV. Some characteristics of our sample of models

Having made the elementary statistical analysis of our sample, we could derive some conclusions about the connections among various properties of the models. Obviously the properties of models form the basis of their groupings; since we put in a specific group those models which have similar characters from some points of view. (A particular model can be in our system element of more than one group, i.e. the groups are not separated.) Here we give some results of the analysis based on the main codes only and then a tentative classification is given.

IV.1. Results of the analysis of frequency tables

We give (just very briefly) the main characteristics of the sample, as follows:

A great majority of models handles a single item and single location. Most of the models considers deterministic input and stochastic output. Static models are more common than dynamic ones. The models are mostly cost-minimizing, there is a considerable number of reliability type models and a few descriptive or other types. The most common ordering rule is s;q (recorder point-order quantity), but almost the same number of t;s models (reorder time - order level) can be found. These two groups take 60 % of all models, the remaining part is equally distributed between s;S, t;q and other type of models. Ratio of models with periodic review and those with continuous review is 2:1. Shortage is allowed and demand is backlogged in the majority of models. If lead time is considered (it occurs in less than half of the models), it is constant in most cases, there can be found only a few models with stochastic lead time.

IV.2. Results of analysis of contingency tables

While in the previous part we have characterized the sample of models by the distribution of individual codes, now we turn to the examination of connections among the various characteristics of the models. Some aspects of analysis are given as follows:

- Complexity

We have analysed the effects of three properties which obviously make the model more complex. These properties are: multi-item, multi-location and dynamic character. If any of the three properties are handled in the model quite generally one will find that there is no lead time in the model, input is not treated at all, or it is deterministic in one lot, and there is a prescribed order period.

- Objective function and mechanism

By mechanisms we mean the ordering rules and specify them exactly as it is used in the book of E. Naddor. (Inventory Systems, Wiley, New York, 1966).

We have found that there is a group of mechanisms, (namely $t;q$, $t_p;q$, $s_p;q$), which is characteristical for the elementary models. In these models input and output processes are deterministic, shortage is not allowed, reorder (scheduling) periods are equal. These simple mechanisms can be also found in some models which are very complex from other points of view.

303

Models of t;S type normally have equal reorder periods, continuous demand and orders usually filled in one lot.

More complex models are built usually on the s;q and s;S mechanisms. These models have generally stochastic output, continuous reviewing period, backlogged orders (i.e. in case of shortage demand is recorded and filled when the next shipment arrives), non-prescribed and non-equal reorder periods. For s;q models characteristical are also the positive lead time and that demand occurs in random intervals, while (s,S) models shipment normally arrive in one lot.

The vast majority of models is cost minimizing. There is one exception: But as we have already mentioned, there is a special group of models with the objective to satisfy a reliability equation instead of minimizing a cost function. This set consists of models almost exclusively t,S type, and has the following other characteristics: input is stochastic there is a reliability constraint for occurance of shortage, both input and demand are either continuous or occur in several lots.

- Input output processes

One of the features having the most important influence on the structure of models is the characteristics of output. Most of the models with deterministic output are of $t:q$, $s_p;q$ type, do not allow shortage, have zero lead time. Models with stochastic output can generally be characterized by s;S, s;q, or t;S mechanisms, allowed shortage and non-zero lead time.

As for the input, most of the models are deterministic. Those having stochastic input are mostly of reliability type, with characteristics described in the previous chapter. Cost minimizing models with stochastic input are generally based on s;q ordering rule.

V. A tentative classification

On the basis of the analyses made up till now some groups of models can already be defined.

Beside the results of analysis of frequency and contingency tables we have already obtained some results from multi-variable statistical analysis (i.e. factor-, and cluster-analysis) as well. We have still made only the first step in using these methods (there are rather heavy difficulties, in scaling and defining distances for example), but our results until now seem to strengthen the ones obtained by traditional methods.

In our classification below there appear the results of both investigation mentioned. We have found that there is a strong tendency that models in a specific group are very close to each other as for their structure, i.e. their features and the connections between these features. Our classification is as follows:

1.) Simple deterministic models

2.) Deterministic, multi-item models

3.) Stochastic output- deterministic input, (t_p, S) models

4.) Stochastic output, multi-item models

5.) Dynamic (s, S) models

6.) Stochastic output and input models

7.) Reliability-type models

Although this classification is supported by a thorough analysis we emphasize that this is not our final word on the subject.

We expect changes first of all on the basis of further factor-
and cluster-analyses which are still to be carried out.

VI. Comparison of models to the "typical" models

We have defined two different "typical" models and have
examined the differences between these typical models and the
models of the whole sample. The first hypotetical typical
model has been determined by the most frequent values of the
forty-five variables, (i.e. codes characterizing the models).
The second one has been defined by those code-values which
chan be considered the most commonly applicable for input inventories at Hungarian enterprises. (We could find a model in
the sample which exactly corresponds to the first kind of our
typical models, but no model corresponding to the second one
was found.)

We have examined how many models in the sample differ from
the typical ones in one, two, etc. codes. We have evaluated
frequency distributions of these differences. We have found
that the density functions were very close to the normal distribution in both cases, and the standard deviation was higher in case of the model created by us than by the one having
the most frequent parameters.

VII. Computerized library of inventory models

From the point of view of practice the first and basic
result of our work is the knowledge of over 330 models. Using
these models we have created a model-library which consists of
four subsystems.

1.) Library of verbal descriptions of models.

From the verbal description one can see the main characteristics of a model, even if he is not a specialist of models. There is, of course an exact reference to the origin of description, i.e. to the complete, original model.

2.) Library of code-descriptions of models which has two forms:

- system of code-sheets filled in manually;
- the computerised code-description which have been created by an appropriate transformation from the above one, excluding or transforming most of the verbal information. We have created a computer program which is able to answer many different questions and through which we have access to models of various types, defined from various points of view.

3.) Library of flow-charts of models, It is for technical purposes to help transformations of models from the first to the fourth subsystem.

4.) Library of operating models. It consists of computer programs of algorithms for determining optimal values of decision variables of the models. That is directly for practical use.

We have in our mind the following way of application: The manager decides to use our model-library to specify optimal parameters for a given product. He is to turn to the "librarian" who gives him a questionnaire, which corresponds to our code-system but it is written in a language appropriate for communication between people of practice and theory. Then on the basis of this questionnaire the model(s) having properties specified by the manager is requested from the computer. If there are such models, it is all right - if not, the computer will print the models "closest" to the requested one. Then there must be a discussion on the applicability of the model. If all involved can agree, the model can be called from library-4, to put appropriate input parameters into it and obtain the optimal values of decision variables. (We do not deal here with such questions of implementation as for example availability of data, putting optimal decision rules force, etc. - which are very important, but not closely connected to the problems of our research.)

We have already carried out an application, for a subset of our models, which have been built into the inventory control subsystem of a complex computerized management system, created by the Computer Development Association of the Chemical Industry, which is a joint venture of 14 Hungarian companies in the chemical industry. Our experimental results were quite promising.

VIII. Conclusion

Our objective was to give an overview of the scope, aims and results of our long-term research project. We emphasize that we consider most of our statements and reasonings as tentative ones, and we are to carry out more analyses before drawing up "final results".

Proc. First Int. Symp. on Inventories
Budapest, Hungary 1980

SOME INVENTORY MODELS

E. V. BULINSKAYA

Moscow State University, Moscow, USSR

One often deals practically with substitution of products. A well-known example of substitution is based on the possibility of transfusion of compatible blood groups. The same feature is inherent to a system of single-product stores interchanging their supplies (not arbitrarily!) to meet demand. In the sequel we treat multi-product inventory models with periodical inspection of supplies.

Assume that the store has the quantity x_i of the i-th product ($i = \overline{1, \tau}$, $\tau = $ const.) and the orders for refilling can be made at fixed moments separated by equal time periods. These orders are fulfilled immediately, though we can more generally consider deterministic or stochastic delays in delivery. Let $\bar{\xi}^\kappa = (\xi_1^\kappa, \ldots, \xi_\tau^\kappa)$ denote the demands to the store within the κ-th period of operation; we assume $\bar{\xi}^\kappa$ to form a sequence of independent random vectors possessing the distribution density $\mathcal{Y}_\kappa (\vartheta_1, \ldots, \vartheta_\tau)$.

For the unit of the i-th product let κ_i be the cost of order, h_i - the cost of storage within a period and p_i - the charge for the lack.

In addition to standard assumptions made by many authors

(see references) we suppose that the graph of possible substitutions of products is given along with the costs q_{ij}
due to the substitution of j-th product for the i-th
one (taken in the same quantity, thereby the model handles
the system of interacting stores as well).

As to the demands that still could not be met after permitted substitutions one may suppose that either they were
lost or remained waiting for new replenishments, i.e. we can
have a system with refusals or with queueing.

The problem is to determine a policy of refilling the
store minimizing the total average costs for n periods.

For arbitrary τ the equations specifying the minimal average costs are too involved so we shall give them explicitly
only for $\tau = 2$ in case of system with refusals and nonstati-
onary distribution of demands. It is convenient to denote the
density of demands in the first period as φ_n, in the second as φ_{n-1} and so on. The ordered supplies are delivered
without delays.

Let $f_n(x_1, x_2)$ be the minimal n-periods average costs
corresponding to initial level (x_1, x_2) of supplies and put

$$q_1 = q_{12}, \quad q_2 = q_{21}.$$

One easily obtains

$$f_n(x_1, x_2) = \min_{\substack{y_1 \geq x_1 \\ y_2 \geq x_2}} G_n(y_1, y_2) \tag{1}$$

where

$$G_n(y_1, y_2) = \kappa_1(y_1 - x_1) + \kappa_2(y_2 - x_2) + \mathcal{L}_n(y_1, y_2) + \hat{\mathcal{L}}_{n-1}(y_1, y_2) \tag{2}$$

The first two terms in the right hand side of (2) determine

the costs of the order. The next formula (3) gives the average costs of storage within the first period plus payments
for the substitutions and the lack of supplies provided the
level of supplies (after immediate delivery) is (y_1, y_2) at
the beginning of the period.

$$\mathcal{L}_n(y_1, y_2) = \int_0^{y_1} \int_0^{y_2} \left[h_1(y_1 - s_1) + h_2(y_2 - s_2) \right] \mathcal{G}_n(s_1, s_2) ds_1 ds_2 +$$

$$+ \int_0^{y_2} \int_{y_1}^{y_1 + y_2 - s_2} \left[q_1(s_1 - y_1) + h_2(y_1 + y_2 - s_1 - s_2) \right] \mathcal{G}_n(s_1, s_2) ds_1 ds_2 +$$

$$+ \int_0^{y_1} \int_{y_2}^{y_1 + y_2 - s_1} \left[q_2(s_2 - y_2) + h_1(y_1 + y_2 - s_1 - s_2) \right] \mathcal{G}_n(s_1, s_2) ds_1 ds_2 +$$

$$+ \int_0^{y_2} \int_{y_1 + y_2 - s_2}^{\infty} \left[q_1(y_2 - s_2) + p_1(s_1 + s_2 - y_1 - y_2) \right] \mathcal{G}_n(s_1, s_2) ds_1 ds_2 +$$

$$+ \int_0^{y_1} \int_{y_1 + y_2 - s_1}^{\infty} \left[q_2(y_1 - s_1) + p_2(s_1 + s_2 - y_1 - y_2) \right] \mathcal{G}_n(s_1, s_2) ds_1 ds_2 +$$

$$+ \int_{y_1}^{\infty} \int_{y_2}^{\infty} \left[p_1(s_1 - y_1) + p_2(s_2 - y_2) \right] \mathcal{G}_n(s_1, s_2) ds_1 ds_2 \tag{3}$$

$$\hat{\mathcal{L}}_{n-1}(y_1, y_2) = \int_0^{y_1} \int_0^{y_2} f_{n-1}(y_1 - s_1, y_2 - s_2) \mathcal{G}_n(s_1, s_2) ds_1 ds_2 +$$

$$+ \int_0^{y_2} \int_{y_1}^{y_1 + y_2 - s_2} f_{n-1}(0, y_1 + y_2 - s_1 - s_2) \mathcal{G}_n(s_1, s_2) ds_1 ds_2 +$$

$$+ \int_0^{y_1} \int_{y_2}^{y_1 + y_2 - s_1} f_{n-1}(y_1 + y_2 - s_1 - s_2, 0) \mathcal{G}_n(s_1, s_2) ds_1 ds_2 +$$

$$+ \int\int_{s_1 + s_2 > y_1 + y_2} f_{n-1}(0,0) \mathcal{G}_n(s_1, s_2) ds_1 ds_2 \tag{4}$$

The last relation (4) expresses the average costs within

the next $(n-1)$ periods of optimal ordering policy.

We call the optimal policy or optimal control for the first step of the n-step process the values $y_{n1}(x_1, x_2), y_{n2}(x_1, x_2)$ minimizing the right hand side of (1).

With x_1, x_2 fixed we obviously have to choose one of the following strategies as the optimal control:

1) Both products are ordered (in prescribed amount).

2) The first product is ordered (in prescribed amount).

3) The second product is ordered (in prescribed amount).

4) No orders are made.

Thus the region $\{x_1 \geqslant 0, x_2 \geqslant 0\}$ is divided into four corresponding domains: O_{12}^n - the domain of strategy 1, O_1^n - the domain of strategy 2, O_2^n - the domain of strategy 3 and $\overline{O}^n$ - the domain of strategy 4.

The boundaries of these domains are some curves $\ell_{n1} = \{y_1 = g_{n1}(y_2)\}$, $\ell_{n2} = \{y_2 = g_{n2}(y_1)\}$, that can be determined also by the inverse functions $\ell_{n1} = \{y_2 = g_{n1}^{-1}(y_1)\}$, $\ell_{n2} = \{y_1 = g_{n2}^{-1}(y_2)\}$. The functions $y_2 = g_{n2}(y_1)$, $y_2 = g_{n1}^{-1}(y_1)$ are monotonously decreasing and

$$\frac{d}{dy_1} g_{n2}(y_1) > -1, \qquad \frac{d}{dy_1} g_{n1}^{-1}(y_1) < -1$$

The position of the curves depending on the values of parameters κ_i, h_i, p_i, q_i ($i = 1, 2$) and on the distribution densities $\varphi_\kappa(s_1, s_2)$ ($\kappa = \overline{1, n}$) falls into three main patterns.

I. The curves ℓ_{n1}, ℓ_{n2} have one point of intersection $(\overline{x}_{n1}, \overline{x}_{n2})$ whenever $g_{n1}^{-1}(0) > g_{n2}(0)$, $g_{n2}^{-1}(0) > g_{n1}(0)$.

The optimal control takes the form

$$(y_{n1}(x_1,x_2), y_{n2}(x_1,x_2)) = \begin{cases} (\bar{x}_{n1}, \bar{x}_{n2}) & (x_1,x_2) \in O_{12}^n \\ (g_{n1}(x_2), x_2) & (x_1,x_2) \in O_1^n \\ (x_1, g_{n2}(x_1)) & (x_1,x_2) \in O_2^n \\ (x_1, x_2) & (x_1,x_2) \in \bar{O}^n \end{cases} \quad (5)$$

Four distinct cases arise

a) $\quad g_{n1}^{-1}(0) < \infty \;, \quad g_{n2}^{-1}(0) < \infty$

b) $\quad g_{n1}^{-1}(0) < \infty \;, \quad g_{n2}^{-1}(0) = \infty$

c) $\quad g_{n1}^{-1}(0) = \infty \;, \quad g_{n2}^{-1}(0) < \infty$

d) $\quad g_{n1}^{-1}(0) = \infty \;, \quad g_{n2}^{-1}(0) = \infty$

In any case

$$O_{12}^n = \left\{ 0 \leq x_1 \leq \bar{x}_{n1}, \; 0 \leq x_2 \leq \bar{x}_{n2} \right\}$$

In case a) both domains O_1^n and O_2^n are bounded

$$O_1^n = \left\{ 0 \leq x_1 \leq g_{n1}(x_2), \; \bar{x}_{n2} < x_2 \leq g_{n1}^{-1}(0) \right\}$$

$$O_2^n = \left\{ \bar{x}_{n1} < x_1 \leq g_{n2}^{-1}(0), \; 0 \leq x_2 \leq g_{n2}(x_1) \right\}$$

In case b) O_1^n is the same as in previous case but O_2^n is unbounded

$$O_2^n = \left\{ \bar{x}_{n1} < x_1 < \infty, \; 0 \leq x_2 \leq g_{n2}(x_1) \right\}$$

In case c) O_2^n is the same as in case a) and O_1^n is unbounded

$$O_1^n = \left\{ 0 \leq x_1 \leq g_{n1}(x_2), \; \bar{x}_{n2} < x_2 < \infty \right\}$$

At last in case d) both the domains are unbounded.

In each case $\bar{O}^n$ is the complement of $O_{12}^n \cup O_1^n \cup O_2^n$ in $\{x_1 \geq 0, x_2 \geq 0\}$.

II. The curve ℓ_{n2} lies above ℓ_{n1} whenever $g_{n1}^{-1}(0) \leq g_{n2}^{-1}(0)$, $g_{n2}^{-1}(0) > g_{n1}(0)$.

Then only domains O_2^n and $\bar{O}^n$ appear and the optimal control is

$$(y_{n1}(x_1,x_2), y_{n2}(x_1,x_2)) = \begin{cases} (x_1, g_{n2}(x_1)) & (x_1,x_2) \in O_2^n \\ (x_1, x_2) & (x_1,x_2) \in \bar{O}^n \end{cases} \qquad (6)$$

In this situation two cases are possible

a) $\quad O_2^n = \{0 \le x_1 \le g_{n2}^{-1}(0),\ 0 \le x_2 \le g_{n2}(x_1)\}$

b) $\quad O_2^n = \{0 \le x_1 < \infty,\ 0 \le x_2 \le g_{n2}(x_1)\}$

III. The curve ℓ_{n1} lies above ℓ_{n2}, whenever $g_{n1}^{-1}(0) > g_{n2}(0)$, $g_{n2}^{-1}(0) \le g_{n1}(0)$.

The nonempty domains are O_1^n and $\bar{O}^n$. The optimal control is then

$$(y_{n1}(x_1,x_2), y_{n2}(x_1,x_2)) = \begin{cases} (g_{n1}(x_2), x_2) & (x_1,x_2) \in O_1^n \\ (x_1, x_2) & (x_1,x_2) \in \bar{O}^n \end{cases} \qquad (7)$$

Two distinct cases are

a) $\quad O_1^n = \{0 \le x_1 \le g_{n1}(x_2),\ 0 \le x_2 \le g_{n1}^{-1}(0)\}$

c) $\quad O_1^n = \{0 \le x_1 \le g_{n1}(x_2),\ 0 \le x_2 < \infty\}$

We shall refer to the optimal controls (5),(6),(7) corresponding to the relative positions I,II,III of the curves ℓ_{n1}, ℓ_{n2} as to the variants I,II,III respectively.

The further classification of these variants is given in terms of functions $\Psi_{n1}(y_1)$, $\Psi_{n2}(y_2)$:

$$\Psi_{n1}(y_1) = (\kappa_2 - p_2) - (\kappa_1 - p_1) - (q_2 - p_2 + p_1) \int_0^{y_1}\int_0^{\infty} \Psi_n(s_1, s_2)\, ds_1\, ds_2$$

$$\Psi_{n2}(y_2) = (\kappa_1 - p_1) - (\kappa_2 - p_2) - (q_1 - p_1 + p_2) \int_0^{y_2}\int_0^{\infty} \Psi_n(s_1, s_2)\, ds_1\, ds_2$$

Let $\bar{y}_{n1}$ (resp. $\bar{y}_{n2}$) denote the root of the equation $\Psi_{n1}(y_1) = 0$ (resp. $\Psi_{n2}(y_2) = 0$) and put $\bar{y}_{ni} = -\infty$ if $\Psi_{ni}(0) < 0$, $\bar{y}_{ni} = +\infty$ if $\Psi_{ni}(\infty) > 0$ ($i = 1, 2$).

The following <u>theorem</u> is valid:

If the parameters satisfy the relations

1) $\quad K_1 - p_1 < 0, \quad K_2 - p_2 < 0$

2) $\quad p_1 + h_2 > q_1 > max\ (p_1 - p_2,\ h_2 - h_1)$

$\quad\quad p_2 + h_1 > q_2 > max\ (p_2 - p_1,\ h_1 - h_2)$

3) $\quad K_1 + h_1 = K_2 + h_2$

then there exist for any n such curves ℓ_{n_1}, ℓ_{n_2} that the optimal control for the first step of the n-step process coincides either with (5) or (6) or (7).

Furthermore, if condition

A) $\quad K_2 - K_1 = p_2 - p_1$

is satisfied then the variant I is optimal for any n.

Under condition

B) $\quad K_2 - K_1 < p_2 - p_1$

the variant I is optimal if $g_{n_2}(0) > \overline{y}_{n_2}$ and the variant II is optimal if $g_{n_2}(0) \leq \overline{y}_{n_2}$.

Under condition

C) $\quad K_2 - K_1 > p_2 - p_1$

the variant I is optimal if $g_{n_1}(0) > \overline{y}_{n_1}$ and the variant III is optimal if $g_{n_1}(0) \leq \overline{y}_{n_1}$.

If the additional relations are imposed

$$K_1 + h_2 + (m-1)(K_2 + h_2) \leq q_1 < K_1 + h_2 + m(K_2 + h_2)$$

$$K_2 + h_1 + (\ell - 1)(K_1 + h_1) \leq q_2 < K_2 + h_1 + \ell(K_1 + h_1) \qquad (8)$$

then for $n = 1, 2, \ldots, min\ (\ell, m)$ the case d) is realized; next if $m < \ell$ then for $n = m+1, \ldots, \ell$ the case b) takes place and for $n > \ell$ the case a); at last with $m > \ell$ for $n = \ell + 1, \ldots, m$ the case c) obtains and for $n > m$ the case a).

(Whenever $m = 0$ or $\ell = 0$ the inequalities in (8) are

substituted by $q_1 < k_1 + h_2$ or $q_2 < k_2 + h_1$ respectively.)

Note that the condition 3) of the theorem is superfluous for $n = 1$. The conditions 1) and 2) have natural interpretations since $k_i - p_i < 0$ means that the costs of refilling the store is less than the charge for the lack of supplies. If the sign of these inequalities is opposite it is obvious that no refilling is needed for $n = 1$. Analogously $p_1 + h_2 > q_1$ or $p_2 + h_1 > q_2$ imply that the substitution is preferable to payment of fines and storage of excessive other product.

In the stationary case when $\Psi_k \equiv \Psi$, $k = \overline{1, n}$ we can detalize the character of the optimal policy under conditions B) or C).

For instance assuming B) we have II as the optimal variant for all n if $g_{12}(0) \leq \overline{y}_2$ (here $\Psi_2(\overline{y}_2) = 0$, $\Psi_{n2} \equiv \Psi_2$) and therefore $g_{n2}(0) = g_{12}(0)$. If $g_{12}(0) > \overline{y}_2$ then for all n the optimality of I is implied by $g_{n2}(0) > \overline{y}_2$ while with $g_{n2}(0) \leq \overline{y}_2$ the variant II is optimal.

The analogous statement is valid in case C) if we substitute III for II and $g_{n1}(0)$, $g_{11}(0)$, $\overline{y}_1$ for $g_{n2}(0)$, $g_{12}(0)$, $\overline{y}_2$ respectively.

The situation with delays is far more complicated even for the fixed one-step delay. Now

$$f_n(x_1, x_2) = \min_{\substack{z_1 \geq 0 \\ z_2 \geq 0}} \left[k_1 z_1 + k_2 z_2 + \mathcal{L}_n(x_1, x_2) + \hat{\widehat{\mathcal{L}}}_{r-1}(x_1, x_2, z_1, z_2) \right]$$

and the minimized expression is no longer the function of the sums $x_1 + z_1$, $x_2 + z_2$ in contrast to the immediate delivery case.

Indeed

$$\widehat{\mathscr{L}}_{n-1}(x_1, x_2, z_1, z_2) = \int_0^{x_1} \int_0^{x_2} f_{n-1}(x_1 + z_1 - \jmath_1, x_2 + z_2 - \jmath_2) \, \varphi_n(\jmath_1, \jmath_2) \, d\jmath_1 d\jmath_2 +$$

$$+ \int_0^{x_2} \int_{x_1}^{x_1 + x_2 - \jmath_2} f_{n-1}(z_1, x_1 + x_2 + z_2 - \jmath_1 - \jmath_2) \, \varphi_n(\jmath_1, \jmath_2) \, d\jmath_1 d\jmath_2 +$$

$$+ \int_0^{x_1} \int_{x_2}^{x_1 + x_2 - \jmath_1} f_{n-1}(x_1 + x_2 + z_1 - \jmath_1 - \jmath_2, z_2) \, \varphi_n(\jmath_1, \jmath_2) \, d\jmath_1 d\jmath_2 +$$

$$+ \iint_{\jmath_1 + \jmath_2 > x_1 + x_2} f_{n-1}(z_1, z_2) \, \varphi_n(\jmath_1, \jmath_2) \, d\jmath_1 d\jmath_2$$

Again one can prove that the optimal policy is determined by certain partition of the first quadrant into 4 domains O_{12}^n, O_1^n, O_2^n, $\bar{O}^n$ though their boundary curves and the corresponding optimal orders have no compact description.

References

Balintfy J.L. (1964): Management Science v.10, N2, p.287.

Iglehart D. (1965): Management Science v.12, N3, p.193.

Ignall E. (1969): Management Science v.15, N5, p.278.

Ignall E.,Veinott A. (1969): Management Science v.15, N5, p.284.

Johnson E. (1968): Management Science v.15, N1, p.80.

Veinott A. (1965): Management Science v.12, N3, p.206.

Proc. First Int. Symp. on Inventories
Budapest, Hungary 1980

POLICIES OF (MULTI-S) TYPE
IN DYNAMIC INVENTORY PROBLEM

STANISŁAW BYLKA

Institute of Computer Science, Polish Academy of Sciences, Warsaw, Poland

We consider a discrete-time inventory model with one indivisi-
ble commodity. The model is of the type investigated by
Veinott (1966), Johnson (1968), and Tijms (1972). In each period the initial stock is observed. It may be increased to any
amount by placing an order which is delivered immediately. The
demand is met out of the stock on hand after ordering. The
stock which passes to the next period is reduced by the demand.
Any unfilled demand in a period is completely backlogged. The
stock on hand may take on any integral value, where a negative
value indicates the existence of a backlog. We shall assume
that the demands are independent random variables with the same
probability distribution having a finite and positive expected
value.

If the order is positive, a positive setup cost, which
does not depend on the amount ordered, is incurred. There is
no purchase cost. All costs of storage and shortage will be
considered together in the form of a function L expressing the
expectation of those costs depending on the stock on hand after
ordering. The total expected cost is defined as the undiscoun-
ted sum of costs over a finite number of considered periods.

319

We define policies of (multi-S)-type as a generalization (different from that due to (Porteus 1971) of policies of (s,S) -type. Some properties of these policies, analogously for (multi S)-type and (s,S)-type, are given by Theorems 1 and 2. The next Theorems 3 and 4 relate to the existence of optimal policies for the model investigated.

1. Policies of (multi-S)-type

In each period our decision is whether to increase the stock or not. If the initial stock i is observed then by our decision, the stock on hand after ordering will be $f(i) \geqslant i$.

The set of integers we shall denote by I. Any function f defined on I assuming integers as its values and satisfying

$$f(i) \geqslant i \qquad \text{for} \qquad i \in I$$

is called an ordering decision function.

An ordering decision function f is of (s,S)-type if and only if there exist two integers $s \leqslant S$ such that

$$f(i) = \begin{cases} S & \text{for } i < s \\ i & \text{for } i \geqslant s \end{cases}$$

We shall write too (s,S) (i) i.e. $f = (s,S)$.

An ordering decision function f is of (multi S)-type if there exist n+1 integers $S^0 \leqslant S^1 < \ldots < S^n$ such that

$$f(i) = \begin{cases} S^1 & \text{for } i < S^0 \\ i \text{ or } S^r & \text{for } S^{r-1} \leqslant i < S^r \text{ and } r=1,\ldots,n \\ i & \text{for } i \geqslant S^n. \end{cases}$$

By $A(S^0, S^1, \ldots, S^n)$ we shall denote the set of all such functions. We see that if n=1 and $S^0 \neq S^1$ then the policy (S^0, S^1) of (s,S)-type satisfying $(S^0, S^1) \in A(S^0, S^1)$ but there are policies not of (s,S)-type in the set $A(S^0, S^1)$ too.

Any t-tuple ordering decision function $(f_1, \ldots, f_t)$ is called a t-period ordering policy. We assume that in the first period the ordering amount is determined by the function f_t, in the second period by f_{t-1}, and so on, therefore in period t by f_1. If all of the decision functions are (multi S)-type ((s,S)-type) then the policy is (multi-S)-type ((s,S)-type).

2. Total expected cost of an optimal policy

For a given triple (ϕ, K, L) where ϕ is a probability distribution $\phi(n) \geqslant 0$, $\sum_{n=0}^{\infty} \phi(n) = 1$ and $\phi(0) \neq 1$, $K > 0$ is a set-up cost and L is expectation of storage and shortage costs, we shall study finite-period planning problems. The total expected cost of a t-period policy $(\pi_1, \ldots, \pi_t)$ under assumption that the stock on hand at the beginning of the first period is i, may be calculated by an iterative method as follows:

$$C_1(i; \pi_1) = C(i, \pi_1(i))$$

and for $t > 1$

$$C_t(i; \pi_1, \ldots, \pi_t) = C(i, \pi_t(i)) + \sum_{n=0}^{\infty} \phi(n) C_{t-1}(\pi_t(i) - n;$$
$$\pi_1, \ldots, \pi_{t-1})$$

where for $a \geqslant i$

$$C(i,a) = K \delta(a-i) + L(a)$$

with $\delta(0) = 0$ and $\delta(j) = 1$ for $j > 0$.

Let us define by induction on t two sequences of functions $V_t(\cdot)$ and $L_t(\cdot)$, all of them from integers to reals:

$$V_0(i) = 0 \qquad \text{for any integer } i \in I$$

$$L_t(i) = L(i) + \sum_{n=0}^{\infty} \phi(n) V_{t-1}(i-n)$$

$$V_t(i) = \inf_{a \geqslant i} K \, \delta(a-i) + L_t(a) \qquad \text{for} \quad i \in I$$

The quantity $V_t(i)$ expresses the total expected cost of the optimal policy in the t-period planning problem with the initial stock i. The quantity $L_t(i)$ expresses the total expected cost when i is the initial stock achieved by the following policy: In the first period no order is placed, in the subsequent periods an optimal (t-1)-period policy is used.

We see that

$$V_t(i) = \min \left\{ L_t(i), \quad K + \inf_{j > i} L_t(j) \right\} . \tag{0}$$

Assumption 1. There exist integers $m < M$ and a real number $\lambda > 0$ such that

(i) $\qquad L(i) > \inf_{j \in I} L(j) + K \qquad \text{for} \quad i \leqslant m$

and

(ii) $\qquad L(i) \geqslant \inf_{j \in I} L(j) + K + \lambda \qquad \text{for} \quad i \geqslant M.$

This assumption is nearly Johnson's assumption (Johnson 1968):

$$\lim_{|i| \to \infty} L(i) > \inf_{i \in I} L(i) + K,$$

and is weaker than Veinott s assumption (Veinott 1966):

$$\lim_{|i| \to \infty} L(i) = + \infty .$$

Key Lemma. If the function L satisfies Assumption 1 and $\bar{S} = \max \left\{ S \mid L(S) = \inf_{i \in I} L(i) \right\}$ then for any $t = 1, 2, \ldots$ there exist an integer M_t and a real number $\lambda_t > 0$ such that

(a) $\qquad L_t(i) = L(i) + \sum_{n=0}^{\infty} \phi(n) \, V_{t-1}(i-n) \qquad \text{for} \quad i \in I,$

322

(b) $\qquad V_t(i) \geqslant V_t(S) + K + \lambda_t \qquad$ for $\quad i \geqslant M_t$,

(c) $\qquad$ for $\; i \leqslant \bar{s}$

$$V_t(i) - V_{t-1}(i) \leqslant \left[L_t(m) - L_1(m) \right] - \left[V_{t-1}(m) - V_1(m) \right],$$

(d) $\qquad$ for $\; i \leqslant \bar{s}$

$$L_{t+1}(i) - L_t(i) \leqslant \left[L_{t+1}(m) - L_1(m) \right] - \left[V_t(m) - V_1(m) \right],$$

(e) $\qquad$ for $\; i \geqslant M_t$

$$L_t(i) \geqslant \inf_{j \in I} L_t(j) + K + \lambda_t,$$

(f) $\qquad$ for $\; i \leqslant m$

$$L_t(i) > \inf_{j \in I} L_t(j) + K,$$

(g) $\qquad$ there exists $\; S_t \in I \;$ such that for $\; i \leqslant m$

$$V_t(i) = K + \inf_{j \in I} L_t(j) = K + L_t(S_t) =$$

$$= K + \inf_{j \in I} V_t(j) = K + V_t(S_t).$$

Proof. We first prove that (a), (b), (c) and (f) are satisfied
for $t = 1$. Further we can prove the following implications:
(b) $\Rightarrow$ (e); (e) and (f) $\Rightarrow$ (g); (g) for $t \Rightarrow$ (a) for $t+1$;
(a) for t and $t+1$ and (c) for $t \Rightarrow$ (d) for t; (d), (g)
for t and (a) for $t+1 \Rightarrow$ (f) for $t+1$; (b) for t and (a) for
$t+1 \Rightarrow$ (b) for $t+1$; (a), (d), (b) for t and (a) for $t+1 \Rightarrow$ (c)
for $t+1$. This proof is given by Bylka (1979).

Corollary of Key Lemma. For each $\; t = 1, 2, \ldots$ there exists a
sequence of integers $(S^0, S^1, \ldots, S^n, \ldots)$ (infinite or finite)
such that $S^0 \leqslant S^1 < S^2 < \ldots < S^n < \ldots$ and the following four

conditions are satisfied:

(P_t)
$\left\{\begin{array}{l}\end{array}\right.$

(i) If there exist $j_1 < j_2 \leqslant j_3$ such that

$L_t(j_1) > L_t(j_2) + K$ and $L_t(j_3) = \min\limits_{i \geqslant j_1} L_t(i)$ then

there is $k \geqslant 1$ such that

$$\min\limits_{i \geqslant j_1} L_t(i) = L_t(S^k)$$

and if $k > 1$ then $S^{k-1} < j_1 < S^k$,

(ii) $L_t(i) \geqslant L_t(S^1) + K$ for $i < S^0$

(iii) $L_t(S^0) \leqslant L_t(S^1) + K$,

(iv) for any $S^0 \leqslant S^k < S^{k+1}$ there exist integers i_1 and i_2 such that $S^k < i_1 < i_2 \leqslant S^{k+1}$ and $L_t(i_1) > L_t(i_2) + K$.

Remark. The sequence is finite if and only if there is an integer i_1 such that $L_t(i) \leqslant L_t(j) + K$ for each $i_1 \leqslant i < j$ or

$$\inf\limits_{j \geqslant i_1} L_t(j) < L_t(i) \quad \text{for each } i = i_1 + 1,\ i_1 + 2, \ldots \ .$$

Veinott (1966) formulates conditions (P_1) for two integers $s \leqslant S$, with equalities in (ii) and (iii) because of continuity of L.

3. Existence theorems

It can be easily derived from the definitions and the Corollary of Key Lemma.

Theorem 1. Let Assumption 1 be fulfilled; then for each $t = 1, 2, \ldots$ and a sequence $S^0 \leqslant S^1 < \ldots < S^n$ the following three conditions are equivalent:

(i)   the sequence $(S^0, S^1, \ldots, S^n)$ satisfies (P_t) and

$$L_t(i) \leqslant L_t(j) + K \quad \text{for} \quad S^n \leqslant i < j,$$

(ii)   there exists an optimal t-period policy

$(\pi_1, \ldots, \pi_t)$ such that $\pi_t \in A(S^0, S^1, \ldots, S^n)$,

(iii)

$$V_t(i) = \begin{cases} L_t(S^1) + K & \text{for} \quad i < S^0 \\ \min\{L_t(i), L_t(S^k) + K\} & \text{for} \quad S^{k-1} \leqslant i < S^k \\ & \text{and} \quad k = 1, \ldots, n \\ L_t(i) & \text{for} \quad i \geqslant S^n. \end{cases}$$

For policies of (s, S)-type we have:

Theorem 2. Let Assumption 1 be fulfilled; then for each $t = 1, 2, \ldots$ and a pair $S^0 \leqslant S^1$ the following three conditions are equivalent:

(i)   the sequence (S^0, S^1) satisfies (P_t) and

$$L_t(i) \leqslant L_t(j) + K \quad\quad \text{for} \quad S^0 \leqslant i < j;$$

(ii)   there exists an optimal t-period policy

$(\pi_1, \ldots, \pi_t)$ such that $\pi_t = (S^0, S^1)$.

(iii) $V_t(i) = \begin{cases} L_t(S^1) + K & \text{for} \quad i < S^0 \\ L_t(i) & \text{for} \quad i \geqslant S^0 . \end{cases}$

To establish the existence of an optimal policy of (multi-S)-type some additional assumptions for L are needed.

Assumption 2. There exist integers $M_0 < M^0$ such that

(i) $L(i) \leqslant L(j)$ for $M_0 \leqslant i < j$

(ii) $L(i) > L(M_0) + K$ for $i \geqslant M^0$.

Theorem 3. Let the function R satisfy both Assumption 1 and 2. If a sequence $S^0 \leqslant S^1 < S^2 \leqslant \ldots$ satisfies conditions (P_t) then it is a finite sequence $S^0 \leqslant S^1 < \ldots < S^n$ and there exists an optimal t-period policy $(\pi_1, \ldots, \pi_t)$ such that $\pi_t \in A(S^0, S^1, \ldots, S^n)$ and

(i) $m < S^0 \leqslant S^n \leqslant M^0$

and

(ii) $S^{n-1} \leqslant M_0$

Proof. Let $t \in I$. By Assumption 1 there exists a sequence $(S^0, S^1, \ldots)$ satisfying (P_t). Because Assumption 2 then for each $M_0 \leqslant i < j$

$$L_t(j) - L_t(i) = L(j) - L(i) + \sum_{n=0}^{\infty} \phi(n)\left[V_{t-1}(j-n) - V_{t-1}(i-n) \right] \geqslant$$

$$\geqslant L(j) - L(i) - K \geqslant - K .$$

We see that the set $\{ t \,/\, S^t > M_0 \}$ has at most one element. This sequence is finite sequence $(S^0, S^1, \ldots, S^n)$ and (ii) is satisfied.

   For $i > M^0$

$$L_t(i) - L_t(M_0) \geqslant L(i) - L(M_0) - K > 0$$

which means that for any $i \leqslant M^0$

$$\inf_{j \geqslant i} L_t(j) = \min_{i < j \leqslant M^0} L_t(j) \tag{1}$$

and $S^n \leqslant M^0$.

326

By (i) of (P_t) and Assumption 2

$$L_t(i) \leqslant L_t(j) + K \qquad \text{for} \quad S^n \leqslant i < j \qquad (2)$$

Condition (i) follows from Eq. (1) and (f) of the Key Lemma. Equation (2) implies (i) of Theorem 1. This completes the proof.

By Corollary of Key Lemma and Theorem 3 we have

Main Conclusion. If Assumption 1 and Assumption 2 are fulfilled, then for each $t = 1,2,\ldots$ there exists an optimal policy of (multi-S)-type.

Assumption 3. There exist integers $\underline{S} \leqslant \bar{S}$ such that

(i) $\quad L(i) \geqslant L(j)$ $\qquad\qquad$ for $\quad i \leqslant j \leqslant \bar{S}$,

(ii) $\quad L(i) \leqslant L(j)$ $\qquad\qquad$ for $\quad \underline{S} \leqslant i \leqslant j$,

(iii) $\quad L(i) > L(\bar{S})$ $\qquad\qquad$ for $\quad i < \underline{S}$ or $i > \bar{S}$.

In other words, it is assumed that there exists an integer S such that function L is non-increasing for $i \leqslant S$ and is non-decreasing for $i \geqslant S$.
If Assumption 1 then Assumption 3 implies Assumption 2.

Assumption 3 is Veinott's assumption of unimodality of $-L$. Veinott proves the existence of finite period optimal policy of (s,S)-type. As in Veinott s Theorem 1 in (Veinott 1966) we have:

Theorem 4. Let function L satisfy both Assumption 1 and 3. If a sequence $S^0 \leqslant S^1 < \ldots$ satisfies conditions (P_t) then it is a pair $S^0 \leqslant S^1$ and there exists an optimal t-period policy $(\pi_1,\ldots,\pi_t)$ such that $\pi_t = (S^0,S^1)$ and

(i) $\qquad m < s^0 \leqslant s^1 \leqslant M$

and

(ii) $\qquad s^1 \geqslant \underline{s}$.

Proof. If M and $\underline{s}$ satisfy (ii) of Assumption 1 and (ii) of Assumption 3 respectively then the pair M_0, M^0 where $M_0 = \underline{s}$ and $M^0 = M$ satisfies Assumption 2. From Theorem 3 follows that for any $t = 1, 2, \ldots$ and $(s^0, s^1, \ldots, s^n)$ satisfying (P_t) we have

$$s^{n-1} \leqslant \underline{s}.$$

We shall show by induction that for $T = 1, 2, \ldots$

$$L_T(i) - L_T(j) \geqslant L(i) - L(j) \geqslant 0 \quad \text{for} \quad i \leqslant j \leqslant \bar{s}. \qquad (4)$$

For $T = 1$ this is (i) of Assumption 3. Let us suppose that Eq. (4) is satisfied for $T \geqslant 1$. It follows from Eqs. (0) and (4) for T that

$$V_T(i) \geqslant V_T(j) \qquad \text{for} \quad i \leqslant j \leqslant \bar{s}. \qquad (5)$$

Conditions (a) of Key Lemma and Eq. (5) imply that Eq. (4) is satisfied for $T + 1$.

By Eg. (4) and (iii) of Assumption 3 $s^1 \geqslant \underline{s}$ which together with Eq. (3) imply $n = 1$.

Let $s^0 \leqslant i \leqslant s^1$ and $i < j$. It follows from (i) and (iii) of (P_t) and Eq. (4) that

$$- K < L_t(s^1) - L_t(s^0) = [L_t(i) - L_t(s^0)] + [L_t(j) - L_t(i)] +$$

$$+ [L_t(s^1) - L_t(j)] \leqslant L_t(j) - L_t(i).$$

328

Therefore (S^0, S^1) satisfies condition (i) of Theorem 2. The proof is now complete.

REFERENCES

Bylka, S. (1979), "Optimal Policies for Dynamic Inventory Models with Discrete Stochastic Demands", Memo no 76, Københavns Universitets Økonomiske Institut.

Johnson, E.L., (1968), "On (s,S) Policies", Management Sci. 15, 80-101.

Porteus, E.L. (1971), "On the Optimality of Generalized (s,S) Policies", Management Sci. 17, 411-426.

Tijms, H.C. (1972), "Analysis of (s,S) Inventory Models", Centre Tract No 40, Mathematisch Centrum, Amsterdam.

Veinott, A.F. (1966), "On the Optimality of (s,S) Inventory Policies New Conditions and a New Proof", SIAM J. Appl. Math. 14, 1067-1083.

Proc. First Int. Symp. on Inventories
Budapest, Hungary 1980

INVENTORY PLANNING
USING ROLLING PRODUCTION SCHEDULING

ROBERT C. CARLSON[1] and DEAN H. KROPP[2]

[1] *Stanford University, Stanford, CA, USA*
[2] *Dartmouth College, Hanover, NH, USA*

Although algorithms exist for finding optimal solutions to multiperiod
production scheduling problems, the solution found is rarely implemented in
its entirety. Typically, the solution's first period decision is implemented,
the model is updated to recognize the acquisition of new or improved information, and a new (and possibly different) solution is found to the updated
problem. The process then repeats itself. This method of solving a multiperiod problem, implementing the first period decision, updating, and resolving creates what is called a rolling schedule.

Past research has dealt extensively with the optimization of finite
horizon models, but little attention has been paid to the effectiveness of
such solutions when implemented on a rolling basis. Progress has been made
in this direction by Baker (1977) using simulation techniques with a dynamic
lot-sizing model. In this research we further pursue the answer to the
question which Baker (1977, p. 20) posed: "How good are model-optimal
decisions for the actual system, when implemented on a rolling basis?"

Baker found that choosing a proper forecast window length for each problem was important to achieving an efficient rolling schedule. The result of
interest is that Baker found that the longest possible forecast horizon was
not necessarily the best. He encountered large fluctuations in rolling
schedules' effectiveness which depended upon the length of the forecast

331

horizon. In an attempt to smooth these fluctuations, we experimented with forecasting demand beyond the forecast horizon. The results were not always as expected. Some results confirmed Baker's conclusion that less information is better than more, while others pointed toward a conclusion that "the more information, the better."

BAKER'S EXPERIMENTS

The multiperiod planning model used in Baker's experiments, and ours as well, is the Dynamic Lot Size model. Briefly, it is:

$$\text{Minimize} \quad \sum_{t=1}^{N} (k\delta(Q_t) + hI_t) \quad \text{subject to:} \quad I_{t-1} + Q_t - I_t = d_t$$

$$Q_t \geq 0, \ I_t \geq 0$$

where: h = unit holding cost   k = production setup cost

Q_t = production lot size d_t = demand which must be met

I_t = ending inventory level   N = horizon length or forecast window

$\delta(x) = \begin{cases} 0 \text{ for } x = 0 \\ 1 \text{ for } x > 0 \end{cases}$

The Wagner-Whitin (1958) algorithm is used to find the optimal values of Q_t for this model.

Baker's measure of the effectiveness of rolling schedules is the ratio of the cost of the rolling schedule to the cost of the theoretically optimal schedule for the same problem, C_r/C_o. The C_o value is the cost of the Wagner-Whitin optimal policy for a 48-period problem. The C_r value is the cost of a rolling schedule constructed by solving a series of N-period problems, each time saving the first period solution, until a vector of 48 decisions has been formed. To make the comparison with the optimal cost equitable, costs associated with production for periods beyond the 48-period interval are ignored in calculating the cost of the rolling schedule.

Three factors are varied in Baker's experiments. The forecast window, N, is the number of future periods for which demand is known deterministically. In Baker, N is the number of periods of data used by the Wagner-

332

Whitin algorithm; it takes on values of 2,4,6,8,10,12,14, and 24. The second factor varied is the length of the natural cycle, T, which is defined as $T = \sqrt{2k/dh}$; it is the time between successive orders or production setups in an Economic Order Quantity system where demand is constant at d units per period. Baker uses values of 2,4,6,8,10, and 12 for T. Finally, he tests four demand patterns: uniform, trend, seasonal, and trend-seasonal.

ANALYSIS OF BAKER'S RESULTS

Baker (1977) concludes that there is "no simple answer" to the question of how well model-optimal decisions perform on a rolling basis. He does however find that, in many cases, _less information is better than more_ when solving the multiperiod problems to create the rolling schedules. This is especially true for the uniform demand pattern. Table 1 (from Baker, 1977, p. 22) contains results for uniform demand with a range of 75. The tabled values are the average C_r/C_o ratios based on 50 problems. Notice what we refer to as the _diagonal effect_ -- the ratios found along the diagonal where N = T are consistently smaller than the other ratios in their respective rows. The apparent conclusion is that the planning forecast horizon should never be longer than the natural cycle. This conclusion is counterintuitive because it argues in favor of ignoring potentially valuable information.

Table 1

Values of C_r/C_o from Baker: Uniform Demand (range = 75)

T \ N	2	4	6	8	10	12
2	1.002	1.002	1.002	1.002	1.002	1.002
4	1.29	1.004	1.05	1.004	1.03	1.01
6	1.74	1.10	1.004	1.05	1.04	1.01
8	2.21	1.27	1.04	1.003	1.03	1.06
10	2.70	1.48	1.14	1.03	1.007	1.02
12	3.19	1.70	1.27	1.09	1.03	1.003

333

As demand becomes more variable, and in particular when seasonality is added, Baker finds this diagonal effect to be less marked. Nevertheless, he still finds that the choice of an inappropriate forecast window can significantly damage the effectiveness of the rolling schedule. Furthermore, the appropriate window is again not necessarily the longest possible.

Although it is not used in this research, the Period Order Quantity (POQ) lot-sizing technique (Gorham, 1968) offers some useful insights into the diagonal effect. Assume initially that demand is constant. The optimal production schedule in the case of constant demand requires that a setup occur every T periods, or once every natural cycle as it is defined in the POQ context.

In the case of $N < T$, the Wagner-Whitin algorithm processes only N periods of information at each decision point. Clearly, the algorithm will not find the optimal tradeoff duration, T, because it does not have enough information. Instead it will set up once every N periods, thus producing for the longest cycle it possibly can. This results in a cycle shorter than the optimal cycle and a cost larger than the optimal cost. In the case of $N = T$, one expects the algorithm to be able to make approximately the same tradeoffs as a POQ analysis and have a setup every T periods.

The case of $N > T$ is more difficult to analyze. Here the algorithm has more than one full natural cycle of information on future demand; and in making the tradeoff between setup costs and carrying costs, will often choose to produce lot sizes different than those dictated by a POQ analysis. For example, consider a problem in which $k = 1600$, $h = 1$, and demand is given by

Period	1	2	3	4	5	6	7	8
Demand	192	187	195	219	205	180	205	186

The mean demand is 200, which results in a natural cycle of 4. The Wagner-Whitin algorithm yields these optimal values for production in period 1, x_1^*, as a function of N:

N	1	2	3	4	5	6	7	8
x_1^*	192	379	574	793	998	574	574	793

On the average, one would like to produce approximately once every fourth period -- the POQ result -- which means that $x_1^* = 793$ is probably a good selection. For N = 1,2, and 3, not enough data is supplied to the algorithm. This leads to a low, and therefore poor, value of x_1^* as previously discussed.

For N = 5, the algorithm is in the peculiar position of having "not enough" data, but at the same time "too much". There is not enough data in that the Wagner-Whitin algorithm operates on the implicit assumption that demand beyond the horizon equals zero. However, in a rolling scheduling context it is clear that demand after period 5 will not be zero. It is just not yet known. There is too much data in the sense that given this mode of operation of the algorithm and given its implicit assumption, we would have been better off to have had data for only 4 periods. For N = 6, the same analysis holds except in this case the algorithm adjusts by producing too little in period 1 rather than too much. The tradeoff between setup costs and holding costs for the 6-period problem is such that two setups are scheduled and small amounts produced at each. Finally, at N = 8, an integer multiple of the natural cycle, things are back "in phase" again, and $x_1^* = 793$, just as it did for N = 4.

This case is a particularly interesting one. One would expect that giving the Wagner-Whitin algorithm m x T (m integer) periods of demand data would result in decisions close to those made in the optimal schedule, and indeed this result is observed. In examining Baker's results, we notice that the ratios improve at points where N is an integral multiple of T. Unexpectedly, however, the best horizon choice in many of these cases is still the natural cycle, T. Thus, for N > T, when N is "out of phase" with T, there is a likelihood of choosing an incorrect lot size for the first period.

Overall, one can conclude on the basis of such analysis that the ratio values on the diagonal where N = T will be low. Indeed for cases of uniform and trend demand, Baker finds this to be true. However, as demand becomes more variable, as in the case of seasonal demand, one expects these conclusions to be less valid as inventory is no longer drawn down uniformly.

EXTENDING THE HORIZON

The awkward situation of simultaneously having "too much" and "not enough" data is a result of what is called the horizon effect in which the optimal first period lot-size is highly sensitive to the horizon length, N. McClain and Thomas (1977) demonstrated the significance of the horizon effect in rolling scheduling problems. Research to date has concentrated on overcoming this difficulty by specifying a terminal inventory level (a single number) as a constraint on the dynamic programming procedure. However, such research has also demonstrated that cost of the solution obtained is extremely sensitive to the terminal inventory condition imposed upon the problem.

Our approach is to eliminate the horizon effect by extending the horizon. Thus, instead of relying on known demand data for future periods beyond N, we forecast that demand and use the Wagner-Whitin algorithm on a combination of known future demand (through period N) and forecast future demand (beyond N). In this way, we use the data of the problem to implicitly determine terminal conditions. Instead of solving a fixed-horizon problem with a specified terminal inventory level, we extend the horizon of the problem, one period at a time, until a stopping rule condition is met. Each extension creates a new problem to which the Wagner-Whitin procedure is applied.

EXPERIMENTAL SETUP

Our experiments were structured as Baker's, except for the use of forecasting to extend the horizon. For each combination of the 8 values of the forecast horizon, N, (2,4,6,8,10,12,14,24), with the six values of the

336

natural cycle, T, (2,4,6,8,10,12), we solved 20 randomly generated problems and calculated an average C_r/C_o ratio. We conducted tests using uniform demand patterns with ranges of 75 and 400. Demand forecasts were made using a five-period moving average method.

The Wagner-Whitin algorithm is a nearly ideal methodology to use with horizon extension because it is a forward dynamic programming technique. Thus, each extended problem is easily solved using the results of the solutions of all previous problems. Our procedure was to add periods to the problem, one-at-a-time, and to forecast demand for each of these periods, one-at-a-time, each time solving a new problem. Our stopping rule was to extend the problem 5T periods past the horizon, as suggested by Lundin and Morton (1975) unless the process could be stopped earlier. We know from the Wagner and Whitin (1958) horizon theorem that once a setup occurs in the final period of a Wagner-Whitin problem, a setup will occur in that period for all longer (extended) problems. When this happens, the decisions in all prior periods will be fixed and will not change as more periods are added to the problem. Therefore when such an occurrence takes place after the first period, we can discontinue the extensions.

RESULTS

Tables 2 and 3 contain values of C_r/C_o for each type of demand tested for rolling schedules created without forecasting demand beyond the N periods for which data were available. These results are essentially the same as Baker's and are presented primarily for comparison with results achieved when forecasting was used. Two observations are worth noting. First, the diagonal effect described earlier is particularly strong for the uniform demand pattern with range = 75 (Table 2), but it is virtually non-existent for the other more variable demand pattern (Table 3). This would seem to indicate that as demand becomes more variable, more information is better than less in solving the multiperiod problems. Secondly, values for ratios below the diagonal (where N < T) are consistently very large.

Table 2

Values of C_r/C_o Without Forecasting: Uniform Demand (range = 75)

T \ N	2	4	6	8	10	12	14	24
2	1.001	1.001	1.001	1.001	1.001	1.001	1.001	1.0002
4	1.29	1.004	1.05	1.004	1.02	1.008	1.01	1.01
6	1.73	1.09	1.004	1.05	1.04	1.01	1.02	1.01
8	2.21	1.27	1.05	1.003	1.03	1.06	1.02	1.02
10	2.69	1.48	1.14	1.03	1.006	1.02	1.06	1.04
12	3.18	1.70	1.26	1.09	1.03	1.003	1.05	1.04

Table 3

Values of C_r/C_o Without Forecasting: Uniform Demand (range = 400)

T \ N	2	4	6	8	10	12	14	24
2	1.11	1.009	1.003	1.002	1.002	1.002	1.002	1.002
4	1.42	1.10	1.06	1.02	1.01	1.006	1.007	1.008
6	1.87	1.18	1.08	1.09	1.04	1.02	1.01	1.007
8	2.34	1.35	1.11	1.06	1.08	1.05	1.03	1.01
10	2.82	1.55	1.20	1.08	1.05	1.07	1.07	1.03
12	3.31	1.77	1.32	1.13	1.07	1.05	1.09	1.03

For the same demand patterns, we next created rolling schedules using forecasting to extend the number of periods used in the Wagner-Whitin algorithm. For these rolling schedules, the values C_r/C_o are given in Tables 4 and 5. These tables contain some surprising results as well as some which were expected. First, values of C_r/C_o below the diagonal decreased dramatically as expected. It is for these situations where N < T

338

that extending problem horizons via forecasting will be most valuable. Second, for a given T, the minimum C_r/C_o is most often found for N = 24, the largest value of N employed. Furthermore, this rightward movement of the row minima in these tables is much more pronounced for demand with high variability (Table 5). In general, the minimum C_r/C_o ratios are no longer found on the diagonal. All minima have moved to the right, and most to the last column. Thus in general it can be said that more information is better than less when forecasting is used to extend the horizon.

Table 4

Values of C_r/C_o With Forecasting: Uniform Demand (range = 75)

T \ N	2	4	6	8	10	12	14	24
2	1.11	1.04	1.03	1.02	1.01	1.01	1.008	1.003
4	1.19	1.08	1.02	1.01	1.01	1.01	1.01	1.01
6	1.11	1.12	1.04	1.02	1.02	1.01	1.007	1.01
8	1.08	1.10	1.12	1.04	1.02	1.02	1.04	1.01
10	1.10	1.06	1.10	1.11	1.03	1.01	1.01	1.01
12	1.09	1.09	1.11	1.11	1.10	1.03	1.03	1.03

Table 5

Values of C_r/C_o With Forecasting: Uniform Demand (range = 400)

T \ N	2	4	6	8	10	12	14	24
2	1.15	1.01	1.002	1.002	1.002	1.002	1.002	1.002
4	1.29	1.20	1.02	1.01	1.007	1.007	1.008	1.008
6	1.21	1.18	1.08	1.03	1.01	1.01	1.01	1.007
8	1.17	1.17	1.14	1.08	1.04	1.01	1.01	1.01
10	1.15	1.14	1.13	1.10	1.05	1.04	1.02	1.02
12	1.12	1.14	1.12	1.15	1.12	1.08	1.05	1.02

A third result is that the values of C_r/C_o in Tables 4 and 5 exhibit far less fluctuation with changes in N (for a given T) than their counterparts, Tables 2 and 3. Smoothing these fluctuations was one of the objectives of this research, as this will protect the scheduler against the vagaries of having selected a "bad" value of N. Thus it appears that forecasting makes the choice of N less crucial.

CONCLUSIONS

There are some tentative conclusions that can be drawn from our results. First it appears that if N = T and thus the interval over which demand is known deterministically exactly equals the natural cycle, extending the horizon via forecasting is not a good idea. Extending the horizon using forecasting has been shown to be most valuable for cases where N < T. For cases in which N > T, we must be more specific in interpreting our results. When N = mT (m integer), we say that N and T are "in phase" and in general extending the horizon is less valuable than when N and T are out of phase. A relatively clear-cut and important result is that horizon extension via forecasting provides better and better (relative to not extending the horizon) rolling schedules as the variance of demand increases.

REFERENCES

Baker, K. R. (1977): "An Experimental Study of the Effectiveness of Rolling Schedules in Production Planning," Decision Sciences, Vol. 8, pp. 19-27.

Gorham, T. (First Quarter, 1968): "Dynamic Order Quantities," Production and Inventory Management, Vol. 9, pp. 75-81.

McClain, J. O. and Thomas, J. (1977): "Horizon Effects in Aggregate Production Planning with Seasonal Demand," Management Science, Vol. 23, pp. 728-736.

Lundin, R. A. and Morton, T. E. (1975): "Planning Horizons for the Dynamic Lot Size Model: Zabel vs. Protective Procedures and Computational Results," Operations Research, Vol. 25, pp. 711-734.

Wagner, H. and Whitin, T. (1958): "Dynamic Version of the Economic Lot Size Model," Management Science, Vol. 8, pp. 89-96.

Proc. First Int. Symp. on Inventories
Budapest, Hungary 1980

CONTINUOUS REVIEW INVENTORY MODELS WITH STOCHASTIC LEAD-TIME

YVO M. I. DIRICKX[1] and DANIELLE KOEVOETS[2]

[1] *Twente University of Technology, Enschede, The Netherlands*
[2] *Catholic University of Louvain, Louvain, Belgium*

1. THE GENERAL MODEL (M)

The objective of this paper is to present some results on continuous review

inventory models with stochastic lead-time under varying assumptions con-

cerning the demand process and the lead-time distribution. It will be con-

venient to formulate a general model, referred to as (M), of which the

models discussed in Sections 2-4 will be special cases. In Section 5 a

different type of model will be considered (with (s,S)-policies). The paper

concludes with some comparisons. Now we turn to the description of the

general model. To do so, we specify (i) the demand process, (ii) the ordering

process, and (iii) the cost structure.

The demand process

Consider a probability space (Ω, J, P) and random variables

$$X_n : \Omega \to \overline{M}, \quad {}^{*)}$$
$$T_n : \Omega \to R_+, \quad {}^{**)}$$

such that $T_0 = 0$, $T_n \leq T_{n+1}$ for $n = 1, 2, \ldots$ with $T_n \to \infty$ a.s., where T_n

$*$) $\overline{M} = \{1, 2, \ldots, M\}$, $M < \infty$

$**$) Nonnegative reals

denotes the instant of the n-th demand and X_n its size; the interarrival time between successive demands is $Y_n = T_n - T_{n-1}$, the process $\{X_n, Y_n\}$ satisfies the Markov property, i.e.,

$$P(X_{n+1} = j, Y_{n+1} \leq t \mid X_0 = j_0, X_i = j_i, Y_i = t_i, i = 1, \ldots, n)$$

$$= P(X_{n+1} = j, Y_{n+1} \leq t \mid X_n = j_n), \qquad (1)$$

$$\text{for all } j, j_i \in \overline{M}, t, t_i \geq 0.$$

Note that (1) encompasses models allowing for Markovian dependency between sizes of successive demands as well as between demand size and interarrival time, and will be specialized later on.

The ordering process

Only $(S-1, S)$-policies will be considered. The lead-time of a reorder is the sum of the waiting time in a reorder queue and the service time (the service mechanism can be thought of as a repair center). Simplifying assumptions will have to be made to characterize the lead-time distribution.

The cost structure

The cost structure is linear and consists of
- an ordering cost of the form $C_0 + c_0 x$, when x items are ordered,
- a unit inventory carrying cost rate of c_1,
- a unit backorder cost rate of c_2.

The objective is to find a critical number minimizing the exspected average cost.

342

2. A MODEL WITH SEMI-MARKOVIAN DEMAND, (S-1,S) ORDERING POLICY AND EXPONEN-TIAL SERVICE MECHANISM WITH FIFO-SERVICE (K-1)

This is a model described in Koevoets [6]. How this model, referred to as (K-1), is a specialization of (M) is clear from this section's title.

The service time distribution has mean $1/\beta$. As to the cost structure note that the ordering costs are determined by the demand process and not de-pendent of S. So we evaluate the expected inventory carrying costs, $C_1(S)$, and the backorder costs, $C_2(S)$.

If now, $Z(t)$ denotes the on-hand inventory and $N(t)$ the number of units in the reorder process, we have

$$Z(t) = S - N(t). \tag{2}$$

Observe that

$$C_1(S) = c_1 \sum_{k=0}^{S} k \lim_{t\to\infty} P(Z(t) = k),$$

$$C_2(S) = c_2 \sum_{k=-\infty}^{0} k \lim_{t\to\infty} P(Z(t) = k),$$

or, in view of (2), and denoting $p_k = \lim_{t\to\infty} P(N(t) = k)$ (the limit exists under "plausible" assumptions, see below)

$$C_1(S) = c_1 \sum_{k=0}^{S} (S-k) p_k, \tag{3}$$

$$C_2(S) = c_2 \sum_{k=s} (k-S) p_k. \tag{4}$$

To obtain expressions for the p_k's, the results of Çinlar [1] were adapted for bulk arrivals in Koevoets [6]. The underlying idea is to consider a demand, say the n-th of size j with interarrival time Y_n, as j single demands where j - 1 single demands have an interarrival time of zero and 1 with an interarrival time Y_n. This simply means that $\overline{M}$ can be artificially written as

$$\underline{M} = \{1_1, 2_1, 2_2, \ldots, M_1, M_2, \ldots, M_M\}.$$

The results of Çinlar can be applied to $\underline{M}$. There is, however, a technical detail: even if the imbedded Markov chain $\{X_n\}$ defined over $\overline{M}$ is aperiodic, the imbedded Markov chain over $\underline{M}$ may be periodic in which case the limiting results of Koevoets do not apply directly. Nevertheless, Koevoets showed that

$$p_0 = 1 - (\beta\mu)^{-1} \qquad \text{(clearly assuming } \beta\mu > 1)$$

$$p_k = (\beta\mu)^{-1} \lim_{n \to \infty} P(N_n = K-1) \quad \text{for } K \geq 1,$$

(5)

where μ is the steady state expected value of the "extended" interarrival time and where N_n denotes the number of items in the reorder queue at the time of the n-th arrival in the extended process. Actually, (5) only holds under some further technical assumptions. The limiting probability of N_n, can be expressed in terms of the steady-state probabiliting vector of the extended chain, denoted by α, and the matrices Γ and T whose elements are rather complicated. The elements of Γ are the (distinct) roots, say $q_i(s,w)$, of an equation of the form $\det[zI - wA(s+\beta-\beta z)] = 0$ evaluated in $s = 0$, $w = 1$ where $A(\cdot)$ is the matrix of Laplace transforms of the semi-Markov matrix associated with the extended demand process. The elements of T are obtained from the reduced adjoint matrix of $g_i(s,w)I - w A(s+\beta-\beta g_i(s,w))$ again evaluated at $s = 0$, $w = 1$. The technical details are contained in Çinlar [1, p. 372], and the expression takes on the following form:

$$\lim_{n \to \infty} P(N_n = k-1) = \alpha T^{-1}(I-\Gamma)\Gamma^k T\underline{1}'.$$

(6)

344

From (3)-(6), every (S-1),S) ordering policy can be evaluated - at least from a theoretical point of view. Needless to say that for realistically sized models the computational burden becomes overwhelming.

3. (K-1) WITH A COMPOUND POISSON DEMAND PROCESS (K-2)

Here we specialize (K-1), by noting that the interarrival times in a compound Possion process are independent, identically exponentially distributed (with parameter λ), and that the demand sizes are also i.i.d. random variables with

$$\text{Prob}(X_n = j) = f_j \qquad\qquad j \in \overline{M}.$$

It can be shown (recall (5) and (6)) that:

(i)
$$\alpha = (\alpha_{i_k}) = (\frac{f_i}{\delta})$$

with $\delta = E[X_n]$,

(ii)
$$\mu = (\lambda\delta)^{-1},$$

see Koevoets [6].

In view of (6), one is still left with the computation of Γ and T which is still not a trivial task but manageable for reasonable sized problems. If $\overline{M} = \{1,2\}$ a complete analytical solution can be obtained (see also Gross, and Harris [4]). In fact, it is relatively straightforward to show that (6) reduces to

$$\lim_{n\to\infty} P(N_n = k) = \frac{[1-(z_1+z_2)+z_1 z_2][z_1^{k+1}-z_2^{k+1}+f_2(z_1^k-z_2^k)]}{(1+f_2)\,(z_1-z_2)} \tag{7}$$

where z_1 and z_2 are the roots of

$$-\frac{\beta}{\lambda} z^2 + z + f_2 = 0.$$

345

Of course, (7) can be computed recursively, and finding an optimal $(S-1,S)$-policy is straightforward.

4. $(K-1)$ WITH EXPONENTIAL INTERARRIVAL TIME WITH DEPENDENCE ON PRECEEDING DEMAND-SIZE; $\overline{M} = \{1,2\}$ $(K-3)$

Here it is assumed that

$$P(Y_n \leq t \mid X_{n-1} = 1) = 1 - e^{-\lambda_1 t},$$
$$P(Y_n = t \mid X_{n-2} = 2) = 1 - e^{-\lambda_2 t}.$$

It can be shown that

$$\mu = \frac{1}{\delta} \left(\frac{f_1}{\lambda_1} + \frac{f_2}{\lambda_2} \right),$$

and that (6) is of the form given in (7) with z_1 and z_2 as the roots of

$$\beta^2 z^3 - \beta(\beta+\lambda_1+\lambda_2) z^2 + \lambda_1(\lambda_2+\beta f_1) z + f_2 \lambda_2 (\beta+\lambda_1) = 0$$

satisfying $|z_i| < 1$, see Koevoets [6].

5. A MODEL WITH COMPOUND POISSON DEMAND PROCESS, (s,S)-ORDERING POLICY, NO REORDER QUEUE AND GENERAL SERVICE DISTRIBUTION $(D-K)$

The development of this section are, although related, distinct from the assumption that $(S-1,S)$ policies are used. This has the immediate impli-cation that we can no more concentrate on the properties of the demand process alone. Since the results of this section are widely known, see , e.g., Dirickx - Koevoets [3] and Gross - Harris [5], a brief review will suffice. We discuss the D - K model.

No reorder queue is assumed and the lead-time distribution is simply a "well-defined" distribution, say $G(t)$, which is assumed to be independent of the order size (this is consistent with the absence of queues).

A restrictive assumption is needed to obtain workable results, namely:

Assumption. No orders can overlap, i.e., if an order is outstanding the next order can only be placed after the arrival of the outstanding order. The overall cost rate is now

$$C(s,S) = C_0(s,S) + C_1(s,S) + C_2(s,S),$$

since ordering costs can no more be neglected and overall costs are dependent on two critical numbers.

It can be shown that (involving results from Markov renewal theory) that

$$C_0(s,S) = \frac{C_0 + c_o(S - \sum_{j \leq s} j \frac{\pi_j}{\sum_{j \leq s} \pi_j}) \sum_{j \leq s} \pi_j}{\sum_{j=s+1}^{S} \pi_j(m_j - m') + m'},$$

$$C_1(s,S) = c_1 \sum_{j=0}^{S} j P_j^*,$$

$$C_2(s,S) = c_2 \sum_{j=-\infty}^{0} j P_j^*,$$

where

$$m_j = \begin{cases} \int_0^\infty t\, dG(t) \quad (= m') & j \leq s, \\[2ex] \frac{1}{\lambda} & j = s + 1, \\[2ex] \frac{1}{\lambda}(1 + \sum_{k=1}^{j-s-1} \sum_{n=1}^{k} f_k^{(n)}) & j > s + 1 \end{cases}$$

($f_k^{(n)}$ denotes the n-fold convolution of the demand-size distribution); the π_j's are the steady state probabilities associated with the Markov chain $\{z_n\}$ - z_n denotes the inventory level at the time of arrival of the n-th order, and can be computed very easily (see Dirickx - Koevoets [3], Lemma 2); furthermore

$$P_j^* = \lim_{t \to \infty} P(Z(t) = j / Z(0) = i),$$

which, again, can be computed rather easily (see D - K [3] , Theorem 1 and Lemma 5).

If, for instance, $G(t) = 1 - e^{-\mu t}$, results simplify considerably.

6. SOME COMPARISONS

Models of the type considered in Sections 1-4 (S-1,S) and of the type of Section 5 (s,S) deal with different types of methodologies. "(S-1,S)-models" can deal with complex reorderingmechanisms and heavily rely on queueing theory whereas the complexities of "(s,S)-models" can be handled rather satisfactorily by using results from Markov renewal theory. For comparisons with other existing models we can refer to Dirickx - Koevoets [3] and Koevoets [6].

REFERENCES

[1] Çinlar, E., "Queues with Semi-Markovian Arrivals", Journal of Applied Probability, 4, 365-379, (1967).

[2] Çinlar, E., "Markov Reneval Theory", Management Science, 21, 727-752, (1975).

[3] Dirickx, Y.M.I. and D. Koevoets, "Continuous Review Inventory Model with Compound Poisson Demand Process and Stochastic Lead Time", Naval Research Logistics Quarterly, 24, 577-585, (1977).

[4] Gross, D., and C.M. Harris, "On One-for-One Ordering in Inventory Policies with State-Dependent Leadtimes", Operations Research, 19, 735-760, (1971).

[5] Gross, D., and C.M. Harris, "Continuous-Review (s,S) Inventory Models with State-Dependent Leadtimes", Management Science, 19, 567-574, (1973).

[6] D. Koevoets, "A Stochastic Inventory Model with Semi-Markovian Demand", Research Report 7711, Dept. of Applied Economcis, K.U. Leuven, (1977).

Proc. First Int. Symp. on Inventories
Budapest, Hungary 1980

A SPARE PARTS INVENTORY PROBLEM WITH SEASONAL FLUCTUATIONS

L. GERENCSÉR, GY. GYEPESI and F. URBÁNSZKI

Computer and Automation Institute, Hungarian Academy of Sciences, Budapest, Hungary

The purpose of this paper is to give a case study of a practical study of a practical inventory problem. The problem arose in a large agricultural company situated in Nádudvar, East Hungary. This company is responsible to supply about 300 smaller agricultural cooperatives and companies with machines and spare parts for agricultural machines produced by the John Deere Company. The demand processes have heavy seasonal fluctuations, which makes standard methods hard to apply.

The contact between Nádudvar and John Deere Co. has the following main characteristics. Orders can be placed every week. The lead time, i.e. the time between placing and receiving an order may be three weeks or three months. The first kind of orders may make up 20% of the total annual order.

The equipments arriving in Hungary are stored in a special store until they are sold. All machines and spare parts in this special store are the property of John Deere Co. Their prices are paid only when they are actually sold to some of the smaller companies. The consequence of this agreement was that Nádudvar was not motivated to keep the inventory level low. Therefore some additional constraints on the maximum inventory level

351

were introduced by John Deere Co. These constraints work well if the demand process is uniform, but they are unsuitable when heavy seasonal fluctuations are present.

Therefore we propose a new strategy. The requirements on the new strategy are:

- taking into account seasonal fluctuations,
- low inventory level,
- easy implementation.

As for the second demand, the inventory level is evaluated by John Deere in the following way: if the ratio (annual turnover):(average inventory level) is at least 4, then the inventory level is acceptably low.

In the new strategy we shall place orders monthly.

Let us describe our strategy. For a specific article let

$x(t)$ demand of t-th month

$S(t)$ inventory state after placing an order at the beginning of month t

$\xi(t)$ physical inventory at the end of month t.

The inventory state $S(t)$ is the sum of the physical inventory plus the orders that has been placed up to time t. The lead time is three months S t is realized as physical inventory by the beginning of month t+3. Therefore we have

$$\xi(t+3) = S(t) - x(t) - x(t+1) - x(t+2) - x(t+3). \qquad /1/$$

The optimal choice for $S(t)$ would be such that $\xi(t+3)$ becomes O. As at time t future demands are not known, we propose the strategy

$$S(t) = \hat{x}(t) + \hat{x}(t+1) + \hat{x}(t+2) + \hat{x}(t+3), \qquad /2/$$

352

where $\hat{x}(t)$ denotes a suitable predicted value of $x(t)$. If $S(t)$ is greater than $\xi(t-1)$, then $S(t) = \xi(t-1)$, i.e. no order is placed.

There are not sufficient data to perform a refined statistical analysis of the past. Therefore, the predicted values are given by experts with great experience.

The computations for this strategy are very simple, and the strategy is computationally feasible even for those 1000 articles, which make out 40% of the annual capital turnover.

The simulation results have shown that the new strategy ensures a good supply with low inventory costs and it will be used in a one year experimental period.

23

Proc. First Int. Symp. on Inventories
Budapest, Hungary 1980

RELIABILITY TYPE INVENTORY MODELS WITH ORDERING TIME LIMIT

H.-J. GIRLICH and H.-U. KÜENLE

Karl Marx University of Leipzig, Leipzig, GDR

1. Introduction

Most inventory models are concerned with the analysis of systems in which some kinds of costs arise, and are subject to control. But in practice the determination of shortage cost is very difficult. That is why in the early 1960's Hungarian scientists began to construct the so-called reliability type models. The inventory problem in this kind of model is to control the reliability of the system characterized by the probability that no excess demands arise in the time interval T:

$$\propto (z,a) := P \ (\ \sup_{t \in T} (\beta_t - \delta_t(z) - a) \leqq 0), \qquad (1)$$

where β_t is the cumulative demand and $\delta_t(z)$ the total delivery of stock up to the time t.

In the models studied by Prékopa (1973) and Prékopa/Kelle (1978) only the initial stock level a is the decision variable and the delivery process $(\delta_t)_{t \in T}$ is a non-controllable stochastic process. Our goal is to extend the decision rules. We proceed from the ordering time limit condition found in the management of the G.D.R. economy which is analysed by Klemm (1980), and ask for a static ordering rule, ensuring with a prescribed probability that during the time T no shortage occurs. We consider three special models.

Using Model I we show that even under very strong conditions on the demand process the criterion given by Eq.(1) generates considerable numerical inconvenience. In the two other models we take an easier criterion based on

$$\alpha_i(z,a) := P\ (\sup_{t \in T_i}\ (\beta_t - \delta_t(z)-a) \leqq 0),\ i=1,\ldots,n, \qquad (2)$$

obtained from Eq. (1) by decomposing T.

Model II describes a simple system with a deterministic delivery process and a stochastic demand process which may be a good adaptation to different constructions of the production plan

Model III consists of a special stochastic delivery process and a Poisson process as a demand process.

2. The delivery process

In an inventory system with ordering time limit the replenishment action is initiated at time $t_0 = 0$. At this time the decision-maker has to order n quantities $z_1,\ldots,z_n$. The quantity z_i arrives after the passage of a deterministic or stochastic leadtime of $t_i - t_0 \geqq 1 > 0$ time units, i.e. at time t_i the order quantity $z_i \geqq 0$ is available. The quantity z_0 is ordered before t_0 and arrives in the period $(t_0, t_0 + 1)$.

Thus, the delivery process of an ordering time limit model is realized in the simple form

$$\delta_t(z) = \sum_{k=0}^{i} z_k =: v_i \text{ for } t \in T_i = \begin{cases} [1,t_1),\ i=0 \\ [t_i,t_{i+1}),\ i=1,\ldots,n \end{cases} \qquad (3)$$

with $t_0 < t_1 < t_2 < \ldots < t_{n+1}$.

3. The reliabilities

First of all, the demand process $(\beta_t)_{t \geqslant 0}$ may be a stochastic process with left-continuous and monotonically nondecreasing sample paths and $\beta_0 = 0$. If we choose a decomposition of $T = [1,t_{n+1})$ and a delivery process according to Section 2, using the inventory process

356

$$\eta_t(z,a) := a + \delta_t(z) - \beta_t,$$

we obtain for the reliability in view of Eq. (1)

$$\alpha(z,a) = P\ (\inf_{t \in T} \eta_t(z,a) \geqq 0)$$

$$= P\ (\min_{i=1,\ldots,n+1} \eta_{t_i-0}(z,a) \geqq 0)$$

$$= P\ (\max\ (U_1,\ldots,U_{n+1}) \leqq a) =: q(a/z), \qquad (4)$$

where $U_k = \sum_{i=1}^{k} X_i$, $\quad k=1,\ldots,n+1 \qquad (5a)$

with

$$X_{i+1} = \begin{cases} \beta_{t_1} - z_0, & i=0 \\ \beta_{t_{i+1}} - \beta_{t_i} - z_i, & i=1,\ldots,n \end{cases} \qquad (5b)$$

For the reduced reliabilities we have in view of Eq.(2)

$$\alpha_i(z,a) = P\ (\inf_{t \in T_i} \eta_t(z,a) \geqq 0)$$

$$= P\ (\eta_{t_{i+1}-0}(z,a) \geqq 0)$$

$$= P\ (\beta_{t_{i+1}} \leqq a + v_i) =: p_i(a + v_i), \qquad (6)$$

where $p_0, p_1,\ldots,p_n$ are monotonically nondecreasing functions.

4. Optimization

In the reliability type inventory models constructed by
A. Prékopa and co-workers for the safety-stock level a an
optimization problem is to be solved, which we specialize
to

$$a = \min\ ! \qquad (7)$$
$$q(a/z) \geqq 1 - \varepsilon,$$

where q given by Eqs. (4), (5) is a monotonically non-decreasing function of a and $z \in \mathbb{R}_+^{n+1}$ is fixed.

In the ordering time limit models the level a and the quantity z_0 shall not be controlled. But for the order quantities $z_1,\ldots,z_n$ we have to solve the optimization problem

$$\sum_{i=0}^{n} z_i = \min \ !$$

$$\alpha_i(z,a) \geqq 1 - \varepsilon \ , \quad z_i \geqq 0, \quad i = 1,\ldots,n \ . \tag{8}$$

Using Eqs. (3) and (6) wo obtain an equivalent problem

$$v_n = \min \ !$$

$$p_i(a+v_i) \geqq 1 - \varepsilon \ , \quad v_{i+1} \geqq v_i \geqq 0, \quad i = 1,\ldots,n \tag{9}$$

and the iterative solution

$$z_i' = \inf \ (z_i = 0/p_i(a+z_0' +\ldots+ z_{i-1}' + z_i) \geqq 1 - \varepsilon) \tag{10}$$

$i = 1,\ldots,n$, where $z_0' = z_0$ and a are prescribed.

5. Model I

We consider an inventory system under the following assumptions:

(i) The demands $B_0, B_1, \ldots, B_n$ in periods $T_0', T_1, \ldots, T_n$ for a single product are independent random variables with probability density functions $f_0, f_1, \ldots, f_n$.

(ii) Excess demand is backlogged. $- T_0' = [t_0, t_1)$.

(iii) A delivery process according to Section 2 and with fixed order quantities is given.

(iv) The safety-stock level satisfying the optimization problem (7) is to be determined.

This model leads for the reliability q given by Eq. (4) with

$$X_{i+1} = B_i - z_i, \quad i=0,1,\ldots,n \tag{11}$$

to the expression

$$q(a/z) = \int\ldots\int_{R(a)} \prod_{i=1}^{n+1} f_{i-1}(x_i + z_{i-1})\, dx_i,$$

where the region of integration

$$R(a) = (x_1,\ldots,x_{n+1}) / \sum_{k=1}^{i} x_k \leqq a, \quad i=1,\ldots,n+1$$

may be transformed to $\mathbb{R}_+^{n+1}$ according to

$$y_1 = a - x_1, \quad y_i = y_{i-1} - x_i, \quad i=2,\ldots,n+1 .$$

As the transformed multiple integral we obtain

$$q(a/z) = \int_0^\infty f_0(a+z_0-y_1)\, G_n(y_1,z)\, dy_1, \tag{12}$$

where the function

$$G_n(y_1,z) = \int_0^\infty\ldots\int_0^\infty \prod_{i=1}^{n} f_i(y_i-y_{i+1}+z_i)\, dy_{i+1} \tag{13}$$

can generally be calculated only approximately by a quadrature formula or by Monte–Carlo methods.

6. An example

In this section we determine the optimal safety-stock level of Model I for a very special case.

We consider a decomposition of T consisting of only two parts. Let the demands B_0, B_1 obey a normal probability law with parameters

$$m_k = E(B_k), \quad \sigma_k^2 = var(B_k), \quad k=0,1 .$$

We use the symbol φ to denote the probability density function of the standard normal law, i.e.

$$\varphi(x) = (2\pi)^{-\frac{1}{2}} \exp(-\tfrac{1}{2} x^2),$$

and Φ denotes the corresponding distribution function.

Then we have

$$G_1(y_1,z) = \int_0^\infty f_1(y_1-y_2+z_1)\, dy_2 = \Phi\left(\frac{y_1+z_1-m_1}{\sigma_1}\right).$$

Consequently, the reliability is given by

$$q(a/z) = \frac{1}{\sigma_0}\int_0^\infty \varphi\left(\frac{a+z_0-y_1-m_0}{\sigma_0}\right)\Phi\left(\frac{y_1+z_1-m_1}{\sigma_1}\right) dy_1,$$

and may be obtained as a simple expression in the case

$$z_0 = m_0, \quad z_1 = m_1, \quad \sigma_0 = \sigma_1 = 1$$

using the table of integrals given by Khadzhi (1971):

$$q(a/z^0) = \frac{1}{2}\left(\Phi(a) + \Phi^2\left(\frac{a}{\sqrt{2}}\right)\right),$$

where the decision z^0 is of the form $z^0 = (m_0,m_1)$. Therefore, the optimal safety-stock level a' is the unique
solution of the reliability equation

$$\Phi(a) + \Phi^2\left(\frac{a}{\sqrt{2}}\right) = 2(1-\varepsilon). \tag{14}$$

7. Model II

The inventory system of this section modifies that of
Section 5 by passing from the reliability given by Eq. (1)
to the reliabilities of Eq. (2). Thus, in the Model II
only the assumptions (iii), (iv) of Model I will be
changed, and T_0 will be substituted for T_0'.

(iii) A delivery process according to Section 2
      with prescribed z_0 and initial stock a is given.

(iv) A decision $z' = (z_1',\dots,z_n')$ solving the
      optimization problem (9) is to be chosen.

Because of the assumed independence of the demands and
Eq.(6) we determine the function p_i as a convolution of
the density functions $f_0, f_1,\dots,f_i$ by the recurrence
formula

$$p_i(x) = \int_{-\infty}^\infty p_{i-1}(x-u)f_i(u)\, du$$

with $p_0' = f_0$. By $k_i(s)$ we denote the corresponding lowest quantile of order s, i.e.

$$k_i(s) = \inf (x/p_i(x) = s). \qquad (15)$$

Then, in view of Eq. (9) we set

$$a + v_i^* = k_i(1 - \varepsilon), \quad i=1,\ldots,n .$$

If the sequence (p_i) is monotonically nonincreasing, i.e.

$$p_1(x) \overset{\geq}{=} p_2(x) \overset{\geq}{=} \ldots \overset{\geq}{=} p_n(x), \quad x \in \mathbb{R},$$

$$\qquad (16)$$

and holds $k_1(1 - \varepsilon) = a + z_0$

then we have the optimal order quantities

$$z_1' = k_1(1- \varepsilon) - a - z_0 ,$$
$$z_i' = k_i(1- \varepsilon) - k_{i-1}(1- \varepsilon), \quad i=2,\ldots,n . \qquad (17)$$

In the normal case

$$p_i(x) = \Phi\left(\frac{x-\widetilde{m}_i}{\widetilde{\sigma}_i}\right) , \quad \widetilde{m}_i = \sum_{j=0}^{i} m_j, \quad \widetilde{\sigma}_i^2 = \sum_{j=0}^{i} \sigma_j^2$$

it follows immediately that

$$k_i(s) = \widetilde{m}_i + \widetilde{\sigma}_i k(s), \qquad (18)$$

where $k(s)$ fulfill the equation

$$\Phi (k(s)) = .s ,$$

and the Eq. (17) under $z_0 = m_0$ may be reduced to

$$z_1' = m_1 - a + \widetilde{\sigma}_1 k(1- \varepsilon) \qquad (19)$$
$$z_i' = m_i + (\widetilde{\sigma}_i - \widetilde{\sigma}_{i-1}) k(1- \varepsilon), \quad i=2,\ldots,n .$$

If Eq. (16) is not satisfied, we obtain from Eq. (10) for the optimal order quantities

$$z_i' = \begin{cases} 0, & \text{for } a+z_0' +\ldots+ z_{i-1}' \geq \tilde{m}_i + \tilde{\sigma}_i \cdot k(1-\varepsilon) \\ \tilde{m}_i + \tilde{\sigma}_i k(1-\varepsilon) - (a+z_0' +\ldots+ z_{i-1}'), & \text{else.} \end{cases} \tag{20}$$

The reader who is interested in numerical examples and economical interpretations of Model II is referred to Girlich (1980) and Klemm (1980).

8. Model III

In our last section we consider an inventory system where the inventory is replenished at random delivery. We shall proceed from the following assumptions:

(i) The demand process is a Poisson process $(N(t))_{t \geq 0}$ with parameter λ .

(ii) Excess demand is backlogged.

(iii) A delivery process according to Section 2 is given, where the delivery time t_i is uniformly distributed between r_i and $r_{i+1} = r_i + \frac{1}{n}$, $i=1,\ldots,n$, and $r_1 = 1$.

(iv) A decision $z' = (z_1',\ldots,z_n')$ solving the optimization problem (9) is to be chosen, where z_0 and a are prescribed.

In order to find the optimal order quantities, we have to determine the p_i using the formula of total probability

$$p_i(v) = \int_{t_0}^{\infty} P(N(t_{i+1} - 0) \leq v / t_{i+1} = t) d\, P(t_{i+1} \leq t).$$

For $v = m \in N$ we obtain

$$p_i(m) = \int_{r_{i+1}}^{r_{i+2}} \exp(-\lambda t) \sum_{j=0}^{m} \frac{(\lambda t)^j}{j!}\, n\, dt$$

$$= \frac{n}{\lambda} \exp(-\lambda (1+\tfrac{i}{n})) \sum_{j=0}^{m} (h(j/\lambda (1+\tfrac{i}{n})) - e^{-\frac{\lambda}{n}} h(j/\lambda (1+\tfrac{i+1}{n})))$$

$$\text{where } h(j/y) := \sum_{k=0}^{j} \frac{y^k}{k!} . \tag{21}$$

362

If we successively compute $p_i(m)$ for $m = 0,1,2,\ldots$ we arrive at a number n_i with the property

$$p_i(n_i-1) < 1 - \varepsilon \, , \ p_i(n_i) \geqq 1 - \varepsilon \, . \tag{22}$$

These numbers $n_1, n_2, \ldots, n_n$ determine the optimal order quantities in view of Eq. (10) and $z_0' = z_0$ to

$$z_i' = \begin{cases} 0, \ \text{for } a + z_0' + \ldots + z_{i-1}' \geqq n_i \\ n_i - (a + z_0' + \ldots + z_{i-1}'), \ \text{else}. \end{cases} \tag{23}$$

Finally, we give a numerical example (cf. Küenle (1980))

$$\lambda = 2, \ n = 4, \ l = \tfrac{1}{4}, \ \varepsilon = 0,1 \tag{24}$$

m \ i	1	2	3	4
0	0,290	0,175	0,106	0,065
1	0,645	0,479	0,344	0,241
2	0,867	0,743	0,610	0,482
3	0,960	0,898	0,809	0,698
4		0,966	0,921	0,863
5				0,950
n_i	3	4	4	5

For $a + z_0 = 3$, it follows from (23) $z_1' = z_3' = 0$, $z_2' = z_4' = 1$.

9. References

Girlich, H.-J. (1980): Ein einfaches Bestellfristenmodell. Sitzungsbericht "Bestellfristenproblematik",
Mathematische Gesellschaft der DDR, Alt-Reddevitz.

Khadzhi, P.I. (1971): The Probability Integral,
Kishinev, 398p.

Klemm, H. (1980): Der Bestellvorgang bei Bestellfristen
- eine Problemanalyse. First Symposium on Inventory,
Budapest.

Küenle, H.-U. (1980): Ein Bestellfristenmodell mit zu-
fälligen Lieferzeitpunkten. Sitzungsbericht
"Bestellfristenproblematik", Alt-Reddevitz.

Prékopa, A. (1973): Generalization of the Theorem of
Smirnov with Application to a Reliability Type
Inventory Problem. Mathematische Operationsfor-
schung und Statistik, 4, 283.

Prékopa, A. and P. Kelle (1978): Reliability Type
Inventory Models Based on Stochastic Programming.
Mathematical Programming Study 9, 43.

Proc. First Int. Symp. on Inventories
Budapest, Hungary 1980

A SIMPLE METHOD OF DETERMINING
NEARLY OPTIMUM ORDER QUANTITIES
FOR A MULTI-PRODUCT
SINGLE-SUPPLIER SYSTEM

SURESH KUMAR GOYAL

The Polytechnic of Wales, Pontypridd, UK

Abstract

In this paper a simple method has been presented for determining nearly
optimum order quantities for products which are jointly procured
from a single supplier.   The orders are placed upon the supplier at
equal intervals (T), and, each product is replenished at equal intervals
which is restricted to be an integer multiple of T.

An example has been solved to illustrate the method.

Introduction

The problem of determining economic order quantities for a multi-product
single supplier system is akin to the problem of determining economic
packaging frequency for an unpackaged product which is packaged into a
number of packaging sizes immediately after manufacture.   In the
published literature it has been invariably assumed that the cost of
placing a purchase order consists of two components: one which is
independent of the number of products on order and the other which
depends on the products being ordered in a particular order.   Hence,

reduction in cost can be achieved by ordering products jointly. In the published papers, it was assumed that orders are placed on the supplier at equal time intervals, see Goyal (1973, 1974, 1979), Nocturne (1973), Shu (1971) and Silver (1976). Andres et al. (1976) pointed out that when there are more than two products it may not be always optimal to place orders at equal time intervals, furthermore, it may not even be optimal to order each product at equal time intervals. However, in this paper it is being assumed that orders are placed at equal time intervals on the supplier in order to have a simpler operating policy for the buyer as well as for the supplier.

Silver (1976) suggested a heuristic method of determining economic packaging frequencies of jointly replenished items. His method was, however, improved upon by Goyal et al. (1979). In this paper a further improvement in Silver's heuristic method is being incorporated.

An example has been solved and the suggested method has been compared with other heuristic methods.

The Mathematical Models

The following assumptions are being made:

1. Lead time for procuring supplies is zero.

2. Stock outs are not permitted.

3. Time horizon is infinite.

4. Minimisation of cost is taken as the criterion of optimality.

5. The purchase orders are placed at equal time intervals.

6. Demand for each product is constant over time.

7. Each product is ordered at equal time intervals.

366

The following notations are being used in the paper:

n number of items

S that part of cost of placing a purchase order which is
   independent of the number of items on order

T time interval between successive purchase orders (in years),
   for the i th item

Q_i demand per year

h_i stock holding cost per item per year

S_i that part of the cost of placing a purchase order which must
   be incurred whenever the item is ordered

D_i the order quantity.

Let the i th product be ordered in every K_i th purchase order (Note that K_i is restricted to have only integer values), then the total annual variable cost, $V(T, K_i)$ is given by

$$V(T, K_i) = (S + \sum_{i=1}^{n} S_i/K_i)/T + \frac{T}{2} \sum_{i=1}^{n} Q_i H_i K_i \qquad \ldots \ldots (1)$$

At a given value of T, the variable cost for the i th item can be minimised by obtaining $K_i = K_i(T)$ from the following condition:

$$K_i(T).(K_i(T) - 1) \leq \frac{2S_i}{Q_i h_i T^2} \leq K_i(T).(K_i(T) + 1) \qquad \ldots \ldots (2)$$

(See Goyal (1974) for the derivation of such a condition).

For a given set of $K_i(T)$ values the minimum annual variable cost is given by:

$$V^*(K_i(T)) = [2(S + \sum_{i=1}^{n} S_i/K_i(T)) \; (\sum_{i=1}^{n} Q_i h_i K_i(T))]^{\frac{1}{2}} \qquad \ldots\ldots (3)$$

The economic order quantity for the i th product is given by:

$$D^*_i(T) = Q_i \; [2(S + \sum_{i=1}^{n} S_i/K_i(T))/ \sum_{i=1}^{n} Q_i h_i K_i(T)]^{\frac{1}{2}} \qquad \ldots\ldots (4)$$

Silver (1976) suggested that in order to determine K_i values by (2), first identify the item for which the ratio $2S_i/Q_i h_i$ is least (he called it as item 1) and then determine $K_i(T)$ value for each product by (2) after substituting $(2(S+S_i)/Q_i h_i)$ for T^2.

Goyal et al. suggested that the $K_i(T)$ value for each product be obtained after substituting least value of $(2(S+S_i)/Q_i h_i)$ for T^2 in (2).
Their suggested approach resulted in equally good or better results as compared to Silver's method for the 40 examples examined by them.

In this paper the following approach is being suggested for determining T^2 value for substitution in the condition given by (2) for determining $K_i(T)$.

Step 1.　Determine $\text{Min}_i \dfrac{(2(S + S_i))}{Q_i h_i} = T^2_0$.

Step 2.　Arrange products in ascending order of $2S_i/Q_i h_i$ ratio.

Step 3.　Determine the m th product which satisfies the condition

$$\frac{2S_m}{Q_m h_m} \leq T^2_0 \leq \frac{2S_{m+1}}{Q_m h_m}$$

Step 4.   Determine T^2 as follows:

$$T^2 = \frac{2(S + \sum\limits_{i=1}^{m} S_i)}{\sum\limits_{i=1}^{m} Q_i h_i}$$

The value of T^2 as obtained in step (4) is then substituted in the condition given by (2) and hence $K_i(T)$ values for each product is obtained.   The minimum annual cost and the order quantity for each product can be obtained on applying (3) and (4) respectively.

An Example

The data for the example is given in the following table:

TABLE 1

Data for the Example

Item No.	S_i	$Q_i h_i$
1	8	20000
2	13	30000
3	10	18000
4	9	15000
5	8	10000
6	10	4800
7	8	2000
8	8	1500
9	9	1125
10	8	560

S = 45 per order

Determination of K_i values by Silver's Method   METHOD-1

$$T^2 = \frac{2(S + S_i)}{Q_i h_i} = \frac{2(45+8)}{20000} = 0.0053$$

On applying the decision rule (2) the $K_i(T)$ values are obtained as
$1,1,1,1,1,1,1,1,2,2$ and 2 for $i = 1,2,---10$.   The annual cost of
this policy equals 2560.47.

Determination of K_i values by Goyal and Belton's Method   METHOD-2

$T^2 = \text{Min}(2(S+S_i)/Q_i h_i) = 0.003866$ on applying the decision rule (2) the
$K_i(T)$ values are obtained as $1,1,1,1,1,1,2,2,2$ and 3.   The annual
cost of this policy equals 2534.51.

Determination of K_i values by the method given in this paper   METHOD-3

As $\quad \dfrac{2S_5}{Q_5 h_5} \leqslant 0.003866 \leqslant \dfrac{2S_6}{Q_6 h_6}$

so $\quad T^2 = \dfrac{2\left(S + \sum\limits_{i=1}^{5} S_i\right)}{\sum\limits_{i=1}^{5} Q_i h_i} = 0.002$

The following $K_i(T)$ values are obtained on applying the decision rule
given by (2): $1,1,1,1,1,2,2,2,3$ and 4 for $i = 1,2,---,10$.   The annual
cost of this policy equals 2528.72.   The order quantities can be
obtained on applying (4).

The following table gives the summary of results obtained for a sample
of 40 test problems:

TABLE 2

Summary of the results of 40 Test Problems.

Number of Problems		Number of examples where optimal solution was achieved by method			Number of examples having penalty cost less than 0.05% by method			Average % Cost penalty by method		
		1	2	3	1	2	3	1	2	3
4	10	4	4	8	6	6	9	0.27	0.27	0.10
5	10	2	3	5	4	5	9	0.80	0.50	0.12
10	10	1	2	4	2	3	8	1.30	0.75	0.20
20	10	0	0	2	0	1	6	2.00	0.91	0.31

CONCLUDING REMARKS

The method suggested in this paper is capable of achieving nearly optimal order quantities for items procured from a single supplier as is shown by Table 2.

REFERENCES

1.   Andres, F.M., and Emmon, H (1976): On the Optimal Packaging Frequency of Products Jointly Replenished, Management Science, 22, 1165.

2.   Goyal, S.K (1973): Determination of Economic Packaging Frequency for Items Jointly Replenished, Management Science, 20, 232.

3a.   Goyal, S.K. (1974): Determination of Optimum Packaging Frequency of Items Jointly Replenished, Management Science, 21, 436.

Proc. First Int. Symp. on Inventories
Budapest, Hungary 1980

AN IMPROVED PROCEDURE FOR DETERMINING INVENTORY HOLDING COSTS

ROBERT W. GRUBBSTRÖM and ANDERS THORSTENSON

Linköping Institute of Technology, Linköping, Sweden

1. Introduction

The following report summarizes some results from analytical models and from simulation experiments reported in two previous papers [Grubbström, 1980; Grubbström, Thorstenson, 1980]. Apart from this is provided a new analysis of the simulation results.

The objective of the method set forth has been to provide evidence that usual accounting principles tend to give an underestimation of the capital costs associated with inventories and work-in-progress and to point at ways in which traditional accounting procedures might be improved.

The ultimate consequences of decisions in a manufacturing firm are to be found in the form of payments between the firm and its environment. Decisions that have no effect on the monetary stream at some point in time are of no economic importance. In practice, analyses of payment streams (cash flows) are usually carried out for the few infrequent decisions associated with substantial payment consequences, i.e. major investments of different kinds etc. It is argued, however, that payment consequences of the many small everyday production decisions also should be analyzed along similar lines. Payments are characterized by their amount, their temporal allocation and sometimes by additional stochastic properties.

373

It can be shown [Williams, Nassar, 1966] that the only consistent measure evaluating a payment stream, if certain basic axioms are to be satisfied, is the *net present value* (*NPV*) or some positive monotonic transformation of this value. Any such transformation would be equally useful from the point of view of making correct decisions, since the ranking of alternatives will be preserved.

However, one simple transformation translating the net present value into a constant continuous stream of payments, the *annuity stream* (*AS*), has the advantage that this stream usually can be given a direct concrete economic interpretation.

If given a series of payments a_0, a_1, ..., occurring at the times t_0, t_1, ..., the *NPV* of this series is defined as:

$$NPV = \sum_{i=0}^{\infty} a_i \, e^{-\rho t_i} \tag{1}$$

where ρ is the continuous interest rate. The annuity stream providing the same *NPV* is obtained as:

$$AS = \rho NPV = \rho \sum_{i=0}^{\infty} a_i \, e^{-\rho t_i} \tag{2}$$

which for a series of constant payments at constant intervals becomes:

$$AS = \frac{\rho a}{1 - e^{-\rho T}} = a \left(\frac{1}{T} + \frac{\rho}{2} + \frac{\rho^2 T}{12} - \frac{\rho^4 T^3}{720} \ \cdots \right) \tag{3}$$

where a is the amount of each payment and T the time interval between each pair of consecutive payments. The right-hand member being a Maclaurin expansion of the middle member, provides an economic interpretation; the first term being the payment

374

averaged out over the time interval (such as an average depre-
ciation), the second an interest on the average capital associated with this payment, the third an interest on interest, etc.
For example, with an interest rate of ρ = 20 per cent per annum
and an interval of T = 10 years, the first and second terms each
will give a contribution of 10 per cent (of a), the third a
positive contribution of 3.3 per cent and the fourth a negative
contribution of -0.22 per cent. The first two terms would then
provide an error of 13.5 per cent (too low) and the first three
terms an error of 0.9 per cent (too high).

In the case of production situations in which capital is tied
up in inventory and work-in-progress, the first term would
correspond to an average profit and the second to a first approximation of the inventory holding costs.

2. Analytical models and hypotheses

The basic idea in the foregoing section to evaluate payment
streams associated with production decisions was applied in
[Grubbström, 1980] to some simple analytical models of inventory theory.

In figure 1 two elementary cases are shown. In (a) we have the
standard situation with a periodical discrete replenishment and
constant demand and in (b) its mirror image with a constant
production rate and demand taking place in periodic batches.

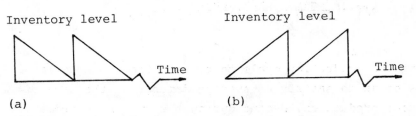

Figure 1. Two elementary inventory models

Applying the *AS*-principle to these two cases shows that inventories in case (a) should be evaluated at unit production (purchase) cost and in (b) at unit sales price. Although the (b)-section shows an unrealistic case, the example does point out that the correct evaluation depends on characteristics of the production process.

Two other analytical models are depicted in figure 2, the first being a batch production model (a) and the second a line production model (b). In the batch case, material is purchased in the beginning of the cycle, after being in inventory for some time it is manufactured during which it increases its value, and finally it is stocked and sold. Also there is one credit period provided by the supplier and one provided to the customer. The figure shows the cumulative cost to date.

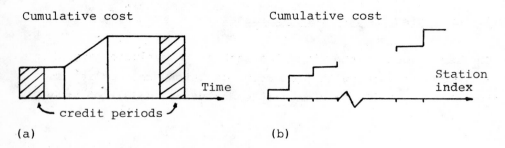

(a)   (b)

Figure 2.   Batch and line production models

If the *AS*-principle is applied to the batch case, it may be shown that the inventories on the average should be evaluated above average cost by an amount of:

$$Marginal\ profit \cdot \left(\frac{Demand\ during\ cycle}{Batch\ quantity} - \frac{1}{2} \right) \qquad (4)$$

assuming the production cycle to repeat itself at regular intervals so as to satisfy an average demand. In the case of continuous production, demand during the cycle coincides with the batch quantity which implies that in such a case the inventories should be assessed at a level of half of the marginal

376

profits above their average cost. In the normal case we would
have a cycle longer than the interval satisfied by the batch
(in any case longer than half of this interval) which means
that inventories certainly should be ascribed values above
average production cost.

In the (b)-section of figure 2 is shown the case of values being
added to the product at different stations in a production line.
Applying the AS-principle shows that inventories at a particular
station should be evaluated at sales price less remaining variable costs to be incurred at later stations. This value will
coincide with variable costs laid down in the product to date
if the sales price equals the total variable costs, i.e.when
the gross profits are zero. Hence the model indicates that
stocked items should be given a value in excess of costs incurred to date.

These analytical models have provided grounds for formulating
two basic hypotheses. On the one hand would traditional accounting procedures, only taking costs incurred to date into consideration, underestimate the correct value for determining the inventory holding costs, and secondly, one would anticipate that
the differential which should be added to costs laid down would
increase with the profit margin of the product. In order to test
these two hypotheses some simulation experiments were carried
out [Grubbström, Thorstenson, 1980].

3.   Simulation models

In order to further investigate the impact of considering payments when evaluating inventory holding costs we carried out
a simulation study thereby regarding stochastic elements underlying the payment consequences. The cases studied include two
different production system structures as shown in figure 3,
where circles denote production stations and triangles denote
intermediate buffer stocks and inventories for finished goods.
Structure (a) is a pure production line in which raw material
is at first purchased and then machined at three consecutive

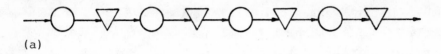

(a)

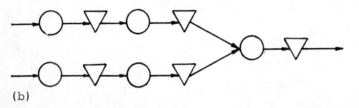

(b)

Figure 3.   Two basic production structures

work stations after which finished products are stocked into a
final inventory in order to satisfy demand. The second structure
(b) consists of two parallel sub-lines in which raw material is
purchased and the components machined at one work station in
each sub-line. The two sub-lines then merge at a third work
station, e.g. a point of assembly, whereupon the finished products are stocked in an inventory from which they finally are
sold.

For each of these two structures the simulations have been run
with respect to two different kinds of models, namely on the
one hand a queueing model using Erlang-distributed interarrival
and service times, and on the other hand a model based on the
physical flows between the stocks and inventories.

The calculation of economic consequences for the four cases
thus created has been carried out both in accordance with standard accounting procedures, first using the value added (at
variable cost) as a base for evaluating inventory holding costs,
and secondly, by considering the payments that occur at different points in time. The ultimate objective of these computations
has been to test the basic hypotheses stated above; on the one
hand that standard procedures underestimate the true inventory
holding costs, and on the other that this underestimation increases with the profit margin.

A number of variations have been included in the cost structures and in the stochastic properties of the different models.
The economic parameters introduced consist of unit purchasing
costs and unit production costs, a given interest rate and a
unit revenue parameter. No credits have been allowed.

4.   Results of simulations

As reported in [Grubbström, Thorstenson, 1980] the first of our
basic hypotheses was given an overwhelming support in all cases
simulated. This was shown using a t-parameter test and a Wil-
coxon test, both of which provided high levels of significance
in favour of the presumption that traditional practices produce
too low holding costs.

In this report, as mentioned earlier, we shall look further into
the simulation results with regard to our second basic hypothesis. Our interest in this respect is to determine characteristics of the relationship between the profit margin, defined
as *(price - variable cost)/price* and an overhead factor. This
overhead factor is the factor costs incurred should be multiplied by in order for this figure to represent the correct capital value on which the capital costs are to be computed. The
overhead *rate* used below is this factor less unity.

From theoretical considerations, we may deduce that the com-
pensatory overhead rate should be zero for a zero profit margin and infinite for a unit profit margin (zero variable costs).
Plotting the overhead rate as a function of the profit margin
(only three points are provided from each simulation case), we
obtain the typical convex pattern as shown in figure 4.

Based on analytical considerations the following mathematical
relationship is hypothesized:

$$\beta = l \, \frac{\alpha}{1-\alpha} \hspace{3cm} (5)$$

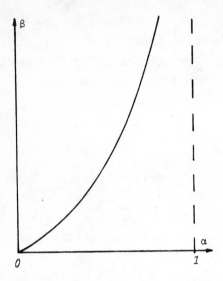

Figure 4. Typical overhead rate as function of marginal profit

where α is the profit margin, β the overhead rate and l a constant depending on other circumstances than the profit margin. It is clear that $\alpha = 0$ yields $\beta = 0$ and that $\alpha \to 1$ requires $\beta \to \infty$ which therefore satisfies our theoretical requirements. The proportional relation between $\alpha(1-\alpha)^{-1}$ and β may then easily be tested by regression analysis from which the constant will be estimated and a coefficient of determination computed.

Applying this procedure to each of the simulation results from the four cases of flow-oriented models (line production and two sub-line cases, each with two different ranges of stochastic disturbances) and from the twelve cases of queueing-oriented models (line production and two sub-line cases, each with two different mean service rates and three different values of the Erlang parameter determining the shape of the service time distribution) gave the results summarized in tables 1 and 2.

From studying the results shown in these two tables we can immediately draw the conclusion that on the one hand, the

Case	Production structure	l	R^2
1	Line	1.53 ± 0.63	0.995
2	Line	1.56 ± 0.63	0.996
3	Two sub-line	1.29 ± 0.54	0.995
4	Two sub-line	1.31 ± 0.55	0.995

Table 1. Estimated values of coefficient l and coefficient of determination R^2 in flow-oriented model cases. Confidence interval of l shown at the 95 % level of significance

Case	Production structure	l	R^2
1	Line	5.33 ± 0.96	0.999
2	Line	4.34 ± 0.75	0.999
3	Line	4.26 ± 0.67	0.999
4	Line	5.16 ± 1.04	0.999
5	Line	4.94 ± 0.93	0.999
6	Line	4.43 ± 0.73	0.999
7	Two sub-line	5.01 ± 0.70	0.999
8	Two sub-line	3.77 ± 0.50	0.999
9	Two sub-line	3.80 ± 0.43	0.999
10	Two sub-line	4.76 ± 0.79	0.999
11	Two sub-line	4.47 ± 0.65	0.999
12	Two sub-line	3.89 ± 0.46	0.999

Table 2. Estimated values of coefficient l and coefficient of determination R^2 in queueing-oriented model cases. Confidence interval of l shown at the 95 % level of significance

mathematical approach given by (5) provides an almost perfect relationship for explaining the dependence of the overhead rate β on the profit margin α (in no case does the coefficient of determination fall below 99.5 per cent), and on the other that the two different kinds of models (flow-oriented versus queueing-oriented) produce significantly different estimated values of the coefficient l, whereas this value varies only slightly between the different stochastic parameter values within each of these two sets of cases ($1.29 \leq l \leq 1.56$ in flow-oriented cases; $3.77 \leq l \leq 5.33$ in queueing-oriented cases).

An intuitive explanation of the difference in l-values is the following. In the flow-oriented cases total holding costs represent a greater share of total costs than in the queueing-oriented cases. This is due to structural discrepancies between the two models. The higher ratio of holding costs over total cost implies that a lower overhead rate β should be applied in order to arrive at a correct capital value, i.e. a correct capital cost for a given profit margin. Therefore, the values of l, which depend on other circumstances than the profit margin, such as the characteristics of the particular model that is being used, should be of a higher magnitude in the queueing-oriented cases.

5. Future research

The results reported here and in the two previous papers referred to indicate that evaluation of payment consequences from production systems may have a significant impact on the determination of capital costs of work-in-progress and inventory. Since the interest of industry in many ways focuses on these costs future research within this area would be highly momentous.

In the first place a wider spectrum of cases should be given care attention both by using an analytical approach and by using simulation approaches as the cases studied have been limited with respect to configuration as well as complexity.

In the second place further sophistication should be brought into the models, thereby enabling the possibility of drawing conclusions from more realistic settings. This could be achieved by means of simulation utilizing existing production simulation models such as the on described in [Andersson, Jönsson, 1979] in which production control in a job-shop is based on material requirements planning.

Finally, an important line of research would be to develop practical accounting procedures based on the ideas presented here that could be applied in industry. Essentially these procedures would have to be simple, compatible with traditional accounting and easy to implement.

6. References

Andersson, R, Jönsson, H, 1979, *PICSIM I: Production Inventory Control Simulator*, Research Report 44, Department of Production Economics, Linköping Institute of Technology

Emskoff, J R, Sisson, R L, 1970, *Design and Use of Computer Simulation Models*, New York: Macmillan

Grubbström, R W, 1967, On the Application of the Laplace Transform to Certain Economic Problems, *Management Science*, Vol 13, pp 558-567

Grubbström, R W, 1976, *On the Balancing of Queueing Costs and Capacity Costs Along the Assembly Line*, 5th International Seminar on Algorithms for Production Control and Scheduling, Karlovy Vary, Czechoslovakia

Grubbström, R W, 1980, A Principle for Determining the Correct Capital Costs of Work-In-Progress and Inventory, *International Journal of Production Research*, Vol 18, pp 259-271

Grubbström, R W, Lundquist, J, 1977, The Axsäter Integrated Production-Inventory System Interpreted in Terms of the Theory of Relatively Closed Systems, *Journal of Cybernetics*, Vol 7, pp 49-67

Grubbström, R W, Thorstenson, A, 1980, *Evaluation of Payment Consequences from the Control and Design of Production Systems*, 6th International Seminar on Algorithms for Production Control and Scheduling, Karlovy Vary, Czechoslovakia

Sprouse, R T, Moonitz, M, 1962, *A Tentative Set of Broad Accounting Principles for Business Enterprises*, New York: American Institute of Certified Public Accountants, pp 27 ff

Tate, T B, 1977, NPV, DCF and the EBQ, *Operational Research Quarterly*, Vol 28, pp 747-748

Williams, A C, Nassar, J I, 1966, Financial Measurement of Capital Investments, *Management Science*, Vol 12, pp 851-864

Proc. First Int. Symp. on Inventories
Budapest, Hungary 1980

RELIABILITY TYPE INVENTORY MODELS FOR RANDOM DELIVERY PROCESS

PÉTER KELLE

Computer and Automation Institute, Hungarian Academy of Sciences, Budapest, Hungary

Summary

Inventory models are formulated in which the order given for the supply of a period arrives until the end of the period but not at one occasion - as supposed usually - but in random time points of the period in random amounts. We give the initial stock level that ensures a continuous material supply in the whole period on a given probability level. Such models have been constructed by some Hungarian authors. We give generalizations of these models which we need for special applications.

1. A practical inventory problem and its model

First we give a general model formulation of an inventory control problem. The factory considered has continuous production and a periodic review inventory system. At every review point an order is given for the supply of the continuous demand of a period with length T, say $[0,T]$. This order amount is denoted by C. The supplier undertakes to deliver

25

the amount C until the end of the period, but it is not to be forced to deliver it in a given time point. There is a typical case in which the delivery happens not at one occasion, as it is assumed by the conventional inventory models, but in random amounts in n equidistant time points of the period $[0,T]$. These delivery time points are usually randomly disturbed, too. The factory plans an initial stock as safety stock for each period to protect itself against the random disturbances in the delivery and demand process. The problem is how to give the minimal level of the initial stock which ensures the continuous supply in the whole period on a given service level.

We formulate a general version of chance constrained inventory models, the so-called reliability type inventory model for m different commodities as follows

$$\text{minimize } f\left(\underline{M}\right), \quad \text{subject to}$$

$$P\left(\sup_{0\leq t\leq T}\left\{\xi_j(t) - \eta_j(t)\right\} \leq M_j \; ; \; j=1,\ldots,m\right) \geq 1-\varepsilon \qquad /1.1/$$

$$\underline{0} \leq \underline{M} \; , \quad \underline{M} \in D.$$

where $\xi_j(t)$ denotes the cumulative amount of demand and $\eta_j(t)$ the cumulative amount of delivery in the time interval $[0,t]$ $/0 \leq t \leq T/$ for commodity $j /j=1,\ldots,m/$, which are stochastic processes; $f(\underline{M})$ is the cost function depending on the initial stock level vector $\underline{M}' = (M_1,\ldots,M_m)$; D is an m-dimensional set, defined by the constraints /e.g. capacity or investment constraint/. The service level is given by the prescribed joint probability $1-\varepsilon$ of the continuous material supply in $[0,T]$, which is formulated in the chance constraint.

The first model of this type was formulated by A.Prékopa /1965/ and M.Ziermann /1963/. Later on some other papers e.g. Z.László /1973/, A.Móritz /1978/ were published, containing solution methods for the one-commodity version of this model under different assumptions concerning the stochastic processes $\xi(t)$ and $\eta(t)$. A more sophisticated multi-commodity version of this model was published by A.Prékopa - P.Kelle /1978/.

We have examined such type of problems in a textile factory and in a steel works. For the solution of the practical problems we have given new models of the demand and delivery process which will be discussed in this paper.

2. Approximation of the delivery process by an empirical distribution function with random jumps

In the published models of random delivery process it is usually assumed, that the deliveries can occur in each point of the interval $[0,T]$ with the same probability. If there are n time points of deliveries, they are considered as the elements of an ordered sample $t_1 < t_2 < \ldots < t_n$ taken from a uniform distribution on $[0,T]$. This is usually an appropriate approximation in our case, too. However, for the amounts delivered at one occasion we allow any kind of distribution, so we can approximate them by help of the statistical data of earlier observations and other informations. This is a generalization of earlier models. Here the amount delivered at the time point t is a random variable denoted by β_i/n.

Thus our model of the delivery process is

$$
\eta(t) = \begin{cases} 0, & \text{if} \quad 0 \leq t \leq t_1 \\[3mm] \dfrac{1}{n} \displaystyle\sum_{i=1}^{k} \beta_i, & \text{if} \quad t_k < t \leq t_{k+1} \ (k=1,\ldots,n) \end{cases} \qquad /2.1/
$$

$/t_{n+1} = T/$, which can be regarded as a generalized empirical distribution function of the uniform distribution in $[0,T]$ with random jumps β_i/n . This stochastic process will be denoted by $F_n^{\frac{\beta}{\cdot}}(t)$.

First we consider only one commodity and a demand with constant intensity $\alpha > 0$, thus

$$
\xi(t) = \alpha t \qquad \left(0 \leq t \leq T \right) \qquad /2.2/
$$

The shape of the cumulative delivery, the cumulative demand and the stock level is illustrated on Figure 1.

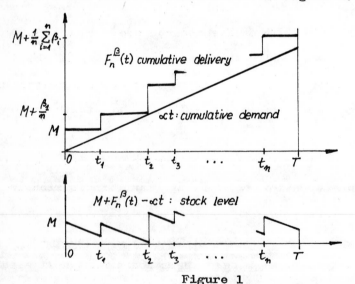

Figure 1

Delivery and demand pattern, stock level

For the solution of the model of type /1.1/ the main problem is to give the probability distribution of the random variable

$$\sup_{0 \leq t \leq T} \left\{ \alpha t - F_m^{\beta}(t) \right\} \qquad /2.3/$$

This is a generalized version of the well-known Kolmogorov-Smirnov statistic used for statistical tests. We can prove the following theorem /owing to the extent of the proof we can only refer to P.Kelle /1979//:

Theorem 1. If the random variables $\beta_i (i=1,\ldots,n)$ are interchangeable, i.e. all of their $n!$ permutations have the same joint probability distribution /or a special case when they are independent, identically distributed/, then

$$P\left(\sup_{0 \leq t \leq T}\left\{\alpha t - F_n^{\beta}(t)\right\} \leq M\right) = 1 - \left(1 - \frac{M}{\alpha}\right)^n -$$
$$- \frac{M}{\alpha} \sum_{k=1}^{n} \binom{n}{k} \int_0^{n(\alpha T - M)} \left(\frac{M + \frac{x}{n}}{\alpha}\right)^{k-1} \left(1 - \frac{M + \frac{x}{n}}{\alpha}\right)^{n-k} dH_k(x) \qquad /2.4/$$

where $H_k(x)$ denotes the distribution function of $\sum_{i=1}^{k} \beta_i$ $(k=1,\ldots,n)$.

This model allows, that the amount ordered might not be totally delivered up to time T as it occurs sometimes in practice, too. The total fulfilment of the order can be prescribed. In this case the random variables β_i $(i=1,\ldots,n)$ are not independent but in some cases they are interchangeable, for example in a model of A.Prékopa /1965/.

The direct application of Theorem 1   is possible for
planning the initial stock of a commodity if we have information concerning the distribution function of the
amounts that will be delivered, and if we know the demand
intensity $\propto$ of the planning period $[0,T]$.

3. Random intensity of demand

In the time point of the decision making, the production
intensity of the future planning period can often be only
roughly estimated. In this case we consider the demand rate
$\propto$ as a random variable which has a distribution function
$G(x)$. For a random delivery process described in the previous chapter the initial stock level of a commodity can be
given as the solution of the following equality

$$\int_0^\infty P\left(\sup_{0 \leq t \leq T}\left\{xt - F_n^{\beta}(t)\right\} \leq M \,\Big|\, \alpha = x\right) dG(x) = 1 - \varepsilon. \qquad /3.1/$$

This is a special case of Model /1.1/. The left-hand side
of Eq. /3.1/ is a monoton increasing function of the initial stock level M, thus Eq. /3.1/ holds for the minimal
M which ensures the continuous supply in the whole planning
period with probability $1-\varepsilon$.

The demanded amounts of the different commodities usually
depend on each other. If we can estimate the joint probability distribution of the demand rates for a group of basic
materials, then we can give a more accurate joint planning
method of the initial stocks. We suppose a random supply
of each material according to Model /2.1/ with different parameters n_j and random variables β_i^j $(i=1,\ldots,n_j)$ which
will be assumed to be stochastically independent for different materials /for different values of j, j=1,...,m/.

The dependence in the demand rates will be considered. Let $V(\underline{x})$ denote the joint probability distribution function of the demand rate vector $\underline{\alpha}' = (\alpha_1, \ldots, \alpha_m)$. The cost optimal vector of the intital stocks $\underline{M}' = (M_1, \ldots, M_m)$ is the solution of Model /1.1/ with the reliability constraint

$$\int_{R_m^+} \prod_{j=1}^{m} \left[P \left(\sup_{0 \le t \le T} \{x_j t - F_{n_j}^{\beta^j}(t)\} \le M_j \,\middle|\, \alpha_j = x_j \right) \right] dV(\underline{x}) \ge 1-\varepsilon \quad /3.2/$$

where R_m^+ denotes the positive orthant of the m-dimensional Euclidean space. The set of vectors $\underline{M}$ satisfying Inequality /3.2/ is in many special cases a convex set, as it has been shown by P.Kelle /1979/. This enables us to find the global optima of Model /1.1/ for a convex set of constraints D and a convex cost function $f(\underline{M})$.

The above methods are too complicated and time consuming for the less important items of the production, so we want to give a simple formula for the approximate solution of Eq. /3.1/. If the delivery amounts are approximately the same C/n at the different random time points of delivery, then the input process can be approximated by the empirical distribution function of the uniform distribution on $[0,1]$ like by A.Prékopa /1965/ and M.Ziermann /1963/ . T = 1 and C = 1 can be reached by an appropiate choice of the units, so this will be assumed in the following part of the paper. We can apply the following asymptotic distribution well known in statistics:

$$\lim_{n \to \infty} P \left(\sup_{0 \le t \le 1} \left\{ \left(1 + \frac{h}{\sqrt{n}}\right) t - F_n(t) \right\} \le \frac{v}{\sqrt{n}} \right) = 1 - e^{-2v(v-h)} \quad /3.\overline{3}/$$

where $F_n(t)$ denotes the empirical distribution function of the uniform distribution on $[0,1]$:

$$F_n(t) = \begin{cases} 0, & \text{if} \quad 0 \leq t \leq t_1, \\ k/n, & \text{if} \quad t_k < t \leq t_{k+1}, \quad k=1,\ldots,n-1 \\ 1, & \text{if} \quad t_n < t \leq 1. \end{cases} \qquad /3.4/$$

Substituting $\alpha = 1+h/\sqrt{n}$ and $M = v/\sqrt{n}$ in Eq. /3.3/ we can get the following approximation for finite values of n

$$P\left(\sup_{0 \leq t \leq 1} \{\alpha t - F_n(t)\} \leq M\right) \approx 1 - e^{-2nM(M+1-\alpha)} \qquad /3.5/$$

for $0 < M < \alpha - 1$. Here α means the ratio of the demanded and the delivered amount in the planning period. Compared to the exact values calculated by means of Eq./2.4/ we have found that in the range of the usual service level 0.75 to 0.97 the approximate formula gives a probability 1 to 10 % less than the exact one for $n=10$. Here and for $n < 10$ a numerical correction can be applied. By greater values of n we have a better approximation. Thus the solution of Eq. /3.1/ can be approximated for deterministic α by the following simple formula

$$M \approx \frac{\alpha - 1}{2} + \sqrt{\left(\frac{\alpha - 1}{2}\right)^2 + \frac{1}{2n} \ln \frac{1}{\varepsilon}} \qquad /3.6/$$

which is a generalized version of the formula given by A.Prékopa /1965/ and M.Ziermann /1963/.

If α is a random variable, then the approximate value of the left-hand side of Eq. /3.1/ is

$$1 - e^{-2nM(M+1)} E\left[e^{2nM\alpha}\right] \qquad /3.7/$$

where E means the expectation. For given distribution of

$\propto$ Eq /3.1/ can be solved by a numerical method,

having the expectation, for given M. In the most important

case, however as $\propto$ has a normal distribution, by elemen-

tary calculations we can get the approximate solution in an

explicit form:

$$M \approx \frac{m-1}{2(1-ns^2)} + \sqrt{\left[\frac{m-1}{2(1-ns^2)}\right]^2 + \frac{1}{2n(1-ns^2)} \; ln \; \frac{1}{\varepsilon}} \qquad /3.8/$$

for s $<$ 1/$\sqrt{n}$, where m means the expectation, and s

means the standard deviation of $\propto$ /assuming T = 1 and

C = 1/. These parameters are usually easily available, they

are estimated in the course of demand forecasting.

4. Application of the models

The application of the above models is in progress in a

big Hungarian textile factory and in a Hungarian iron and

steel works. Both enterprises have had data management sys-

tems for stock control, in course of which all delivery and

demand time points and amounts are registered and stored

on magnetic tapes. These historical data are the base to

choose and to fit the appropriate model for the input and

output process of each item. We need some supplementary data,

such as required service level. The future supply possibili-

ties and demands can be only roughly estimated at most of the

items mainly using past data. A statistical forecasting method

and a modular program system for planning the stock

level has been developed. The models are based on the reliability type inventory models known in literature and the ones presented here. These program models give us the possibility to control a lot of different types of demand and supply variations. On the base of the stock level plan an order recommendation is given for the decision makers.

For the most important groups of basic materials the joint planning model /3.2/ has been tested, still the difficulties in collecting the data and in having a fast working system advise the use of the simple approximate solution method of the models with appropriate numerical corrections.

References

P.Kelle /1979/: "A Contribution to the Theory of Reliability Type Inventory Models", Doctoral Thesis, L.Eötvös University of Budapest

Z.László /1973/: "Some recent results concerning reliability-type inventory models" in A.Prékopa (ed.): Inventory Control and Water Storage, J.Bolyai Math.Soc., Budapest and North Holland Publ.Co., Amsterdam, 179- 187 pp.

A.Móritz /1978/: "Ein mathematisches Modell für die Lager-
haltung im ungarischen Binnenhandel",
Zeitschrift für Operations Research, 22,
B45-B56 pp.

A.Prékopa /1965/: "Reliability Equation for an Inventory
Problem and its Asymptotic Solutions"
in Colloquium on the Application of Mathematics to Economics, Akadémiai Kiadó, Budapest, 313-327 pp.

A.Prékopa, P.Kelle /1978/: "Reliability Type Inventory
Models Based on Stochastic Programming",
Mathematical Programming Study,9, 43-58 pp.

M.Ziermann /1963/: "Application of the Theorem of Smirnov
for an Inventory Control Problem", Publications
of the Math.Inst. of the Hungarian Academy of
Sciences, 8/B. 509-518 pp. /in Hungarian/

Proc. First Int. Symp. on Inventories
Budapest, Hungary 1980

INVENTORY MODELS WITH ORDERING TIME LIMIT. ANALYSIS OF THE PROBLEM

HERMANN KLEMM

VEB Carl Zeiss Jena, Jena GDR

1. Setting the problem

In the socialist economy of the GDR, there exist an ordering time limit for materials in order to plan and balance basic proportions of national economic funds on the state level. According to this ordering system, up to a certain date t_o of the current year the orders for meeting next year's demands are to be placed. It means that until t_o it must be determined what quantities $/z_k/$ and for which time of delivery $/t_k/$ are to be ordered. The trouble is that at the date t_o there is great uncertainty concerning future demand /1/ for the remaining period of the current year and /2/ for the next year. Therefore, the fundamental aspect of resolving the problem is the planning and modelling of requirements. Reordering and storage costs play no considerable role since - due to the great uncertainty - the prior aim is to satisfy demands.

2. Analysis of the problem

2.1. Outline of the problem: Subject of investigation is an item of materials which is needed by a company /consumer/ to fulfil its economic tasks and is to be purchased from another company /manufacturer, supplier/. The intermediator between consumer and supplier is a "disposer" with the following tasks:

- collecting and summarizing information on material demand;
- examining future demand taking into account the available stock, as well;
- supervising of changes in stocks;
- forwarding of orders to suppliers /ordering decision/;
- setting orders and supervising its performance.

Instruments of planning /methods, models, algorithms/ are to be found for the disposer to make decisions of ordering.

2.2. Timing concepts: Three consecutive periods will be taken into consideration: the previous year /79/, the current year /80/ and the next year /81/. These periods are characterized by dissimilar factors determining demands and different variables of stocks /e.g. production program and plan, basic technological data, list of parts, working instruction, norms of material consumption, material demand, service level stock/ concerning

- the previous year: planned and actual quantities of the year before the previous year;
- the current year: planned stock of the previous year corrected by the figures from the beginning of year up to t_o and
- the next year: planning quantities /decision variable/.

Figure 1. Timing pattern and variables

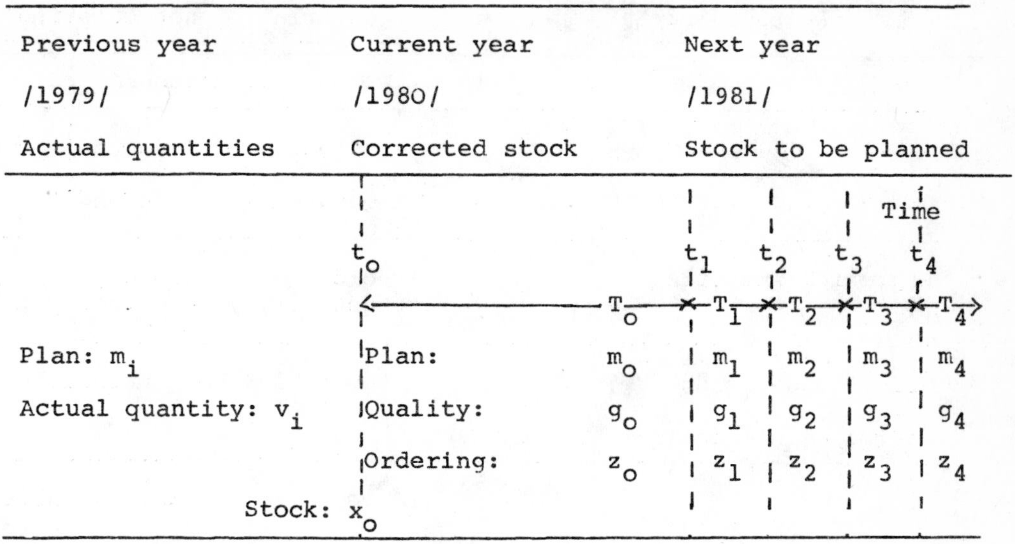

Previous year /1979/ Actual quantities	Current year /1980/ Corrected stock	Next year /1981/ Stock to be planned

The timing diagram shows dates t_0 in the current year and t_1, t_2, t_3, t_4 in the next year along a time axis marked T_0, T_1, T_2, T_3, T_4.

Plan: m_i

Actual quantity: v_i

Plan: m_0, m_1, m_2, m_3, m_4

Quality: g_0, g_1, g_2, g_3, g_4

Ordering: z_0, z_1, z_2, z_3, z_4

Stock: x_0

2.3. Ordering time limit and decision variable: Ordering time limit is the date t_0 until which normal orders are to be placed towards suppliers for meeting next year's demand. An order has to contain the following data: number of shippings /n/, terms for them /t_k/ and quantity /z_k/ of deliveries /k=1,2,...,n/ for the next year.

2.4. Satisfaction or non-satisfaction of demands: The behavior to be followed at ordering and delivering depends on whether the demand of a certain article can be covered by the supplier for all his consumers or not:

	Behaviour at	
Quantity	covering	non-covering
	of demands	
Actual consumption	= demand	< demand[1]
Demand placed by the consumer	= demand	> demand[1]
Replenishment size	= order quantity	< order quantity
Ordering decision /terms, quantities/	possible	impossible
	economic decision	administrative decision

[1] Neither of these data is suitable to estimate demands.

In the case of not satisfying demands, the order placed by consumer company cannot be directly met but negotiations are carried out in order to get an agreement - not discussed in details here - for the final solution. It is required here from an economic aspect that no higher stocks than necessary should be established   /contrary to the general behaviour of the disposer/.

In the following, the tasks to be solved by the company in both cases /covering or non-covering of demands/ will be discussed: to estimate future demand up to date t_o and to make an ordering decision for the next year on the basis of the former year.

3. Planning of demand

In addition to the data related to stock x_o as well as the ordered but still not received quantities z_o /both in the function of date t_o/, the disposer is expected to know the future demand in order to be able to make decisions on ordering. The following aspects are to be considered here:

- the disposer must order a great number of items of different kinds;
- items to be ordered are dissimilar as far their economic importance and, at the same time, the purchasing conditions of them are also varying, thus no unified planning method for all the items is available;
- no planning process /not even the breaking down of the list of parts / yields exact figures of demand /planned quantity/;
- the quality of planning figures has a diminishing character /the so-called time dilemma of material supply - Klemm, 1979/.

Because of the above circumstances, the following proceedings are recommended:

Dissimilar features of items /from the technical point of view of planning/ are to be characterized by criteria K1 -K4:

1. Criteria of economic significance:

K1: Share in total consumption in value terms /ABC-analysis/ /Magee, Boodman, 1967/

Class	Share	Value of consumption (%)	Quantity of items (%)
A	High	80 - 90	10 - 20
B	Medium	10 - 15	20 - 30
C	Low	5	50 - 70

K2: Purchasing conditions

Class	Significance	Determination by
S	Supply is difficult /imports, bottle-neck, difficulties in delivery/	Nomenclature
NS	No difficulties in supply	-

2. Criteria of available information on demand:

K3: Possibilities of forecast /Schodlok 1974/

Class	Significance	
H	Horizontal demand pattern	
T	Trend-type demand pattern	
HS	Horizontal/seasonal demand pattern	predictable /v/
TS	Trend-type/seasonal demand pattern	
STR	Demands with great dispersion	
A	New items	not predictable /nv/
SP	Sporadic demands	

K4: Share of deterministically calculable demand

$$Q = \frac{\text{share of deterministically known demand /plan/}}{\text{total demand /actual/}}$$

Class	Significance	Criterion
HA	High share	Q > limit /60%/
NA	Low share	Q < limit /60%/

Thus, items have been disjunctively ranged into classes. To each class of items, the appropriate method of planning P1 - P5 as well as the number n of next year's deliveries /i.e. the structure of scheduling/ will be adjusted:

Algorithm AUSW	1	2	3	4	5	6	7
K2: Purchasing conditions ?	S	NS	NS	NS	NS	NS	NS
K1: ABC analysis ?	-	A	A	A	B	B	C
K4: Deterministic demand ?	-	HA	NA	NA	-	-	-
K3: Predictability ?	-	-	v	nv	v	nv	-
Planning method	P2 +P1	P2 +P1	P3	P4 +P1	P3	P4	P4 +P5
Number n of deliveries	n^x	4	4	4	2	2	1

n^x = to be determined individually for each item.

Symbols:

P1 : estimated demands /by experts/

P2 : deterministic demands /e.g. breaking down of list of items - Grupp 1976/

P3 : mathematical-statistical forecast /Schodlok 1974/

P4 : average demand of the current year and the previous year

P5 : purchase in case of emergency /no planning/

Each of these planning methods gives plan quantities m_k for the periods T_k, k=0/1/n, for each item. These quantities m_k are deemed forecast demands in T_k which is of course inaccurate. It is hardly possible to find regular statistic methods to estimate the quality of plan quantity m_k since

- no enough data for the individual items are available to apply traditional statistic evaluations;

- the so-called time dilemma of material management /the increasing inaccuracy of planning/ is only a tendency to express groups of items;

- with the individual items, a modified method of estimation can be applied so that errors of forecast cannot be extrapolated.

Two methods are recommended for the quantification of quality g_k of plan quantities m_k, alternatively:

1. Expert estimation of fluctuation for each method of planning:

Examples for g %	Period k /%/				
	0	1	2	3	4
Constant quality	5	5	5	5	5
Decreasing quality	2	5	10	15	20
Strongly decreasing quality	5	50	60	80	100

For each item : $g_k = m_k \cdot \dfrac{g\%}{100}$

    2. Statistic calculation: for each item, planning dimension m_i and the actually existing demands /actual consumption/ v_i are used /referred to period t_o provided that the described instruments of planning in the previous year have already been applied/. Thus:

    2.1. For each commodity: $g = \dfrac{1}{N} \sum_i |v_i - m_i|$, herewith the fluctuation interval is measured.

    2.2. Each period i and planning method p:

$$\bar{g}_i^p = \frac{1}{N_i^p} \sum_a |v_i^{(a)} - m_i^{(a)}|,\ \text{summation over all commodities a,}$$

planning method p.

    Standardizing: selection of a $\bar{g}_i^p : = g^*$ /e.g. the last $\bar{g}_i^p$ chronologically/

$$\gamma_i^p = \frac{\bar{g}_i^p}{g^*}$$

herewith, the chronological development of fluctuation interval for each planning method is measured.

2.3. For each item: $g_k = g \cdot \gamma_i^p$ /i $\hat{=}$ period k of the next year/

Table 1. Example for statistic calculation

i	2	3	4	5	6	7	8	Ø	g	
m_i	400	400	400	400	400	400	400	400	–	
v_i/1/	410	380	420	420	430	350	450	408	29	item 1
v_i/2/	405	410	390	380	450	470	390	414	25	item 2
v_i/3/	395	390	410	440	450	350	450	412	31	item 3
v_i/4/	410	410	395	430	450	390	500	426	31	item 4
$\bar{g}_i$	4.3	7.1	6.4	15.7	25.7	25.7	24.3			
γ_i	0.18	0.29	0.26	0.65	1.05	1.05	1			
g_k/1/	5.2	8.4	7.5	18.9	30.4	30.4	29			item 1
g_k/2/	4.5	7.3	6.5	16.3	26.3	26.3	25			item 2
g_k/3/	5.6	9.0	8.1	20.2	32.6	32.6	31			item 3
g_k/4/	5.6	9.0	8.1	20.2	32.6	32.6	31			item 4

4. Decision model /outline/

The above analysis leads to the following concretizing of the decision problem of a given commodity and ordering time limit t_o:

- The algorithm AUSW establishes an adjustable planning method p which is applied to determine:

  n = number of deliveries in the next year /and timing pattern at the same time: periods $T_o, T_1, \ldots, T_n$/

  m_k = planning quantity for demand T_k

  g_k = quality of the planning quantity m_k.

- Up to date t_o, the stock x_o as well as the ordered but not delivered quantities z_o are known.
- The quantities z_k which will be ordered for the time limit $t_k: = t_{k-1} + T_{k-1}$, $k = 1/1/n$ are yet to be known.
- The simultaneous decisions n on $z_1, z_2, \ldots, z_n$ are to be taken so that in each period T_k a prescribed α-service level α_o is observed.

The few statements on future demand may be interpreted - without contradiction with the real conditions on the basis of existing information - as follows: demand $\xi[T_k]$ in period T_k is a random variable with expected value m_k and dispersion g_k:

$$P \{\xi[T_k] \leq x\} = F_k(x/T_k)$$

with an appropriate distribution function $F_k(x/T_k)$. In addition, it is to be provided that the accidental quantities $\xi[T_o]$, $\xi[T_1], \ldots, \xi[T_n]$ are totally independent.

According to the above reasoning, there is a /S,S/-policy for each k=1/1/n in a periodic /stationary/ inventory model with delivery time lag $\lambda = T_o + T_1 + \ldots + T_{k-1}$ and with length of period $T = T_k$, so that the α-service level is:

$$P \{\xi[\lambda + T] = S\} = F_k(S/\lambda + T) \geq \alpha_o$$

The ordered quantities are then:

$$z_1: = S_1 - (x_o + z_o)$$
$$z_k: = S_k - S_{k-1} \qquad k = 2/1/n$$

Details on the above model see in Girlich, Küenle /1980/ and Klemm /1980/.

5. Safety stocks /Sv/

Safety stocks are of special importance if the recommended strategy is followed depending on the situation of ordering time limit t_0 and uncertainty in planning. For each distribution $F_k(x|T_k)$ safety stock Sv_k can be calculated:

$$Sv_k : = S_k - \sum_{j=0}^{k} m_j$$

Explicit statements on Sv are given by accepting $F_k(x|T_k)$ as normal distribution. Then:

$$E \, \xi[T_k] = m_k, \qquad var \, \xi[T_k] = \sigma_k = 1.25 \, g_k$$

$$S_k = \sum_{j=0}^{k} m_j + k(\alpha_0) \sqrt{\sigma_0^2 + \sigma_1^2 + \ldots + \sigma_k^2}$$

$$Sv_k = k(\alpha_0) \sqrt{\sigma_0^2 + \sigma_1^2 + \ldots + \sigma_k^2}$$

with $\Phi(k(\alpha_0)) = \alpha_0$, Φ = standardized normal distribution $N(0.1)$.

Several numeric examples /ZB/ are demonstrated in Tables 2-4; where $\alpha_0 = 0.84$, i.e. $k(\alpha_0) = 1$.

ZB 1.0 : constant m_k, decreasing quality $\sigma\%$

ZB 1.1 : Continuation of ZB 1.0 in the second following year

ZB 1.2 : ordering date t_0 is 2 quarters later, quality of planning figures is better

ZB 1.3 : Ordering date is 2 quarters later, quality unchanged

Table 2. Numeric example 1

	T_2^0	T_3^0	T_4^0	T_1^1	T_2^1	T_3^1	T_4^1	T_1^2	T_2^2	T_3^2	T_4^2	ZB
m_k^0	400	400	400	400	400	400	400	400	400	400	400	1.0
$\sigma\%$	2%	3%	4%	5%	10%	15%	20%					
Sv^0	8	14	22	30	50	78	112					
z_k^0	408	406	408	[408]	[420]	[428]	[434]					
$\sigma\%$					2%	3%	4%	5%	10%	15%	20%	1.1
Sv^1					8	14	22	30	50	78	112	
z_k^1					408	406	408	408	420	428	434	
$\tilde{z}_k^1$	with $x_0^1 = 30$						-90	[318]	[420]	[428]	[434]	
$\sigma\%'$			2%	2.5%	5%	7.5%	10%					1.2
$Sv^{0'}$			8	13	24	38	55					
$z_k^{0'}$			408	[405]	[410]	[414]	[417]					
$\sigma\%''$			4%	5%	10%	15%	20%					1.3
$Sv^{0''}$			16	27	47	77	111					
$z_k^{0''}$			416	[411]	[420]	[430]	[434]					
$\tilde{Sv}^0$	8	14	22	30	30	30	30					1.4
$\tilde{z}_k^0$	408	406	408	[408]	[400]	[400]	[400]					
$\tilde{k}_s$	1	1	1	1	0.60	0.38	0.27					
$\tilde{\alpha}$	0.84	0.84	0.84	0.84	0.73	0.65	0.61					

Table 3. Numeric example 2

	T_2^o	T_3^o	T_4^o	T_1^1	T_2^1	T_3^1	T_4^1	T_1^2	T_2^2	T_3^2	T_4^2	ZB
m_k^o	400	400	400	400	400	400	400	400	400	400	400	2.0
$\sigma\%$	5%	5%	5%	50%	60%	80%	100%					
Sv^o	20	28	35	203	314	449	601					
z_k^o	420	408	407	$\boxed{568}$	$\boxed{511}$	$\boxed{535}$	$\boxed{552}$					
$\sigma\%$					5%	5%	5%	50%	60%	80%	100%	2.1
Sv_k^1					20	28	35	203	314	449	601	
z_k^1					420	408	407	568	511	535	552	
z_k^1							−566	$\boxed{2}$	$\boxed{511}$	$\boxed{535}$	$\boxed{552}$	
$\sigma\%'$			1%	20%	30%	40%	50%					2.2
$Sv_k^{o'}$			4	80	144	215	293					
$z_k^{o'}$			404	$\boxed{476}$	$\boxed{464}$	$\boxed{471}$	$\boxed{478}$					
$\sigma\%''$			5%	50%	60%	80%	100%					2.3
$Sv^{o''}$			20	201	313	448	600					
$z_k^{o''}$			420	$\boxed{581}$	$\boxed{512}$	$\boxed{535}$	$\boxed{552}$					

$x_o^1 = 203$

Table 3 /cont./

	T^0_2	T^0_3	T^0_4	T^1_1	T^1_2	T^1_3	T^1_4	T^2_1	T^2_2	T^2_3	T^2_4	zB
$\tilde{S}v^0_k$	20	28	35	203	203	203	203					2.4
$\tilde{z}^0_k$	420	408	407	[568]	[400]	[400]	[400]					
$\tilde{k}_s$	1	1	1	1	0.65	0.45	0.34					
$\tilde{\alpha}$	0.84	0.84	0.84	0.84	0.74	0.67	0.63					
m^1_k				600	600	600	600	600	600	600	600	2.5
$\sigma\%$					5%	5%	5%	50%	60%	80%	100%	
Sv^1_k					30	42	52	304	471	673	901	
z^1_k					630	612	610	852	767	802	828	
$\tilde{z}^1_k$							+51	[903]	[767]	[802]	[828]	
$m^{1'}_k$				200	200	200	200	200	200	200	200	2.6
$\sigma\%'$					5%	5%	5%	50%	60%	80%	100%	
$Sv^{1'}_k$					10	14	17	101	157	224	300	
$z^{1'}_k$					210	204	203	284	256	267	276	
$\tilde{z}^{1'}_k$							-1384	[-1100]	[-844]	[-577]	[-301]	

$x^1_0 = 203$

Table 4. Numeric example 3

	T^o_2	T^o_3	T^o_4	T^1_1	T^1_2	T^1_3	T^1_4	T^2_1	T^2_2	T^2_3	T^2_4	ZB
m^o_k	250	400	150	600	200	450	150	150	700	800	200	3.0
$\sigma\%$	5%	5%	5%	5%	10%	15%	20%					
Sv^o_k	13	24	25	39	44	80	86					
z^o_k	263	411	151	614	205	486	156					
$\sigma\%$					5%	5%	5%	5%	10%	15%	20%	3.1
Sv^1_k					10	25	26	27	75	141	147	
z^1_k					210	465	151	151	748	866	206	
z^1_k	$x^1_o = 39$						-60	91	748	866	206	
$\sigma\%'$			2%	2.5%	5%	7.5%	10%					3.2
$Sv^{o'}$			3	15	18	38	41					
$z^{o'}_k$			153	612	205	470	153					
$\sigma\%''$			5%	5%	10%	15%	20%					3.3
$Sv^{o''}$			8	31	37	77	83					
$z^{o''}_k$			158	627	206	490	156					
$\tilde{S}v^o_k$	13	24	25	39	39	39	39					3.4
$\tilde{z}^o_k$	236	411	151	614	200	450	150					
$\tilde{k}_s$	1	1	1	1	0.89	0.49	0.45					
$\tilde{\alpha}$	0.84	0.84	0.84	0.84	0.81	0.69	0.67					
m^1_k				660	220	495	165	165	770	880	220	3.5
$\sigma\%^1$					5%	5%	5%	5%	10%	15%	20%	
Sv^1_k					11	27	28	30	82	156	162	
z^1_k					231	511	166	167	822	954	226	
z^1_k	$x^1_o = 39$						+22	189	822	954	226	
$m^{1'}_k$				540	180	405	135	135	630	720	180	3.6
$\sigma\%^{1'}$					5%	5%	5%	5%	10%	15%	20%	
$Sv^{1'}_k$					9	22	23	24	67	127	132	
$z^{1'}_k$					189	418	136	136	673	780	185	
$z^{1'}$	$x^1_o = 39$						-143	-7	666	780	185	

ZB 1.4 : modified strategy: from T_1^1, Sv remains constant /e.g. in case of non-covering of demand/

ZB 2.0 : constant m_k, strongly decreasing quality $\sigma\%$

ZB 2.1 : analogous versions to ZB 1.1 - 1.4

Continuation of ZB 2.0 in the second following year:

ZB 2.5 : demand m_k: + 50% in comparison to planning figures till now

ZB 2.6 : demand m_k: - 50% in comparison to planning figures till now

ZB 3.0 : fluctuating m_k, decreasing $\sigma\%$

ZB 3.1 - 3.6 : analogous versions to ZB 2.1 - 2.6

The following consequences may be drawn from the above examples:

- The safety stocks are very big and are growing /1/ because the increasing of inaccuracy of planning figures and /2/ because the periods $T_o + T_1 + \ldots + T_k$ increase.
- The shortening of periods alone /later date of ordering t_o/ has no significant effect on Sv; a determinant effect is felt only if the quality of planning figures improves /what can be expected/, at the same time.
- If the estimated Sv will not be ordered the service level decreases accordingly. Thus, the disturbances in production may be quantified.

413

References

Girlich, H.-J., Küenle, K.-U. /1980/: Ein Bestellfristen-
    Lagerhaltungsmodell. Symposium on Inventory Control,
    Budapest.

Grupp, B. /1976/: Elektronische Stücklistenorganisation in der
    Praxis. Forkel-Verlag, Stuttgart, p. 274.

Klemm, H. /1979/: Vollständige Materialbedarfsermittlung durch
    Klassifikation und Kombination verschiedener Planungs-
    methoden. Sitzungsbericht der Fachtagung "Entwicklungs-
    tendenzen der betrieblichen Materialwirtschaft", Merse-
    burg, pp. 33-42.

Klemm, H. /1980/: Sitzungsbericht des Arbeitsseminars "Bestell-
    fristenproblematik", Alt-Reddevitz, IGr "Lagerhaltungs-
    modelle" der Mathematischen Gesellschaft der DDR.

Magee, J.F., Boodmann, D.M. /1967/: Production Planning and
    Inventory Control. New York, London, Toronto.

Schodlok, H. /1974/: Materialbedarfsermittlung, Kap. 3 in:
    Klemm, Linke /Hrsg./: Lagerhaltungsmodelle - Neue
    Anwendungen, Erfahrungen und Erkenntnisse. Verlag Die
    Wirtschaft, Berlin.

Proc. First Int. Symp. on Inventories
Budapest, Hungary 1980

AN ANALYTICAL INVENTORY MODEL WITH STOCHASTIC LEAD TIME

TAMÁS KULCSÁR

Institute for Applied Computer Sciences, Budapest, Hungary

Introduction

The inventory model presented in this paper is to a great extent similar to that of Liberatore [2]. The most important difference is that, in the model to be presented, distribution of the lead time is given in a finite interval, contrary to that in [2]. Interpretations of ordering cost and lot size are also different. Besides, this model is the cost optimization version of the simplest member [4], [5], or the model-group of Prékopa and Ziermann.

Analysing this model, we succeeded in proving   in an analytical way that if some assumptions are fulfilled, there exists an optimal solution. A new result is, compared with those in [2], that limits can be given to the optimal values of parameters. Structure of the limits is the same as in the model given by Gerencsér [1], which assumes continuous reviewing and stochastic demand.

In the last part of this paper we also show an approximative solution, which is easier to treat.

1. Model Formulation

The model is based on the following assumptions:

/1/ The model deals with stocking of a single item.

/2/ Demand is deterministic, with the uniform rate x.

/3/ The amount ordered is delivered in a single lot.

/4/ Date of delivery, denoted by ρ, is a random variable in the interval $[0,\gamma]$, with the known probability distribution $G(\rho)$. Let M_1 and D^2 designate the expected value and variance of the distribution, respectively.

/5/ There is a continuous reviewing.

/6/ Shortages are allowed; all the shortages are to be made up.

/7/ Costs taken into account are [$]:

c_1 - holding cost per unit quantity, per unit time

c_2 - shortage cost per unit quantity, per unit time

c_3 - ordering cost per order.

/8/ The decision variables are as follows:

s - safety stock; we order when the inventory level reaches this value /i.e., s: reorder point/, $s \geqq 0$

q - lot size, $q > 0$.

Before writing down cost function of the model, we also need the following assumption:

$$q \geqq \gamma\, x \qquad\qquad /1/$$

This assumption ensures that there can be only one ordered lot that has not been delivered.

Now we can compose the cost function showing the expected total costs per unit time:

$$K(s_1 q)=c_1\frac{q}{2}+c_1 s-c_1 M_1 x+(c_1+c_2)\frac{1}{2q}\int_{s/x}^{\gamma}(\rho x-s)^2 dG(\rho)+c_3\frac{x}{q} \qquad /2/$$

In the following section of this paper we deal with the optimization of cost function /2/.

2. The Optimal Solution

Analysing cost function /2/ with the classical methods of analysis, we arrive at the following statement:

Theorem 1.

If $G(\frac{s_o}{x}) < \frac{c_2}{c_1+c_2}$, the optimal value s_o can be obtained by solving the following equation:

$$c_1(c_1+c_2) \int_{s_o/x}^{\gamma} (\rho x-s_o)^2 \, dG(\rho)+2c_1c_3x=(c_1+c_2)^2 \left[\int_{s_o/x}^{\gamma} (\rho x-s_o)dG(\rho) \right]^2 \qquad /3/$$

In turn, the optimal q_o can be calculated in the following way:

$$q_o = \sqrt{\frac{c_1+c_2}{c_1} \int_{s_o/x}^{\gamma} (\rho x - s_o)^2 \, dG(\rho) + \frac{2c_3}{c_1} x} \qquad /4/$$

Proof: Let us calculate partial derivatives of cost function /2/, with respect to s and q, respectively.

$$\frac{\delta K(s,q)}{\delta q} = \frac{c_1}{c_2} - \frac{c_1+c_2}{2q^2} \int_{s/x}^{\gamma} (\rho x - s)^2 \, dG(\rho) - \frac{c_3x}{q_2}$$

$$\frac{\delta K(s,q)}{\delta s} = c_1 - (c_1+c_2) \frac{1}{q} \int_{s/x}^{\gamma} (\rho x - s) \, dG(\rho)$$

Having these derivatives to be equal to zero and solving the system of equations gained in this way, we get /4/ from the first equation, and /3/ from the second one.

In order that the solution of the equation system should really be an optimum, it is necessary that the Hessian matrix of function /2/ should be a positive definite one. It assumes the derivatives of second order to be positive, and determinant of the Hessian matrix to be greater than zero.

Let us check these assumptions, one by one.

$$\frac{\delta^2 K(s,q)}{\delta q^2} = \frac{c_1+c_2}{q^3} \int\limits_{s/x}^{\gamma} (\rho x - s)^2 \, dG(\rho) + \frac{2c_3 x}{q^3}$$

This is obviously positive, when

$$s < \gamma \, x \qquad\qquad\qquad\qquad /5/$$

This condition formulates the economically reasonable assumption that one should not hold safety stock of amounts greater than the total demand occurring during the maximum lead time.

This is so much an evident assumption that even the optimum of function /2/ will be sought only in interval $[0, \gamma x]$.

$$\frac{\delta^2 K(s,q)}{\delta s^2} = (c_1+c_2) \frac{1}{q} \int\limits_{s/x}^{\gamma} dG(\rho)$$

Again, this term is positive if the condition /5/ is fulfilled.

$$\frac{\delta^2 K(s,q)}{\delta q \delta s} = (c_1+c_2) \frac{1}{q^2} \int\limits_{s/x}^{\gamma} (\rho x - s) \, dG(\rho)$$

On the basis of the above, we can determine the value of determinant of the Hessian matrix belonging to cost function /2/:

$$\left(\frac{c_1+c_2}{q_o^3} \int\limits_{s_o/x}^{\gamma} (\rho x - s_o)^2 \, dG(\rho) + \frac{2c_3 x}{q_o^3} \right)(c_1+c_2) \frac{1}{q_o} \int\limits_{s_o/x}^{\gamma} dG(\rho) -$$

$$- (c_1+c_2)^2 \frac{1}{q_o^4} \left[\int\limits_{s_o/x}^{\gamma} (\rho x - s_o) \, dG(\rho) \right]^2 > 0$$

This, by small alterations, can be transformed to the following form:

$$(c_1+c_2) \int\limits_{s_o/x}^{\gamma} (\rho x - s_o)^2 \, dG(\rho) \left[(c_1+c_2) \int\limits_{s_o/x}^{\gamma} dG(\rho) - c_1 \right] +$$

$$+ 2c_3 x \left[(c_1+c_2) \int\limits_{s_o/x}^{\gamma} dG(\rho) - c_1 \right] > 0$$

This term is positive, if

$$(c_1+c_2) \int\limits_{s_o/x}^{\gamma} dG(\rho) - c_1 > 0$$

from which the condition $G(s_o/x) < \dfrac{c_2}{c_1+c_2}$ can be gained immediately.

Q.e.d.

That is, if there is an s_o, corresponding to Theorem 1, we know that this and q_o belonging to it are optimal solutions of cost function /2/. Now it only remained to study the problem: on what conditions has equation /3/ a root in the interval $[0, \gamma x]$. Regarding this, the following theorem can be proved.

Theorem 2. Let s^* denote the value of s, for which

$$G\left(\frac{s^*}{x}\right) = \frac{c_2}{c_1+c_2} \qquad\qquad /6/$$

Then, if the condition

$$\frac{2c_1 c_3}{c_1 + c_2} < [c_2 M_1^2 - c_1 D^2] \; x \qquad\qquad /7/$$

is fulfilled, equation /3/ has one and only one root (s_o), in the interval $[0, \gamma x]$, for which: $0 < s_o < s^*$.

$\underline{\text{Proof:}}$ Let $L(s)$ denote the following function:

$$L(s) = c_1(c_1 + c_2) \int_{s/x}^{\gamma} (\rho x - s)^2 \; dG(\rho) + 2c_1 \, c_3 \, x \; -$$

$$- (c_1 + c_2)^2 \left[\int_{s/x}^{\gamma} (\rho x - s) \; dG(\rho) \right]^2$$

Let us calculate the first derivatives of this function.

$$L'(s) = 2(c_1 + c_2) \int_{s/x}^{\gamma} (\rho x - s) \; dG(\rho) \left[(c_1 + c_2) \int_{s/x}^{\gamma} dG(\rho) - c_1 \right]$$

Sign of this term is obviously determined by the sign of function

$$L_1(s) = (c_1 + c_2) \int_{s/x}^{\gamma} dG(\rho) - c_1$$

As $L_1(s) = 0$, when $s = s^*$, $L_1(s) > 0$, when $s < s^*$, and $L_1(s) < 0$ when $s > s^*$, the following can be stated about the behaviour of function: $L(s)$ is monotonically increasing in the interval $[0, s^*]$, monotonically decreasing in the interval $[s^*, \gamma x]$ and has a maximum at s^*.

It results from this that if $L(s)$ is negative at $s = 0$, and is positive at $s = \gamma x$, then $L(s)$ has only one root in the interval $[0, \gamma x]$, and this root is in the interval $[0, s^*]$.

420

That is:

$$L(\gamma x) = 2c_1 c_3 \; x > 0$$
$$L(0) = (c_1 + c_2) \; x^2 \; [c_1 \; D^2 - c_2 \; M_1^2] + 2c_1 \; c_3 \; x$$

By transforming $L(0) < 0$ we get condition /7/.

Q.e.d.

It is worth to compare equation /6/ defining s^* with a result of L.Gerencsér [1], who, in the case of stochastic demand process used $s_0 < s^*$, where s^* is defined by the following equation

$$F(s^*) = \frac{c_2}{c_1 + c_2} \qquad\qquad /8/$$

where $F(x)$ is the distribution function of demand.

Structural and essential identity of equations /6/ and /8/ is clear-cut. The question arises whether the models with continuous reviewing have an unchanging property of giving similar limits to optimal values of parameters, independently of the nature of stochastic process which is influencing it.

Thus far we treated this model in its most general form. We had not even assumed that the probability distribution is continuous; the statements made so far are valid for both discrete and continuous distributions.

However, in order to exceed equation /3/ in solving this problem it is necessary to specify the distribution function. In the case of equation /3/, this hardly seems to be a practicable way, because assuming even the uniform distribution, one arrives at an equation of fourth degree in s_0. This is why solution of equation /3/ can rather be achieved by using a computer. In doing that, Theorem 2 may prove to be useful, since the root-seeking procedure can be limited to the interval $[0, s^*]$.

At the same time, however, demand of finding an approximative solution, easier to be treated, is also arising. In the following section of the paper we deal with this problem.

3. Approximative Solution

Basis of the approximative solution is to assume: $q_o = \gamma x$. This is a reasonable assumption, when the demand rate is uniform and known.

Having altered all the equations according to this assumption, we gain that optimal s_o should satisfy the following equation:

$$\frac{c_1}{c_1 + c_2} \gamma x = \int_{s_o/x}^{\gamma} (\rho x - s_o) \, dG(\rho) \qquad /9/$$

For solving this, we can make use of the following theorem.

__Theorem 3.__ If $M_1 \geqq \dfrac{c_1}{c_1 + c_2} \gamma$, equation /9/ has one and only one root in the interval $[0, \gamma x]$.

Proof: Be now

$$L_2(s) = (c_1 + c_2) \int_{s/x}^{\gamma} (\rho x - s) \, dG(\rho) - c_1 \gamma x$$

As $L_2'(s) = - (c_1 + c_2) \int_{s/x}^{\gamma} dG(\rho) < 0$, so $L_2(s)$ is a monotonically decreasing function. Now $L_2(\gamma x) = - c_1 \gamma x < 0$, so if

$L_2(0) = (c_1 + c_2) x \int_o^{\gamma} \rho dG(\rho) - c_1 \gamma x > 0$ - which is equivalent to the condition in the theorem - the existence of the unique solution - because of the monotony of the function - is guaranteed.

$$\text{Q.e.d.}$$

This model is really easier to treat. Let us take an example now, where we suppose that $G(\rho)$ is a distribution function of a random variable, uniformly distributed in the interval $[0, \gamma x]$. In this case condition in Theorem 3 takes the following form:

$$\frac{\gamma}{2} \geq \frac{c_1}{c_1 + c_2} \gamma$$

and it is fulfilled, when $c_2 > c_1$, a relation which is quite reasonable to assume.

Now the equation corresponding to /9/ is of form:

$$c_1 \gamma x - (c_1 + c_2) \frac{1}{\gamma} \int_{s_0/x}^{\gamma} (\rho x - s_0) \, d\rho = 0$$

Solution of this is:

$$s_0 = \left[1 - \sqrt{\frac{2c_1}{c_1 + c_2}}\right] \gamma x \qquad /10/$$

When examining this result, we find that it is always smaller than 1, that is, it should never be stocked as a safety stock, an amount of inventories equal to the total demand during the maximum lead time. In addition, we see that the right side in /10/ is an increasing function of c_2, that is, the inventory level s_0 is increasing when c_2 is increasing, the probability of not having any shortages is increasing, too.

Let us take a numerical example. One might demand that the probability of the stockout should not exceed 5 per cent. Then, if the probability of stockout is approached by the ratio $c_1/(c_1+c_2)$, a feasible solution of equation $c_1/(c_1+c_2) = 0.05$ is e.g. $c_1 = 1$ and $c_2 = 19$. The value of s_0 belonging to this is $s_0 = 0.75 \, \gamma x$.

Let us compare this result with that of the simplest model of Prékopa and Ziermann. This model is based on conditions that are definitely the same as in our model. Solution of that model is $M = [1 - \xi] \, \gamma x$, where M is the initial inventory, ξ is the probability of stockout. When substituting the above data into this model, we get $M = 0.95 \, \gamma x$.

It can be seen that using the cost optimization version of the model results in nearly 20 per cent inventory level reduction.

Simulation tests of this model are to demonstrate whether it is true or not.

References

[1] L.Gerencsér: Egy folyamatos nyilvántartásu sztochasztikus készletgazdálkodási modell ismertetése és érzékenységi vizsgálata /Introduction of a Continuous Reviewing Stochastic Inventory Model and Examination of its Sensitivity/. MTA SZTAKI Közlemények, 10 /1973/.

[2] M.J.Liberatore: The EQQ Model Under Stochastic Lead Time. Operations Research 27, pp. 391-396 /1979/.

[3] T.Kulcsár: Egy sztochasztikus késési idős, folytonos készletellenőrzéses költségoptimalizáló készletmodell /A Continuous Reviewing, Cost Optimization Inventory Model with Stochastic Lead Time/. IX. Magyar Oparációkutatási Konferencia, Győr /1979/.

[4] A.Prékopa: Reliability Equation for an Inventory Problem

and its Asymptotic Solutions. Colloquium on

Appl. of Math. to Economics, Budapest /1963/.

[5] M.Ziermann: Készletgazdálkodási és sorbanállási modellek,

"Operációkutatás" /Inventory and Queuing

Models, "Operations Research"/, Chapter VI,

pp. 309-312, SZÁMOK /1972/.

Proc. First Int. Symp. on Inventories
Budapest, Hungary 1980

ABOUT THE OPTIMUM EXECUTION
OF STOCK KEEPING PROCESSES
BY MEANS OF PLANNED MODEL TESTS

JOHANN-ADOLF MÜLLER

B. Leuschner College of Economics, Berlin, GDR

1.Problem

The solution of a series of economical problems like those
of the stock keeping and operating type,for instance,cause
to study stochastic systems,whose essential system qualities
are characterized by a parameter vector c.Supposing Q to be
the characteristic value of efficiency,we will deal with the
following stochastic optimum problem:

$$J(c_o) = \min \left\{ J(c) \; / \; c \in C \wedge h(c) \geq 0 \right\} \qquad (1a)$$

$$J(c) = E_z \left\{ Q(z,c) \right\} \quad , \quad h(c) = E_z \left\{ g(z,c) \right\} \; . \qquad (1b)$$

The mathematical structure obtained is often too complicated
to permit any analytical solution at all or under restrictive
conditions only.

Especially the development of computer engineering brings
about some possibilities of extending the scope of the mathematical model analysis beyond the limits of performance of
the mathematical optimization procedures, provided that the
mathematical model is realized by a computer and that an
approximation solution of the problem concerned is found out
by means of planned model tests.

Instead of a simple comparison of variants aimed at solving
this problem, test planning intended for reaching the admissible target zone by as few tests as possible becomes necessary.

The amount of rules for choosing the system out of the system family given, which the suitable dimensional variable is
to be determined for by means of the model test, is called

a search plan. This article is intended to demonstrate, how
to apply sequential and simultaneous search plans to the execution of production and stock keeping processes. Therewith
sequential search plans lay down the following test on the
basis of the results obtained by the tests carried out hither
to ,where methods of planning optimizing tests and search
methods, respectively, are adequate to establish them in
addition to heuristic statements.

2. Stock Keeping System To Be Studied

Conditions:

A stock is being considered. Let the demand R for a definite
article within the order period $[th, (t+1)h]$ be a time-inde-
pendent random variable $R=R_1+R_2$, in connection with which
R_1 and R_2 are independent random demands at the intervals
$[th, (t+1-\lambda)h]$ and $[(t+1-\lambda)h ,(t+1)h]$, respectively,
with the probability density functions $f_1(R_1), f_2(R_2)$. Orders
for recharging the stock are possible to be passed at fixed
order times $(t+1-\lambda)h$, let the order time be constant λh. The
stock keeping causes the expenditure of storage costs k_L,
which are proportional to the mean stock, as well as that of
procurement costs k_B. The normal procurement costs consist of
a constant part k_B^o , which has to be expanded for each supply
and of a part k_B^1 ,which is proportional to the amount ordered.

If the stock is empty ,the demand has to be met by a special
procurement and the costs k_F^1 for special supply are proportional to the mean stock shortage.

Aim of the study:

It is required to establish an order rule (s,S), whose application at the interval Th keeps the mean costs for stock
keeping and procurement per period of order as low as possible,with s being the critical stock and S the order level.
Therewith $J(S,s)= E\{Q(T,S,s)\}$,in connection with which
$Q(T,S,s)$ are the random total costs to be expanded at the
interval $[0 ,Th]$ applies to the expected value of the total
costs at the interval Th. It holds true:

$$Q(T,S,s) = \sum_{t=0}^{T-1} Q(x[th], R_1^t, R_2^t, S, s),$$

in connection with which $x[th]$ is the stock at the beginning
of the order period $[th, (t+1)h]$, R_i^t (i=1,2) is the realization of the demands at $[th, (t+1-\lambda)h]$ and $[(t+1-\lambda)h,$
$(t+1)h]$, respectively. Therewith to the stock $x[th]$ applies
$x[(t+1)h] = x[th] + p(t+1,h) - R_1^t - R_2^t$, in connection with which
are $p(t+1,h) = \{S - x[th] + R_1^t\} H[x[th] - R_1^t - s]$ as well as
$H(z)=1$ for $z > 0$ and $H(z)=0$ for $z \leq 0$.

There are even with simple probability density functions
$f_1(R_1)$ and $f_2(R_2)$ obvious considerable difficulties in the
analytical solution of the stochastic optimum problem. That
is why an algorithmic model was programmed in ALGOL and PL 1,
respectively, and was realized by the computer R 300 and
EC 1020, respectively.

3. Adaptive Trial Solution

The model (in general an algorithmic one) of the stock keeping system to be studied, is realized by the computer.
As a result of the model tests a realization of samples taken
at random of the model state development is yielded for each
realization of samples taken at random of the influencing
variables. Depending on which efficiency criterion is choosen,
we will get a realization $Q(z^r,c)$, in connection with which
$Q(z^r,c)$ is a random variable of an unknown partition. The optimum problem Eq./1a,1b/ to be solved turns out to be a stochastic optimum one of an insufficient a-priori-information.
If the complexity of the model does not permit sequential
search plans to be supplied, it is possible to make use of the
well-known regular search methods, provided that they are combined with a suitable statistic test. For this purpose a combination was made between

a. the search algorithm after Nelder/Mead and a sequential
   test for equality of two mean values (NS),

b. the gradient method and a statistic estimation of the gradient (orthogonal test planning) (BW).

In addition to this, stochastic search methods are adequate, whereby a modified algorithm of the stochastic approximation (S) was applied to the case in question.

In conformity with these possibilities, programmes were developed in PL 1 and were realized for different problems of the stock keeping and operating type.

For the purpose of illustration /Müller,1978/ indicates the mean optimum strategies for the example by means of stochastic simulation and by the application of sequential search plans (NS,BW and S) to different partition functions and model parameters.

4. Probability Theory Approach

Another possibility is offered by the probability theory approach to the simulation / -,1971/ ,which does not use any realizations of the random variables unlike the stochastic simulation, but makes use of their probability functions as original information. The transformation of the probability functions in the way adequate to the system logic, yields the desired probability functions of the state variable concerned. Thus the solution of the optimum problem does not differ any longer from the solution of the deterministic optimum problem Eq./1a/.

The task of the algorithmization is to determine the transformation of the probability functions and to realize them by the digital computer. Therewith it becomes evident, that a small number of typical operations, which can be pre-programmed as macro-orders, will have to be carried out, if circumstances are favourable. A suitable programme is available ,with the most important macro-orders being in PL 1.

This programme was applied to the study of operating and stock keeping problems. In order to determine the optimum critical stock and the optimum order level in a stochastic demand of the example, the stock keeping system was modeled in the specified way and was combined with the search method after Rosenbrock.

For the determination of the expected value of costs we need
the probability function of stock (and stock shortage, respectively), that of ordered quantity as well as the   probability
of an order to be passed. These variables can be   determined
by realizing the following operations:

$$X(5,L) = SUB (X(3,I), X(4,K))$$
$$X(L)   = SUB (S, X(5,L))$$
$$X(1,L) = SCW (S-s, X(I), 0)$$
$$H(L)   = SCW (s, X(5,I), S)$$
$$X(3,L) = SUB (H(I), X(6,I)) ,$$

in connection with which the following probability functions
are used:

X(1,L) -Consignment at the beginning of the order period
$$p_t = [t, \ t+h)$$
X(3,L) -Stock at the beginning of the order period
X(L), H(L) - Auxiliary variables
X(4,L) -Demand in $[t, \ t+(1-\lambda)h]$
X(5,L) -Stock at the time of order passing
X(6,L) -Demand in $[t+ (1-\lambda)h, \ t+h)$.

Besides this there is the following meaning of the operators:

$$SUB \quad (Y(L) = SUB \{X(I), Z(I)\}) :$$

$$Y(L) = \sum_M X(I) Z(K) \quad , \quad M = \{(I,K) \ / \ I-K = L\}$$

as well as

$$SCW \quad (Y(L) = SCW \{P, \lambda(I) , R\}) :$$

$$Y(R) = \sum_{I=x_{min}}^{P} X(I) \quad , \quad Y(L) = X(L) \quad for \quad L > P .$$

Basing on the defined initial state, the probability functions
of the desired stable state are yielded after an adequate number of iterations.

The programme for the realization of the given operations was
combined with a regular search method after Rosenbrock (T).
The mean optimum parameters (s_0, S_0) for $T \to \infty$ (stationary
state), which were obtained, are shown in /Müller, 1978/.

5. Application Of Simultaneous Search Plans

The partially considerable computing times needed by the electronic data processing equipment EC 1020- for one example, even the determination of the mean optimum order strategies for the stock keeping system shown in /Müller,1978/(2 decision variables) took 5 to 20 minutes depending on the search method and the model parameters - reveal the bounds of the application of such sequential search plans to complicate algorithmic models and to a great number of decision variables, respectively. In many cases, however, simultaneous search plans are adequate to attain a desired improvement of the characteristic value of efficiency.

Generally, the application of simultaneous search plans is aimed at approximating to the complicate functional J(c) Eq. /1b/ by a simpler one, e.g. by a polynominal in c. Therewith the number of test points has to be fixed until active model test is started. Within the scope of the theory of test suitable search plans, which are used to avoid systematic errors in the experimental arrangement, were developed. If it is known in advance, that not all the decision variables (factors) exercise an equally strong influence on the characteristic value concerned, use can be made of the method of random balance/Nalimov,1971/, which eliminates the essential factors relative to a given characteristic value from the totality of influencing factors. The method of random balance is here a heuristic one.

The application of such simultaneous search plans is necessary in order to determine optimum order strategies within the stock keeping system concerned, if several storage goods are considered. To give further information, let us study a stock in conformity with passage 2, but of M storage goods. In this case the order strategy includes 2 M variables (S_i, s_i) (i =1 (1) M). Let the optimization of every storage article in ones be excluded, as the storage capacity K_o of the stock is restricted. If the storage demand is

$$B = \sum_{i=1}^{M} f_i S_i > K_o \text{ ,there will be additional costs of rent}$$

$c_L(B-K_o)$ due to the removal of a portion of storage goods.
Therewith f_i is the specific storage demand of the i-th sto-
rage article, c_L the costs of rent per storage unit.
The function of costs obviously turns out to be

$$J(S,s) = \sum_{i=1}^{M} J_i(S_i,s_i) + c_L\left(\sum_{i=1}^{M} f_i S_i - K_o \right) \, \text{sign}\left(\sum_{i=1}^{M} f_i S_i - K_o \right) \, .$$

In this case the following approach is to be recommended:
A.Repetitive combination of the method of random balance
   with the orthogonal test planning /Martin,1980/

For the stock keeping system of M storage goods an algorithmic model is set up. Active model tests in the original
state by means of the random balance permit to choose N_1 factors, which have an particularly strong influence on the
costs $J(S,s)$, from among the 2M factors S_i, s_i (i=1 (1) M).
The use of the orthogonal test planning for the N_1 factors
will result in an analytic (linear and quadratic ,respective-
ly) model, by means of which it is possible to determine a
zone close to the optimum. As this zone may eventually be
under the particularly strong influence of other factors, it
is recommended to apply random balance to orthogonal test
planning repeatedly as often as sufficiently good results
will be obtained. The method presented under /Martin,1980/
yielded satisfying results for a stock keeping system of 15
storage goods at a computing time of about 3 hours by means
of the computer EC 1020.

B.Hierarchic optimization

For the M storage goods the partial mean optimum strategies
(S_i^p, s_i^p) (i=1 (1) M) are separately determined without regard
to the capacity bound K_o, whereby the methods described in
passage 2 and 4 respectively, are applied. For a stock keeping system of 14 storage goods the mean optimum order strategies were yielded by means of the search algorithm NS in
combination with a statistic test. Without regard to the capacity bound nor to the increase of costs caused by this,
the following estimation of costs is therewith yielded:

$m=268.12$, $\sigma=12.37$ (m - mean value, σ - standard deviation).

If the yielded unconditional mean optimum strategy does not comply with the specified auxiliary condition $\sum_{i=1}^{M} f_i S_i^p \leq K_o$, a second stage is carried out to determine the quadratic approximation of the costs of all storage goods to a sufficient vicinity of the optimum (S_i^p, s_i^p) by means of the orthogonal test planning (for two factors S_i, s_i):

$$\tilde{J}_i(S_i, s_i) = a_o^i + a_1^i S_i + a_2^i s_i + a_3^i S_i^2 + a_4^i s_i^2 + a_5^i S_i s_i .$$

For this purpose the search algorithms NS and S were combined with the orthogonal test planning, so that the quadratic approximation of each optimum solution is additionally yielded in the vicinity of the optimum.

The exposed example showed with $K_o = 700$ the available storage capacity to be insufficient for the unconditional mean optimum strategy, that means to be exceeded by 102.1 on the mean. This accordningly results in an increase of costs by 204.2 ($c_L = 2$) on the mean. By the application of the very efficient regular search algorithm after Powell , the mean quasi-optimum order strategy (S_i^o, s_i^o) (i=1 (1) M) was determined

$$J(S_i^o, s_i^o) = \min \left\{ \sum_{i=1}^{M} \tilde{J}_i(S_i, s_i) + c_L \left(\sum_{i=1}^{M} f_i S_i - K_o \right) \text{sign} \left(\sum_{i=1}^{M} f_i S_i - K_o \right) \right\}.$$

It is obviously necessary to verify after the determination of S_i^o, s_i^o (i=1 (1) M) ,wether this strategy is within the range of validity of the partial quadratic models or not. The mean quasi-optimum order strategies, which were yielded is: the required storage demand is 700, the costs amount to $m = 270.21$, $\sigma = 14.03$.

The computing time required to determine the optimum order strategies for all the 14 storage goods was 124 minutes, that required to determine the partial quadratical models by means of the orthogonal test planning was 21 minutes and that required to determine the quasioptimum strategy was 14 minutes.

Table : Stock Keeping System /Müller,1978/

Partition	k_B^0/k_L	k_B^1/k_L	k_F^1/k_L	λ	T	s	S	J(s,S)	Method
g					10	6.1	12.0	6.92	S
	1	0.01	0.5	0.3	10	6.1	13.0	6.91	BW
					10	7.2	12.6	6.93	NS
					–	5.0	14.4	6.89	T
					10	23.3	49.9	188.1[x]	S
					10	20.0	50.0	189.7[x]	NS
g	50	5	10	0.5	–	22.0	50.0	185.0[x]	T
					10	9.2	93.3	158.3	NS
					10	18.1	60.3	185.6	BW
					10	16.5	36.6	53.4	BW
g	10	1	5	0.3	10	17.0	34.0	53.3	NS
					–	19.8	34.0	52.9	T
					10	32.1	40.0	63.1	BW
d_r	10	1	5	0.3	10	25.7	38.9	63.3	NS
					–	22.2	41.9	62.4	T
					10	9.3	19.9	61.9	BW
d_l	10	1	5	0.3	10	8.5	27.1	62.3	S
					10	9.9	27.0	62.5	NS
					–	21.6	36.0	56.5	T
					10	3.3	20.2	21.9	BW
					10	0.4	16.5	22.0	S
e	10	1	5	0.3	10	2.3	14.8	21.6	NS
					–	1.0	17.0	21.3	T

g – Equipartition $R \in [0 , 50]$
d_r – Triangular partition right-hand oblique $R \in [0 , 50]$
d_l – Triangular partition left-hand oblique $R \in [0 , 50]$
e – Exponential partition $E(R) = 7.2$
x – with auxiliary condition $S \leq 50$

Bibliography

--- (1971): Digital Simulation .Berlin, Heidelberg 1971.
Martin,W.(1980): Ermittlung der wesentlichen Faktoren und
ihrer Wirkungsweise mit Hilfe von Modellexperimenten am Bei-
spiel von TUL-Prozessen (Determination Of the Essential
Factors and Their Mode Of Action By Means Of Model Tests In
the Example Of TUL-Processes).VIth Scientific Congress
"Mathematics and Cybernetics In the Economy",Rostock .
Müller,J.A.(1978):Optimale Gestaltung von Produktions- und
Lagerhaltungsprozessen mit Hilfe geplanter Modellexperimen-
te (Optimum Execution Of Stock Keeping Processes Production
Processes By Means Of Planned Model Tests).Mitteilungen der
Mathematischen Gesellschaft der DDR,vol.1,p.81.
Nalimov,V.V.(1971): Теория эксперимента.
(Theory Of the Test).Moscow .

Proc. First Int. Symp. on Inventories
Budapest, Hungary 1980

A FRAMEWORK FOR EVALUATING
SCHEDULING ALGORITHMS
IN MULTI-LEVEL PRODUCTION SYSTEMS

ELIEZER NADDOR

The Johns Hopkins University, Baltimore, MD, USA

1. Introduction to Multi-Level Production Scheduling

We introduce the reader to a framework for multi-level systems by considering a system with four levels, 24 parts, and eight lines on which the parts can be produced. The framework can be used to evaluate scheduling algorithms for systems with any number of levels, parts, and production lines. It is currently operational at The Johns Hopkins University. Figures 2 to 4 are copies of computer outputs generated for this report for the four-level system from a program called INVLEV.

Figure 1 illustrates some of the characteristics of the parts in our system. The first eight parts, at Level 1, are the finished products. The last four parts, at Level 4, are bought parts - for these only a purchasing schedule has to be provided. Parts at any level G, except those in the last level, may require for their production parts at levels G+1, G+2, etc. For each part, the figure also lists the lines on which it can be produced, the cost of the part, the cost to set up a production run, and the average expected weekly shipments (in units of 100). The shipments of the finished products (parts 1 to 8) depend on external customers, but those of the other parts are determined by internal scheduling.

The rate of production of a line depends on whether production is normal, a setup occurs, or overtime is authorized. For lines 1 to 4 the normal and setup rates are 10. The normal rate of lines 5 and 8 is 20, and the setup rate is 15.

For lines 6 and 7 the corresponding rates are 25 and 20. The additional rate for overtime on all lines is 5.

Our production system includes numerous other characteristic that are usually encounterd in real production systems such as leadtime and shipping forecasts.

Part	Level	Parts needed	Lines	Cost	Setup	Ship
1	1	9,13,21,22,23,24	1	250	450	10
2	1	10,24	1,2	50	100	25
3	1	11,22,33	1,2	100	300	28
4	1	12,21,22,23	1,2,3	200	350	20
5	1	12,21,22,24	1	200	400	15
6	1	14,24	1,2,3,4	50	150	35
7	1	15,23,24	1,2,3,4	100	250	40
8	1	16,24	1,2,3,4	50	200	25
9	2	17,21,22,23,24	5,6	100	400	10
10	2	20,22	5,6	30	200	35
11	2	17,21,24	5,6	60	300	28
12	2	18,21,22,23,24	5,6	120	400	35
13	2	17,21,22,24	5,6	75	300	10
14	2	19,23	5,6	30	200	35
15	2	19,22,24	5,6	60	300	40
16	2	20,24	5,6	30	200	25
17	3	22,23,24	7,8	30	200	48
18	3	21,22,23,24	7	38	150	35
19	3	21,22	7,8	20	50	75
20	3	23	7,8	8	100	50
21	4	–	–	6	60	238
22	4	–	–	4	60	351
23	4	–	–	1	60	311
24	4	–	–	3	30	371

Figure 1. Parts' Requirements, Costs, and Shipments

2. Production Scheduling

In this report the term production scheduling means the assignment of parts to production lines on every day of a planning horizon. For parts in the last level, the bought parts, the production schedule includes the purchased quantities and the days on which they are due. Mathematically, the corresponding schedule is an array $U(L,I)$ indicating the part that has to be produced on Line L, Day I. Figure 2 illustrates a portion of a production schedule for the parts and lines in Level 1 of the the system described in Section 1.

438

DAY	L01	L02	L03	L04	P01	P02	P03	P04	P05	P06	P07	P08
-1	1	2	7	6	1	2				4	3	
1	3	3	7	6				12		4	3	
2	7	3	4	7			2	3		14		
3	5	2	4	6		2		3	1	4		
4	5	2	4	6		2		3	1	4		
5	1	3	7	6	1		2			4	3	
6	8	3	7	7			2				34	1
7	8	2	8	7		2				4	13	
8	8	2	8	6		2				4	13	
9	5	3	4	6			2	3	1	4		
10	1	3	7	6	1		2			4	3	

Figure 2. Production Schedule of Lines and Parts in Level 1

Scheduling algorithms generate schedules meeting the following requirements:

(a) On a given day, a line is assigned to only one part, or it is idle. No fractional assignmnets are allowed.

(b) No part is assigned to a line on which it cannot be produced.

(c) One part may be assigned to several lines on a given day.

A scheduling algorithm need not guarantee that all shipping requirements are met. For example, if insufficient production capacity is available then shortages inevitably arise. The total shortage for Part R is entered in the array I(R).

Our general framework allows the handling of numerous scheduling algorihms. Each algorithm is expected to return a scheduling array U(L,I) and a shortage array I(R). A costing routine is then used to evaluate the effectiveness of any scheduling algorithm.

(Ideally, one would wish to find U(L,I) and I(R) optimally by solving an appropriate mathematical programming problem. It is known, though, that such an approach leads to an NP complete problem [1]. Note that Reference [1] also gives a bibliography on mathematical programming approaches to production planning problems.)

Two heuristic scheduling algorithms are currently incorporated in our framework. One of them, the LINE algorithm, produces schedules similar to that in Fig-

439

ure 2, and the costs in figures 3 and 4. The other, the DAY algorithm, is compared to the LINE algorithm in Section 5. Both algorithms use a lot-sizing algorithm to schedule the purchasing of the parts in the last level (the bought parts). This algorithm produces a schedule which minimizes the total carrying and setup costs.

Both algorithms review the parts and lines level by level. First the schedule in Level 1 is determined. The shipping requirements for the parts in this level are known. The schedule in any Level G determines shipping requirements in Levels G+1, G+2, etc. The algorithms thus proceed from Level 1 to the last but one level, and then the lot-sizing algorithm mentioned above is used.

The DAY Algorithm

The DAY algorithm produces a schedule by examining shipping requirements on a day to day basis, hence its name. On Day I of the planning horizon, one part at a time is reviewed. If no shipments of the part are needed then the next part is reviewed. If a shipment is needed and there is sufficient inventory available, then the amount shipped is deducted from the inventory and the next part is reviewed.

If there is insufficient inventory for some Part R, then all lines on which the part can be made are checked. A Line L which has available capacity is then scheduled (i.e., $U(L,I) = R$), and the available inventory is updated accordingly. If inventory is still insufficient to meet the shipment, further lines are checked and, possibly, scheduled. If there still is need for more production, the same process is repeated for days I-1, I-2, ..., 1. If necessary, and if overtime is authorized, the whole procedure is repeated once again for the days and lines which have already been scheduled for Part R, and overtime production is added accordingly. Finally, if any shortages still exist then they are accumulated in the shortage array I(R).

The LINE Algorithm

This algorithm examines one line at a time, rather than one day at a time as the DAY algorithm does. For each Line L, every Part R that can be produced on it is selected. Dynamic Programming is then used to determine the optimal schedule $U(L,I)$ for that part on Line L during the whole horizon. This schedule minimizes the total carrying and setup costs. If insufficient capacity is available to meet all the requirements of the part, the remaining requirements are recorded, and an attempt is made to schedule them on the next appropriate line.

After all the lines have been scheduled, the remaining requirements for each Part R are recorded in the shortage array $I(R)$. If overtime is authorized, the LINE algorithm attempts to reduce the amounts in $I(R)$ by adding overtime production on the lines and days in which Part R has been scheduled by the Dynamic Programming procedure.

3. Carrying, Setup, Shortage, and Overtime Costs

In this report we assume that there are five work-days in a week, and 50 work--weeks in a year. We also assume that the annual cost of carrying inventory is a percentage P of the part's cost.

The cost of starting a new production run is called the setup cost. That is, if a Part R is not produced on Line L on Day I-1, and is produced on this line on days I, I+1, I+2, etc., then one setup cost on Day I is incurred.

The assignment of shortage costs in inventory systems in general depends on whether shortages are backordered or not. In multi-level production systems this assignment is even more complex since production at any Level G causes demands for shipments in levels G+1, G+2, and so on. In the present framework we assume that shortages are overcome by an additional inventory which is made available at the beginning of the planning horizon. In our illustrative system the unit shortage cost is assumed to be nine times the unit cost of carrying inventory.

Our present framework also makes a rather simplified assumption with regard to the method of charging for overtime production. It assumes that this cost is linearly dependent on the amount produced.

Some of the details on the inventory fluctuations, production, shipments, and the corresponding costs of Part 18 during a planning horizon of 35 days are given in Figure 3. This figure shows how the various costs are computed and how the initial inventories are handled.

LEV	PAR	DAY	BEG	PROD	SHIP	END	CAR/C	SET/C	SHO/C	OVE/C	TOT/C
3	18	-4	15	25	0	40	0	0	615	0	615
3	18	-3	40	0	0	40	0	0	0	0	0
3	18	-2	40	0	0	40	0	0	0	0	0
3	18	-1	40	20	0	60	0	0	0	0	0
3	18	1	60	0	20	40	182	0	0	0	182
3	18	2	40	0	0	40	182	0	0	0	182
3	18	3	40	20	20	40	182	150	0	0	332
3	18	4	40	0	0	40	182	0	0	0	182
3	18	5	40	20	20	40	182	150	0	0	332
3	18	6	40	0	0	40	182	0	0	0	182
3	18	7	40	0	20	20	91	0	0	0	91
3	18	8	20	0	0	20	91	0	0	0	91
3	18	9	20	0	20	0	0	0	0	0	0
3	18	10	0	20	0	20	91	150	0	0	241

Figure 3. Inventory and Cost Details on Part 18

Computations similar to that in Figure 3 are made for all parts in the system. A summary of these, for the first five days of the horizon, is given in Figure 4. The reader should be able to check some of the entries in the figure.

LEV	PAR	DAY	BEG	PROD	SHIP	END	CAR/C	SET/C	SHO/C	OVE/C	TOT/C
1	1	5	10	10	5	15	1200	450	0	0	1650
1	2	5	20	20	25	15	450	100	0	0	550
1	3	5	0	40	30	10	1080	900	0	0	1980
1	4	5	15	30	15	30	2160	350	0	0	2510
1	5	5	15	20	15	20	1560	400	0	0	1960
1	6	5	20	40	35	25	630	150	0	0	780
1	7	5	20	40	40	20	1440	750	0	0	2190
1	8	5	20	0	20	0	480	0	0	0	480
2	9	5	0	20	10	10	840	400	0	0	1240
2	10	5	20	20	20	20	324	200	0	0	524
2	11	5	55	0	40	15	900	0	0	0	900
2	12	5	35	60	50	45	3096	1200	0	0	4296
2	13	5	10	0	10	0	360	0	0	0	360
2	14	5	40	15	40	15	378	200	0	0	578
2	15	5	30	80	40	70	1980	300	0	1900	4180
2	16	5	105	0	0	105	1890	0	1458	0	3348
3	17	5	20	45	20	45	792	200	0	0	992
3	18	5	60	40	60	40	912	300	615	0	1827
3	19	5	80	75	95	60	852	100	0	0	952
3	20	5	65	0	20	45	273	0	0	0	273
4	21	5	315	200	255	260	1004	120	0	0	1124
4	22	5	575	245	440	380	945	120	0	0	1065
4	23	5	375	340	300	415	246	120	0	0	366
4	24	5	445	330	355	420	720	90	32	0	842
4	24	5	2350	1670	1940	2080	24513	6450	2106	1900	34969

Figure 4. Inventory and Cost Summaries for Five Days

4. Sensitivity of Scheduling Algorithms and Options

Currently, a user may select the following options for costing a production system during the running of Program INVLEV:

ALG The scheduling algorithm. At present only the DAY and the LINE algorithms are available.

SEQ The sequences (orderings) in which parts and lines are considered by the scheduling algorithm. Any consistent sequences may be specified.

HOR The number of days in the planning horizon. Any number may be specified. However, shipments of the finished parts must be known during the entire horizon.

TIM The length of the time of production. Either a normal (NOR) rate or overtime (OVE) may be specified.

CAR The annual carrying cost percentage. Any percent may be specified.

In Figure 5 we present the total costs of our illustrative system when two alternatives are selected for each of of the above options. We discuss the significance of these results in the following sections.

ALG	SEQ	HOR	TIM	CAR	CAR/C	SET/C	SHO/C	OVE/C	TOT/C
DAY	1	25	NOR	20	17436	6640	5760	0	29836
DAY	1	35	NOR	20	19806	6290	10080	0	36176
DAY	1	25	OVE	20	17571	6590	4730	1375	30267
DAY	1	35	OVE	20	18550	6650	6890	1375	33465
DAY	1	25	NOR	30	25966	6640	8640	0	41246
DAY	1	35	NOR	30	29110	6290	15120	0	50520
DAY	1	25	OVE	30	26090	6620	7095	1375	41181
DAY	1	35	OVE	30	27670	6620	10335	1375	46001
LIN	1	25	NOR	20	16433	6250	1368	0	24051
LIN	1	35	NOR	20	16928	6110	2520	0	25558
LIN	1	25	OVE	20	16219	6250	669	4650	27788
LIN	1	35	OVE	20	16549	6160	1425	4650	28785
LIN	1	25	NOR	30	23918	6740	988	0	31646
LIN	1	35	NOR	30	24692	6450	2538	0	33680
LIN	1	25	OVE	30	23820	6740	664	0	31224
LIN	1	35	OVE	30	24513	6450	2106	1900	34969
DAY	2	25	NOR	20	18841	5110	10080	0	34431
DAY	2	35	NOR	20	22129	5540	16380	0	44049
DAY	2	25	OVE	20	17324	5760	7200	1375	31659
DAY	2	35	OVE	20	19893	5850	11700	1375	38818
DAY	2	25	NOR	30	28150	5540	15120	0	48810
DAY	2	35	NOR	30	33268	5600	24570	0	63438
DAY	2	25	OVE	30	25832	5790	10800	1375	43797
DAY	2	35	OVE	30	29893	5970	17550	1375	54788
LIN	2	25	NOR	20	16440	4640	2376	0	23456
LIN	2	35	NOR	20	17836	4920	4392	0	27148
LIN	2	25	OVE	20	16456	4700	1882	4650	27689
LIN	2	35	OVE	20	17485	4920	3178	3275	28859
LIN	2	25	NOR	30	23808	6680	2964	0	33452
LIN	2	35	NOR	30	25458	5900	4752	0	36110
LIN	2	25	OVE	30	23800	6430	2424	1375	34029
LIN	2	35	OVE	30	24894	5900	3456	1375	35625

Figure 5. Sensitivity of Costs to Algorithms and Options

(1) The DAY and LINE Algorithms. As one expects intuitively, the LINE algorithm (which contains significant attempts at suboptimization) gives lower total costs than the DAY algorithm (which does not).

The differences between the algorithms are especially noticable when comparing the results for carrying cost percentages of 20 and 30. Since the Dynamic Programming procedure in the LINE algorithm minimizes carrying and set up costs, one expects somewhat more setups for 30% as compared to 20%.

In the DAY algorithm hardly any costs are considered and one should therefore expect no differences in the setup costs when comparing 20% and 30% carrying costs. The small differnces that can still be noted are due to the lot-sizing algorithm for bought parts, which does consider costs.

(2) Sequencing of Parts and Lines. Both the DAY and LINE algorithms produce schedules which consider parts and lines in certain sequences. In the results of Figure 5 two different sets of sequences are used in Level 1 only:

Level	SEQ	Parts	Lines
1	1	1,5,2,3,4,6,7,8	4,3,2,1
	2	5,1,2,3,4,6,7,8	1,2,3,4

From Figure 5 we can see that although there is a relatively small difference in the sequences, the corresponding costs are quite different - 26% in one case.

(3) The Planning Horizon. Two planning horizons are considered: 25 days and 35 days. (But note that all the costs are given for the first five days only.) Invariably, the larger the horizon the more costly is the schedule. This does not seem to be an unexpected result. The DAY algorithm in particular is very sensitive to the length of the horizon.

For both algorithms the increase in costs is reflected mostly in the shortage costs. The longer the horizon the more difficult it is to meet the shipping requirements.

(4) Normal and Overtime Production. It will be recalled that both algorithms consider overtime only after normal production is scheduled, and then only if shortages occur. Thus, it is not surprising that whenever overtime is used the cost of shortages is reduced. Since shortages also affect the amount carried initially, the carrying costs are also reduced somewhat.

445

(5) <u>Carrying Costs</u>. In Figure 5 we consider two percentages of carrying costs per year: 20 and 30. Thus, in comparing the results for these options one should expect an increase of 50% in the carrying costs and in the shortage costs, and a substantial increase of costs in general.

5. Conclusion

The framework presented in this report is mainly intended as a planning tool for evaluating scheduling algorithms for multi-level production systems. The framework includes many of the elements, if not most, which exist in real production environments.   In the following comments we mention a number of possible extensions that seem worth considering:

(1) The current DAY algorithm is extremely fast. It takes between 0.50 and 0.95 DEC-10 CPU seconds to produce each of the schedules for which the costs are given in Figure 5. Although the algorithm does not consider costs, the schedules that it produces are reasonably good. It can probably be greatly improved by the addition of heuristic routines which do consider costs. Our LINE algorithm is, of course, slower.   It takes between 2.69 to 6.64 seconds to produce each schedule in Figure 5. The performance of the algorithm can, no doubt, be improved. Its running time can be speeded up, and one should also be able to include shortages and overtime in the optimization phase. A related question is finding the optimal sequence of parts and lines in both scheduling algorithms. We have seen that a minor perturbation in the sequence leads to a great change in costs.

(2) Our current treatment of shortages may not be appropriate in some applications. When production capacities significantly exceed shipping requirements, then shortages will rarely occur. Whenever exessive shortages do occur, the following approaches may be considered:

(a) Modifying shipping requirements. This option either postpones or sometimes even cancels shipments. If the option is exercised at some Level G, then the

446

appropriate adjustments have to be made in levels G-1, G-2, etc.

(b) Authorization of special overtime. Such extra overtime may include additional shifts and/or week-end production.

(c) On-line scheduling. The user is permitted to evaluate on-line the options (a) and (b), and, possibly, others. Extensive and ingenious computer programming is required for the implementation of this approach.

(3) We have seen that when a 35-day horizon is used, as compared with a 25-day horizon, then the total costs increase. Since shipping forecasts are known to be notoriously inaccurate and subject to many fluctuations, an interesting question arises: What is the optimal length of the planning horizon? We have used the first five days of a planning horizon for cost comparisons. This was done with assumption that during these five days the production schedule is not subject to change. In reality this assumption may not be valid. Another interesting question then arises: What is the optimal length of the period to be used for comparing scheduling alternatives?

(4) The constraints imposed on our scheduling algorithms do not include provisions for desired ending inventories. Thus, both in the DAY and LINE algorithms inventories at the end of the planning horizon tend to approach zero. In some production environments this may not be appropriate. It should be relatively easy to include in an algorithm a desired minimum inventory for each part. But what should this minimum be? This, too, is an interesting optimization problem for which no simple answer seems to be readily available.

Reference

[1] Jacqueline McKinney, "Optimal Multi-Product Scheduling on One Machine Over a Finite Horizon", Doctoral Dissertation, The Johns Hopkins University, 1980.

Proc. First Int. Symp. on Inventories
Budapest, Hungary 1980

QUEUEING MODELS FOR CONTROLLING PERISHABLE INVENTORIES[1]

STEVEN NAHMIAS

University of Santa Clara, Santa Clara, CA, USA

1. Introduction

The purpose of this paper is to explore the potential for utilizing a certain class of queueing models for determining operating rules to control the stocking of perishable goods.

In practice, many types of inventory items can be retained in stock only a limited amount of time, after which they can no longer be used to satisfy demand and must be discarded. Foodstuffs, blood, photographic film, and drugs are just a few examples.

Recently, there has been a fairly considerable interest in the analysis of analytical models which result in optimal and sub-optimal ordering rules for perishable goods. Early unpublished work by Van Zyl (1964) gave the optimal order policy for a single product with a lifetime of two periods. This model was later generalized and extended by Nahmias (1975) and Fries (1975). Considerable additional work was reported by a number of researchers on both optimal order policies for more complex models and a variety of different types of approximations. A recent review article by Nahmias (1980) details the existing work in the field and contains 75 references. A difficult and unsolved problem is determining suitable ordering policies for a

[1]This work was supported by a Grant from the National Science Foundation.

fixed life commodity when inventory levels are reviewed continuously and there is a positive leadtime for placing an order.

This current paper will describe the analogy between the perishable inventory problem and queueing models with customer impatience. We hope to show what specific results from queueing could be useful in the inventory context and how the queueing methodology might provide some clues for dealing with the unsolved continuous review problem mentioned above.

2. The Queueing-Inventory Analogy

Consider the following single server queue: customers arrive to a single channel system according to some stationary stochastic process, and proceed to queue up for service on a first come first served basis. If a customer has not completed service by the end of a fixed time, say L, he exits from the queue never to return.

If we identify the arrival of customers with the replenishment process, the total number of customers in the system with the level of inventory, the times of completion of service with times of demand and the impatience time with the lifetime of the fresh units, then the analogy is complete. However, this does not imply that the queueing results will automatically give operating rules for the inventory problem. On the contrary, the queueing models have only a somewhat limited utility in the inventory context, since in queueing it is generally assumed that the arrival rate is known and fixed, while in inventory this is the primary control variable.

Early work on inventory models with impatience is due to Barrer (1957) and Gnedenko and Kovalenko (1968) who treated the M/M/1 system with impatience. (Note that although Barrer's results appear to be correct, Gnedenko and Kovalenko point out that his method of analysis may not be entirely correct.) Extensions of the results of these studies to more general systems are due to Finch (1960), Loris-Teghem (1972), Cohen (1969),

Gavish and Schweitzer (1977) and Stanford (1979). Note that some of these models do not precisely fit into the analogy described above since in many cases it is assumed that the customer completes service once he enters even if his total waiting time plus service time exceeds L .

In most queueing systems, the stochastic process which specifies the total number of customers in the system is Markovian. That is, if one knows the number in the system at time t then the probabilistic evolution of the process beyond t is independent of the history prior to time t . In the inventory context, this would mean that the level of on hand (or on hand and on order) stock is Markovian.

However, when impatience is imposed on the system, the number of customers in the queue is no longer a Markov process. To analyze the queueing system in this manner would require keeping track of not only each customer individually, but the amount of time elapsed since each joined the queue. Fortunately, there is a single dimensional process that still remains Markovian when there is impatience. That process is the virtual waiting time process. The virtual waiting time is equivalent to the actual waiting time in a system in which the times of service are realized when customers arrive rather than when they enter service.

A closely related process is the age of the oldest unit in the queue, say $A(t)$, which (if no other information is available) will also be Markovian. A typical realization of the process $A(t)$ is pictured below. Note that $A(t)$ will increase at a unit rate and will jump downward at either times of demand (i.e., times of completion of service) or at times of outdating (i.e., times when customers exit from the queue due to impatience). The magnitudes of the jumps correspond to the times between successive arrivals.

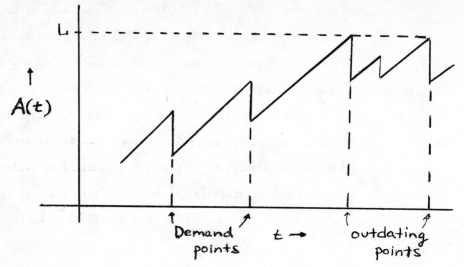

The virtual waiting time process, say $W(t)$, may have a typical sample path as pictured below. The virtual waiting time decreases at a unit rate

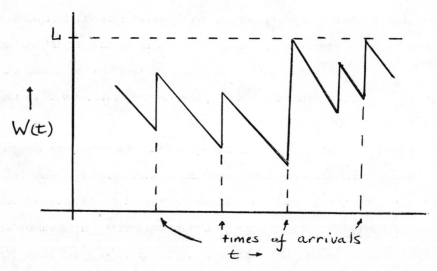

and jumps at times of arrivals of customers. One can see that $\{L - W(t)\}$ for an M/G/1 system has the same distribution as $A(t)$ for a G/M/1 system, so that $A(t)$ and $W(t)$ are, in some sense, dual processes.

Graves (1968) has analyzed the process $A(t)$ directly to obtain various characteristics of interest for the perishable inventory problem [many of his results duplicate those of Barrer (1957) and others]. In the next section we will show how these results can be used to construct an optimization model for a perishable inventory system.

3. An Optimization Model

As a prototype problem in which queueing theory might be used, consider a central blood bank in which donors arrive completely at random and donate one pint of blood. Demand requests are also assumed to occur on a random basis and are also for one unit. Blood has a legal lifetime of exactly 21 days. The manager of the bank may affect the arrival rate by calling registered volunteers or announcing to the public at large that a need exists. Excess demand is assumed to be filled from emergency orders outside the system.

Assume fresh units arrive to the system at rate λ and demand requests occur at rate μ. Suppose that the shelf life of new units is L. A common approach in managing such systems is to assume that stocking levels are chosen to meet some trade-off between shortages (under-stocking) and outdates (over-stocking). [See Jennings (1973) for a discussion of this type of methodology applied to blood banking.] Hence we will assume that there are known costs of stockout at p per unit per unit time and outdating at θ per unit per unit time. Let $G(\rho)$ be the expected cost incurred per unit time expressed as a function of the traffic intensity $\rho = \lambda/\mu$. Using known results for the M/M/1 queue with impatience [see Barrer (1957) or Graves (1968)] we will find that

$$G(\rho) \;=\; \begin{cases} \dfrac{(\rho-1)\mu}{\rho\, e^{\alpha(\rho-1)} - 1}\;\{\rho\theta\, e^{\alpha(\rho-1)} + p\} & \text{if } \rho \neq 1 \\[4ex] \dfrac{\mu}{\alpha+1}\;\{\theta + p\} & \text{if } \rho = 1 \end{cases}$$

where $\alpha = \mu L$. [Note that $G(\rho)$ is continuous at $\rho = 1$.] The objective is to determine ρ (and hence the arrival rate λ) to minimize $G(\rho)$.

Differentiation gives $G'(0) = \mu e^{-\alpha}(\theta - p) - p$ so that a sufficient condition that $G'(0) < 0$ is that $p > \theta$. Since $G(\infty) = +\infty$, it is clear that the value of $\rho > 0$, say ρ^* , which minimizes $G(\rho)$ solves $G'(\rho^*) = 0$. [It appears that G is strictly convex, so that the equation $G'(\rho^*) = 0$ has exactly one root. However we have been unable to develop a proof of this result.]

As an example, suppose $\mu = 1$, $L = 1$, $\theta = 1$, and $p = 4$. For this case the function $G(\rho)$ is pictured below.

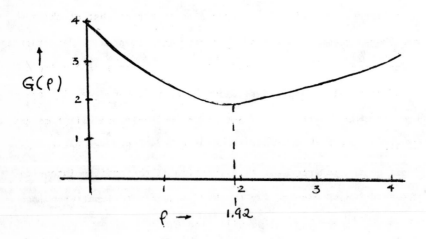

The optimal $\rho^* = 1.92$ for the example. Note that in general the actual values of the shortage and outdate costs are not significant. In this case we are simply saying that the relative cost of shortages to out-dates is 4 to 1.

This approach can be easily expanded to include procurement costs and holding costs. It can be extended to certain other cases — some results are known when the service distribution (i.e., times between demands) is arbitrary. However, it should be recognized that these types of queueing models are only useful if items are resupplied on a one at a time basis. In most inventory problems, stock is replenished on a lot-sizing basis according to a specified control rule, such as an (s,S) policy. Hence, the queueing models are of only limited value and can be applied only when a rather special problem structure exists such as in the blood bank problem.

4. Directions for Further Work

That the virtual waiting time process gives sufficient information to analyze the queue with impatience suggests a rather intriguing approach to the inventory problem. In the inventory context we may think of the virtual waiting time as the virtual lifetime of the on hand inventory; that is, the amount of time remaining until the inventory has been depleted either by demand or outdating. If we were able to determine the expected remaining lifetime of the stockpile, this quantity could be used to develop a new type of control rule which might be more appropriate for perishables than control rules based on stock levels.

In particular, what we hope to investigate in future research is the feasibility of a control rule of the form: when the expected remaining lifetime $\leq W$, then place an order for Q units. It is interesting to note that when there is no perishability, this rule will be equivalent to the standard (Q,r) stocking policy [see Hadley and Whitin (1963)] since when units have an infinite lifetime there is a one to one correspondence between the expected lifetime of the stockpile and numbers of units in inventory.

References

Barrer, D. Y. (1957): "Queueing With Impatient Customers and Ordered Service," Operations Research, 5, 650-656.

Cohen, J. W. (1969): "Single Server Queues With Restricted Accessibility," Journal of Engineering Mathematics, 3, 265-284.

Finch, P. D. (1960): "Deterministic Customer Impatience in the Queueing System GI/M/1," Biometrika, 47, 45-52.

Fries, B. (1975): "Optimal Order Policy for a Perishable Commodity With Fixed Lifetime," Operations Research, 23, 46-61.

Gavish, B. and Schweitzer, P. D. (1977): "The Markovian Queue With Bounded Waiting Time," Management Science, 23, 1349-1357.

Gnedenko, B. and Kovalenko, I. N. (1968): Introduction to Queueing Theory, Israel Program for Scientific Translation.

Graves, S. C. (1968): "Simple Analytical Models for Perishable Inventory Systems," Technical Report No. 141, Operations Research Center, Massachusetts Institute of Technology.

Hadley, G. and Whitin, T. M. (1963): Analysis of Inventory Systems, Prentice-Hall.

Jennings, J. B. (1973): "Blood Bank Inventory Control," Management Science, 19, 637-645.

Loris-Teghem, J. (1972): "On the Waiting Time Distribution in a Generalized Queueing System With Uniformly Bounded Sojourn Times," Journal of Applied Probability, 9, 642-649.

Nahmias, S. (1975): "Optimal Ordering Policies for Perishable Inventory — II," Operations Research, 23, 735-749.

Nahmias, S. (1980): "Perishable Inventory Theory: A Review," submitted for publication.

Stanford, R. E. (1979): "Reneging Phenomena in Single Channel Queues," Mathematics of Operations Research, 4, 162-178.

Van Zyl, G. J. J. (1964): "Inventory Control for Perishable Commodities," unpublished Ph.D. Dissertation, University of North Carolina.

Proc. First Int. Symp. on Inventories
Budapest, Hungary 1980

OPTIMAL ESTIMATION OF INTER-MACHINING INVENTORY LEVELS USING DISCRETE STATE VARIABLE CONTROL THEORY

P. J. O'GRADY and M. C. BONNEY

University of Nottingham, Nottingham, UK

1 ABSTRACT

Effective scheduling relies on the accurate determination of the size and location of in-process inventory levels. In practice, in-process inventory levels may be determined either from estimates based on expected system behaviour or by directly measuring the inventory levels or by some combination of estimation and measurement. In this paper the estimates of the states of the production system are combined together to form a best least squared error estimate. This is achieved using an extended Kalman filter. The use of the filter to determine the optimum choice of measurements to be taken is illustrated by the use of a numerical example.

2 INTRODUCTION

Actual production system behaviour results from the expected system behaviour together with the inherent random variations in the manufacturing process. These random variations degrade our knowledge of the system but it is possible to improve the accuracy of the estimation procedure by physically measuring the system. Measurement, though, has two disadvantages which limit its usefulness; firstly it is generally economically impractical to measure at every work station, and secondly the measurement itself is prone to error. Essentially therefore, we have two estimates of system behaviour. The first estimate is based on expected

459

system behaviour and the second estimate is based on measurement at selected points. The problem is how to combine these estimates so as to produce a best least squared error estimate.

The powerful filtering techniques proposed by Kalman (1960) and Kalman & Bucy (1961), together with the state variable approach of control theory, are in fairly wide use in many fields. The possibility of using these techniques in production control is suggested by Koivo & Hendricks (1973). However actual applications are few: Tapiero (1977) derives the optimum inventory measurement interval and Stohr (1979) extends this to the multi-product inventory case.

In this paper we also approach the problem by utilising the state variable approach of discrete control theory. But we treat the production system (manufacturing, inventory and delivery) as a whole. Initially we give the deterministic and stochastic system matrix equations which are capable of describing a wide range of production systems. We then revert back to the original problem, i e. to obtain the best estimate of the state of the system given estimates based on expected system behaviour and estimates based on measurements of the system. We achieve this using a filter, capable of handling non-stationary systems, to optimally combine these estimates. This multi-level, multi-product filter is, in effect, a Kalman filter extended to incorporate deterministic inputs. The use of the filter is described by a numerical example.

3 STATE VARIABLE REPRESENTATION OF PRODUCTION SYSTEMS

A deterministic system can be expressed in the following form-

$$\underline{X}(N+1) = \underline{A}(N)\underline{X}(N) + \underline{B}(N)\underline{U}(N) \dots\dots\dots\dots\dots\dots(3.1)$$

where $\underline{X}(N+1)$ is the n state vector for period N+1, and $\underline{X}(N)$ that for period N. $\underline{A}(N)$ is an n x n matrix and $\underline{B}(N)$ an n x m matrix, both defined at period N. The m vector $\underline{U}(N)$ indicate the system inputs. For a production control system these may be, for example, the work force level or the level of schedules.

The measurements of the deterministic system can be described by the equation-

$$\underline{Y}(N) = \underline{H}(N)\underline{X}(N)\dots\dots\dots\dots\dots\dots(3.2)$$

where $\underline{Y}(N)$ is an h vector of the measurements and $\underline{H}(N)$ is an h x n matrix defined at period N. In view of possible random disturbances the deterministic system equations, (3.1) & (3.2), have to be amended to:-

$$\underline{X}(N+1) = \underline{A}(N)\underline{X}(N) + \underline{B}(N)\underline{U}(N) + \underline{C}(N)\underline{W}(N)\dots\dots\dots(3.3)$$

$$\underline{Y}(N) = \underline{H}(N)\underline{X}(N) + \underline{V}(N)\dots\dots\dots\dots\dots(3.4)$$

$\underline{W}(N)$ and $\underline{V}(N)$ are vectors of purely random numbers having zero mean value with covariance matrices $\underline{Q}(N)$ and $\underline{R}(N)$ repectively. Matrices $\underline{A}(N),\underline{B}(N),\underline{C}(N)$ & $\underline{H}(N)$ are abbreviated to $\underline{A},\underline{B},\underline{C}$ & $\underline{H}$ respectively in the following sections.

4 SYSTEM ESTIMATES

We will consider two possible ways of obtaining estimates of the values of the state variables:-

(a) the first estimate, $\underline{X}_p(N)$, is obtained from the extrapolation of the present best estimate of the state vector to the next time period, using eq.(3.3), with the noise $\underline{W}(N)$ taking its mean value of zero, so that-

$$\underline{X}_p(N+1) = \underline{A}\,\hat{\underline{X}}(N) + \underline{B}\,\underline{U}(N)\dots\dots\dots\dots(4.1)$$

where $\underline{X}_p(N+1)$ is the estimate for time period N+1 and $\hat{\underline{X}}(N)$ is the 'best' estimate for time period N.

(b) the second independent estimate, $\underline{X}_r$, is obtained from measurements made on the system, with the value of $\underline{V}(N)$ taken to be the mean value of zero, so that from (3.4)

$$\underline{Y}(N) = \underline{H}\underline{X}_r\dots\dots\dots\dots\dots\dots(4.2)$$

where $\underline{X}_r(N)$ is the estimate for the time period N, $\underline{H}$ is the measurement matrix, and $\underline{Y}(N)$ are the measured values of the system's state.

One way of reducing the system error is to combine these estimates, $\underline{X}_p(N)$ and $\underline{X}_r(N)$, and this process is described in the next section.

5 MULTI-DIMENSIONAL COMBINATION OF SYSTEM ESTIMATES

5.1 Use of the Optimum Filter

The multi-dimensional combination of the system estimates for a production system is achieved by an optimum filter given in Appendix 1. This optimum filter (in effect a Kalman filter extended to incorporate deterministic inputs) combines the estimates of the state of the system, $\underline{X}_p(N)$ and $\underline{X}_r(N)$ from eqs.(4.1) & (4.2), into a 'best' estimate, $\hat{\underline{X}}(N)$.

The best estimate, $\underline{X}(N)$ is obtained by using the equation:-

$$\hat{\underline{X}}(N) = \underline{A}\hat{\underline{X}}(N-1) + \underline{BU}(N-1) + \underline{K}(N)\{\underline{Y}(N) - \underline{HA}\hat{\underline{X}}(N-1) - \underline{HBU}(N-1)\}........(5.1)$$

where $\underline{K}(N)$ is the Kalman gain matrix. It can be calculated as shown in Appendix 1. Equation (5.1) is shown diagramatically in Fig 5.1.

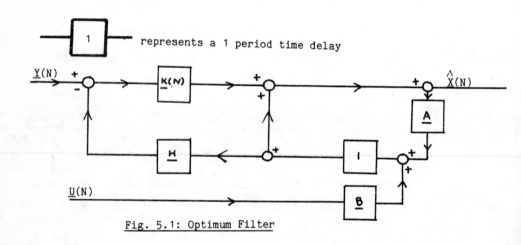

Fig. 5.1: Optimum Filter

Matrices $\underline{A}$, $\underline{H}$, $\underline{B}$ can be made time varying. If measurements are not taken at every time period then either matrix $\underline{H}$ can be altered at different time periods to take into account the different measurements or else the error variance of the missed measurements can be increased to a very large number.

Essentially matrix $\underline{K}(N)$ operates to lower the best estimate error covariance matrix, $\underline{G}(N)$, to the minimum least squares form and a new best estimate is obtained using eq.(5.1), taking as inputs the schedules, the measurements and the old best estimate. The order of events, therefore, in calculating the best estimate is as follows:-

- Determine the system structure and errors and express these in the form of eqs.(3.3) & (3.4), with the associated error covariance matrices $\underline{Q}(N)$ and $\underline{R}(N)$. The system structure and errors will be constant for a stationary system.

- Evaluate matrix $\underline{K}(N)$ as detailed in Appendix 1. If the system is stationary matrix $\underline{K}(N)$ attains a steady state within a few time periods.

- Substitute in the values of the schedules, measurements and the previous best estimate in (5.1) and, by the use of a computer program, produce the value of the new best estimate of the system's state.

In a stationary system matrix $\underline{K}(N)$ tends to the steady state necessary to keep matrix $\underline{G}(N)$ at the minimum least squares value. For a stationary system, therefore, after an initial settling down, matrices $\underline{A}$, $\underline{G}(N)$, $\underline{H}$, $\underline{B}$ and $\underline{K}(N)$ are constant with time.

463

5.2 Cost of Misinformation

It is assumed that the cost of system misinformation in each time period using the best estimate is a quadratic relationship, i.e.:-

$$\text{Cost} = \underline{D}(N)' \, \underline{L} \, \underline{D}(N) \dots\dots\dots\dots\dots (5.2)$$

where $\underline{L}$ is a matrix cost function which can be time varying and $\underline{D}(N)$ is the n vector of the major diagonal elements of $\underline{G}(N)$, the error covariance matrix of the best estimate of the system. The prime symbol,', indicates the transpose of the matrix.

6 EXAMPLE OF THE USE OF THE OPTIMUM FILTER

We will consider the production system described by Fig 6.1, with a manufacturing delay of 8 time periods and the orders being moved from the inter-machining stock after a 1 period delivery delay. This stationary

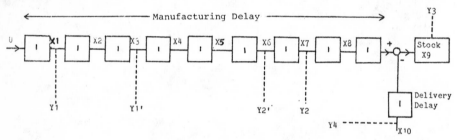

Fig. 6.1: Example

system can be expressed in the form of eqs.(3.3) & (3.4). Matrix $\underline{C}$ is a constant unit identity matrix. The system extrapolation error variance is taken to be 1.0 for each stage, that is $\underline{Q}(N)$ is a constant unit identity matrix. Initially we will take the 4 measurement positions to be Y1, Y2, Y3 & Y4. Y4 is deterministic with the error variance of the other measurements 0.5, and this is expressed as matrix $\underline{R}$.

Starting with the assumed value for $\underline{G}(N)$ taken to be $\underline{A}(N)$, successive values of $\underline{K}(N)$ are calculated by the iterative use of eqs.(8.3) (8.4) &

464

(8.5). Since the system is stationary both matrices $\underline{K}(N)$ and $\underline{G}(N)$ attain a steady state. The diagonal elements of $\underline{G}(N)$ give the variance of the best estimate of the state variables. After several iterations these were found to be:-

X1	0.33	X6	5.33
X2	1.33	X7	0.46
X3	2.33	X8	1.46
X4	3.33	X9	0.43
X5	4.33	X10	0.0

As can be seen the error variances cascade along the system in the absence of any measurements. At the measuring points, (X1, X7, X9 & X10), the measurements lower the error variance of the best estimate. With matrix $\underline{K}(N)$ evaluated, the values of the schedules, the system measurements and the best estimate $\hat{\underline{X}}(N-1)$ can be substituted in eq.(5.1) and, using a computer program, the value of the new best estimate of the state of the system, $\hat{\underline{X}}(N)$, can be produced.

One set of results for the stock level, X9, is shown in Fig 6.2. The

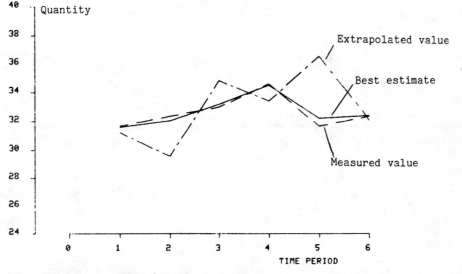

Fig. 6.2: Stock Level

'Extrapolated Value' is the value obtained using eq.(4.1) and the 'Measured Value' that obtained using eq.(4.2). Since the measured values have a lower error variance than the extrapolated values, the values of the best estimate are allied more closely to the former.

If we take matrix $\underline{L}$ to be a unit diagonal matrix but with elements L(10,10) = 0.0 and L(9,9) = 9.5 then the cost of misinformation, given by eq.(5.2), can be calculated. To reduce the cost of misinformation then the positions of the measurements Y1 & Y2 can be altered on a trial and error basis. The cost of misinformation is found to be a minimum when measurements Y1' and Y2' are taken.

The expected misinformation costs can be calculated for this system with different measuring configurations. The results, with misinformation cost matrix $\underline{L}$, are shown below.

EXPECTED MISINFORMATION COSTS PER TIME PERIOD

1. Measurements Y1,Y2,Y3,Y4, no optimum filtering   76.3
2.   "   "   "   with optimum filtering   69.78
3.   "   Y1',Y2',Y3,Y4   "   "   "   23.18

If the costs of taking each measurement were known, further analysis could be undertaken to produce both the optimum number and optimum choice of measurement.

7 CONCLUSION

The use of the filtering techniques is shown to reduce the cost of misinformation. Greater cost reductions can be achieved by an optimum selection of the measurement positions. In the simple example considered, the expected misinformation cost reduction using filtering techniques is about 8 per cent. However this is increased to about 70 per cent by an optimal choice of measurements.

8 APPENDIX 1 - OPTIMUM FILTER

The full derivation of the basic Kalman filter is contained in Kalman (1960) and Kalman & Bucy (1961). The basic Kalman filter is used to obtain the best estimate of the state vector, $\underline{X}(N)$, using the equation:-

$$\hat{\underline{X}}(N) = \underline{A}(N-1)\ \hat{\underline{X}}(N-1) + \underline{K}(N)\{\underline{Y}(N) - \underline{H}\ \underline{A}(N-1)\ \hat{\underline{X}}(N-1)\}\dots\dots\dots(8.1)$$

where $\hat{\underline{X}}(N)$ is the optimum linear estimate, $\underline{Y}(N)$ is the h measurement vector and $\underline{K}(N)$ the n x h Kalman gain matrix, both defined at time period N. $\underline{A}(N-1)$ is a n x n matrix defining the system.

With a deterministic input m vector $\underline{U}(N-1)$, (8.1) can be extended to:-

$$\hat{\underline{X}}(N) = \underline{A}(N-1)\ \hat{\underline{X}}(N-1) + \underline{B}(N-1)\ \underline{U}(N-1) + \underline{K}(N)\{\underline{Y}(N) - \underline{H}\ \underline{A}(N-1)\ \hat{\underline{X}}(N-1)$$

$$+ \underline{H}\ \underline{B}(N-1)\ \underline{U}(N-1)\}\dots\dots\dots\dots(8.2)$$

The following equations, with nomenclature as in eqs.(3.3) and (3.4), are used iteratively to determine matrix $\underline{K}(N)$, the Kalman gain matrix:-

$$\underline{P}(N) = \underline{A}(N-1)\ \underline{G}(N-1)\ \underline{A}(N-1)' + \underline{C}(N-1)\ \underline{Q}(N-1)\ \underline{C}(N-1)'\dots\dots\dots(8.3)$$

$$\underline{K}(N) = \underline{P}(N)\ \underline{H}'\ \{\underline{H}\ \underline{P}(N)\ \underline{H}' + R(N)\}'\dots\dots\dots\dots\dots\dots(8.4)$$

$$\underline{G}(N) = \underline{P}(N) - \underline{K}(N)\ \underline{H}\ \underline{P}(N)\dots\dots\dots\dots\dots\dots\dots(8.5)$$

The prime, ', indicates the transpose of the matrix. $\underline{G}(N)$ is the n x n error covariance matrix of the best estimate, $\hat{\underline{X}}(N)$. $\underline{P}(N)$ is the n x n error covariance matrix of the extrapolated estimate X_p. The iteration is started by assuming an initial estimate of $\underline{G}(0)$ in (8.3) to calculate $\underline{P}(1)$. This is then substituted in (8.4) and (8.5) to obtain values of $\underline{K}(1)$ and $\underline{G}(1)$. The best estimate of the state, $\hat{\underline{X}}(1)$, can then be obtained from (8.2). The iteration can be repeated to give further values of $\underline{K}(N)$, $\underline{G}(N)$ and $\hat{\underline{X}}(N)$.

9 REFERENCES

Aoki M. & Mu Tung Li (1969): 'Optimal Discrete Time Control System With Cost for Observation', IEEE Trans. Auto. Control, Vol. AC-14, 1969.

Coggan G.C. & Wilson J.A. (1971): 'On Line State Estimation With a Small Computer', Computer Journal, Vol. 14, No. 1, p61-64.

Kalman R.E. (1960): 'A New Approach To Linear Filtering & Prediction Problems'. ASME Journal of Basic Engineering, March 1960, p35-40.

Kalman R.E. & Bucy R.S. (1961): 'New Results in Linear Filtering and Prediction Theory'. ASME Journal of Basic Engineering, March 1961, p95-108.

Koivo A.J. & Hendricks C.L. (1973): 'On Optimisation of Sales, Production & Inventory Using a Stochastic Model', Int. J. Sys. Sci., Vol. 4, No. 3, p407-416.

O'Grady P.J. & Bonney M.C. (1980): 'An Introduction to the Application of Modern Control Theory To Production Control', Working Paper 80/1, Dept. Production Engineering & Production Management, University of Nottingham, 1980.

Stohr E.A. (1979): 'Information Systems for Observing Inventory Levels'. Operations Research, Vol 27, No 2, p242-259.

Tapiero C.S. (1977): 'Optimisation of Information Measurement with Inventory Applications'. INFOR, Vol 15, No 1, p50-61.

Proc. First Int. Symp. on Inventories
Budapest, Hungary 1980

A BATCH SIZE MODEL
FOR THE HOSPITAL PHARMACY

C. CARL PEGELS

State University of New York at Buffalo, Buffalo, NY, USA

Introduction

The newsboy problem is a classic example of how to apply a tabular
model to determine the number of newspapers a newsboy should acquire so
that he can maximize his expected profit. Unfortunately, the application
of the newsboy problem model is rather limited because of several limitations inherent in the model. Limitations consist of assumed perishability
of the product, a fixed time period, knowledge of sales level probabilities,
and others.

In this paper we shall show the development of a model to determine the
optimum batch size of a pharmaceutical product for use in a hospital setting.
The model is a variation of the newsboy problem model with important differences and similarities. Similarities include the perishability of the product and the use of discrete usage (demand) probabilities. However, the
differences create some real problems. Whereas the newsboy problem is a
profit maximization problem, the hospital pharmaceutical problem is a cost
minimization problem. Also, there is no fixed planning period in the hospital pharmaceutical problem, only a maximum length planning period. Hence,
the model to be developed for the hospital pharmaceutical model is substantially more extensive and complex than the newsboy problem model.

The Hospital Pharmaceutical Model

The model considers two cost components. The one cost, batch preparation cost, decreases as batch size increases, and the other cost, waste cost, increases as batch size increases.

The planning period has a maximum length determined by the length of time the pharmaceutical product is viable. Since batches of the pharmaceutical product can be prepared at any time, the length of an actual planning period is determined by the usage rate of the pharmaceutical product during the respective planning period. Whenever a batch is used up, or whenever the batch reaches its maximum lifetime, a new batch is prepared. Hence, the hospital pharmaceutical product model is essentially a variable planning period model.

Operationally, a batch size will be determined, and this batch will be prepared. When this batch is used up, another batch of equal size will be prepared. If a batch is not used up during the life of the batch, then a waste cost is incurred. The central problem is how a model can be formulated that will allow us to determine an optimal batch size for a variable planning period.

The optimal batch size model that is developed uses a variable planning period but a fixed planning horizon. The length of the planning horizon must at a minimum be several multiples of the maximum length of the planning period. For instance, if the maximum length of the planning period is 96 hours or four days, then a reasonable planning horizon is 30 days (one month) or 60 days (2 months).

As we stated above, the pharmaceutical product model is a tabular model. It has m demand levels, identified as y_i, $i = 1,\ldots,m$. For each demand level, y_i there is associated a probability of demand $P_i(y)$ such that,

$$\sum_{i=1}^{m} P_i(y) = 1 .$$ (1)

The demand levels and their respective probabilities are for a fixed period equal to the life of the pharmaceutical product. The expected demand during the fixed period will therefore be,

$$E(y) = \sum_{i=1}^{m} y_i P_i(y) .$$ (2)

The planning horizon will be defined as a multiple of the planning periods such that the length of the planning period is equal to the life of the pharmaceutical product. If the planning horizon is equal to n planning periods, then the expected demand during the planning horizon will be,

$$E(Y) = nE(y) .$$ (3)

The expected requirements of the pharmaceutical product during the planning horizon will be somewhat larger than the demand because $E(Y)$ does not include the number of units that will be outdated and thus wasted. The amount of waste will depend on the batch size selected.

If the selected size of the batch to be prepared is B, then the expected number of batches $E[z(B)]$, based on demand only, during the planning horizon will be,

$$E[z(B)] = E(Y)/B .$$ (4)

Note that B will lie in the range from the minimum value of y to the maximum value of y .

The expected number of units wasted, $E(W,B)$, for batch size B during a planning horizon is then,

$$E(W,B) = \sum_{i=1}^{m} (B - y_i) \, P_i(y) \, E[z(B)]/[1 - P_i(y)] \; . \tag{5}$$

In each instance that the term $B - y_i < 0$, it should be set equal to zero.

We can now determine the expected requirements during the planning horizon. Note that requirements include both demand and units wasted. For batch size B, expected requirements are,

$$E(Y,B) = E(Y) + E(W,B) \; . \tag{6}$$

The expected number of batches of size B, $E[z'(B)]$, during the planning horizon will now amount to,

$$E[z'(B)] = E(Y,B)/B \; . \tag{7}$$

Note that $E[z'(B)] \geq E[z(B)]$.

If we define the preparation cost of batch B to be $PC(B)$, then the total expected preparation cost during the planning horizon for batch size B will amount to,

$$E[TPC(B)] = E[z'(B)] \; PC(B) \; . \tag{8}$$

Similarly, if the waste cost per unit wasted is WC, then the expected waste cost during the planning horizon for batch size B will amount to

$$E[TWC(B)] = E(W,B) \; WC \; . \tag{9}$$

The total expected cost for batch size B, during the planning horizon

472

will therefore amount to,

$$E\big[TC(B)\big] = E\big[TPC(B)\big] + E\big[TWC(B)\big] \ . \qquad (10)$$

Since the objective is cost minimization, we select that batch B which will minimize total expected cost during the planning horizon.

The Batch Sizing Model for the Hospital Pharmaceutical Product

Although there were numerous pharmaceutical products to which the model could be applied, we shall illustrate the model by just applying it to one of these products. The demand during the 96 hour lifespan of the pharmaceutical product ranged from 90 to 149 units. To include each one of the demand levels between 90 and 149 in a tabular array clearly would have been prohibitive because it would have made the application too extensive and difficult to comprehend. For that reason the 60 demand levels from 90 to 149 were grouped into six demand ranges as shown in Table 1. The midpoint for each demand range was also determined to assist in determining the expected demand during the planning period.

Table 1 Expected Demand Calculation -- Pharmaceutical Product

Demand Range $(y_L - y_H)$	Demand Midpoint (y)	Probability of Demand $P(y)$	Expected Demand $yP(y)$
90 – 99	94.5	.071	6.71
100–109	104.5	.107	11.18
110–119	114.5	.286	32.75
120–129	124.5	.286	35.61
130–139	134.5	.143	19.23
140–149	144.5	.107	15.46
			120.94

A planning horizon of 30 days was selected. Since the expected demand during the four day planning period is 120.94 units, the expected demand during the planning horizon will amount to 907.05 units.

The calculations for the expected units wasted during the planning horizon are shown on Table 2. Note that the batch sizes are not set at the midpoints of each demand range but at the maximum of each demand range.

Table 2   Expected Waste Calculations — Pharmaceutical Product

Batch Size (B)	Monthly Expected Demand* E(Y)	Expected Number of Units Wasted per Month E(W,B)
99	907.05	4.5[.071(9.16)/(1 - .071)] = 3.150
109	907.05	14.5[.071(8.32)/(1 - .071)] + 4.5[.107(8.32)/(1 - .107)] = 13.706
119	907.05	24.5[.071(7.62)/(1 - .071)] + 14.5[.107(7.62)/(1 - .107)] + 4.5[.286(7.62)/(1 - .286)] = 41.242
129	907.05	34.5[.071(7.03)/(1 - .071)] + 24.5[.107(7.03)/(1 - .107)] + 14.5[.286(7.03)/(1 - .286)] + 4.5[.286(7.03)/(1 - .286)] = 92.676
139	907.05	44.5[.071(6.53)/(1 - .071)] + 34.5[.107(6.53)/(1 - .107)] + 24.5[.286(6.53)/(1 - .286)] + 14.5[.286(6.53)/(1 - .286)] + 4.5[.143(6.53)/(1 - .143)] = 156.116
149	907.05	54.5[.071(6.09)/(1 - .071)] + 44.5[.107(6.09)/(1 - .107)] + 34.5[.286(6.09)/(1 - .286)] + 24.5[.286(6.09)/(1 - .286)] + 14.5[.143(6.09)/(1 - .143)] + 4.5[.107(6.09)/(1 - .107)] = 219.783

*Based on 30 days which equals 7.5 stability lifetimes of 4 days each.

The calculations for determining the optimal batch size are shown on Table 3. The preparation cost formula is,

$$PC(B) = 5.40 + 0.05B , \qquad (11)$$

Table 3   Optimum Batch Size Calculations — Pharmaceutical Product

Batch Size (B)	Expected Monthly Demand E(Y)	Expected Monthly Number of Units Wasted E(W,B)	Expected Monthly Number of Units Required E(Y,B)	Monthly Number of Batches E[z´(B)]	Preparation Cost per Batch PC(B)	Expected Monthly Preparation Cost E[TPC(B)]	Expected Monthly Waste Cost E[TWC(B)]	Expected Monthly Total Cost E[TC(B)]
99	907.05	3.150	910.200	9.194	$10.35	$95.16	$ 7.56	$ 102.72
109	907.05	13.706	920.756	8.447	10.85	91.65	32.89	124.54
119	907.05	41.242	948.292	7.969	11.35	90.45	98.98	189.43
129	907.05	92.676	999.726	7.750	11.85	91.85	222.42	314.27
139	907.05	156.116	1063.166	7.649	12.35	94.47	374.68	469.15
149	907.05	219.783	1126.833	7.563	12.85	97.18·	527.48	624.66

and the cost of each unit wasted, $WC = 2.40$. The optimal batch size is 99 units. Note that increasing the batch size to 109 units only increases total cost by a small amount. However, increases in batch size beyond 109 units increase cost considerably.

Conclusion

The batch sizing model developed for the hospital pharmaceutical product problem has been instrumental in assisting the pharmacy staff of a large general hospital to deal with a problem they were unable to solve on their own. The model developed is a variation of the basic tabular profit maximization model, also called the newsboy problem, which was developed years ago. The unusual situation that necessitated development of a unique model, resulted from the need to consider a variable planning period. However, the variable planning period could be transformed into a fixed planning horizon.

Proc. First Int. Symp. on Inventories
Budapest, Hungary 1980

RELIABILITY TYPE INVENTORY MODELS.
A SURVEY

ANDRÁS PRÉKOPA

Computer and Automation Institute, Hungarian Academy of Sciences,
Budapest, Hungary

1. Introduction. In the early sixties the National Planning
Board in Hungary raised the problem that how much the
inventory levels of basic materials (or semi-products) should
be increased at a factory if its production is increased
according to a given rate. The answer to this question lead
to the formulation of some new inventory models [9] where also
the applied mathematical tool is different from those used in
conventional inventory control theory.

After an almost a year diagnostical activity of the
research group dealing with the problem it was recognized that
no backorder cost would have been available. Furthermore
material deliveries did not occur so that to every order there
would have corresponded one (or a few) fixed delivery time
point(s) with fixed delivered amounts.

The typical situation that existed and still exists to
some extent can be described as follows: Factory A supplies
Factory B by some material that Factory B uses with constant
intensity in time (this assumption was dropped later on).
Contracts are made between these two partners so that before
every quarter of a year, say, the amount that is needed by
Factory B will be delivered by Factory A. There is no agreement,
however, regarding the number of, time points of and amounts of
deliveries. The question is now, how large we have to choose
the initial inventory level (existing beginning of the actual
quarter of a year) so that Factory B should be able to use

continuously the material in question.

2. The basic models.

Let us consider one quarter of a year or more generally one time interval for which such a problem is formulated and assume that this is the interval $(0,T)$. We will assume that the number of deliveries is fixed and is equal to n. In the first model published later on by M.Ziermann and the author of this paper it was assumed that

a.) the delivery time points are random and they are distributed on the interval $(0,T)$ similarly as are n randomly and on this interval uniformly distributed points;

b.) the individually delivered amounts are equal to each other;

c.) the use of the material at Factory B is continuous and has a constant intensity c (the amount used in unit time). Thus during time T Factory B needs the amount cT.

The initial inventory level, that will be the single decision variable in the model, will be denoted by M. If we denote by $\xi(t)$ the amount delivered up to time t then our problem can be formulated in the following way [10], [18] : find M such that

(2.1)
$$P\left(\inf_{0\leq t\leq T}\ (M+\xi(t)-ct)\geq 0\right) = 1-\varepsilon$$

where $1-\varepsilon$ is a prescribed probability, near unity in practice. The probability levels for $1-\varepsilon$ that are primarily used are 0.8, 0.9 and 0.95. Requirement (2.1) means that the random broken line $M+\xi(t)$ has to be above the straight line cT in the whole time interval $(0,T)$ (see Fig.1).

It was shown in [10] and [18] that (2.1) is equivalent to

(2.2)
$$P\left(\sup_{0\leq t\leq T}\ \left(\frac{t}{T} - \frac{1}{cT}\xi(t)\right)\leq \frac{M}{cT}\right) = 1-\varepsilon$$

This equation is called the reliability equation. The random function $\frac{1}{cT}\xi(t)$ can be considered as an empirical distribution function belonging to a sample of size n taken from a

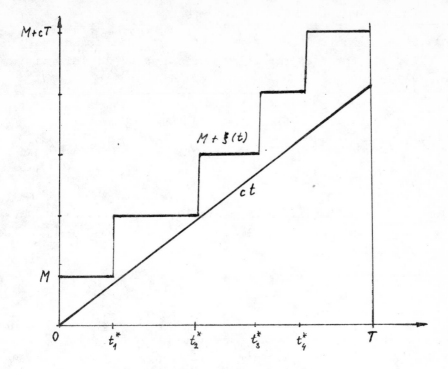

Figure 1

The material supply is ensured in the
time interval $(0, T)$ if the broken
line $M + \xi(t)$ is above the straight
line ct in the whole interval $(0, T)$.

population uniformly distributed in the interval $(0, T)$. By the application of results in order statistics [1] we immediately obtain a formula for the probability standing on the left hand side of (2.2):

(2.3)
$$P\left(\sup_{0 \leq t \leq T}\left(\frac{t}{T} - \frac{1}{cT}\xi(t)\right) \leq \frac{M}{cT}\right)$$
$$= 1 - \frac{M}{cT}\sum_{i=0}^{\left[n\left(1 - \frac{M}{cT}\right)\right]}\binom{n}{i}\left(1 - \frac{M}{cT} - \frac{i}{n}\right)^{n-i}\left(\frac{M}{cT} + \frac{i}{n}\right)^{i-1}$$

that provides us with another form of the equation (2.1).

For large n (roughly $n \geq 10$) a simple approximation can be given for the above mentioned probability. In fact by the theorem of Smirnov we have

(2.4)
$$\lim_{n \to \infty} P\left(\sqrt{n}\sup_{0 \leq t \leq T}\left(\frac{t}{T} - \frac{1}{cT}\xi(t)\right) \leq y\right) = 1 - e^{-2y^2}$$

if $y > 0$ and the limit is equal to zero if $y \leq 0$. Assuming n large enough to have good approximation in (2.4) without the lim sign and setting $y = \sqrt{n}\frac{M}{cT}$, we obtain the following approximate form of the reliability equation:

$$1 - e^{-2\left(\sqrt{n}\frac{M}{cT}\right)^2} \approx 1 - \varepsilon$$

from where we get

(2.5)
$$M \approx cT\sqrt{\frac{1}{2n}\ln\frac{1}{\varepsilon}}.$$

To answer the original practical problem we now assume that if the production at Factory B increases then c increases proportionally, furthermore n also increases proportionally with c. This means

$$M = K\sqrt{c}$$

where K is a constant. For the elasticity of M with respect to c we get

$$\frac{dM}{dc}\frac{c}{M} = \frac{1}{2}.$$

Thus, roughly speaking, if the production at Factory B is increased by 1% then the inventory level M has to be increased only by 1/2%.

In case of a more general delivery process $\xi(t)$ and an $\eta(t)$ consumption (use) process of the material, the reliability equation can be written in the following more general form:

$$(2.6) \qquad P\left(\inf_{0 \leq t \leq T} (M + \xi(t) - \eta(t)) \geq 0\right) = 1 - \varepsilon.$$

The first generalization of the above described model given by the author [10] dropes the rectrictive condition b. Instead, it is assumed that if a delivery occurs then there is a minimum amount delivered that is denoted by δ and the remaining amount $cT - n\delta$ is delivered at the n delivery occasions in random quantities so that an interval of length $(0, cT - n\delta)$ is subdivided into n parts by $n-1$ independent and uniformly distributed random points and these parts are added subsequently to the already fixed δ amounts.

Let $c = T = 1$ in the sequal, for the sake of simplicity, furthermore $\lambda = n\delta$. Define the following "generalized empirical distribution function":

$$(2.7) \qquad F_n(t, \lambda) = \begin{cases} 0 & , \text{ if } 0 \leq t \leq t_1^* \\ \lambda \frac{k}{n} + (1-\lambda) \tau_k^* & , \text{ if } t_k^* < t \leq t_{k+1}^*, \quad k = 1, \ldots, n-1, \\ 1 & , \text{ if } t_n^* < t \leq 1, \end{cases}$$

where $\tau_1^*, \tau_2^*, \ldots, \tau_{n-1}^*$ and $t_1^*, t_2^*, \ldots, t_n^*$ are independent ordered samples taken from the interval $(0, 1)$. The following generalization of the theorem of Smirnov was first mentioned in [10] and proved in [11]:

$$(2.8) \quad \lim_{n \to \infty} P\left(\sqrt{\frac{n}{1+(1-\lambda)^2}} \sup_{0 \le t \le 1} \left(t - F_n(t,\lambda)\right) \le y\right) = 1 - e^{-2y^2}$$

if $y > 0$ and the limit equals zero if $y \le 0$.

Using (2.8) we can obtain an approximate formula for $M = M_\lambda$:

$$(2.9) \quad M_\lambda \approx \sqrt{1 + (1-\lambda)^2} \sqrt{\frac{1}{2n} \ln \frac{1}{\varepsilon}}$$

In case of a random consumption process $\eta(t)$, similar modelling is possible. In the case where we apply this kind of modelling for both $\xi(t)$ and $\eta(t)$, keeping the stochastic independence of these two processes, the approximate formula for the initial inventory level is given in [10], [11]. This reads as follows:

$$(2.10) \quad M_{\lambda,\mu} = \sqrt{\frac{1 + (1-\lambda)^2}{n} + \frac{1 + (1-\mu)^2}{m}} \sqrt{\frac{1}{2} \ln \frac{1}{\varepsilon}}$$

where μ and m correspond to the process $\eta(t)$ similarly as λ and n correspond to the process $\xi(t)$.

3. Further results. The special case $\lambda = 0$ was investigated in more detailed by Z.László [4], [5]. He derived the formula

$$(2.11) \quad P\left(\sup_{0 \le t \le 1} \left(t - F_n(t,0)\right) \le M\right) = 1 - (1-M)^n (1+M)^{n-1}$$

if $0 < M < 1$ and is equal to 0 if $M \le 0$. Similar formula was derived for the case where the total delivered amount is not the same as the amount used by Factory B but M and c satisfy the relation: $\max(0, c-1) < M < c$. Various other special problems were solved too in this connection in the work [4].

Approximating the stochastic processes $\xi(t)$ and $\eta(t)$ by Wiener processes , Gy.Németh obtained simple expression for M [7]. J.Pintér dealt with the problem of determining an inventory level ensuring the continuous production in many subsequent periods [8] .

A generalization of the above-mentioned reliability type models was formulated in [12] and developed in more detail in [15] . The generalization consists on one hand side in dropping the condition of homogenity of the delivery process and on the other hand in formulating the problem for more than one kind of material. To describe this we assume that the number of delivery time points is equal to (the fixed number) n and the consumption process at Factory B has a constant intensity. We also keep the convention $c = T = 1$ (the units can always be chosen in such a way that these equalities hold). Let δ be the same as before and choose in the interval $(0, 1-n\delta)$ independently of each other L random and in this interval uniformly distributed points. Then from ordered sample $y_1^* < y_2^* < ... < y_L^*$ we select those that correspond to subscripts $i_1 < i_2 < ... < i_{n-1}$ and define the random variables:

$$\eta_1 = y_{i_1}^* \quad , \quad \eta_2 = y_{i_2}^* - y_{i_1}^* \quad , \quad ... \quad , \quad \eta_n = 1 - n\delta - y_{i_{n-1}}^* .$$

The amounts delivered at the subsequent delivery time points are then defined so that these are

$$\delta + \eta_1 \quad , \quad \delta + \eta_2 \quad , \quad ... \quad , \quad \delta + \eta_n .$$

Similar is the modelling of the delivery time points where instead of δ, L we use γ, N which are not necessarily the same as those in case of the delivery amounts. The delivery time points will be the partial sums of the sequence:

$$\gamma + \xi_1 \quad , \quad \gamma + \xi_2 \quad , \quad ... \quad , \quad \gamma + \xi_n$$

Introducing the random variables

$$\zeta_1 = \xi_1 ,$$
$$\zeta_2 = \xi_1 + \xi_2 - \eta_1 ,$$
$$\vdots$$
$$\zeta_n = \xi_1 + \xi_2 + ... + \xi_n - \eta_1 - \eta_2 - ... - \eta_{n-1} .$$

We can formulate the condition of the safe material supply by the system of inequalities

$$(3.1) \qquad \xi_j \leqq M + (j-1)\delta - j\gamma \quad , \quad j=1, \dots, n.$$

Let $h(M)$ denote the probability that the inequalities (3.1) hold jointly. Then the reliability equation reads as

$$(3.2) \qquad h(M) = 1 - \varepsilon.$$

In case of k different materials we have k different functions: $h_1(M), \dots, h_k(M)$ and to determine $M^{(1)}, \dots, M^{(k)}$ we formulate the following stochastic programming problem:

$$(3.3) \qquad \text{minimize} \sum_{i=1}^{k} d_i M^{(i)}$$

$$\text{subject to}$$

$$H(\underline{M}) = h_1(M^{(1)}) \dots h_k(M^{(k)}) \geqq 1 - \varepsilon,$$

$$\underline{M} \geqq \underline{0}, \quad \underline{M} \in D,$$

where $\underline{M}$ is the vector of components $M^{(1)}, \dots, M^{(k)}$; D is some set in the k-dimensional Euclidean space and $d_1, \dots, d_k$ are some (nonnegative) numbers that somehow penalize the unit inventory levels.

Note that the random vectors:

$$\underline{\eta} = (\eta_1, \dots, \eta_{m-1}) \qquad \text{and} \qquad \underline{\xi} = (\xi_1, \dots, \xi_m)$$

are assumed to be stochastically independent. Both $\underline{\eta}$ and $\underline{\xi}$ have Dirichlet distributions (see [17]).
It is shown in [12] , [13] , [14] that $H(\underline{M})$ is a logarithmically concave function of the vector valued variable $\underline{M}$ thus the probabilistic constraint in Problem (3.3) determines a convex set of the vectors $\underline{M}$. If furthermore D is a convex set then

(3.3) is a convex programming problem.

In $[12], [15]$ further similar stochastic programming models are also mentioned.

The numerical evaluation of Problem (3.3) and the other problems mentioned in $[12]$ and $[15]$ goes via combination of nonlinear programming and Monte Carlo technique. The SUMT method is particularly well suited with logarithmic penalty function because then the individual unconstrained problems involve convex functions to be minimized which is a favoured task in numerical analysis.

Among the further results regarding these reliability type inventory models most significant is the explicit formula obtained by P.Kelle and Z.László $[3]$, $[6]$. We assume again $T = 1$. The symbol c will kept because we will not assume now that the total delivery during time T equals the total demand at Factory B. The formula given below will be somewhat more general also in the sense that we require the permanent material supply only in the subinterval $(0, s)$ of the interval $(0, 1)$ i.e, $s \leqq 1$. We have

$$P\left(\sup_{0 \leqq t \leqq s} \left(ct - F_n(t, \lambda)\right) \leqq M\right) = 1 - \left(1 - \frac{M}{c}\right)^n - \frac{M}{c} \sum_{k=1}^{r} k \binom{n}{k} \binom{n-1}{k} \cdot$$

(3.4)

$$\cdot \int_0^{a_k} \left(\frac{M + (1-\lambda)z + \lambda \frac{k}{n}}{c}\right)^{k-1} \left(1 - \frac{M + (1-\lambda)z + \lambda \frac{k}{n}}{c}\right)^{n-k} z^{k-1} (1-z)^{n-k-1} dz,$$

where it is assumed that $\max(0, s-1) < M < cs$ and the symbols a_k, r are defined as $(0 < \lambda < 1)$:

$$a_k = \min\left(\frac{cs - M - \lambda \frac{k}{n}}{1 - \lambda}, 1\right);$$

$$r = \min\left(\left[\frac{n}{\lambda}(cs - M)\right], n-1\right).$$

If $\lambda \varnothing 0$ then $r = \hbar - 1$ and if $\lambda = 1$ then $a_k = 1$ by definition.

To prove (3.4) László applied a direct reasoning whereas Kelle based his consideration on some results of Takács concerning the maximum functional of stochastic processes [16]. Kelle obtained a formula that is more general than (3.4) and from where (3.4) is easily derivable [3] .

P.Kelle also found formula and application for the case when the consumption intensity is random [3] and solved an asphalt mixing problem [2] by a variant of the reliability type models mentioned in this paper.

4. Applications. Since the formulation of the models described in Section 2. and the first applications mentioned already in [9] these models became very popular and widely used in Hungary. In the mid sixties an unofficial report estimated the total national saving obtained by the reduction of the superfluous stock on the basis of the reliability type model to be about 4-5 billion (10^9) Forints. Many further applications are reported so far so that we may say these models became quite standard. Attempts were made several times to apply models where costs are involved, only a few of them were successful, however.

Among the most significant applications of the reliability type models described in this paper the following should be mentioned.

The Kerinforg Systems Research Company in Budapest belonging to the Ministry of Internal Trade created the DORIS (Demand Oriented Inventory System) program system [21],[25], at the end of the sixties, where the general formulas first published in [10] are applied to determine safety stock. This was successfully applied at several wholesale companies (radioelectricity, sport goods and toys etc.). Researchers who participated in this work are L.Gerencsér, Sz.Halász, A,Móricz, Á.Skrabszki, I.Vass and the author.

Another system was developed by the Vilati (Institute for Electrical Automation) with the name STOMCOS (Stock Management and Control System) where also the formulas in [10] were applied to determine the safety stock level. The system was applied among others for the Metalloglobus Company in Budapest. Similar system was developed for some central means of production trade companies at the Institute for Automation of the Technical University of Budapest with the participation of T.Gál, P.Kelle and T.Kovács [22] .

An application for the general model described in Section 2. for a sulphuric acid producing factory was made by Z.László [4] . In that special problem his formula for the case of $\lambda \cdot 0$ had to be applied (see in Section 3.).

In the Hungarian Synthetic Material Processing Firm the safety stock is permanently determined on the basis of reliability type models. This application work aiming several other objectives was directed by A.Chikán and E. Megyeri of the Economic University of Budapest [19] .

The Chemical Computing and Development Trust in Budapest worked out a complex system for production control in chemical companies. Reliability type inventory models are heavily used in this. A report on this is written by M.Preisich, A.Szalai, B.Pompéry and G.Szatmári [24].

The Danube Cement Company has determined the safety stock levels for more than 10000 materials by the use of the reliability models.

Recently in the Danube Steelwork, the largest steelwork in Hungary introduced an inventory system using reliability models. The programs were prepared in the Computer and Automation Institute of the Hungarian Academy of Sciences.

Several application were done by M.Ziermann, one of the initiator of this kind of model family. The names of Gy. Meszéna, Z.Kelemen, G.Bodnár, Gy.Németh sould also be mentioned among the names of principal contributors to the applicational results.

487

Many further important applicational results could be listed.
It is perhaps needless to continue to describe them, the
practical significance of the reliability type models family
is well illustrated by the above mentioned examples.

References

1   Z.W.Birnbaum and F.H.Tingey, One-Sided Confidence Contours
    for Probability Distribution Functions, Annals of Mathe-
    matical Statistics 22(1951) 592-596.

2   P.Kelle, Chance Constrained Inventory Model for an Asphalt
    Mixing Problem, Recent Results in Stochastic Programming,
    Proceedings Oberwolfach 1979, Lecture Notes in Economics
    and Mathematical Systems 179, 179-189.

3   P.Kelle, On a Reliability Type Inventory Model, Submitted
    for publication in European Journal of Operations Research

4   Z.László, A Completely Random Reliability Type Inventory
    Model, Thesis, Hungarian Academy of Sciences, Budapest,
    1970, (in Hungarian).

5   Z.László, Some Recent Result Concerning Reliability Type
    Inventory Models, Colloquia Mathematica Societatis János
    Bolyai 7. Inventory Control and Water Storage, North
    Holland Publishing Company 1973, 179-187.

6   Z.László, On Reliability Type Inventory Models, Paper
    presented at the 9th Hungarian Operations Research
    Conference, Szeged, Hungary, 1978.

7   Gy.Németh, Investigations Concenring Stochastic Inventory
    Models, MTA Matematikai és Fizikai Tudományok Osztályának
    Közleményei (Publications of the Department of Mathematics
    and Physics of the Hungarian Academy of Sciences) 20 (1971)
    133-135.

8   J.Pintér, Investigation Concerning the Maximum Deviation
    of Sequences of Empirical Distribution Functions; Appli-

cation for a Multi Period Reliability Type Inventory
Model, Alkalmazott Matematikai Lapok (Journal of Applied
Mathematics) 1 (1975) 189-197. (in Hungarian).

9   A.Prékopa and M.Ziermann, On the Minimal Inventory Level
Ensuring Continuous Production, National Planning Board,
Budapest, 1962 (in Hungarian).

10   A.Prékopa, Reliability Equation for an Inventory Problem
and its Asymptotic Solutions, Colloquium on the
Application of Mathematics to Economics, Publ. House of
the Hungarian Academy of Sciences 1965, 317-327.

11   A.Prékopa, Generalizations of the Theorems of Smirnov with
Application to a Reliability Type Inventory Problem,
Mathematische Operationsforschung und Statistik 4(1973)
283-297.

12   A.Prékopa, Stochastic Programming Models for Inventory
Control and Water Storage Problems, Colloquia Mathematica
Societatis János Bolyai 7.Inventory Control and Water
Storage, North Holland Publishing Company 1973, 229-247.

13   A.Prékopa, Logarithmic Concave Measures with Application
to Stochastic Programming, Acta Scientiarum Mathematicarum
32 (1971) 301-316.

14   A.Prékopa, On Logarithmic Concave Measures and Functions,
Acta Scientiarum Mathematicarum 34 (1973) 283-297.

15   A.Prékopa and P.Kelle, Reliability Type Inventory Models
Based on Stochastic Programming, Mathematical Programming
Study 9 (1978) 43-58.

16   L.Takács, Combinatorial Methods in the Theory of Stochastic
Processes, Wiley, 1967.

17   S.S.Wilks, Mathematical Statistics, Wiley, 1962.

18   M.Ziermann, Application of the Theorem of Smirnov for an
Inventory Problem, MTA Matematikai Kutató Intézetének
Közleményei (Publications of the Mathematical Institute
of the Hungarian Academy of Sciences) 8(1963)509-516.

Applicational Reports

19   A.Chikán and E.Megyeri, Development of the Inventory
     Control System of the Hungarian Synthetic Material
     Processing Company, Institute for Industrial Economics,
     Economic University of Budapest, 1971 (in Hungarian).

20   A.Chikán, J.Berács, P.Kelle, M.Nagy, I.Vass, Integrated
     Inventory Control System for Machine Manufacturing
     Companies, Gépipari Technológiai Intézet,(Machine
     Technological Institute) Budapest, 1976.

21   DORIS (Demand Oriented Inventory System) Inventory
     Control System, Kerinforg, 1971 (in Hungarian).

22   T.Gál, P.Kelle, T.Kovács, The STOMCOS Inventory Control
     Program System and its Application to the Metalloglobus
     Company, Institute for Automation, Technical University
     of Budapest, 1977 (in Hungarian).

23   I.Nagy and A.Prékopa, Investigations on Optimal Inventory
     Control at Mine Machine Manufaturing Companies, Institute
     for Industrial Economics, Organization and Computing
     technique, Ministry of Heavy Industry, Budapest, 1968
     (in Hungarian).

24   M.Preisich, A.Szalai,B.Pompéry, G.Szatmáry, Production
     Control at Chemical Companies, Lecture held at the
     Conference on Production Control, Hungarian Academy of
     Sciences, Budapest, 1978.

25   I.Vass, Application of an Inventory Control Model Based
     on a Stochastic Input-Output Process in the Distribution
     Industry, Keirnforg, 1973.

Proc. First Int. Symp. on Inventories
Budapest, Hungary 1980

ON THE MULTICOMMODITY
ARROW-KARLIN INVENTORY MODEL

RYSZARDA REMPAŁA

Institute of Mathematics, Polish Academy of Sciences, Warsaw, Poland

§1. Summary

The aim of this paper is to present some properties of the optimal solution of a generalization of Arrow and Karlin's inventory problem.

§2. Formulation of the problem

Let us suppose that n commodities are produced continuously during a time period $[0,T]$.

The cost of production per unit of time when the rate of production is $u = (u_1, \ldots, u_n)$ is equal to $c(a_1 u_1 + \ldots + a_n u_n)$ where a_i are some positive constants and the function $c(\cdot)$ is assumed to be nonnegative, monotone increasing, strictly convex and twice continuously differentiable.

The commodities may be kept in magazine. Hence holding cost is incorporated. The positive numbers h_i denotes unit cost of holding of the i-th commodity. It is supposed that the rate at which the commodities are demanded is known, the rate is denoted by the vector-function $r(t) = (r_1(t), \ldots, r_n(t))$, $r_1(t), \ldots, r_n(t)$ being positive. All demands are assumed to be met, so at time t the inventories denoted by the vector $Y(t) = (Y_1(t), \ldots, Y_n(t))$, are equal to

$$Y(t) = y_0 + \int_0^t (u(s) - r(s)) ds, \quad \text{where} \quad y_0 = (y_1, \ldots, y_n)$$

denotes the initial value of inventories.

The problem is to schedule the production so as to minimize the production and holding costs under the conditions of satisfying demands for every commodity in any time. In other words a production policy is required to be chosen so as to minimize

$$I(u) = \int_0^T \{c(a_1 u_1(t) + \ldots + a_n u_n(t)) + h_1 Y_1(t) + \ldots + h_n Y_n(t)\} dt; \quad (1)$$

under the constraints $(i = 1, 2, \ldots, n)$

$$\frac{d}{dt} Y_i(t) = u_i(t) - r_i(t), \quad Y_i(0) = y_i; \quad (2)$$

$$Y_i(t) \geq 0, \quad u_i(t) \geq 0 \quad \text{for} \quad t \in [0, T]. \quad (3)$$

Let us note that one may take $Y_i(0) = 0$ and

$$\tilde{r}_i(t) = \begin{cases} 0 & \text{if} \quad y_i - \int_0^t r_i(s) ds > 0 \\ r_i(t) & \text{otherwise} \end{cases}$$

instead of r_i and $Y_i(0) = y_i$, $(i = 1, 2, \ldots, n)$.

§3. The case $a_1 = \ldots = a_n$, $h_1 = \ldots = h_n$

The assumption stated in the subtitle means that the commodities are identical with respect to the production and holding costs but they may be different with respect to the demands (e.g. the same kind of product but of different colours, this latter fact being of importance for a consumer).

In such a situation optimization may be carried on in two steps. First, one can obtain the optimal solution of the one commodity problem with the initial inventory $Y(0) = 0$ and demand $\tilde{r}(t) = \tilde{r}_1(t) + \ldots + \tilde{r}_n(t)$, where $\tilde{r}_i$ were defined above. The optimal solution of such an optimization problem has been well known since the paper of Arrow and Karlin (1958). This solution gives the production u^* which obviously satisfies the summary demand $\tilde{r}$, i.e.

$$Y^*(t) = \int_0^t (u^*(s) - \tilde{r}(s)) ds \geq 0 \quad \text{for} \quad t \in [0, T].$$

In the second step the production plan u_i^* for each i-th commodity is constructed in such a way that $u_i^* \geq 0$, $u_1^* + \ldots + u_n^* = u^*$ and

$$Y_i^*(t) = \int_o^t (u_i^*(s) - \tilde{r}_i(s))ds \geq 0, \quad \text{for } t \in [0,T], \ i = 1,2,\ldots,n.$$

For a detailed construction and the proof of its optimality see Rempała (1975).

§4. The case $a_1 = \ldots = a_n = 1$, $h_1 < h_2 \ldots < h_n$

It is easy to see that the assumption $a_1 = \ldots = a_n = 1$ does not decrease generality of the problem (1)-(3) and so it will be assumed in the sequel.

Under the assumption $h_1 < h_2 \ldots < h_n$ the problem (1)-(3) cannot be reduced to a one-dimensional problem in a straightforward manner. The full construction of the optimal solution for $n = 2$ was given in Rempała (1977). Some properties of the optimal solution for arbitrary $n \geq 1$ will be considered here. In what follows we shall assume that the function r is bounded and has both one sided limits at each point. Due to assumptions on the costs and the constraints the problem (1)-(3) is a convex optimal control problem with constraints on the state of the system. The production u is considered as a control variable and inventory Y as a state variable. So if u is treated as a function from $L^2(0,T;R^n)$ and Y from $H^1(0,T;R^n)$ then by the maximum principle (cf. Bensoussan et al. 1974) the following theorem may be obtained

Theorem. If $u = (u_1,\ldots,u_n) \in L^2(0,T;R^n)$ is an optimal solution of the problem (1)-(3), then there exist functions λ_i, $i = 1,2,\ldots,n$ such that

(i) λ_i is non-decreasing and right-continuous,

(ii) λ_i is constant in any interval of time where

$$Y_i(t) = y_i + \int_o^t (u_i(s) - r_i(s))ds > 0.$$

(iii)   For almost all   t

$$\max_{w_1,\ldots,w_n \geq 0} [v_1(t)w_1+\ldots+v_n(t)w_n-c(w_1+\ldots+w_n)] =$$

$$= v_1(t)u_1(t)+\ldots+v_n(t)u_n(t)-c(u_1(t)+\ldots+u_n(t)),$$

where $v_i(t) = h_i t - \lambda_i(t)$, $i = 1,2,\ldots,n$.

Let $u \in L^2(0,T;R^n)$ and $Y \in H^1(0,T;R^n)$ satisfy conditions
(2)-(3)   and moreover there exist functions v_i satisfying
(i)-(iii)   of the Theorem. It is easy to get the following
corollaries:

(I)   At every point $t \in (0,T)$ the functions v_i have both
        one-sided limits and $v_i(t-) \geq v_i(t+) = v_i(t)$

(II)   If $v_i(t_0) < \max(v_1(t_0),\ldots,v_n(t_0))$ then $u_i = 0$ in
        $[t_0,t_0+\varepsilon)$ for some $\varepsilon > 0$.

(III) $u_1 + \ldots + u_n = \hat{c}(\max(v_1,\ldots,v_n))$, where

$$\hat{c}(z) = \begin{cases} 0 & \text{for } z < c'(0) \\ (c')^{-1}(z) & \text{for } z \geq c'(0) \end{cases}$$

In the sequel $\max(v_1,\ldots,v_n)$ will be denoted for simplicity
by v_{max}.
    For the proof of (II) and (III), let   W   denote the set of
vectors $w = (w_1,\ldots,w_n)$ which maximize the left hand side
of (iii) at t_0.   Let $I = \{i : v_i(t_0) = v_{max}(t_0)\}$.
Statement (II) follows from the easy observation that for every
$\bar{w} \in W$ if $i \notin I$ then $\bar{w}_i = 0$. Indeed, if $\bar{w}_i > 0$ and $i \notin I$
then, putting $w_i' = 0$ and $w_k' = \bar{w}_k + \bar{w}_i$ for some $k \in I$ and
$w_j' = \bar{w}_j$ for $j \neq k$ and $j \neq i$,   one obtains $c(\bar{w}_1 + \ldots + \bar{w}_n) =$
$= c(w_1' + \ldots + w_n')$ and $v_1(t_0)\bar{w}_1 + \ldots + v_n(t_0)\bar{w}_n < v_1(t_0 w_1' + \ldots$
$+ v_n(t_0)w_n'$.   This gives $\bar{w} \notin W$.   Hence instead of left hand side
of (iii)   it is sufficient to consider the expression

$$\max_{v_i \geq 0, i \in I} \{v_{max}(t_o) \cdot \sum_{i \in I} w_i - c(\sum_{i \in I} w_i)\}$$

From this (III) follows immediately.

Now some important properties of functions v_i will be given.

<u>Lemma.</u> If $v_j(t_o) \geq v_i(t_o)$ for some $t_o \in [0,T)$ and $j > i$, then $v_j(t) \geq v_i(t)$ for $t \in [t_o,T)$

Proof. The proof will be carried out by contradiction. Let us suppose that there exists $t_1 \in [t_o,T)$ such that $v_j(t_1) < v_i(t_1)$. Obviously, by (I) this inequality holds also in $[t_1, t_1 + \epsilon)$ for some $\epsilon > 0$. Thus by (II) $u_j = 0$ on $(t_1, t_1 + \epsilon)$ and so $Y_j(t_1) = Y_j(t) + \int_{t_1}^{t} r_j(s) ds > 0$ because $r_j > 0$.

Let $Z = \{t < t_1; Y_j(t) = 0\}$ and put $s = \sup Z$ if $Z \neq \emptyset$ and $s = 0$ if $Z = \emptyset$. Then $s < t_1$ and $Y_j(t) > 0$ for $s < t \leq t_1$. Thus, by (ii) and (i) of the Theorem, $v_j(t) = h_j t - a_j$ for some a_j and $t \in [s,t_1]$. The supposition $v_j(t_1) < v_i(t_1)$ implies also that $v_j(t) < v_i(t)$ on $[s,t_1]$. Indeed, if $v_j(t) \geq v_i(t)$ for some $t \in [s,t_1)$, then $v_i(t_1) = h_i t_1 - \lambda_i(t_1) + + v_i(t) - v_i(t) = v_i(t) + h_i(t_1-t) - \lambda_i(t_1) + \lambda_i(t) \leq$
$\leq v_i(t) + h_i(t_1-t) < v_j(t) + h_j(t_1-t) = h_j t - a_j + h_j(t_1-t) = v_j(t_1)$.
By (II) and the fact that $r > 0$ the inequality $v_j < v_i$ on $[s,t_1]$ implies $Y_j(s) > 0$. Thus $Z = \emptyset$ and $v_j < v_i$ on $[0,t_1]$. This contradicts the hyphothesis of this lemma.

The Lemma yields the following results:

(IV) If $v_j(t_1) \geq v_i(t_1)$ with $j > i$ and $\lambda_j = $ constant on
$[t_1,t_2)$ then $v_j > v_i$ on (t_1,t_2).

Proof. By the Lemma $v_j \geq v_i$ on $[t_1,t_2)$. Let $t \in (t_1,t_2)$
$v_j(t) = h_j(t-t_1) + v_j(t_1) > h_i(t-t_1) + v_i(t_1) = h_i(t-t_1) + h_i t_1 - \lambda_i(t_1) =$
$= h_i t - \lambda_i(t_1) \geq h_i t - \lambda_i(t) = v_i(t)$.

(V) If $i < j$ and $v_j(t_o) < v_i(t_o)$ for some $t_o \in (0,T)$ then
$v_j < v_i$ on $[0,t_o]$.

The proof is obvious.

(VI) If $Y_i(t_o) = 0$ for some $t_o \in [0,T]$, then $v_i(t_o) = $
$= v_{max}(t_o)$.

The proof follows from (II) and $r > 0$.

Let now the vector u be an optimal solution of (1)-(3) and Y be a respective vector of inventories.

Definition. t_o is an extreme point of u iff for every $i = 1,2,\ldots,n$ $Y_i(t_o) = \max(0,R_i(t_o))$, where $R_i(t) = Y_i(0) - \int_o^t r_i(s)\,ds$.

Remarks

(A) If $Y_i(t_o) = R_i(t_o)$ then $u_i = 0$ on $[0,t_o)$ and
   $Y_i = R_i > 0$ on this interval

(B) $t = 0$ and $t = T$ are extreme points.

Proposition 1. If $j > i$ and $Y_i(t_o) = 0$ then

$$Y_j(t_o) = \max(0,R_j(t_o)).$$

Proof. If $t_o = T$ then the statement follows from Remark (B). Let $t_o \in [0,T)$. From (VI) $v_i(t_o) \geq v_j(t_o)$.

(a) Let $v_i(t_o) = v_j(t_o)$. If $Y_j(t_o)$ were positive then by (IV) we would have $v_j > v_i$ on $(t_o,t_o+\varepsilon)$ for some $\varepsilon > 0$ and hence $u_i = 0$ in this neighbourhood what is impossible because $Y_i(t_o) = 0$ and $r_i > 0$. Thus $Y_j(t_o) = 0$.
   Moreover, observe that $0 = Y_j(t_o) = Y_j(0) + \int_o^{t_o}(u_j(s) - r_j(s)\,ds) \geq R_j(t_o)$.

(b) Finally, let $v_i(t_o) > v_j(t_o)$. By (V) and (II)
   $0 \leq Y_j(t_o) = R_j(t_o)$.

Proposition 2. Let for every t, $r_1(t) + \ldots + r_n(t) \leq B$ for a constant B. In any interval $[t_1,t_2] \subset [0,T]$ such that $t_2 - t_1 \geq (c'(B) - c'(0))/h_1$ there exists extreme point.

Proof. Let us suppose t_1,t_2 satisfy the hypothesis and there is no extreme point on $[t_1,t_2]$.

Let $t_1' = \sup\{t < t_1;\ t$ is an extreme point$\}$
   $t_2' = \inf\{t > t_2;\ t$ is an extreme point$\}$.

From Remark (B) t_1',t_2' are well defined. It is easy to see

496

that t_1', t_2' are extreme points

(a) Let us note that $v_{max}(t_1') \geq c'(0)$. Otherwise $u_i=0$ for all i, in $(t_1', t_2'+\varepsilon)$ for some $\varepsilon > 0$. This gives $Y_i(t_1') > 0$ and since t_1' is extreme point $Y_i(t) = R_i(t)$ for $t \in (t_1', t_1'+\varepsilon)$ and $i = 1, \ldots, n$. So all points in $[t_1', t_1'+\varepsilon)$ are extreme what contradicts the definition of t_1'.

(b) Let $k = \min\{i; v_i(t_1') = v_{max}(t_1')\}$. Now it will be shown that $Y_k > 0$ in a right neighbourhood of t_1'. For the proof let $t_n \longrightarrow t_1'$, $t_n > t_1'$ be such that $Y_k(t_n) = 0$. By Prop. 1 for $j \geq k$ we have $Y_j(t_n) = \max(0, R_j(t_n))$. From the definition of k and from (I) it follows that for $i < k$, $v_i < v_k$ on $(t_1', t_1'+\varepsilon)$ with some $\varepsilon > 0$. Thus, by (II) and since t_1 is an extreme point, $Y_i(t) = R_i(t)$ on $(t_1', t_1'+\varepsilon)$. Hence each $t_n \in (t_1', t_1'+\varepsilon)$ is an extreme point what contradicts the definition of t_1'. Thus $Y_k(t) > 0$ for $t_1' < t < t_1'+\varepsilon$ with some $\varepsilon > 0$.

(c) Next it will be proved that $Y_k(t) > 0$ on the whole interval (t_1', t_2'). Let $t_1'' = \inf\{t; t_1' < t \leq t_2', Y_k(t) = 0 \text{ or } t=t_2'\}$. If $t_1'' < t_2'$ then by Prop. 1 $Y_j(t_1'') = \max(0, R_j(t_1''))$ for $j > k$ and by (IV) $Y_j(t_1') = R_j(t_1'')$ for $j < k$. This implies that $t_1'' \in (t_1', t_2')$ is an extreme point what contradicts the definition of this interval. Hence $t_1'' = t_2'$ and $Y_k(t) > 0$ for $t \in (t_1', t_2')$ and so $v_k(t) = h_k t + a_k$ for some a_k.

(d) Since t_2' is an extreme point, the sum $Y_1 + \ldots + Y_n$ attains minimum over $(0, t_2')$ at t_2'. Thus $\hat{c}(v_{max}(t_2'-)) \leq r_1(t_2'-) + \ldots + r_n(t_2'-)$. This gives $h_k t_2' + a_k \leq v_{max}(t_2'-) \leq c'(r_1(t_2'-) + \ldots + r_n(t_2'-))$. By part (a) $v_{max}(t_1') = v_k(t_1') = h_k t_1' + a_k \geq c'(0)$. Hence

$c'(B) - c'(0) \geq c'(r_1(t_2'-) + \ldots + c'(r_n(t_2'-)) - c'(0) \geq$
$v_{max}(t_2'-) - v_{max}(t_1') \geq h_k t_2' + a_k - h_k t_1' - a_k =$
$h_k(t_2' - t_1') > h_k(t_2-t_1) > h_1(t_2-t_1)$ what contradicts the hypothesis of this proposition.

§5. The horizon problem

Proposition 2 plays an important role in the so-called horizon problem (Modigliani and Hohn 1955, Blikle and Łoś 1967,

Rempała 1979). As an ilustration we consider very briefly only the case $n = 1$ (by remarks in §3 this also contains the case $n > 1$ with $a_i = 1$ and $h_i = h$). For this let $H \geq c'(B) - c'(0)$, and $T' < T-H$, (the constant B was defined in Prop.2). Prop.2 allows us to find an optimal solution of (1)-(3) on any subinterval $[0,T'] \subset [0,T]$ with the demand being known only on the interval $[0,T'+H]$. For the proof, let $\bar{u}$ and $\bar{\bar{u}}$ be some optimal solutions of (1)-(3) for $[0,T]$ and $[0,T'+H]$ respectively, and let $\bar{Y}, \bar{\bar{Y}}$ be respective inventories. By Prop.2 on the interval $[T',T'+H]$ there exist t_1 and t_2 such that $\bar{Y}_i(t_1) = \max(0, R_i(t_1))$ and $\bar{\bar{Y}}_i(t_2) = \max(0, R_i(t_2))$. In accordance with Remark (B) the point $T'+H$ is an extreme point for $\bar{\bar{u}}$. Thus there exist $t_3 \in [T',T'+H]$ such that $\bar{Y}(t_3) = \bar{\bar{Y}}(t_3)$. Hence the optimality principle gives that

$$\bar{\bar{\bar{u}}} = \begin{cases} \bar{\bar{u}} & \text{on} \quad [0,t_3) \\ \bar{u} & \text{on} \quad [t_3,T] \end{cases}$$

is an optimal solution of the problem (1)-(3) on $[0,T]$.

§6. Final remark

The case $a_1 = \ldots = a_n = 1$, $h_1 \leq \ldots \leq h_n$ can be considered as a combination of the cases of §§3 and 4. If for some of the commodities the holding costs are identical then we treated them as one commodity and thus reduce the original problem to the one of §4 with less n. The production plan for the separated commodities can be obtained in a similar way as in §3.

References

1. Arrow K.J and Karlin S. (1958), Studies in the Mathematical Theory of Inventory and Production, California: Stanford University Press, p.61.

2. Bensoussan A., Hurst Jr E.G. and Naslund B. (1974), Management Applications of Modern Control Theory, North-Holland (American Elsevier) p.240.

3. Blikle A. and Łoś J. (1967), Horizon in Dynamic Programs with Continuous Time, Bull. Acad. Polon. Sci. Ser. Math. Vol. 15 p.513.

4. Modigliani F. and Hohn F. (1955), Production Planning over Time and Nature of the Expectations and Planning Horizon, Econometrica, Vol. 23, p.46.

5. Rempała R. (1975), On Some Integral Inequalities Related to Multicommodity Inventory Model, Preprint 82, Inst. of Math. Pol. Acad. of Sci.

6.   (1977), Minimization of the Cost in Two-Commodity Inventory System, Preprint 106, Inst. of Math. Pol. Acad. of Sci.

7.   (1979), A Dynamic Programming Problem for a Two--Commodity Inventory Model, New Trends in Dynamic System Theory and Economics, Academic Press, New York, p.269.

SOLVING A CAPACITY CONSTRAINED DETERMINISTIC DYNAMIC INVENTORY PROBLEM

KNUT RICHTER

College of Technology, Karl-Marx-Stadt, GDR

1. The problem

We shall consider the problem (A)

$$\sum_{t=1}^{T}(d_t \operatorname{sign} x_t + c_t x_t + L_t y_t) \quad \dashrightarrow \quad \min, \qquad (1)$$

$$y_t = y_{t-1} + x_t - B_t , \qquad (2)$$

$$\left. \begin{array}{l} 0 \leq x_t \leq x_t^+, \; 0 \leq y_t \leq y_t^+ \end{array} \right\} \quad t=1,2,\ldots,T, \qquad (3)$$

$$y_0 = y_T = 0, \qquad (4)$$

where the real numbers B_t, d_t, c_t, L_t are nonnegative and where the upper bounds x_t^+, y_t^+ are finite real numbers.

Economic interpretation: A product may be produced on a machine in T time periods. For every period t the demand B_t is known. The store y_t of the period t equals the store y_{t-1} plus the production x_t minus the demand B_t. x_t^+ denotes the production and y_t^+ denotes the inventory capacities for the period t. Fixed costs are given by d_t, linear costs by c_t and inventory costs by L_t.

The problem is to find a production and inventory plan that minimizes all costs.

Investigations of the problem (A) for $x_t^+ = y_t^+ = +\infty$, $t=1,2,\ldots,T$, are known by Wagner/Whitin (1958), Wagner

(1960), Zabel (1964), Eppen et al. (1969), Richter (1978)
etc. The case $x_t^+ = +\infty$, t=1,2,...,T, with a special subject function is considered by us (Richter, 1978). Baker et.
al. (1978) propose a branch and bound method for $y_t^+ = +\infty$,
t=1,2,...,T.

The set of feasible solutions (2)-(4) is a closed convex
polyhedron. The subject function (1) is concave. If the set
(2)-(4) is not empty an optimal solution of (A) is in one of
its extreme points. Such solution we shall call **extreme optimal.**

We have a simple solubility condition for the problem
(A): The set (2)-(4) is not empty if and only if

$$s_o = 0 \quad \text{and} \quad s_t \leqslant y_t^+ , \quad t=1,2,\ldots,T-1,$$

where $s_T := 0$ and

$$s_{t-1} := \max(0, B_t + s_t - x_t^+), \quad t=T,T-1,\ldots,1, \qquad (5)$$

(Richter, 1976).

2. The equivalent problem (B)

Let (B) the problem

$$\sum_{t=1}^{T} L_t s_t + \sum_{t=1}^{T}(d_t \operatorname{sign} z_t + c_t z_t + L_t v_t) \;\to\; \min, \qquad (6)$$

$$v_t = v_{t-1} + z_t - W_t , \qquad \qquad (7)$$

$$0 \leqslant z_t \leqslant z_t^+, \; 0 \leqslant v_t \leqslant v_t^+ , \qquad \left.\right\} \; t=1,2,\ldots,T, \qquad (8)$$

$$v_o = v_T = 0, \qquad\qquad\qquad\qquad (9)$$

where $W_t = B_t + s_t - s_{t-1}$ and $v_t^+ = y_t^+ - s_t$, t=1,2,...,T,
$z_t^+ = x_t^+$, t=1,2,...,T.

We consider two maps, where

$$\bar{A}(\{x_t, y_{t-1}\}_{t=1}^{T}) = \{x_t, y_{t-1} - s_{t-1}\}_{t=1}^{T}$$

and $\overline{B}(\{z_t, v_{t-1}\}_{t=1}^T) = \{z_t, v_{t-1}+s_{t-1}\}_{t=1}^T$.

Theorem 1: The problems (A) and (B) are $(\overline{A}, \overline{B})$-equivalently (Richter, 1980).

Remarks 1: (i) If $\{z_t, v_{t-1}\}_{t=1}^T$ is optimal for the problem (B) then $\{z_t, v_{t-1}+s_{t-1}\}_{t=1}^T$ is optimal for the problem (A). (ii) In (B) we have

$$W_t \leq x_t^+ = z_t^+ , \quad t=1,2,\ldots,T, \tag{10}$$

because from (5) follows $s_{t-1} \geq B_t + s_t - x_t^+$ and

$$x_t^+ \geq B_t + s_t - s_{t-1} = W_t , \quad t=1,2,\ldots,T.$$

The remark 1(ii) allows consider the problem (A) or (B) with the additional condition $B_t \leq x_t^+$, $t=1,2,\ldots,T$. (11)

3. The equivalent shortest path problem (C)

If in (A) or (B) holds $x_t^+ = y_t^+ = +\infty$, $t=1,2,\ldots,T$, an extreme solution is given if and only if for a feasible solution comes true $y_{t-1}x_t = 0$, $t=1,2,\ldots,T$, (Wagner/Whitin, 1958). In the other case a feasible solution is extreme if and only if between two periods $k < l$, $y_i \in \{0, y_i^+\}$, $i=1,k$, with $0 < y_i < y_i^+$, $i=l+1,\ldots,k-1$, exists at most one period $k < t \leq l$: $0 < x_t < x_t^+$ (Love , 1968).

Let be the subject function (1) dynamic constrained, i.e.

$$c_t + L_t \geq c_{t+1} \quad , \quad t=1,2,\ldots,T, \tag{12}$$

then exists a special extreme optimal solution with

$$(x_t^+ - x_t)x_t y_{t-1} = 0, \quad t=1,2,\ldots,T, \tag{13}$$

or, in other notions,

$$y_{t-1} > 0 \quad \Longrightarrow \quad x_t \in \{0, x_t^+\}, \quad t=1,2,\ldots,T, \tag{14}$$

(Richter, 1978)

We shall investigate the problem (A) under additional

conditions (11)-(14). It is denoted by (A) too.

For further investigations we shall need the following subproblems $(H_{i-1,j})$, $1 \leqslant i < j \leqslant T$,

$$c_{i-1,j} := \min \left\{ \sum_{t=i}^{j} (d_t \text{sign } x_t + c_t x_t + L_t y_t), \right. \tag{15}$$

$$y_t = y_{t-1} + x_t - B_t, \quad t=i,i+1,\ldots,j, \tag{16}$$

$$x_t \in \{0, x_t^+\}, \quad t=i+1,\ldots,j, \quad 0 \leqslant x_i \leqslant x_i^+, \tag{17}$$

$$0 < y_t \leqslant y_t^+, \quad t=i,i+1,\ldots,j-1, \tag{18}$$

$$y_{i-1} = y_j = 0, \tag{19}$$

where $c_{i-1,j} := +\infty$ if (16)-(19) is empty.

We introduce the problem (C) with

$$\sum_{i=1}^{s} c_{t_{i-1}, t_i} \longrightarrow \min, \tag{20}$$

$$0 = t_0 < t_1 < \ldots < t_s = T, \tag{21}$$

$$c_{t_{i-1}, t_i} < +\infty, \quad i=1,2,\ldots,s, \tag{22}$$

$$s \in \{1,2,\ldots,T\}.$$

The problem is a shortest path problem on a network with the vertices $0,1,\ldots,T$, arcs (i,j), $0 \leqslant i < j \leqslant T$, and costs c_{ij}.

Now we consider the maps $\overline{\overline{A}}$ and $\overline{\overline{B}}$, where

$$\overline{\overline{A}}(\{x_t, y_{t-1}\}_{t=1}^{T}) = \{(t_1, t_2, \ldots, t_s): y_{t_i} = 0, \ i=0,1,\ldots,s,$$
$$y_t \neq 0, \ t \neq t_i, \ i=1,2,\ldots,s\}$$

and

$$\overline{\overline{B}}(z) = \overline{\overline{B}}(t_0, t_1, \ldots, t_s) = \{\{x_t y_{t-1}\}_{t=1}^{T} : (2)-(4),$$
$$y_{t_i} = 0, \ i=0,1,\ldots,s, \ y_t \neq 0, \ t \neq t_i, \ i=1,2,\ldots,s,$$
$$x_t \in \{0, x_t^+\}, \ t=t_i+1, t_i+2, \ldots, t_{i+1}, \ i=1,2,\ldots,s-1.$$

Theorem 2: The problems $((A),(11)-(14))$ and (C) are $(\overline{\overline{A}}, \overline{\overline{B}})$-equivalently.

Remarks 2: (i) If $z=(t_0, t_1, \ldots, t_s)$ is an optimal solution of

(C) and

$$\{z_i\} = \{x_t, y_{t-1}\}_{t=t_{i-1}+1}^{t_i} \quad , \quad i=1,2,\ldots,s$$

are optimal solutions of (H_{t_{i-1}, t_i}), then

$$\{z_i\}_{i=1}^{s} = \{x_t, y_{t-1}\}_{t=1}^{T}$$

is an optimal solution of $((A),(11)-(14))$.

(ii) From the transitivity of equivalent relations follows that $((A),(12)-(14))$ and (C) are $(\overline{\overline{AA}}, \overline{\overline{BB}})$-equivalent. It means that from an optimal solution of (C) we can get an optimal solution of $((A),(11)-(14))$ and that this solution gives an optimal solution of $((A),(12)-(14))$.

4. Solving the equivalent problem (C)

In (C) the costs c_{ij} are not given but have to compute. Therefore the efficiency of methods for solving (C) can be reduced to two problems:

(i)   to find conditions that shut out the problems (H_{ij}) or stop the computing process   and

(ii) to solve the problems (H_{ij}) efficiently.

Let solve the problem (C) by following method:

$$f_T := 0, \qquad f_t := \min(c_{tj} + f_j : t < j \leq T), \qquad (24)$$

$t=T-1,\ldots,1,0.$ f_o is the minimal value of function (1). If $f_t < +\infty$ we denote the optimal parameters by $j(t)$:

$$f_t = c_{t,j(t)} + f_{j(t)} \cdot$$

From these parameters we get the optimal solution of (A).

(i)   Suppose that the costs $c_{tj} + f_j$ are computed for $t < j \leq k$. Denote $\bar{c}_{tk} := \min(c_{tj} + f_j : t < j \leq k)$.

Let $c_{tk}^{*} = \bar{c}_{tk} - f_k,$

$$\bar{\bar{c}}_{tk} := \sum_{j=t+1}^{k} (d_j \text{sign } B_j + c_j B_j),$$

and u_{ij} lower bounds for the costs c_{ij}, $0 \leq i < j \leq T$.

Theorem 3 (Richter,1978): Suppose that the problem (A) is solvable. If for a pair (i,j) with $0 \leq i < k < j \leq T$ holds true

$$u_{ij} \geq \min(c_{ik}^{*}, \bar{\bar{c}}_{ij}), \tag{25}$$

then exists a shortest path that is not going over the arc (i,j).

Remark 3: If the inequality is not holding true its right side may be used in the method for solving (H_{ij}) as upper bound.

(ii)   Let f^{*} be an upper bound from the right side in (25) and from the value of a known feasible solution of (H_{ij}). The values of the variables x_t, y_t, $t=j,j-1,\ldots,s$, $s \geq i$, that are feasible in (16)-(19), are called s-partial solution. For s=i we get a feasible solution of $(H_{i-1,j})$.
Denote

$$q_{sj} := \sum_{t=s}^{j} (d_t \text{sign } x_t + c_t x_t + L_t y_t).$$

The values of x_t, y_t, $t=s-1,s-2,\ldots,i$, that complete a given s-partial solution to a feasible solution of $(H_{i-1,j})$, is called its complement.

Theorem 4 (Richter,1978): (i) For all $j \leq T$, $B_j > y_{j-1}^{+}$, $i < j$, the problems $(H_{i-1,j})$ are unsolvable and $c_{i-1,j} := +\infty$.
(ii) Assume that is given a (s+1)-partial solution of $(H_{i-1,j})$ and that is computed $y_s = y_{s+1} - x_{s+1} + B_{s+1}$.
    a) If $y_s = 0$ or $B_s + y_s - x_s^{+} > y_{s-1}^{+}$ or

$$y^+_{s-1} < B_s + y_s < x^+_s \quad \text{or} \quad q_{s+1,j} + c_{i-1,s} + L_s y_s \geq f^*_i,$$

the given (s+1)-partial solution has not complement.

b) If $\max(y^+_{s-1}, x^+_s) < B_s + y_s \leq y^+_{s-1} + x^+_s$,

then follows $x_s = x^+_s$.

c) If $B_s + y_s \leq y^+_{s-1}$, follows $x_s = 0$.

Remark 4: (i) An efficient enueration algorithm based on this theorem for solving the problems $(H_{i-1,j})$ is described by us (Richter,1978).

(ii) If we get a new feasible solution in this algorithm we lower the upper bound appropriatly. We change the given (s+1)-partial solution, if states one of the cases (ii)a).

5. Numerical results

A problem with the parameters

	t=1	2	3	4	5	6	7	8
B_t	10	8	4	5	2	10	3	1
x^+_t	15	10	8	8	8	20	5	2
y^+_t	5	7	7	7	7	10	10	10
d_t	10	10	50	50	50	50	50	50
L_t	2	2	2	2	2	2	2	2
c_t	0	0	0	0	0	0	0	0

we have solved by a FORTRAN-program on the computer EC1020 in 0,46 sec. The optimal solution is

$(x_1,\ldots,x_8) = (12,10,\ 0,\ 7,\ 0,14,\ 0,\ 0)$

with the value of the objective function 146.

For further planning horizons T we have the following computer times: $T=12$: 1,62 sec, $T=16$: 7,86 sec, $T=24$:

26,6 sec   and   T=48: 19,7 sec.

The results show that the two-stage algorithm for solving problem (A) (Richter,1978) is efficiently.

References:

1   Baker K.R., Dixon P., Magazine M.J., Silver E.A.(1978):
An algorithm for the dynamic lot size problem with
time-varying production capacity constraints, Man.
Science 24,10, 1710-1720

2   Eppen G.D., Gould F.J., Pashigian B.P., Extensions of
the planning horizon theorem in the dynamic lot size
model, Man. Science 15(1968)5, 268-277

3   Love S.F. (1968): Dynamic deterministic production and
inventory models with piecewise concave costs, Stanford University, Department of Oper. Research, Techn.
Report 13

4   Richter K. (1976): Untersuchungen eines linearen dyna-
mischen Produktionsplanungsmodells, Wiss. Zeitschrift
TH Karl-Marx-Stadt 18, 4, 399-402

5   Richter K. (1978): Untersuchungen zur Lösung determini-
stischer dynamischer Produktions- und Lagerhaltungsauf-
gaben, Dissertation B, TH Karl-Marx-Stadt

6   Richter K. (1980): Äquivalente Optimierungsaufgaben
und Dekomposition. Teil I, Math. Operationsforschung
und Statistik, Series Optimization 11, 3, 1-14

7   Wagner H.M., Whitin T.M. (1958): Dynamic problems in
the theory of firm, Naval Research Logistic Quarterly
5, 1, 53-74

8   Wagner H.M., Whitin T.M. (1958): Dynamic version of the

economic lot size model, Man. Science 5, 1, 89-96

9   Wagner H.M. (1960): A postscript to dynamic problems
in the theory of the firm, Naval Research Logistic
Quarterly 7, 1, 7-12

10   Zabel E. (1964): Some generalization of an inventory
planning horizon theorem, Man. Science 10, 3, 465-
471

Proc. First Int. Symp. on Inventories
Budapest, Hungary 1980

PRACTICAL INVENTORY POLICIES
FOR THE STOCKING OF SPARE PARTS

E. RITCHIE

University of Lancaster, Bailrigg, Lancaster, UK

Summary

A very common and difficult inventory problem is that of designing a policy for the stocking of spare parts.   Spare parts typically have a life cycle consisting of a period of rising demand, followed by a period of steady demand and finally a stage of declining demand eventually to zero. Some progress has been made in obtaining mathematical solutions to simplified deterministic models of stages of this life cycle, but these solutions are not suitable for practical application.   This paper considers some practical methods which give almost optimal solutions for the simplified deterministic models throughout all stages of the life cycle of a spare part.   Performance of these methods is also explored   using actual data on the demand history of spare parts for electical appliances.

The Life Cycle of Spares Demand

A typical demand life cycle for a spare part for a machine is shown in idealised form in figure 1.

When an item is introduced for the first time on a new machine, spares demand increases from zero as the production of the new machine builds up (Phase I).   Then follows a period of relative stability corresponding to the period of steady production of machines (Phase II).   Eventually the machine is withdrawn when a new model is introduced.   If any items on the old machine are not used in the new model then demand for these items will decline, eventually to zero.

It is ususally necessary and profitable to supply spare parts throughout the whole life cycle of demand. Thus it is also necessary to devise stock holding and replenishment policies for all phases I to III of demand and there are practical considerations which suggest that phase I and II should be considered together and phase III separately.

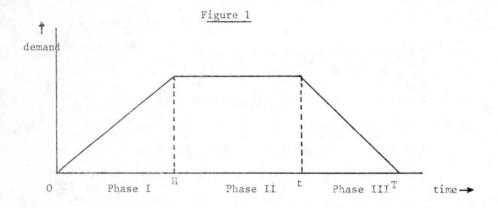

Figure 1

During phases I and II, all parts are being produced during the course of normal production runs for use as spares or for incorporation into new machines. As a consequence the unit cost of items is low. After phase II, all items must be specially made for spares provisioning and much smaller production runs are needed for this purpose. The unit costs for such runs are then generally higher than in phases I and II. Indeed the unit costs may be so high that it is worthwhile producing enough in the final production run to supply demand throughout phase III. The transition from phase II to III is thus seen as a major decision epoch and naturally separates phases I and II from phase III.

Stock Replenishment Policies for Idealised Phases I to III

Consideration of the life cycle of demand for spare parts suggests that stock replenishment policies need to be developed for phase I and II taken together and for phase III separately.

There are a number of publications which are relevant to this question. All consider idealised forms of demand. They further assume that shortages are not allowed and the lead time for stock replenishments is zero.

A policy for Phase II on its own has been established since 1915 with the derivation of the Lot-Size formula or Economic Batch Quantity (E.B.Q). More recently Donaldson (1977) and Silver (1979) have considered phase I on its own: demand increasing deterministically up to a known time horizon H and then ceasing. Donaldson derived an optimal strategy for stock replenishment for the case of known linearly increasing demand up to the time horizon H. Silver showed that a simple rule, based on minimising the cost of stock-holding and replenishments per unit time, gave almost optimal results when compared with Donaldson's method on a number of examples. Ritchie (1980) has shown that it is possible to derive an optimal policy for the more realistic situation of phases I and II taken together. He considers linear increasing demand in phase I up to a known time horizon H, followed by steady demand from H to t. The optimal policy for phases I and II together gave a lower cost than was obtained by applying Donaldson's method up to time H and then following an optimal policy from H to t.

Stock replenishment policies for phase III, the phase of declining demand have been considered by Smith (1977) and Barbosa and Friedman (1979). Barbosa and Friedman derived the optimal replenishment policy for the class of demand function represented by:

$$b(t') = k' (t'-T)^r \quad \ldots\ldots \quad (1)$$

where k' and r' (≥ 0) are known parameters, t' is time into phase III, T is the predicted life span of the item in phase III until demand ceases and b(t') is demand at t'.   Smith

concerned himself with the important question of <u>when to make the final</u>

<u>production run</u>.   For the same class of demand function considered by

Barbosa and Friedman and also for exponential decay of demand, Smith

showed than an almost optimal rule which he called "The stopping rule"

was as follows:

If Total Future Demand $\leq$ 5/4 E.B.Q. then make the final run; other-

wise make the normal stock replenishment.

A total policy for phases I to III could therefore consist of using

Ritchie's method for phases I and II and then the method of Barbosa and

Friedman for phase III.   This combination of policies would be optimal

provided demand increased linearly in phase 1, and the decay in phase III

could be modelled by the demand functions shown in equation (1).   All par-

ameters of the demand functions would of course need to be known <u>exactly</u>

in advance since these are necessary for deriving the optimal policies.   In

addition no shortages would be allowed and all replenishments would have

to take place instantaneously.   Clearly this combination of methods or

indeed the methods on their own are not of any practical use.   In a real-

life situation one would not know the form and parameters of the demand

life cycle which could well span up to ten or more years.   The real

value of these methods is in providing a yardstick for assessing more

practical stock replenishment policies.

Practical Stock Replenishment Policies

In a real-life situation the charactersitics of demand would not be

known exactly in advance but would be subject to random error.   It is

normal practice to estimate the level of demand, trend in demand and

standard error by a forecasting system, and then use these estimates as

the basis for stock replenishment decisions.   Leaving aside questions of lead-time, of variation in the lead-time and in demand, which influence

the level of safety stocks, a prime question is to decide upon the lot

size to be ordered at each replenishment point.   In practical stock

replenishment schemes this decision needs to be based on estimates of

level and trend in demand.

Three practical stock replenishment schemes will be considered. The

first of these is the well known economic batch quantity or E.B.Q. Al-

though this method is strictly only applicable to steady demand situations

it can be and is used when there are trends in demand.   The second meth-

od is the Silver-Meal heuristic which is based on minimising the cost per

unit time over the next replenishment period.   This heuristic calculates

the next replenishment period Δs iteratively using the equation below:

$$\Delta s^{(k)} = \left[\frac{c_1}{c_2(a/2 + 2b\Delta s^{(k-1)}/3)} \right]^{\frac{1}{2}}$$

where $\Delta s^{(k)}$ is the value obtained on the kth iteration

c_1 is the fixed cost of replenishment per lot in £'s

c_2 is the cost of holding inventory   in £/unit per unit time

a   is the current level of demand

b   is the current trend in demand.

The third method to be considered is a modification of the E.B.Q.

The E.B.Q. method does not use the estimate of trend in determining stock

replenishment quantities.   As a consequence when demand is rising the

E.B.Q. method tends to give less than optimal quantities and when demand

is falling it gives larger than optimal quantities.   The author showed

in an earlier paper (Ritchie 1980) that the E.B.Q. could be modified in

a simple way to incorporate trend.   The resulting calculation is in two

stages but the main principle is to base the stock replenishment quantity on the <u>estimated average demand</u> over the next replenishment period. The method, which is termed the Modified Economic Batch Quantity or MEBQ, is as follows. First estimate the replenishment interval

$$\Delta s = \sqrt{\frac{2c_1}{c_2 a}}$$ Then base the stock replenishment on

the interval

$$\Delta s' = \sqrt{\frac{2c_1}{c_2(a+b\Delta s/2)}}$$

The only problem to be overcome in using all three methods is when to make the final stock replenishment. In all cases Smith's stopping rule will be used so that all the methods then yield a complete policy for all stages of the life cycle of demand.

To show how these policies compare with the optimal policy for deterministic demand situations, two examples of their application will be given; the first example for the joint phases I and II and the second for phase III.

<u>Example 1 - Phases I and II</u>

Consider the demand situation shown in figure 2 below

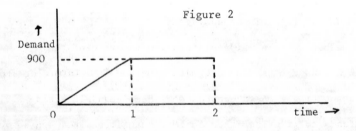

Figure 2

If $c_1 = 9$ and $c_2 = 2$ the optimal number of replenishments is 16 and the total cost of stock holding and set-ups for the optimal policy is 305.2.

The Silver-Meal heuristic yields 17 stock replenishments and a total cost of 307.5.

516

The M.E.B.Q. method requires 15 replenishments and gives a total cost of 305.3.

Finally the E.B.Q. method gives 17 replenishments and a cost of 308.4. These results are summarised below:

METHOD	No. of REPLENISHMENTS	TOTAL COST
E.B.Q.	17	308.4
M.E.B.Q.	15	305.3
Silver-Meal	17	307.5
Optimal	16	305.2

Example 2 - Phase III Declining Demand

$c_1 = 42$ and $c_2 = 0.56$ and the demand in phase III is as shown in figure 3 below.

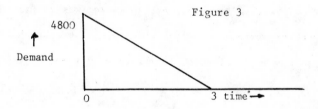

Figure 3

The performance of all policies except the Silver-Meal are shown in the table below. At the tenth replenishment interval the Silver-Meal iterations failed to converge. It proved impossible therefore to complete the calculations for the Silver-Meal heuristic to the point where the stopping rule would have been invoked.

METHOD	No. of REPLENISHMENTS	TOTAL COST
E.B.Q.	10	930.1
M.E.B.Q.	10	926.7
OPTIMAL	10	926.4

517

Performance of the Policies on Actual Demand Data

All policies performed reasonably well on the deterministic examples above with the exception of the Silver-Meal heuristic on example 2. The M.E.B.Q. method performed particularly well given almost optimal results in both cases. To give some guide to their performance in real-life situations the E.B.Q. and the M.E.B.Q. methods will be compared on two examples using actual demand data for spare parts for electrical mach ines. The Silver-Meal heuristic will not be compared on example 4 because of the problem of its nonconvergence in certain circumstances.

Obviously when using actual data an optimal policy cannot be determined. It is also necessary, in order to simulate the operation of the policies, to estimate from the demand data the trend and level of demand at each replenishment point. These estimates were made in the simulation using an exponential forecasting system with trend adjustment and with smoothing parameters of 0.1. This forecasting system was in fact the one used by the inventory system from which the demand data was obtained. In all comparisons made, the final stock levels were adjusted to the same level.

Example 3 Rising Demand

The demand data is shown graphically in figure 4. For this data c_1 = £50 and c_2 = 0.4 £s/unit per year. The E.B.Q. method required 27 replenishments over the 43 months and gave a total cost after adjusting the final stock level of £2830. The M.E.B.Q. method produced 28 stock replenishments and a total cost of £2789. The Silver-Meal heuristic gave 27 stock replenishments and an adjusted total cost of £2796.

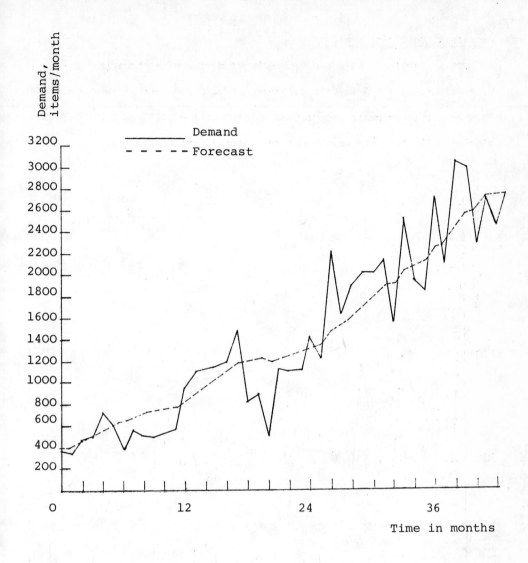

FIGURE 4

Demand v Time

Example 4   Declining Demand

This example is based on 42 months of demand data shown in figure 5. C_1 = £25 and c_2 = 0.5 £s/unit per year.   The E.B.Q. method gave rise to 13 stock replenishments and yielded a total cost of £642.   The M.E.B.Q. also gave 13 stock replenishments and a total cost of £634.

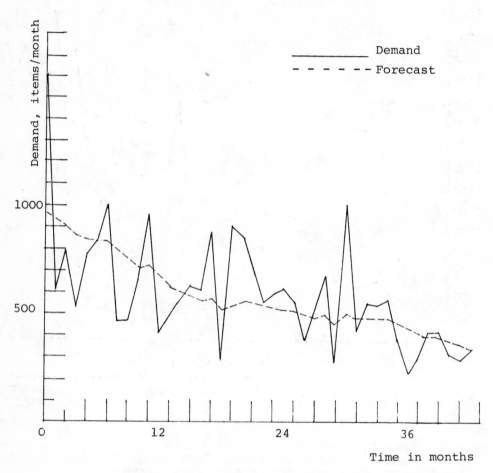

FIGURE 5

Demand v Time

Conclusion

The M.E.B.Q. method has performed well on deterministic examples for both rising and falling demand situations. Indeed the M.E.B.Q. method gave almost optimal results. It also performed well on actual demand data and yielded a small but clear cost advantage over the E.B.Q. method. Even though the cost advantage appears to be small it would give rise to worthwhile savings with the large inventories commonly held. The method is moreover completely practical and easy to use and requires little extra computation compared with the E.B.Q. method: an important point for large inventory systems.

References

L.C. Barbosa and M. Friedman (1979) "Inventory Lot-Size Models with Vanishing Market". J.O.R.S 30 No. 12 Dec. 1129-1132

W.A. Donaldson (1977) "Inventory Replenishment Policy for a Linear Trend in Demand - An Analytical Solution". J.O.R.S 28 663-670.

E. Ritchie (1980) " Practical Inventory Replenishment Policies for a Linear Trend in Demand followed by a Period of Steady Demand" J.O.R.S 31 No. 7 July 605-614.

E.A. Silver (1979) "A Simple Inventory Replenishment Decision Rule for a Linear Trend in Demand". J.O.R.S. 30 No. 1.71-75.

P. Smith (1977) "Optimal Production Policies for Items with Decreasing Demand" E.J.O.R. 1 No. 6 365-367.

Proc. First Int. Symp. on Inventories
Budapest, Hungary 1980

ON OBTAINING A REQUIRED SERVICE-LEVEL IN A PERIODIC INVENTORY MODEL

HELMUT SCHNEIDER

Free University of Berlin, Berlin West

A central problem in inventory practice is the prevention of stock on hand from becoming frequently negative. In inventory theory stockout costs are usually specified in order to guarantee a certain service-level. But in practice it is often extremely difficult to assign a stockout cost. Thus a stockout constraint is often required by the management. However little has been done so far in inventory theory to find an appropriate inventory policy when a service-level is pre-determined.

Brown [1962] has suggested a method of computing a reorder point when a certain service level is required. But this method only holds for a continuous review model. Klemm [1974] considered the periodic review case but the practical results are limited to the case where there are no fixed order costs.

This paper is focused on determining the reorder point when a certain service-level is required, with particular emphasis on the periodic review case with fixed order costs.

In this paper we consider a stationary inventory model for a single item with periodic review. Demands for a product in each of the periods are independent, identically distributed continuous random variables, with known distribution function. If we assume a fixed set-up cost, a linear purchase cost, a convex expected holding and penalty cost function, and total backlogging of unfilled demand, the results of Iglehart [1963] imply that there is an optimal policy of the (s,S)-type. When the stockout cost is substituted by a stockout constraint Beesack [1967] has shown that an (s,S)-policy is still optimal.

Often in practice the amount D = S-s is predetermined by a lot size formula and the problem arises as to how to determine the reorder point to achieve a desired service-level.

Before analysing the inventory problem we have to notice that this service can be measured in different ways (see Rényi and Ziermann [1960], Klemm [1971], Schneider [1980]).

Firstly it may be necessary that there is no stockout say in about 90% of the inspection periods. In this case we are referring to a α-service-level with α = 0.9. Secondly we may want on the average 90% of the demand in a period to be satisfied. This is usually called a β-service-level of 90%. Lastly we may require that at the end of a period only 10% of the mean demand be backordered.

Let us call that a γ-service-level of 90% (see Schneider [1980]). Notice that the γ-service-level is a time-dependent service measure, since all backorders are counted even when they are backdated.

The β-service-level is most often applied in practice and shall be considered in this paper. In many inventory programs there is a method used to determine the reorder point when a certain β-service-level is required which has been derived by Brown [1962]. He suggested using the formula

$$(1-\beta)Q = \int_s^\infty (t-s) \; \varphi(t|\lambda) \; dt \tag{1}$$

where Q is the order quantity, and where $\varphi(t|\lambda)$ is the p.d.f. of demand in lead time λ.

But since that formula is derived from a continuous review system it has to be adjusted when one wants to use it in a periodic review system. The most common correction in practice is that the density on the right-hand side of Eq. (1) is substituted by $\varphi(t|\lambda+T)$, the p.d.f. of the demand in lead-plus review time. In an empirical study Kleijnen [1976] has shown that this correction is not satisfactory in order to obtain the desired service in a periodic review system.

In this paper the exact formula for determining the reorder point when a β-service level is required will be presented. Afterwards approximations are given which, in a periodic review system work better than formula (1).

Some restrictions have to be made. First we consider a stationary inventory system with known demand distribution $\Phi(t|T)$ where T is the review time. We consider an (s,S)-system where the amount D = S-s is predetermined by any method. At the beginning of every period the inventory position x (stock on hand plus on order) is inspected.

When x has fallen to x $\leq$ s the amount S-x is ordered; otherwise nothing is ordered. Our problem is how to determine s, such that a preassigned fraction β of the mean demand is on the average satisfied.

The methods presented in this paper are mainly based on results of Karlin [1958]. The approach we chose is based on our aim to make clear the differences of Brown's [1962] (s,Q)-model and the (s,S)-model.

β-service-level

The β-service-level is defined by the fraction of demand
satisfied immediately in a period. If we define 1-β as the
fraction of demand not being satisfied in a period, then we
obtain, on the average,

$$\mu(T)(1-\beta) = \frac{\text{expected backorder per order cycle}}{\text{expected length of time of an order cycle}} \qquad (2)$$

as we can see in Figure 1.

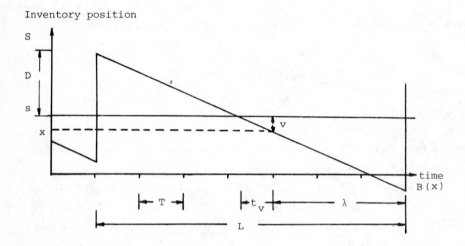

Figure 1

Backorders in an (s,S,T)-system

Notation:

λ lead time, L order cycle, v = s - x excess, T review time,
B(x) backorder

r_i = demand in period i with mean $\mu(T)$ and variance $\sigma^2(T)$.

Now let us evaluate that expression (2). In doing so we first
consider the conditional expected backorder at the end of the
order cycle, given that the inventory position is x, at the
beginning of the period in which an order is placed.

526

$$B(x) = \int_x^\infty (t-x) \; \varphi(t|\lambda) \; dt \tag{3}$$

To find the total expected backorders per order cycle we have to average (3) with respect to the stationary p.d.f. $f(x)$ of the inventory position. We notice that $x = s-v$, where v is the excess shown in figure 1. The distribution of that excess random variable is derived by Karlin [1958]. It satisfies the equation

$$H(D,v) = \Phi(D+v|T) - \Phi(D|T) + \int_0^D H(D-\xi,v) \; d \; \Phi(\xi|T) \tag{4}$$

where $D = S-s$. Differentiating $H(D,v)$ we obtain the density of the inventory position as

$$f(x) = h(D,s-x) \qquad\qquad x \leq s \tag{5}$$

The expected length of an order cycle can be derived from well known results in renewal theory. Let R_n be the n-th partial sum of the $\{r_i\}$. Then R_n is the amount of demand in n periods. For a positive D, define N_D as the largest value of n for which $R_n \leq D$. Then N_D is the number of periods, for which D was enough to satisfy the demand. In the next period the inventory position falls to $x \leq s$ and a new order must be placed. The expected value of N_D is called the renewal quantity and is denoted by $M(D)$. It satisfies the equation

$$M(D) = \Phi(D|T) + \int_0^D M(D-t) \; d \; \Phi(t|T) \tag{6}$$

It follows that the expected length of an order cycle is

$$M(D) + 1 \tag{7}$$

Combining Eqs. (3) to (7) and substituting in (2) we obtain

$$(1-\beta) \; \mu(T) = \frac{\int_{-\infty}^s B(x) \; h(D,s-x) \; dx}{1+M(D)} \tag{8}$$

527

We notice that Eq.(8) is a rather complex equation. In order to derive an equation which is easier to evaluate we make use of the following asymptotic expansion which can be found by Feller [1971].

$$\lim_{D \to \infty} [M(D) - \frac{D}{\mu}] = \frac{\mu_2}{2\mu^2} - 1 \tag{9}$$

$$\lim_{D \to \infty} h(D,v) = \frac{1}{\mu} [1 - \Phi(v)] \tag{10}$$

Hence, for large D we are allowed to replace Eq.(7) by $\frac{1}{\mu} [D + \frac{\mu_2}{2\mu}]$ and Eq.(5) by the right-hand side of Eq.(10). Then we are able to derive an approximation for large D

$$(1-\beta)\mu = \frac{\mu}{D + \frac{\mu_2}{2\mu}} \int_{-\infty}^{s} \int_{x}^{\infty} (t-x)\; \varphi(t|\lambda)\; dt\; \frac{(1-\Phi(s-x))}{\mu}\; dx \tag{11}$$

Substituting v = s-x and denoting

$$\bar{Q} = D + \frac{\mu_2}{2\mu} \tag{12}$$

as the mean order quantity we obtain

$$(1-\beta)\; \bar{Q} = \int_{0}^{\infty} \int_{s-v}^{\infty} (t-(s-v))\; \varphi(t|\lambda)\; \frac{1-\Phi(v)}{\mu}\; dtdv \tag{13}$$

and hence

$$(1-\beta)\; \bar{Q} = \int_{0}^{\infty} \int_{s}^{\infty} (t-s)\; \varphi(t-v|\lambda)\; \frac{1-\Phi(v)}{\mu}\; dtdv \tag{14}$$

and thus we have the following equation to calculate the reorder point s.

$$(1-\beta)\; \bar{Q} = \int_{s}^{\infty} (t-s)\; \{\int_{0}^{t} \varphi(t-v|\lambda)\; \frac{1-\Phi(v)}{\mu}\; dv\}\; dt \;. \tag{15}$$

The function

$$g(t) = \int_{O}^{t} \varphi(t-v|\lambda) \frac{1-\Phi(v)}{\mu} \, dv \tag{16}$$

can be interpreted as the (asymptotic) p.d.f. of the demand in time $\lambda+t_v$ (see figure 1). In general $g(t)$ is not easy to find.

But we are able to determine the variance and mean of the random variable v. Straightforward calculations show

$$E[v] = \frac{\mu_2}{2\mu_1} \tag{17}$$

$$v[v] = \frac{1}{3\mu} \{ (\frac{\mu_2}{2\mu_1})^3 + \mu_3 \} \tag{18}$$

where μ_i is the i-th moment of the demand random variable.

In the special case that demand in a period is exponential distributed with p.d.f.

$$\varphi(t|T) = \frac{1}{\mu} e^{-\mu t} \tag{19}$$

we have

$$\frac{1-\Phi(t|T)}{\mu} = \frac{1}{\mu} e^{-\mu t} = \varphi(t|T) \tag{20}$$

Thus $g(t)$ is the gamma p.d.f. with mean $(\lambda+1)\mu$ and variance $(\lambda+1)\mu^2$.

It follows that Eq.(15) can be reduced to

$$(1-\beta)\overline{Q} = \int_{s}^{\infty} (t-s) \, \varphi(t|\lambda+T) \, dt . \tag{21}$$

The last result shows that in the case that demand is exponential distributed there is no difference in formula (21) and formula (1) which is used in practice.

Before considering the cases when demand is not exponentially distributed let us derive another equation for determining the reorder point which was suggested by Schneider [1978]. If we integrate $g(t)$ we obtain

$$g(t) = \frac{1}{\mu} \{ (1-\Phi(t|\lambda+T)) - (1-\Phi(t|\lambda)) \} \tag{22}$$

Substituting (22) into (15) and integrating by parts yields

$$(1-\beta)\overline{Q} = \frac{1}{2\mu} \{ \int_s^\infty (t-s)^2 \varphi(t|\lambda+T)\,dt - \int_s^\infty (t-s)^2 \varphi(t|\lambda)\,dt \} \tag{23}$$

Still this equation is not easy to solve. But if we take into consideration the fact that the last term on the right-hand side does not usually contribute much we have

$$(1-\beta)\overline{Q} \cdot 2\mu = \int_s^\infty (t-s)^2 \varphi(t|\lambda+T)\,dt \tag{24}$$

This equation was previously suggested by Schneider [1978].

In practice formula (1) is often employed with the correction that the p.d.f. of the lead time plus review time $\varphi(t|\lambda+T)$ is used. By doing so we would assume that mean demand in time $\lambda+t_v$ is $(\lambda+1)$. But as we have seen it follows from Eq.(17) that the mean demand in time $\lambda+t_v$ is given by

$$\lambda\mu + \frac{\mu^2+\sigma^2}{2\mu} = \lambda\mu + \frac{\mu}{2} + \frac{\sigma^2}{2\mu} \tag{25}$$

Let us consider three possible cases:

a) In the case $\mu = \sigma$ (exponential) there is no difference.

b) If $\sigma >> \mu$ we have

$$(\lambda+1)\ \mu\ <\ \lambda\mu + \frac{\mu}{2} + \frac{\sigma^2}{2\mu} \tag{26}$$

Let us consider, for instance, a sporadic demand case:
$\sigma = 1.7\mu$

$$\lambda\mu + \frac{\mu}{2} + \frac{\sigma^2}{2\mu}\ \approx\ \lambda\mu + 2\mu \tag{27}$$

Thus in sporadic demand cases the expected demand is much higher than $(\lambda+1)\mu$.

Therefore the reorder point calculated by the adjusted formula (1) is much too low which results in a service-level lower than required.

c) If $\sigma << \mu$ we obtain

$$\lambda\mu + \frac{\mu}{2} + \frac{\sigma^2}{2\mu} \approx \lambda\mu + \frac{\mu}{2} \tag{28}$$

which is smaller than $(\lambda+1)\mu$.

In this case (normal demand) the reorder point derived from the corrected version of Brown's formula is too high and thus the service-level is much higher than desired.

Let us consider the following example to demonstrate the differences between the formulas (1), (15) and (24) where we use Eq.(15) according to the suggestion made below. The demand is assumed to be normal distributed with mean $\mu = 300$, standard deviation $\sigma = 100$. The mean order quantity is $Q = 600$, the lead time is three weeks and the review period is one week. The desired service-level is $\beta = 0.9$.

In the following table the mean demand and the standard deviation is given for time $\lambda+T$ and $\lambda+t_v$ respectively

Table 1: Data for example

	$\lambda+T$	$\lambda+t_v$
expected demand	1200	1167
standard deviation	200	187

Using the extensive tables given in Schneider [1979] the reorder point can be calculated as

$s_1 = 1200 + 0.065 \cdot 200 = 1213$ formula (24)

$s_1 = 1167 + 0.632 \cdot 187 = 1185$ formula (15)

$s_1 = 1200 + 0.671 \cdot 200 = 1334$ formula (1)

When we use formula (23) to determine the true β-service-levels corresponding to the reorder points given above we obtain the protection level β which is accurate to two digits.

formula (24) $\beta = 0.95$

formula (15) $\beta = 0.95$

formula (1) $\beta = 0.98$

Conclusion

In this paper we have derived three formulas for determining the reorder point when a ß-service-level is required. Formula (8) is rather difficult to solve. In order to solve (15) one first has to determine the demand distribution in time $\lambda+t_v$. Since that is usually very difficult we suggest using the underlying demand distribution with the corrected mean (25) and variance $\lambda\sigma^2+V(v)$. The formula (24) is considered in Schneider [1978], [1979] extensively and it is found that it yields good results as far as the ß-service-level is concerned.

References

Beesack, P.R. [1967]. A Finite Horizon Dynamic Inventory Model with a Stockout Constraint. Mgmt.Sci. 13, 618-630.

Brown, R.G. [1962]. Smoothing Forecasting and Prediction of Discrete Time Series. Englewood Cliffs: Prentice-Hall.

Feller, W. [1971]. An Introduction to Probability Theory and its Application. Bd. 2, New York: John Wiley & Sons.

Iglehart, D. [1963]. Dynamic Programming and Stationary Analysis of Inventory Problems: chapter 1 in: Multistage Inventory Models and Techniques, ed. H.E. Scarf, D.M.Gilford and M.W.Shelly, Stanford, Calif.: Stanford University Press.

Karlin, S. [1958]. The Application of the Renewal Theory to the Study of Inventory Policies. Chapter 15 in: Studies in the Mathematical Theory of Inventory Production, ed. K.J.Arrow, S.Karlin and H.Scarf. Stanford: Stanford University Press.

Kleijnen, J.P.C. [1976]. Computerized Inventory Management: A Critical Analysis of IBM's IMPACT System. Reeks Ter Diskussie No. 76. 045, Katholieke Hogeschool Tilburg.

Klemm, H. [1971]. On the operating characteristic "service level". Colloquia Mathematica Societatis János Bolyai, 7. Inventory Control and Water Storage, Győr (Hungary).

Klemm, H. [1974]. Lieferbereitschaft und Vorratsnorm in Lager-
        haltungsmodellen. Chapter 13 in: Lagerhaltungsmodel-
        le,   ed. P. Linke und H. Klemm. Berlin: Verlag die
        Wirtschaft.

Rênyi, A., M. Ziermann [1960]. Über einige Lagerhaltungspro-
        bleme eines Magazins, (ungarisch). Publications of
        the Math. Institute of Hungarian Academy of Sciences,
        5 B, Y, 495-506.

Schneider, H. [1978]. Methods for Determining the Re-order
        Point of an (s,S) Ordering Policy when a Service
        Level is Specified. J.Opl.Res. Soc. Vol. 29, 12,
        pp. 1181-1193.

Schneider, H. [1979]. Dissertation. Servicegrade in Lagerhal-
        tungsmodellen. M+M Wissenschaftsverlag Berlin.

Schneider, H. [1980]. A Survey of Service-Levels in Inventory
        Models. Diskussionspapier Nr. 5/80 des Instituts für
        Quantitative Ökonomik und Statistik der Freien Uni-
        versität Berlin.

Proc. First Int. Symp. on Inventories
Budapest, Hungary 1980

SIMULATION EXPERIMENTS IN INVENTORY CONTROL

KLAUS SIEGEL

Combinate for Microelectronics, Erfurt, GDR

In the process of permanent increase of the productivity of labour, the interlacing of transport turnover and inventory control processes with production processes, which are becoming closer and closer, must be taken into consideration. There are still significant differences in level between these two processes /technical equipment, working conditions, penetration of scientific results into processes, and so on/. As a result of mature forms of organization and technologies, an adequate rationalization can be reached very often through transport turnover and inventory control processes. Transport turnover and inventory control processes are characterized by a variety of business particularities, complicated structures, and stochastic /random/ influences and dependencies. Appreciating this fact in recent years has led to a more extensive use of modeling methods in the optimization of transport turnover and inventory control processes, for instance with the use of digital simulation. Digital simulation tests have become an important, inseparable means of work in the area of transport turnover and inventory control. By the help of digital simula-

tion, existing processes can be examined, and problems of
dimensioning and optimal co-ordination, especially in complex
stochastic processes, can be solved in the phase of planning.
In order to diminish programming work which is necessary for
digital simulation special simulation programming systems were
developed.

1. Inventory control bank system

Stochastic features of inventory control bank systems
were dealt with extensively in /1, 2/, and under the conditions
of carrying out a digital simulation the author has represented
them in a shortened form.

It should be kept in mind that decisions regarding the
problem of inventory control involve two questions: "when" and
"how much" should be ordered? The first question normally will
be answered by one of the following two answers:

- stocks will be replenished, if stock level is equal with s,
  or if it is smaller than s,
- the stock will be replenished at every time unit t.

The second question usually is answered in one of the
following two ways:

- quantity of orders is a constant quantity of q,
- quantity ordered should be as high as to replenish stock
  level up to level S.

Inventory control system, in which t and S are to be
determined, is called system with a /t, S/ inventory strategy
/stock-holding policy/. The policy which is required for the
replacement of inventories should be a modified /t, S/ policy.
At every time unit t an ordering decision will be made. The

quantity of order at time i fills up the stock A_i until it becomes a "bank" B_i. Returns are allowed. Thus the quantity of delivery which replenishes again the stock is given by the formula

$$P_i = \max[B_i - A_i] \qquad /1/$$

In order to make discussion easier and to represent the inventory control bank system during the weeks 11 to 17 the time unit t was defined to be one week. Thus our analysis will only deal with the "bank" B_i which is controlled by a clerk. The "bank" should be as large as to include average weekly demand of several weeks. That is

$$B_i = \overline{N S}_i \qquad /2/$$

where N is the number of weeks and $\bar{S}_i$ is the average demand of week i. Several methods could be used to determine the average demand $\bar{S}_i$. In this case only one method will be studied. Average demand of interval i will be covered by the medium sized demand over a period of M weeks preceding directly interval i.

$$S_i = \frac{1}{M} \sum_{j=i-M+1}^{i} S_j \qquad /3/$$

Parameters N and M define the horizon of decisions.

Table 1 illustrates the system when demand, for instance, varies from 0 to 300. The time of procurement amounts to two weeks, M = 4 and N = 6. Thus, additionally to equations /1/, /2/ and /3/ we shall get

$$q_i = Q_i - S_i \qquad\qquad\qquad /4/$$

$$A_i = \begin{cases} q_i & i-1 \\ q_i + \sum\limits_{j=i-L} P_j & \end{cases} \qquad \begin{array}{l} \text{for } L = 0 \\[4pt] \text{for } L > 0 \end{array} \qquad /5/$$

$$R_i = P_{i-L} \qquad\qquad\qquad /6/$$

$$Q_{i+1} = q_i + R_i \qquad\qquad\qquad /7/$$

The quantities I_1 /expected stock levels/, I_2 /expected missing quantity/ and I_3 all depend on manipulated variables N /prediction time/ and M /retrospective time/.

The main subject of this chapter is to find explicit functions of $I_1 = I_1(M,N)$, $I_2 = I_2(M,N)$, and $I_3 = I_3(M,N)$ according to /2/. When these relations are known, the total expected costs of the system could be described in the following way

$$C(M,N) = c_1 I_1(M,N) + c_2 I_2(M,N) + c_3 I_3(M,N) \quad /8/$$

Equation /8/ can be used to find the optimum values of M_o and N_o. /See Table 1./

2. Simulation of inventory control bank system

The simulation method will be demonstrated for L=2, M=4, and N=6 with the help of Table 1. In order to be able to simulate the system given in the table, one must:

- generate the random parameters of demand S_i of the distribution P(S), and

- define them with starting conditions.

Table 1. Inventory control bank system with L=2, M=4, and N=6

i	Q_i	S_i	q_i	$\bar{S}_i$	B_i	A_i	$B_i - A_i$	P_i	R_i
1	2	3	4	5	6	7	8	9	10
8	.	100	.	.	.	.	.	.	.
9	.	100	.	.	.	.	.	100	.
10	.	100	300	.	.	.	.	100	100
11	400	100	300	100	600	500	100	100	100
12	400	300	100	150	900	300	600	600	100
13	200	100	100	150	900	800	100	100	100
14	200	100	100	150	900	800	100	100	600
15	700	100	600	150	900	800	100	100	100
16	700	100	600	100	600	800	200	0	100
17	700	200	500	125	750	600	150	150	100
18	600	0	600	100	.	.	.	.	0
19	600	100	500	100	.	.	.	.	150
20	650	100	550	100	.	.	.	.	.
.	.	.	.	.	.	.	.	.	.

Calculations result directly from the equations /1/ to /7/. When simulation run is carried out, then it is easy to estimate the parameters I_1, I_2, and I_3. We suppose that in ordering cycles have been simulated starting with cycle a /in Table 1/ /m=10 and a=11/. Then parameters I_1, I_2, and I_3 can be determined in the following way:

$$I_1(M,N) = \frac{1}{m} \sum_{i=a}^{a+m-1} I_{ji}(M,N), \quad j=1,2,3 \qquad /9/$$

with

$$
I_{1i} = \begin{cases}
(Q_i + q_i)/2 & \text{for } q_i \geqq 0 \\
2/2S_i & \text{for } q_i \leqq 0 \text{ and } Q_i \geqq 0 \quad /10/ \\
Q_i & \text{for } q_i \leqq 0 \text{ and } Q_i \leqq 0 \\
0 &
\end{cases}
$$

$$
I_{2i} = \begin{cases}
0 & \\
2/2S_i & \text{for } q_i \geqq 0 \\
q_i & \text{for } q_i \leqq 0 \text{ and } Q_i \geqq 0 \quad /11/ \\
-(Q_i + q_i)/2 & \text{for } q_i \leqq 0 \text{ and } Q_i \leqq 0
\end{cases}
$$

and with

$$
I_{3i} = \begin{cases}
0 & \text{for } A_i \geqq B_i \\
& \quad\quad\quad\quad\quad\quad\quad\quad\quad /12/ \\
1 & \text{for } A_i < B_i
\end{cases}
$$

In the program flow chart the simulation of the system is illustrated. The top part on the left side of the flow chart will be used for reading in of data and for reading in of the starting conditions. The right side of the flow chart is reserved for the actual simulation over m weeks starting with week a.

The printing of the parameters i, Q_i, S_i, and so on, for every i is also included for sake of check and illustration. In case of a larger simulation run printing, of course, will be omitted. The calculation of parameters S_i, I_{1i}, and I_{2i} is carried out according to a special program flow chart /2/.

In the investigation of transport turnover and inventory control processes conducted by the author, the following

Program flow chart

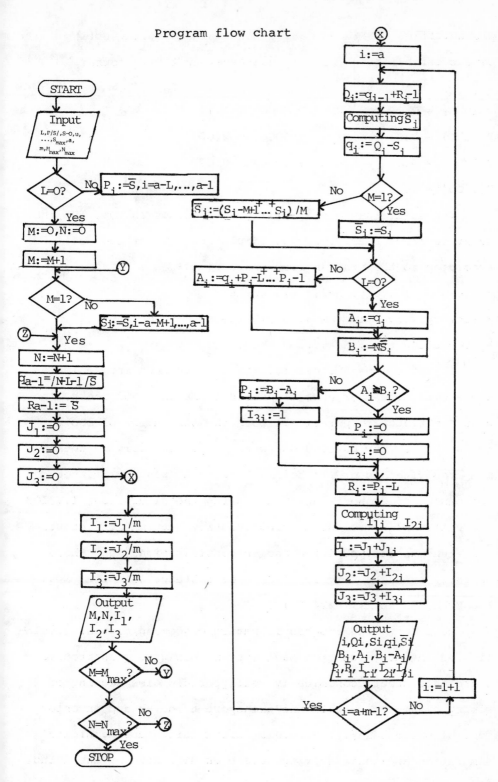

probabilities for the demand of bag cargoed quick-setting cement per building assembly container unit were found:

P(1000) = 0.07	P(3000) = 0.14
P(1500) = 0.08	P(4000) = 0.08
P(2000) = 0.21	P(8000) = 0.07
P(2500) = 0.35	

The significance probability α was fixed as 90%, and the relative error ε as 0.05. The simulation was carried out according to the program flow chart, where
- time of delivery: L=2,...,8 weeks
- retrospective time: M=6,...,10 weeks
- prediction time: N=4,...,8 weeks.

If not all parameters I_1, I_2, I_3 have been met, calculations were done over a total period of maximum 500 weeks. In order to reduce computational work the simulation of 100 to 500 weeks was not carried out weekly, but in every 10 weeks. Compared with Naddor /1/ column 8 (B_i - A) was not printed due to reasons of economizing. When during the simulations 1...100 there is no I_2, i.e. no missing quantity occurred, the simulation run was stopped for economic considerations, and there appeared the sign "Divisor = 0", for instance with L=2, M=4, N=8 ERROR IN ADDRESS 6224 "DIVISOR = 0".

Despite the stochastic nature of demand, digital simulation of inventory control bank systems can give quantitative statements about economically well-grounded dimensioning of memory parameters within the transport turnover and inventory control processes /3/. Problems which occurred during digital simulation and their solving have been discussed by the author

542

in detail in /4/. In the digital simulation of the inventory control bank system calculations were carried out up to that point of time, where, for the first time, the following conditions were reached:

$$\frac{1.65 \, s(I_j, n)}{\bar{x}(I_{j,n}) \sqrt{n}} \leq 0.05 \qquad\qquad \text{for } j = 1,2,3 \qquad /13/$$

3. Summary

As a result of the above statements the following general conclusions could be made for the simulation of inventory control bank systems:

- when increasing fluctuations are concerned, stock levels and shortages will increase, whereas the number of delays will decrease,

- the inventory control system is more sensitive about the number /prediction time/ of weeks in the bank than about the number /retrospective time/ of weeks required for the calculation of average demand,

- if N increases, then also I_1 /the expected stock level/ increases, whereas I_2 /the expected shortage/ and I_3 /the number of deliveries expected per week/ will decrease,

- if M increases, I_1 will decrease, though I_1 first increases later decreases. If this assumption is made we can state an increase of I_3.

The selection of the optimum values M and N will substantially depend on the cost units of the inventory control bank system as a specified model of stock-keeping taking into consideration the possible synchrony of delivery of goods produced by enterprises of the national economy.

543

With the help of this special model of inventory control
it is possible
- to quantify the significance and role of the important factors
  in the process of stock-keeping,
- to allow calculation of ordering strategies and thus to allow
  the derivation of algorithms which are used to print out
  ordering recommendations for managing clerks in the scope of
  computer systems, and
- to consider the constituents of inventory norm as entity and
  derive them from the ordering strategy. Thus it is possible
  to provide a connection between ordering activity and
  normalization of inventories /5,6/.

4. Application of variance-reducing methods for simulation
tests of inventory control systems

4.1. Variance-reducing methods

Variance-reducing methods will be applied in order to
reduce sample size N, which is necessary to reach a given
variant of the sample mean Var $/\bar{X}/$. On the other hand they will
reach the lowest variance of the sample mean for a given sample
size. When independent observations exist, the variance of the
sample mean will be defined as

$$\text{Var } /\bar{X}/ = \frac{\text{Var } /X/}{N} \qquad\qquad /14/$$

In the present work which was carried out under guidance of
Geissendorf, the following variance-reducing methods have been
tested:

1. the antithetic method /"antithetic sampling"/,

2. the selective method /"selective sampling"/,

3. the method of stratified sampling /"stratified sampling"/,

4. the regressive method or the method of accompanying
   auxiliary variables /"regression sampling"/.

   While the antithetic and selective methods are based on a
modification of the stochastic exogenous variables, the method of
stratified sampling and the regressive method are based on the
incorporation of additional information in the form of stratify-
ing or accompanying auxiliary variables in detecting the sample
mean.

   4.2. Input-oriented techniques

   4.2.1. The antithetic method

   A random number X will be generated, and its complementary
random number $Y = 1 - X$ will be formed. Both random numbers are
negatively correlated, i.e. they behave stochastic-diametrical-
ly. These random numbers are necessary to find the array element
index j, which represents the normal parameter of demand, and
on the other hand, to find the index k, which defines the
antithetic parameter of demand. It was found that the variance
of the antithetic sample mean $\overline{\overline{GK}}_{x,y}$ is smaller than the variance
of the sample mean $\overline{GK}$, which was formed in a simple way.

$\underline{X}$: vector of the random numbers $/\underline{x} = x_1,\ldots,x_{50}/$

$\underline{Y}$: complementary vector of the random numbers

$\underline{B}_x$: normally generated stochastic vector of parameters of demand

$\underline{B}_y$: antithetically generated stochastic vector of parameters of
   demand

GK_x, GK_y: medium total costs on the basis of antithetic method

$GK_{x,y}$: arithmetic average of the medium total costs in inventory control systems for a simulation run.

Figure 1: The antithetic method

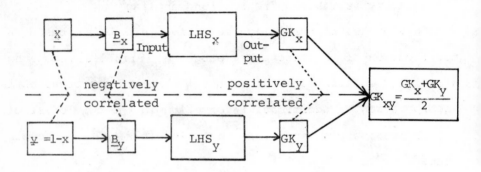

4.2.2. The selective method

The selective method could be characterized according to /6/ as taking a parameter of demand from a fictive urn without returning to it. The variance of the medium total costs GK_z for a simulation run is influenced by:

- the deviations of the relative frequencies of the demand parameters in vector $\underline{B}_z$ from their probabilities, and
- the number of permutations of the demand parameter at given relative frequencies of the demand parameters within the vector $\underline{B}_z$.

The selective method eliminates the first variance source for the medium total costs of a run.

Thus, for the variance of the selective sample mean GK_z the following inequality will apply:

$$\text{Var } /\overline{GK}_z/ = \frac{\text{Var } /GK_z/}{N} < \frac{\text{Var } /GK/}{N} \qquad /15/$$

As a result the selective sample mean GK_z has a smaller variance than the simple sample mean $\overline{GK}$, and thus a variance reducing effect will be reached.

Figure 2: Selective method

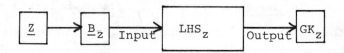

$\underline{Z}$: vector of the random numbers $/\underline{z} = z_1, z_2, \ldots, z_{50}/$

$\underline{B}_z$: selectively generated stochastic vector of the demand parameters

GK_z: medium total costs on the basis of the selective method.

4.3. Output-oriented techniques

The output-oriented techniques use additional information on the input in the form of auxiliary variables, but they do not affect it.

4.3.1. The method of stratified sampling

In this method the auxiliary variable H will be used as stratification variable, which means, the medium total cost values of simulation runs will be divided into strata as a function of their value.

The sample means and empirical variances for the strata first will be found separately, and after that an aggregation to the total mean of the sample and to the empirical total mean variance of the sample will take place. The sum of the random number of vector $\underline{x}$ will be used as auxiliary variables

$$H = \sum_{i=1}^{N} x_i, \qquad N = 50 \qquad\qquad /16/$$

H is thus approximately normally distributed, and has an expectation value $E(H) = 25$.

At the method of stratified sampling the medium total cost values for simulation runs are divided into two strata depending on whether H is smaller and equal to or greater and equal to 25. Thus two strata can be formed, which have the same probability:

$$
\begin{array}{lll}
\text{strata I} & \text{H } 25 < p_1 = 0.5 & \\
& & /17/ \\
\text{strata II} & \text{H } 25 \geq P_2 = 0.5 &
\end{array}
$$

Now we shall test   in which of the strata the medium total value will fall, that means, the total cost values will be assigned to the two above mentioned strata as a function of the assigned values of auxiliary variables.

4.3.2. The regressive method

The basis of the regressive method is correlation. If it is necessary to estimate the expectation value by frequent simulation runs the case could occur that a random variable H could be found which can be simulated together with the medium costs and which has the following characteristics:

- H will be used as accompanying auxiliary variable; H is highly correlated with the medium total costs, that means, the
  correlation coefficient Cor /H, GK/ is approximately one,
- H has the expectation value $E/H/ = 25$.

On the basis of the regressive method the medium total costs GK_R then will be

$$GK_R = GK - \alpha\, H{-}E/H/ \qquad\qquad /18/$$

H : accompanying auxiliary variable

α : coefficient

Since $E\left(\alpha\, H{-}E/H/\right) = 0$, the expectation value GK_R will be

$$E/GK_R/ = E/GK/ \qquad\qquad /19/$$

5. The effectiveness of the individual variance-reducing techniques

In finding out the effectiveness of the variance-reducing methods a difference will be made between effectiveness I and effectiveness II. The effectiveness I will be determined in the following way:

$$E_I = 1 - \frac{\text{variance with application of a reducing method}}{\text{normal variance}} \cdot 100\% \qquad /20/$$

As a result it measures only the net variance-reducing effect of a method, neglecting the occurring additional computation work. Thus the effectiveness I can be considered only as an illustrative parameter, since it indicates generally whether a variance reduction has occurred at all. For finding out the effectiveness II the following scheme will be used:

$$E_{II} = \left[1 - \frac{\text{variance with application of a reducing method}}{\text{normal variance}} \; 1 + \frac{\text{additional computational time}}{100} \right] \cdot 100\%$$

$$/21/$$

Effectiveness II thus measures the variance-reducing effect and compares it with the additional computational work /Table 2/.

Table 2. Results

Variance-reducing methods	$\overline{GK}$	$s^2/\overline{GK}/$	Effectiveness I	Estimated additional computational time	Effectiveness II
-	686.80	869.18	-	-	-
Antithetic	667.73	350.89	61%	90%	26%
Selective	604.97	625.41	30%	10%	23%
Stratified	686.80	763.52	15%	5%	11%
Regressive	665.33	578.35	35%	5%	32%

Therefore, it can be characterized as a realistic parameter for the evaluation of the effectiveness of a variance-reducing method. The detected values for $\overline{GK}$, $s^2/\overline{GK}/$, E_I, E_{II} the additional computational time which was evaluated by usual /conventional/ Monte-Carlo-simulation when using variance-reducing methods, can be taken from Table 2. It must be pointed out that these values were obtained with ordering point z = 10 units and an ordering level Z = 14 units.

6. References

/1/ Naddor, E.: Lagerhaltungssysteme, Leipzig: BSG Teubner
        Verlagsgesellschaft 1971.

/2/ Siegel, K.: Digitalsimulation eines Lagerhaltungs-Bank-
        Systems auf einer mittleren EDVA, Hebezeuge und
        Fördermittel 17/1977/5, pp. 135-139.

/3/ Siegel, K.: Digitalsimulation der Lagerhaltung mit mehreren
        Warenarten, Hebezeuge und Fördermittel 16/1976/9,
        pp. 276-278.

/4/ Siegel, K.: Applikation, Genauigkeitsbetrachtungen und
        Auswertung der Digitalsimulation des Lagerhaltungs-
        Bank-Systems, Hebezeuge und Fördermittel
        19/1979/1, pp. 13-17.

/5/ Lange, P.: Monte-Carlo-Simulation eines LHS unter Verwendung
        varianzreduzierender Techniken, Jena: FSU- WiWi
        1976.

/6/ Siegel, K.: Einiges zur Modellagerung in einer Giesserei
        mit einer Gusskapazität von 30 000 t/a, Giesserei-
        technik 20/1974/2, pp. 54-58.

Proc. First Int. Symp. on Inventories
Budapest, Hungary 1980

SETTING OF PARAMETER VALUES IN COORDINATED INVENTORY CONTROL BY MEANS OF GRAPHICAL AND HAND CALCULATOR METHODS

EDWARD A. SILVER[1] and NEAL E. MASSARD[2]

[1] *University of Waterloo, Waterloo, Ont., Canada*
[2] *Canadian National Railways, Montreal, Que., Canada*

I. INTRODUCTION

In this paper we consider a group (or family) of inventoried items where coordination of replenishments can lead to reduced costs of replenishment. More specifically, there is a major fixed cost associated with any replenishment of the family and a minor fixed cost associated with each separate item included in a group replenishment. The point of coordination is to reduce the number of occasions per year that the major cost is incurred. This structure is applicable in two contexts

  i) A group of items are purchased from the same supplier –
     in this setting the major cost and the minor cost are often
     denoted as the header cost and the line cost respectively.

 ii) A group of items share a common production facility – here the
     major cost is associated with the production setup to move from
     one family to another while the minor cost is for shifting from
     one item to another within the same family.

Other possible reasons for coordination are provided by Peterson and Silver (1979, pp. 495-6).

A reasonable type of coordinated control system to consider is what is called an (S,c,s) system. In such a system we have continuous review (i.e.

transactions recording) of the stock status of each of the items in a family. Whenever the inventory position (on-hand plus on-order minus back-orders) of any item i drops to its must-order point s_i or lower, a group replenishment is initiated. Enough of item i is ordered to raise its inventory position to its order-up-to-level S_i. At the same time any other item j in the family is considered for inclusion in the replenishment. If its inventory position is low enough, namely at or below its can-order point c_j, then item j is included in the group order with enough being ordered to raise its inventory position to S_j. Further details concerning the literature on (S,c,s) and other coordinated control systems can be found in Silver (1974).

Ignall (1969) has shown that the cost-minimizing control policy need not be of the (S,c,s) form. However, the (S,c,s) system, as we shall see, is difficult enough to analyze, let alone having to consider a more complicated system. This philosophy of developing reasonable solutions, that take account of the system control costs, is a central idea in the book by Peterson and Silver (1979).

In an (S,c,s) system, if there are n items in a family, then there are 3n control variables whose effects are all interrelated, thus making an exact mathematical analysis of the problem out of the question. Silver (1974) has proposed an iterative procedure, requiring a computer, for ascertaining reasonable (not necessarily optimal) values of the parameters. In the current paper we present a much simpler approach that makes use of a graphical aid (indifference curves) to establish the values of some of the parameters (the S's and c's) and a programmable calculator routine to determine the settings of the others (the s's). Besides being much simpler to implement, this new approach does as well as the earlier iterative, computer method in terms of required replenishment and carrying costs to achieve a specified service level.

554

In the next section we present the assumptions underlying the model as well as the notation to be used. Then Section III deals with the case of a negligible lead time where indifference curves are developed to find the S and c combinations. Summary results of a number of test examples are presented, including a comparison with the computerized iterative approach of Silver (1974). Next, Section IV is concerned with a calculator program for finding the s values when the lead time is no longer negligible. The paper terminates with a summary in Section V.

II. ASSUMPTIONS AND NOTATION

Assumptions

The model considered is identical with that utilized in Silver (1974) where considerable discussion of the assumptions is provided. Therefore, we simply list the assumptions here.

1. As discussed earlier, the replenishment cost structure is such that there is a major fixed cost A associated with any group replenishment and a minor fixed cost a_i if item i is included in a replenishment.

2. Demand for each item follows a Poisson process where the rate can vary from item to item.

3. The unit variable cost of an item does not depend on the size of the replenishment, ie. there are no quantity discounts.

4. The replenishment lead time is of known length and does not depend upon which subset of the items of the family are involved in the order.

5. Inventory carrying costs are proportional to the average inventory level.

6. Rather than explicitly costing shortages we assume instead that the control parameters are selected so as to provide customer service

555

at or above a prescribed level. For each item, service is defined in
one of two ways:

  i) Probability of no shortage per replenishment cycle.

ii) Fraction of demand to be satisfied directly from shelf.

7.   All demands when out of stock are back ordered. However, the
model could easily be adapted to cope with complete or partial lost
sales.

8.   From the viewpoint of any particular item the sequence of group
replenishments triggered by _other_ items can be approximated by a
Poisson process.

Notation

A, major fixed cost per replenishment (independent of the number of
    items involved), in $.

a_i, minor fixed cost when item i is involved in a replenishment, in $.

c_i, can-order point of item i.

EC_i, expected relevant costs per unit time for item i, in $/yr.

$\acute{E}C_i(c)$, minimum expected costs per unit time for item i when a particu-
    lar c value is used.

$G = 2A\lambda/vr$

L, replenishment lead time, in years.

n, number of items in the family under consideration (i.e. a replen-
    ishment can include up to n different items) - the items are
    numbered i = 1,2,..., n.

NT_i, expected number of replenishments _triggered_ by item i per year.

P_1, desired probability of no shortage per replenishment cycle.

P_2, desired fraction of demand to be satisfied directly from shelf.

$P_{po}(x_0|z) = \dfrac{z^{x_0} \exp(-z)}{x_0!}$, probability that a Poisson variable with

parameter (mean) z takes on a value of x_0.

$P_{po \leq}(x_0|z)$, probability that a Poisson variable with parameter z

takes on a value less than or equal to x_0.

r, inventory carrying charge, in \$/\$/yr.

s_i, must-order point of item i.

S_i, order-up-to-level of item i.

$\hat{S}(c)$, the best S value when a specific c value is used.

v_i, unit variable cost of item i, in \$/unit.

λ_i, Poisson demand rate for item i, in units/yr.

μ_i, the expected number of orders per year triggered by all items

other than item i.

$\rho_i = \lambda_i/(\lambda_i + \mu_i)$

III. THE CASE OF NEGLIGIBLE LEAD TIME

In theory one should select all 3n parameters simultaneously, recognizing the interactions among them. Instead, we follow the pragmatic approach of first finding reasonable settings for the S's and c's by considering the special case of a negligible lead time. Then, in the next section we shall find the s values for a non-zero lead time given the S's and c's already determined. This is identical with the approach adopted and discussed in further detail in Silver (1974).

Development of Indifference Curves

For the case of a negligible lead time, and recognizing that demand transactions are always of unit size (a property of Poisson demand) it follows that all of the s's should be set to zero. From Eq. (13) of Silver (1974) we have that the expected costs per year of item i are given by

$$EC_i = \{S-c+\rho(1-\rho^c)/(1-\rho)\}^{-1}\{(S-c)(S+c+1)vr/2$$

$$+ \rho[c-\rho(1-\rho^c)/(1-\rho)]vr/(1-\rho) + \lambda\rho^c A + \lambda a\}, \quad \ldots (1)$$

where, for simplicity in notation, we have suppressed the subscript i in a_i, c_i, S_i, λ_i, and ρ_i.

Note that EC_i, in principle, depends upon the S's and c's of the other items in the family through μ_i (which is included in ρ_i). For the moment we shall assume that ρ_i is known and we shall return to this point later.

Now, continuing as in Silver (1974), the best _continuous_ S value for a given c, denoted by $\hat{S}(c)$, is given by Eq. (16a) of the earlier paper, namely

$$\hat{S}(c) = c - \rho(1-\rho^c)/(1-\rho) + \sqrt{[2\lambda(a+A\rho^c)/vr + 2c\rho^{c+1}/(1-\rho)}$$

$$- \rho(1-\rho^c)(1+\rho^{c+1})/(1-\rho)^2] \quad \ldots (2)$$

Physically S cannot be smaller than c. When this occurs in Eq. (2), including the case where S becomes imaginary, one can show (Silver, 1974) that the best S is given by

$$\hat{S}(c) = c \quad \ldots (3)$$

Substitution of Eq. (2) into Eq. (1) gives us $\hat{EC}_i(c)$, the best cost for the given c value. It can be shown that this expression is simply

$$\hat{EC}_i(c) = vr[\hat{S}(c) + \tfrac{1}{2}]. \quad \ldots (4)$$

For the case where Eq. (3) is valid, its substitution into Eq. (1) gives

$$\hat{EC}_i(c) = \{\rho(1-\rho^c)/(1-\rho)\}^{-1}\{\rho[c-\rho(1-\rho^c)/(1-\rho)]vr/(1-\rho)$$

$$+ \lambda\rho^c A + \lambda a\}. \quad \ldots (5)$$

We are indifferent between c and c+1 where

$$\hat{EC}_i(c) = \hat{EC}_i(c+1) \quad \ldots (6)$$

For the case where Eq. (2) is valid for both c and c+1, we obtain from Eq. (6) a complicated condition that the 7 parameters a, A, c, S, v, λ and ρ must satisfy. As Massard (1979) has shown, the number of parameters can be reduced to only 4, namely a/A, c, ρ and

$$G = 2A\lambda/vr \qquad \qquad \ldots \text{(7)}$$

where the latter is seen to be the square of an economic order quantity.
Suppose we represent the indifference condition by

$$f(a/A,c,\rho,G) = 0 \qquad \qquad \ldots \text{(8)}$$

For a given value of c Eq. (8) represents an indifference (between c and
c+1) surface in a 3-dimensional space of a/A, ρ and G. For practical
purposes, one uses a set of 2-dimensional plots of G versus ρ, one for
each of several reasonable values of a/A.

It turns out to be easiest to solve Eq. (8) for G in terms of the
other parameters. As Massard has shown,

$$G = (-k_1 + \sqrt{k_1^2 - 4k_2 k_3})/2k_2 \qquad \qquad \ldots \text{(9)}$$

where

$$k_1 = 2k_4 k_5 - k_7 k_8 - k_6 k_9$$

$$k_2 = k_4^2 - k_7 k_9$$

$$k_3 = k_5^2 - k_6 k_8$$

$$k_4 = (k_7 + k_9)/2$$

$$k_5 = (k_6 + k_8 - k_{10}^2)/2 \qquad \qquad \ldots \text{(10)}$$

$$k_6 = 2c\rho^{c+1}/(1-\rho) - \rho(1-\rho^c)(1+\rho^{c+1})/(1-\rho)^2$$

$$k_7 = a/A + \rho^c$$

$$k_8 \text{ is } k_6 \text{ with c replaced by c+1}$$

$$k_9 = a/A + \rho^{c+1}$$

and

$$k_{10} = 1 - \rho^{c+1}$$

In the case where the condition of Eq. (3) holds, then use of Eq. (6)
leads to the following result

$$G = \frac{\dfrac{\rho}{(1-\rho^c)(1-\rho)}[c - \dfrac{\rho(1-\rho^c)}{1-\rho}] - \dfrac{\rho}{(1-\rho^{c+1})(1-\rho)}[c + 1 - \dfrac{\rho(1-\rho^{c+1})}{1-\rho}]}{[\dfrac{\rho^{c+1} + a/A}{2(1-\rho^{c+1})} - \dfrac{\rho^c + a/A}{2(1-\rho^c)}]} \qquad \ldots \text{(11)}$$

It is seen that again there is no difficulty in plotting G versus ρ for a given c and a fixed value of a/A.

Thus Eqs. (9) and (11) allow us to plot indifference curves for various values of c. An illustration (for a/A = 0.1) is shown in Figure 1 for c values up to 30. The apparent discontinuity at ρ = 0.85 is simply a consequence of the change of the scale of ρ at that point. (We introduced this change to permit coverage of a broader range of ρ values on the single graph).

Use of curves

To use the indifference curves for any particular item i we need to know the value of ρ_i. As mentioned earlier, ρ_i depends on μ_i which, in turn, depends upon the S's and c's of all the other items. Fortunately, our research showed that total costs are very insensitive to the value of ρ. Thus we are able to use a very crude value of ρ, based on assuming independent control of all other items in the family. Under independent control the number of orders triggered per year by item j, denoted by NT_j, is given by

$$NT_j = \lambda_j / EOQ_j = \sqrt{\frac{\lambda_j v_j r}{2(A+a_j)}} \qquad \ldots (12)$$

Hence

$$\rho_i = \frac{\lambda_i}{\lambda_i + \mu_i} \simeq \frac{\lambda_i}{\lambda_i + \sum\limits_{j \neq i} \sqrt{\frac{\lambda_j v_j r}{2(A+a_j)}}} \qquad \ldots (13)$$

Once the appropriate c value is found from using the indifference curves then the associated S follows from Eq. (2).

Numerical Illustration

Consider a family of 3 items with A = $25, r = 0.25 $/$/yr. and item characteristics as follows:

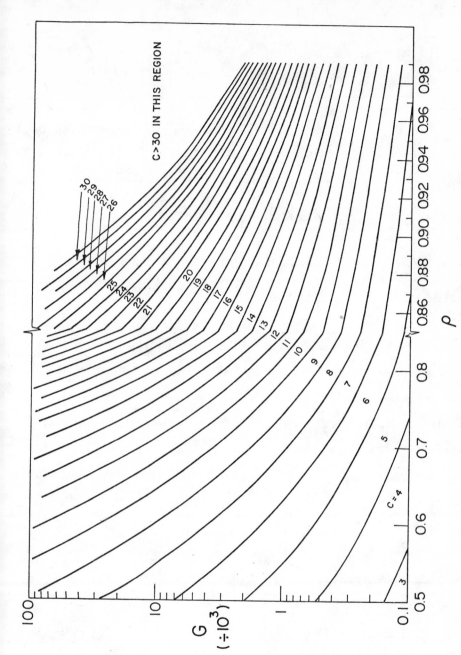

Fig. 1 Indifference Curves to Find the Best c for a/A = 0.1

Item, j	Q_j $\\$	λ_j units/yr.	v_j \$/unit
1	2.50	11	10.00
2	2.50	20	5.00
3	2.50	15	2.00

Consider the determination of c and S for item 3. First, from Eq. (12) we have $NT_1 = 0.707$ and $NT_2 = 0.674$. Hence, from Eq. (13) there results

$$\rho_3 = 15/(15 + 1.381) = 0.916$$

Now, for item 3 Eq. (7) gives a G value of 1500. Furthermore a/A = 0.1 . Thus, from Figure 1 we find that $c_3 = 17$. Then Eq. (2) gives $S_3 = 30$.

Results of a Number of Test Examples

Two sets of examples were used for test purposes. First, the 22 examples originally presented by Silver (1971) were analyzed. These cover family sizes ranging from 4 to 10 and a/A ratios from 0.1 to 0.64 . In each case independent control (ie. ignoring the benefits of coordination) was used as a benchmark. The savings from using the method of this paper ranged from 7.4 to 24.8% with an average of 14.7%. Of perhaps more interest is the fact that in all 22 cases the indifference curves approach did slightly better than Silver's iterative, computerized algorithm (Silver, 1974) despite the latter being much more complex to use. (The average savings of the iterative method over independent control were 14.1%.) In retrospect the reason lies in the fact that the iterative method is based on finding the (S,c) pair for each item that minimize costs for that item only without explicitly taking account of the indirect effects of the particular (S_i, c_i) pair on the costs of the other items ($j \neq i$). Details of the examples and results can be found in Massard (1979).

In the above set of examples it was not possible to find the optimal

solutions because of the computational difficulties involved. Therefore,
a special set of 5 examples, each with only 2 items in a family, was constructed. In each case the small n value permitted the determination of
the optimal set (S_1, c_1, S_2, c_2) by a steepest descent technique (Gottfried
and Weisman, 1973). The results are as shown in Table 1. Further details
can be found in Massard (1979).

Table 1 - Results of 2-Item Examples
Percent Cost Penalty Compared with Exact Solution

Example	Independent Control	Iterative Algorithm	Use of Indifference Curves
1	9.6	0.4	0.2
2	6.9	0.2	0.1
3	4.6	0.08	0.07
4	3.3	0.07	0.02
5	2.5	0.02	0.02
Averages	5.4	0.15	0.08

Again, it is seen that the simple indifference approach slightly outper-
forms the iterative method. Moreover, both give negligible cost penalties
compared with the computationally impractical exact procedure.

IV. THE CASE OF A SIGNIFICANT LEAD TIME

As argued at the beginning of Section III, when the lead time (denoted by L) becomes non-zero we use a sequential approach of finding the
s values given the S and c values found from the case of negligible lead
time (L = 0). More precisely we use

Case of Negligible Lead Time	Case of Significant Lead Time
S(for L = 0)	S(for L = 0) + s
c(for L = 0)	c(for L = 0) + s
s = 0	s

This is comparable, in the case of independent control, to the widely
used approach of first finding an economic order quantity (EOQ) and then
putting an s below it (S becomes EOQ + s).

We considered two of the more common service measures, namely

    i) Specified probability (P_1) of no shortage per replenishment

       cycle.

    ii) Specified fraction (P_2) of demand to be satisfied directly from

        shelf.

Under the assumptions of this paper Eqs. (22) and (24) of Silver
(1974) give that we wish to find the smallest value of s for each item
(the subscript i has been suppressed to keep the notation simpler) such
that

for service measure P_1

$$(1/\rho)^c p_{po\le}(s+c|\lambda L) - p_{po}(s+1|\lambda L) - \rho^{s+1} \sum_{x_0=s+2}^{s+c} p_{po}(x_0|\lambda L) (1/\rho)^{x_0}$$

$$\ge P_1/\rho^c \qquad \ldots \ (14)$$

where $p_{po}(x_0|\lambda L)$ = prob{ Poisson variable with parameter λL

                               takes on a value equal to x_0}

and $p_{po\le}(x_0|\lambda L)$ = prob{ Poisson variable with parameter λL

                               takes on a value less than or equal to x_0}.

for service measure P_2

$$\rho^c[\lambda L-s-\lambda L p_{po\le}(s-1|\lambda L) + s p_{po\le}(s|\lambda L)] + (1-\rho)\rho^{c+s} \sum_{x_0=s+1}^{s+c}$$

$$\rho^{-x_0}[\lambda L - x_0 - \lambda L p_{po\le}(x_0-1|\lambda L) + x_0 p_{po\le}(x_0)] \le [S-c+\rho(1-\rho^c)/(1-\rho)]\cdot$$

$$(1-P_2). \qquad \ldots \ (15)$$

Obviously neither of these equations are practical to solve by hand.
Silver (1974) had their solution programmed for computer solution. Here
we have developed routines on a much simpler and portable device, namely
the Hewlett-Packard HP-97 electronic calculator.

Numerical Illustration

In our 3-item example of Section III suppose that a lead time of 3 months (ie. L = 0.25 years) is appropriate and a P_1 value of 0.95 is desired. We consider the determination of the must-order point s for item 3. From Section III we have

$$S_3 \ (L = 0) = 30; \ c_3 \ (L = 0) = 17; \ \rho_3 = 0.916 \ .$$

The HP-97 program output for this example is as follows (we have retyped the output because the original is on thermal-sensitive paper that would not properly duplicate! In addition we have added the alphabetic symbols as the HP-97 does not have alphabetic characters):

$$\lambda \to 15.00 \ ***$$

$$L(\text{months}) \to 3.00 \ ***$$

$$\rho(\text{to 2 significant digits}) \to 0.92 \ ***$$

$$c(L = 0) \to 17.00 \ ***$$

$$P_1 \to 0.95 \ ***$$

$$s \to 5.00 \ ***$$

It is seen that the final parameter settings for item 3 are thus

$$S_3 = 35, \qquad c_3 = 22, \qquad s_3 = 5 \ .$$

The execution times of the two programs can be significant, particularly for large values of s and c. Based on a limited set of examples we estimate running times (T) approximately by

for P_1 case $\qquad T \simeq 4.8 \ s + 2.0 \ c + 3.7 \qquad$ (in seconds)

for P_2 case $\qquad T \simeq 6.2 \ s + 4.0 \ c + 3.6 \qquad$ (in seconds)

Work is under way on using much simpler expressions than Eqs. (14) and (15). These simpler formulae would make the execution times negligible, in fact, eliminating the need for the calculator assistance.

V. SUMMARY

In this paper we started with a complex problem of coordinated inventory control. For a group of n items the decision problem involved 3n interrelated control variables. We have been able to reduce its solution to a form not even requiring computer assistance. The solution involves two steps. First there are n separate uses of indifference curves, then the second stage is n separate runs of one of two programs on an electronic calculator.

ACKNOWLEDGEMENTS

The authors wish to express their thanks to Neil Freiter for his programming work on the HP-97 calculator. The research leading to this paper was partially supported by the Natural Sciences and Engineering Research Council of Canada under Grant No. A7417.

REFERENCES

Gottfried, B.S. and Weisman, J. (1973): Introduction to Optimization Theory, Prentice-Hall, Englewood Cliffs, N.J., Chapter 3.

Ignall, E. (1969): "Optimal Continuous Review Policies for Two Product Inventory Systems with Joint Set-Up Costs", Management Science, 15, 277.

Love, S, (1979): Inventory Control, McGraw-Hill, New York, N.Y., Chapter 5.

Massard, N.E. (1979): "New Solution Approaches for the (S,c,0) Inventory Problem", unpublished M.A.Sc. project, Department of Management Sciences, University of Waterloo, Waterloo, Ontario, Canada.

Peterson, R. and Silver, E.A. (1979): Decision Systems for Inventory Management and Production Planning, John Wiley, New York, N.Y.

Silver, E.A. (1971): "Some Findings Relative to a Joint Replenishment Inventory Control Strategy", Proceedings of the 14th Annual International Conference of the American Production and Inventory Control Society, 12.

Silver, E.A. (1974): "A Control System for Coordinated Inventory Replenishment", International Journal of Production Research, 12, 647.

Proc. First Int. Symp. on Inventories
Budapest, Hungary 1980

WAREHOUSE REPLENISHMENT USING THE COST-SERVICE TRANSPORTATION MODEL

CHARLES J. TEPLITZ

State University of New York at Albany, Albany, NY, USA

Introduction

It is well known that inventories play an important role in the economy. They are of great importance for both corporate managers and economic policy makers. Since costs associated with maintaining inventories are directly related to the prime interest rate via the opportunity cost of capital, inventory management becomes increasingly important as that prime rate rises. With the prime rate in the United States having reached an unprecedented 20 percent, it is no wonder that emphasis should be placed on minimizing the amount of inventory being carried. But to simply cut inventories in an effort to reduce costs can be dangerous. Lack of inventory will lead to reduced customer service. This, in turn, will result in lost sales leading ultimately to the financial collapse of the firm. Instead, inventories must be reduced while keeping customer service levels as high as possible. Unfortunately, a model has yet to be developed which can optimize these two factors (inventory levels and service levels).

The following model, the cost-service transportation model, originally developed by the author to optimize the tradeoff between transportation cost and service levels, can be adapted to optimize the tradeoff between warehouse service levels and the costs of expediting and shipping goods to those warehouses.

567

The following example was designed to illustrate all phases of the model.

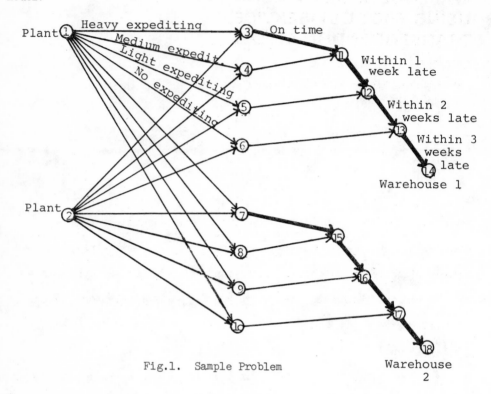

Fig.1. Sample Problem

In Figure 1 we see two production facilities, the first with a production capacity of 78 units, the second with a capacity of 136 units. Two warehouses, each ordering 107 units, would like their orders filled as soon as possible (i.e., during the promised lead time). While it is possible to deliver all goods on time, it would require heavy expediting and rapid transportation resulting in a total cost of \$101,851. On the other hand, all goods could be shipped for only \$1,536 but they would all arrive about 3 weeks later than promised. The question becomes, are we sure its worth \$100,000 in order for our warehouse to experience perfect customer service? The likely answer is <u>no</u>. A compromise between cost and service must be made. The optimal strategy will have some, but not all, units arriving on schedule with the remaining units drifting in over the next few weeks. While this strategy may reduce customer service, it will definitely reduce the cost of expediting production and the cost of employing speedier transportation methods. Also, this shipping strategy will result in reduced inventories on-hand at the warehouse.

Using the least-cost solution and the maximum-flow solution, the production manager can list various combinations of cost and service with which he is indifferent. Table 1 depicts the cost-service tradeoff matrix for our example. As can be seen, the manager derives more satisfaction from lower costs than from higher costs and more satisfaction with timely deliveries than with less-timely deliveries. Using these satisfaction levels, the cost-service transportation model (CST) will attempt to locate the allocation method resulting in equal satisfaction between costs and service.

Table 1. User Tradeoff Matrix

Weeks Late	0%	20%	Satisfaction 40%	60%	80%	100%
Within 3	107.00	107.00	107.00	107.00	107.00	107.00
Within 2	.00	25.40	50.29	72.28	97.66	107.00
Within 1	.00	21.84	43.54	69.15	94.61	107.00
Within 0	.00	20.87	40.66	60.05	80.10	107.00
Cost Equals	$101851	91184	78670	67166	55432	1536

Algorithm

Figure 2 depicts the flow diagram for the cost-service transportation algorithm.

Step 1 (Min Cost/Max Flow). Find the least-cost distribution and the maximum-flow distribution via Fulkerson's out-of-kilter algorithm. If no feasible solution exists, terminate the algorithm, otherwise go to Step 2.

Step 2 (Initialize Bounds). Set the upper bounds of the tradeoff arcs (shaded arcs in Figure 1) equal to the maximum flows through those arcs as determined in Step 1. Set the lower bounds of the tradeoff arcs equal to the least-cost flows through those arcs as determined in Step 1. Go to Step 3.

Step 3 (New Distribution). Using the least-cost distribution from above and the new tradeoff arc bounds, determine a new distribution via Fulkerson's out-of-kilter algorithm. Go to Step 4.

Step 4 (New Bounds). Compute the degree of satisfaction π^{TC} based upon the total cost of distribution TC_n found in Step 3. If this cost-satisfaction exceeds the flow-satisfaction $[\pi_n^{TC} > \pi_n^{F}]$, leave the upper bounds on the tradeoff arcs unchanged. Increase the lower bounds such that $\pi_{n+1}^{F} = (\pi_n^{TC} + \pi_n^{F})/2$. Go to Step 3. If $\pi_n^{TC} < \pi_n^{F}$, set the upper bounds of the tradeoff arcs equal to the lower bounds $[\pi_{n+1}^{TC} = \pi_n^{F}]$ and set the lower bounds equal to the previous lower bounds $[\pi_{n+1}^{F} = \pi_{n-1}^{F}]$. Go to Step 3. If $\pi_n^{TC} = \pi_n^{F}$, go to Step 5.

Step 5 (Optimal Solution). The optimal solution has been found with a cost of TC_n at a satisfaction level of $\pi_n^{TC} = \pi_n^{F}$. Terminate the algorithm.

Example

Returning to our example, we set the bounds on the tradeoff arcs as per Step 2 of the algorithm. The new distribution, restricted by these arc bounds, has a flow-satisfaction of 0 percent and a cost-satisfaction (TC = \$1536) of 100 percent. Since $\pi^{TC} > \pi^{F}$, we increase the lower bounds from 0 to that level corresponding to $\pi^{F} = (100+0)/2 = 50$ percent. Returning to Step 3 we determine a new distribution restricted by the new trade-off arc bounds.

This procedure continues until a feasible distribution is determined which results in $\pi_n^{TC} = \pi_n^{F}$. Such a distribution would leave the manager equally satisfied between cost of expediting and warehouse service levels. Note, the optimal distribution will cost more than \$1,500 but less than

101,000 and the service level will be more than 0 percent but less than 100 percent. Tables 2 and 3 illustrate the optimal expediting schedule and receiving schedule for our example.

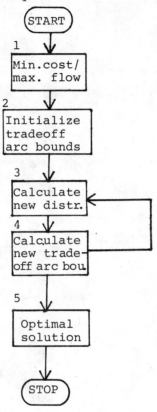

Fig.2. Flow Diagram CST Model Algorithm

Table 2. Expediting Schedule

From To	Warehouse 1	Warehouse 2	Total Supply	Cost
Plant 1				
Heavy	0	1.22	1.22	839.46
Medium	11.42	11.42	22.84	3100.87
Light	3.10	3.10	6.20	210.43
No	23.87	23.87	47.74	405.07
Plant 2				
Heavy	68.61	67.39	136.00	57521.99
Medium	0	0	0	
Light	0	0	0	
No	0	0	0	
Total Demand	107	107	214	62077.82
Cost Satisfaction				68.6%

Table 3. Receiving Schedule

Shipment Arrival	Warehouse 1	Warehouse 2	Satisfaction
On time	68.61	68.61	68.6%
Within 1 week late	80.03	80.03	68.6%
Within 2 weeks late	83.13	83.13	68.6%
Within 3 weeks late	107.00	107.00	100%

Computational Efficiency

The cost-service transportation model algorithm is very efficient.
Since we are using a bisection technique in Step 4 of the algorithm, the
interval of uncertainty ($|\pi^{TC}-\pi^{F}|$) is at least halved each time Step 4 is
entered. Since the original interval of uncertainty is at most 100 percent,
Step 4 is entered only a finite number of times. In fact, it has been
found that the efficiency of the algorithm is only dependent upon the precision desired. Therefore, an upper bound on the number of times Step 4
must be entered is at most $6.8 + 3.38$ X where X is the precision desired.
For example, if we wanted the optimal difference between π^{TC} and π^{F} to be
less than .001 (3 significant digits) it would require at most $6.8 + 3.38$
$(3) = 16.94 \cong 17$ iterations of Step 4. The correlation between the
desired precision and the number of iterations was found to be quite high
($R^2 = .999$), which is to say that 99.9 percent of the variance in the
number of iterations can be attributed to the desired precision. Thus,
the cost-service transportation model algorithm is extremely efficient.

Conclusion

While the cost-service transportation model does not pretend to
explicitly maximize customer service, it does attempt to maximize the
manager's perception of how customers will feel if less than adequate
supplies are available while also maximizing the manager's own feelings
about the added cost of expediting production and shipping. By utilizing
the CST model, the producer will fill warehouse orders at less than desired
levels. This will result in lower inventory levels at the warehouses
thereby reducing total inventory carrying costs. (Details of the model
and computational experience are available directly from the author.)

Proc. First Int. Symp. on Inventories
Budapest, Hungary 1980

APPROXIMATIVE METHODS
OF MULTI-ITEM INVENTORY MANAGEMENT

LADISŁAV UNČOVSKÝ

College of Economics, Bratislava, Czechoslovakia

The question of multi-item inventory models is one of
those problems on which it is possible to show the most important
problem of operations research: the problem of low level of applications in comparison with the sophisticated, but from the
point of practical needs, very problematic mathematical models.

In the last twenty years a new branch of models of
operation research was developed: the mathematical theory
of inventory. On the other hand, the problems of inventory management belong to the most serious problems of management theory and practice all over the world. If we compare the existing
apparatus of mathematical inventory theory with the situation of
management of inventory systems, the great gap between those
two areas is obvious. The reason is perhaps, that new development in mathematical inventory theory means new complicated
models, which need information and data, processing of which
is not worthwhile in comparison to the effects for practice.

One of the most important real problems of inventory management comes from the fact, that real inventory systems are always multi-item systems. In many factories the number of inventory items is at about 20 000 - 60 000. Nevertheless the "classical" inventory theory is a theory of one-item inventory models.
Only in the last years models of multi-item systems were developed. Comparing these models to the possibilities and needs of

practice, it is hardly possible to expect their real application. For the needs of practice less complicated approximate approaches and models are necessary.

If we want to analyse some types of multi-item models from the viewpoint of possible practical application, especially three types of models come into consideration:

1. Models of common reordering of more items of stock. The aim is to combine more deliveries, as a rule, from one factory in order to reduce costs of ordering or in some cases even set-up costs. In the theory the most advantageous approach would be to order all items at the same time with the same lead time. An approach acceptable for practical use is to combine several items into a group of items, which is ordered at the same time. Such types of models were published by Ryžikov /1966/. The model supposes that all items of the group were delivered from one supplier and the costs of order are a linear function of the number of items:

$$C_{A_i} = C_A \left(1 + ig \right)$$

where i = number of items in the group

g = coefficient of equality.

Without demonstrating the whole model which is theoretically and numerically rather complicated, from our point of view it is quite clear, that even after solving all these problems of the model, its applicability is very narrow. Only in the rare cases when really one supplier is delivering all items of the group is it advantageous to use it.

Less complicated are some models, developed by firms, supplying computers in their software for users. The condition, that all items are supplied by one supplier is still valid.

2. Models of modified economic order sizes in case of limitations are the "classical" models of multi-item inventory theory. In the case of limitations on invested money, as in the

case of limitations on total storage space and on aggregate set-up time the mathematical apparatus of finding minimum of the cost function under restrictions by Lagrangean multipliers is used. In this case there is even an interesting interpretation of those multipliers from the viewpoint of economic theory.

On the other side, from the point of practical needs these models hardly can solve the problem of management of multi-item systems. The main problem is, that these models are based on the condition, that all individual optimal order quantities are known, the limitations are set afterwards and optimal quantities are reduced. The number of calculations is even larger than in the case of individual models.

3. Much promising are approaches to multi-item systems modelling based on some economic indices, especially on the turnover rate D and the turnover time D_t /in days/:

$$D = \frac{\text{average stock level /or average invested money/}}{\text{demand /in a time unit/}} = \tag{/1/}$$

$$= \frac{\bar{s}_b}{Z} \quad \text{and} \quad D_t = D \cdot d \tag{/2/}$$

where d = number of days in a time unit /i.e. in a year/.

The use of these indices in some computer oriented inventory management systems, without a use of other mathematical methods, shows that they are effective especially for analytic purposes. So, if

$D \geq C$ the item is dead /where C is a number with value depending on particular circumstances - as a rule between 3 - 10/

by $C \leq D \leq 1,5$ -the item is slowly moving

by $1,5 \leq D < 1$ - the item is normally moving

by $D \leq 1$ the item is moving rapidly.

The advantage of those indices is that they are available nearly in all firms. On the other hand a lot of practical problems are to be solved for their analytical use. Especially the problems of using them for a normative use is important. Other questions are connected with finding values, which influence the indices.

The most intensively studied connections are those of the turnover rate, the reorder quantity and the number of orders. From Eq. /1/ we get

$$D = \frac{Q}{2Z} \qquad\qquad /3/$$

or

$$D = \frac{1}{2r} \qquad\qquad /4/$$

In the literature there are approaches to aproximative models of multi-item systems based especially on correlation between turnover rate and number of orders. | So we may mention the model of J. Murdoch described in Lewis /1970/.

Another interesting approach is based on some remarks of Whithin and on the article of Dellepiane /1967/. The model uses two values: the average stock level $\bar{s}$ or the sum of invested money $\bar{s}_{mi}$ and the number of orders.

$$\bar{s}_i = \frac{Q_i}{2} \qquad\qquad /5/$$

$$s_{mi} = \frac{Q_i P_i}{2} \qquad\qquad /6/$$

where Q_i = reorder quantity of the item i

P_i = price of the item i

and the number of orders

$$r = \frac{Z_i}{Q_i} \qquad Q_i > 0 \qquad\qquad /7/$$

where Z_i = total demand for the i-th item.

We can then formulate the problem

$$\min \sum_{i=1}^{L} \frac{Q_i P_i}{2} \qquad\qquad /8/$$

under

$$\sum_{i=1}^{L} \frac{Z_i}{Q_i} = k_1$$

where k_1 = the given number of orders

and dual problem

$$\min \sum_{i=1}^{L} \frac{Z_i}{Q_i} \qquad Q_i > 0 \qquad \qquad /9/$$

under

$$\sum_{i=1}^{L} \frac{Q_i P_i}{2} = k_2$$

k_2 = given average value of invested money.

By the means of Lagrange multipliers with the primal problem it is possible to find a new distribution of orders and with the dual problem a new number of orders. The product of invested money and the number of orders are in both cases the same.

Some experiments with these models and their further development show good possibilities of using them in some cases.

A precondition of the use of models of this type is that the numbers of deliveries or their size can be influenced. If this is not possible the only controlled variable is morely the total ordered quantity. In such cases for determination of the level of average inventory the most convenient way is to start from the procurement lead time τ and to determine the level of inventory by the equation:

$$\bar{s}_b = \frac{Z_d}{2} \tau \qquad \qquad /10/$$

where τ is the procurement lead time
Z_d = consumption in one day.

This relation is used when $\tau < T$ /where T = cycle between the procurements/.

In case that $\tau > T$ Eq./7/ must be set up as

$$\bar{s}_b = \frac{Z_d}{2} \left(\tau - mT \right) \qquad \qquad /11/$$

where

$$[m] \lessgtr \frac{\tau}{T}$$

i.e. the largest integer less than an equal to τ/T.

In case that T is changing we must sometimes count with the mean value T or the influence of repeated procurements must be taken into consideration by estimation.

Equations /10/ and /11/ are also used with multi-item systems where they are related to the particular items. The particular values are obtained by a one-time computation for each item separately.

Determination of the inventory level on the basis of Eq. /10/ resp. Eq. /11/ touches only average inventory. For determination of safety stock we can use the equations derived on the basis of known stochastic models. When we determine safety stock in case of a large number of items we usually must differentiate according to the importance of the particular items. The ABC rule appears to be a proved criterion of classification here.

The safety stock of the items of the A-group can be determined on the basis of more complicated types of models requiring informations on the distribution of consumption or also on the costs by means of which we can determine the optimal level of safety stock. Using such techniques with the items of group C is usually too claiming.

What comes into consideration is to order all the items according to the value of demand. When there is an appropriate choice of classification intervals we can choose a representant in each interval for which we determine the level of safety stock. This value can then be used for computing of the safety stock for the whole group of items. If this procedure is complicated, too, the safety stock can be determined in group C by a qualified estimation.

The items belonging into group B can be determined according to concrete situations by more exact methods similar to those used for group A or on the contrary by approximate methods

introduced in connection with group C. As particular approximate
methods for this group the techniques based on the differences
of extremal and mean values can be considered.

Because of the reasons of changes in consumption the safety stock can be determined on the basis of the equation

$$s_1 = \left(Z_{d\ max} - Z_d\right) \tau \qquad \text{/12/}$$

or

$$s_1 = \left(Z_{d\ max} - Z_d\right) \left(\tau - mT\right) \qquad \text{/13/}$$

where $Z_{d\ max}$ = maximum daily consumption.

Similarly because of the reasons of fluctuation in procurement lead time the safety stock will be determined as

$$s_2 = \left(\tau_{max} - \tau\right) Z_d \qquad \text{/14/}$$

τ_{max} = maximum length of the procurement lead time.

In case of practical applications the representative character of extremal values must be taken into consideration and
they must be corrected in a way that their use does not result
in an unqualified increase in safety stock.

The total safety stock is then

$$s = s_1 + s_2 \qquad \text{/15/}$$

The total inventory is

$$\bar{s}_c = \bar{s}_b + s \qquad \text{/16/}$$

The turnover coefficient is

$$D = \frac{\bar{s}_c}{Z} \qquad \text{/17/}$$

The turnover coefficient given by Eq. /17/ or the turnover
time P_t are of great importance for the analysis of effectivity
of the work of the supply system. The computation of the real
turnover coefficient can be enclosed into the program systems
for management of multi-item systems in a relatively simple way
and thus a rapid signalisation of irregularities in supply can
be secured.

1. Dellepiane, N.: Metodi di soluzione di problemi di scorte
   senza formulazione esplizita della funzione di costi.
   Note economiche IV, No 2. Torino 1967.
   /Methods of solution of inventory problems without explici-
   te formulation of the cost function/.

2. Lewis, C. D. : Scientific Inventory Control. London, Butterworths 1970.

3. Rishikow, Yu.: Mnogonomenklaturniye zadatschi ob uprawle-
   niyi zapasami. Izwestiya AN SSSR, Tekhnitsheskaya kiberne-
   tika, No 6. Moskva 1966.

Proc. First Int. Symp. on Inventories
Budapest, Hungary 1980

AGGREGATE INVENTORY MANAGEMENT.
A CASE STUDY

JACQUES VANDER EECKEN

Catholic University of Louvain, Louvain, Belgium

I. INTRODUCTION

This paper describes an O.R. study carried out for ABC, one of the major

full-line farm equipment manufacturers in the U.S. (Vander Eecken, 1980).

Using forecasts of annual U.S. tractor industry sales, seasonality of

demand and ABC's market penetration, the model develops optimal ABC dealer

stock levels and stock mix which minimize the cost of lost sales and in-

ventory connected finance and deterioration charges. The model assumes

that ABC's penetration declines at an accelerated rate with declining field

inventory and that optimal inventory levels and profits are quite insensi-

tive to minor errors in the rate of decline, which is estimated from past

experience. Optimal inventory levels and near-optimal inventory ranges for

major product lines are determined by marginal analysis which balances de-

terioration and finance costs against the opportunity cost of lost sales.

It is essential to keep in mind that the final goal of every inventory

study must be to make statements about the total system rather than the in-

dividual items. Management is not and cannot be interested in detail in-

formation but will base the ultimate acceptance or rejection of a proposed

control system on a few characteristics. It is of great importance that

the aggregate evaluation be given in terms which are meaningful to manage-

ment. Typically, management wishes answers to the following types of
questions :

- What will be the average inventory investment ?
- What percentage of the total number of demands per year will be filled
  directly from stock and/or will be lost ?
- How does this compare with present performance ?

To make such an aggregate approach meaningful the following steps must
be carried out (Hausmann, 1962) :

- Given the cost characteristics of the individual products, derive the
  cost function(s) for the whole system and/or a relatively small number
  of meaningful subsystems. Show that these cost functions depend only on
  aggregate quantities.
- Given an overall decision in terms of aggregate inventory levels, trans-
  late this decision into decisions for the individual products.

The Total Inventory Cost Curves obtained in the Tractor Dealer Stock
Model (cfr. infra) pertain to ABC's six major product lines (tractors with
different horsepower engines). From these, optimum inventory decisions
can be made for these major product lines. Using the forecast of the
model-option combination mix, optimum inventory levels can then be computed for all individual models.

II. TRUE INVENTORY HOLDING COSTS

This study estimates the relationship between field inventory levels and
ABC's portion of field inventory costs. The relationship between field
inventory levels and production costs is the subject of another study, the
Divisional Production-Field Inventory Model, which will not be discussed
here.

For each tractor class and each month of the year there exists a field

584

inventory which balances inventory carrying costs against the cost of lost
sales, to minimize ABC's total inventory costs in that month.

A. Holding too much inventory

Primarily incurs :

    A1. The cost of tied-up capital.

    A2. The cost of refurbishing old inventory prior to sale -- i.e., the
        cost of deterioration.

B. Holding too little inventory

Primarily incurs :

    B1. The cost of lost sales.

    A summary follows of how these individual costs were estimated.

A1. Inventory level versus cost of capital

Following competitive practice, ABC finances dealers' stocks up to 12
months. That is to say, the company finances every unit wholesaled until
it is retailed, with a maximum of 12 months.

    The cost of capital sunk in inventory was taken to be the cost of fi-
nancing the average wholesale price through ABC's credit division.

    There will be a cost of capital curve for each horsepower class.

    Figure 1 shows the cost of capital curve for horsepower class I and
was plotted for a cost of .69 % per month (i.e., 8-1/4 % per annum) on a
wholesale price of $ 2,250.

A2. Inventory level versus cost of deterioration

The sophistication of the method chosen to develop this cost curve will
depend on the sensitivity of the over-all cost picture to this cost element.

    The simplest method of incorporating this cost is to assume that a unit in inventory deteriorates by a fixed amount each month, to estimate this amount and to draw a cost line in a similar manner to that for the cost of capital.

A more sophisticated approach would require a detailed analysis of warranty cost and other data to establish the undoubtedly more complex relationship between size of inventory and refurbishing and allied costs.

The curve drawn in Figure 2 is for the horsepower class I and assumes a uniform deterioration of $ 5 per month.

B1. Inventory level versus cost of lost sales

Some assumptions as to market behavior are unavoidable.

In our reasoning, lost sales will at first rise very gradually, as inventory levels are lowered. At this stage ABC's market segment is adequately covered and only a somewhat narrowed choice of uncommon options within each horsepower class may affect sales.

Substantial cuts in inventory, however, will drastically narrow the chance of meeting a specific option demand out of field inventory. A large portion of our customers would then be forced to order from the plant or switch to a competitor.

As field inventory drops to zero, only direct customer orders remain. Presumably, such "mail-order" marketing would not meet the Division's objectives.

Figure 3 expresses these qualitative ideas.

III. TOTAL INVENTORY COST CURVE

The total inventory cost is the sum of the cost of capital, the cost of deterioration and the cost of lost sales.

The Total Cost Curve is U-shaped. The bottom of the trough marks the optimum inventory for the given month and model. Lowering the inventory from this optimum level will result in lost sales and the cost curve will rise steeply. Raising inventory will raise total costs by increasing carrying and deterioration costs.

A typical total inventory cost curve is shown in Figure 4. On the following pages, a quantitative estimate is developed of the Cost of Lost Sales Curve, and the resulting Total Inventory Cost Curve.

IV. ESTIMATING THE COST OF LOST SALES

A cost of lost sales was associated with each inventory level in the following manner.

It was postulated that at each inventory level there was a market share which represented the Best Possible Sales Performance (BPSP) at that inventory level. In most cases the performance would be below this level due to mix, pricing and other factors.

There will also be a market share above which it is not possible to go irrespective of the inventory level - the Absolute Maximum Market Share (AMMS).

It was also postulated that with decreasing inventory the BPSP would fall below the AMMS level at an accelerated rate.

The Market Share difference between these two curves (the BPSP and the AMMS) for each inventory level will be a measure of the sales lost due to holding inventory at that level.

Figure 5 shows these values for the H.P. I class.

V. FITTING THE BEST POSSIBLE SALES PERFORMANCE CURVE (BPSP)

The BPSP curve was fitted around the data points in the following manner (see Figure 6).

Exclusing two data points because of a sales contest and pent-up demand from previous shortages, the Absolute Maximum Market Share (AMMS) level was drawn through the data point with the highest demonstrated market penetration. For very high inventories, the BPSP and the AMMS coincide.

With decreasing inventory, the Best Possible Sales Performance (BPSP) drops off at an accelerated rate. It must pass through at least one actual data point called the Optimum Point in the following way.

1. No other actual data point may lie above the BPSP.

   Otherwise, this would mean that we have actually done better than what we defined as our best performance.

2. At that Optimum Point, the profit contribution related to the BPSP curve must rise at the same rate as the costs associated with finance and deterioration charges.

   This is so for the following reason. Starting from a high inventory level and lowering that level gradually, we reach an optimum level when, with any further decrease, lost sales would erode profits more rapidly than could be offset by savings in finance charges and deterioration expenses. Or conversely, starting from zero inventory, an optimum level is attained when with further increase in inventory the total finance and deterioration expenses would rise more rapidly than the contribution of any added sales.

The following method of locating the optimum point is then "mathematically" guaranteed :

Converting sales in dollars, into average market share and inventory in units into inventory in terms of average months of supply for the entire industry, draw a line which rises at the same rate as the cost of finance and deterioration charges. Move this line up (see Figure 6), until at least one data point lies on it, but none above it. That data point is the Optimum Point. Should two points lie on this line (called the Optimum Profit Line), take the point half way between them.

At the Optimum Point, profits are actually maximized. It is possible that a higher market share could be attained with higher inventory, but to do so would reduce profits since inventory carrying and deterioration costs would rise more rapidly than profits related to higher sales.

The BPSP must then coincide with the AMMS (Absolute Maximum Market Share) for higher inventories, touch the Optimum Profit line in the Optimum Point, and envelope all other data points from above. The BPSP is arbitrarily drawn in Figure 6 at an accelerated downward slope for decreasing inventory.

The exact fitting of the BPSP curve has no critical effect on profits as is shown in a sensitivity analysis associated with the fitting of the BPSP curve around the data points.

We must now convert the relationship, lost market share versus inventory level in months of industry supply to lost sales in dollars versus inventory in units.

Since a month's supply means a different number of units at different times of the year, and since the dollar loss associated with a given lost market share depends on the economic profit of the horsepower class and the size of the market at different times of the year , a different cost curve will exist

a) for each horsepower class

b) for each month of the sales year.

Figure 7 shows the lost sales cost curve for the horsepower class I for the months of January and March.

VI. TOTAL INVENTORY COST CURVE

For each inventory level of the horsepower class I for the indicated months, we can now add the capital cost, cost of deterioration, and cost of lost sales. This results in the true total cost curves. As observed before, these curves will vary for each month and each horsepower class, and are dependent on the industry volume forecast.

From these curves, an optimum of 2,200 units for March and 1,200 units for January is suggested. (see Figure 8)

VII. CONCLUSIONS AND RECOMMENDATIONS

Total inventory profit curves have flat tops, allowing for substantial deviations from optimum inventory levels at little actual cost, i.e. profits are insensitive to inventory fluctuations within considerable limits.

Exceeding the limits can be very expensive. A loss of $ 10,000 per horsepower class amounts to $ 600,000 annually in the U.S. Market alone.

On the assumption that deterioration and capital costs rise linearly while lost sales rise at an accelerated rate with falling inventory, understocking is generally more expensive than overstocking.

Sensitivity analysis shows that possible inaccurracies of the basic data and the amount of arbitrariness of fitting the lost sales curve have no serious effect on the optimal inventory levels.

Production fluctuations can be minimized if we absorb seasonal or other sales fluctuations by adjusting field levels. Within limits this can be done at little actual cost. How field inventory costs are best balanced against production change costs is the subject of a Production/ Inventory Model. A major input to this intertemporal L.P. model consists of the piecewise-linear approximations of the total inventory cost curves, by product category.

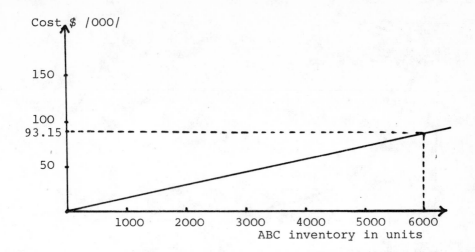

FIGURE 1
Cost of capital curve
/Horsepower Class I/

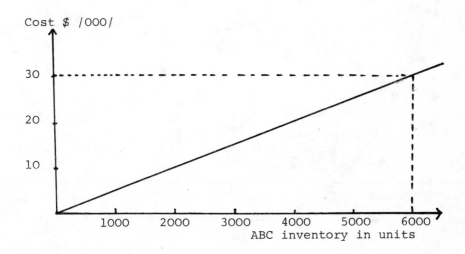

FIGURE 2
Cost of deterioration curve
/Horsepower Class I/

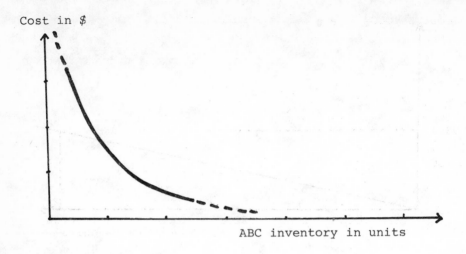

FIGURE 3
Cost of lost sales

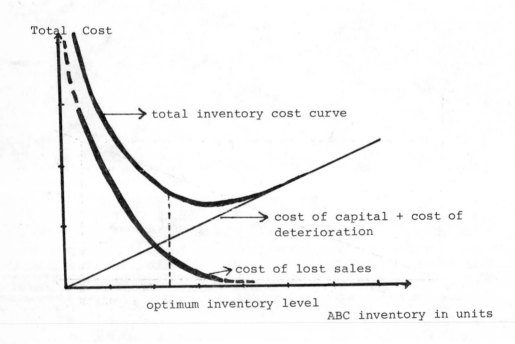

FIGURE 4

Total inventory cost curve

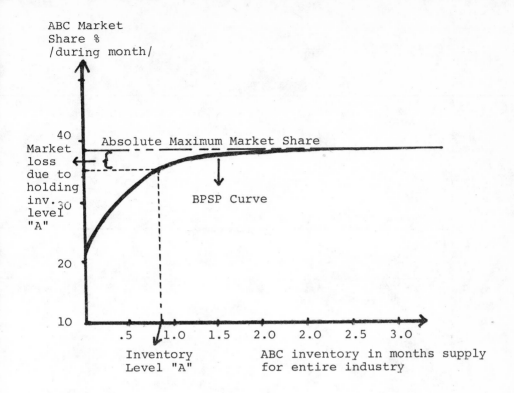

FIGURE 5

Estimating the cost of lost
sales

/Horsepower Class I/

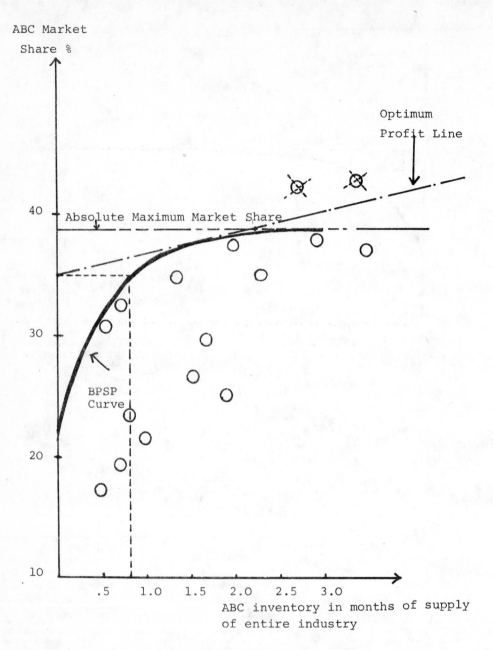

FIGURE 6

Fitting BPSP Curve

/Horsepower Class I/

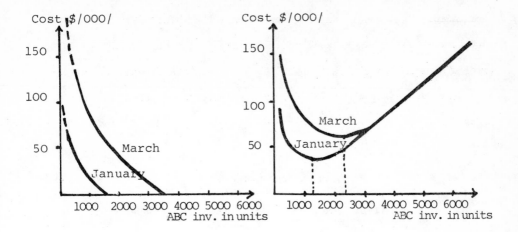

FIGURE 7
Lost sales curve
(Horsepower Class I, January and
March)

FIGURE 8
Total inventory cost curve
(Horsepower Class I, January and
March)

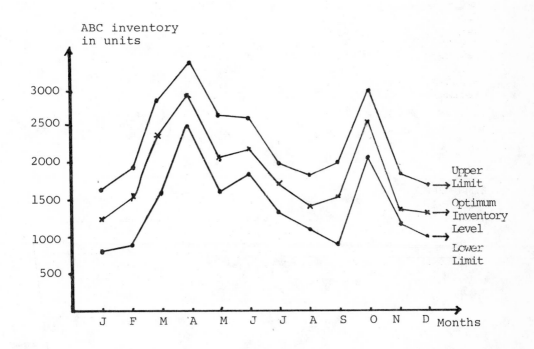

FIGURE 9
Inventory Guidelines
(Horsepower Class I)

Inventory Guidelines can be obtained from the total field inventory cost curves, which can be used manually in planning the monthly production levels, of each product category. Table I gives the recommended guidelines for horsepower class I. They are graphically represented in Figure 9.

TABLE 1

Inventory Guidelines
(Horsepower Class I)

Month	Lower Inventory Level at which Monthly Profits Will Drop $ 3,000 Below Maximum Profits	Optimum Inventory Monthly Profits are Maximized	Upper Inventory Level at which Monthly Profits Will Drop $ 3,000 Below Maximum Profits
January	800	1,200	1,600
February	900	1,450	1,900
March	1,600	2,200	2,700
April	2,450	2,800	3,100
May	1,600	2,000	2,550
June	1,800	2,050	2,550
July	1,300	1,600	2,000
August	1,100	1,400	1,800
September	950	1,500	2,050
October	2,200	2,500	2,850
November	1,100	1,300	1,800
December	950	1,250	1,600

BIBLIOGRAPHY

Hausmann F. , (1962), Operations Research in Production and Inventory Control, John Wiley & Sons, New York, pp. 165.

Vander Eecken J., (1980), Tractor Dealer Stock Model, Tijdschrift voor Economie en Management, Vol. XXV, Nr. 1, pp. 119-135.

Proc. First Int. Symp. on Inventories
Budapest, Hungary 1980

OPTIMAL POLICIES FOR SPARES IN MULTI-ECHELON REPAIR INVENTORY SYSTEMS

PREM VRAT and A. SUBASH BABU

Indian Institute of Technology, New Delhi, India

I   INTRODUCTION

Systems having one or more items stocked at several locations in a hierarchical manner with demands occurring at each
location have been termed multi-echelon inventory systems.
Aggarwal /1974/, Attila Chikán /1970/, Clark /1972/ and Hollier
and Vrat /1976/ have surveyed the literature available on the
multi-echelon inventory systems. Multi-echelon repair inventory system is an important class of multi-echelon inventory
systems. In such systems, the concurrent repair and resupply
is the unique feature.

It is typical of transport organisations, where the re-
coverable items, such as the complete assemblies or engines,
gear boxes, etc. are removed from the facility for repair/over-
haul, after completion of certain hours in operation or upon
premature failure. To minimise the down time of the facility,
it is effective to replace the removed item by a serviceable
spare. Obviously, it would require a reasonable number of
serviceable spares be kept in serviceable spare store, so that,
by and large, an item would be available for fitting into the

facility as and when needed. The failed units upon removal from the facility are sent to the repair facility, located at one or more locations in the system for repair/overhaul.

II THE OBJECTIVES OF THE STUDY

In the existing literature on multi-echelon inventory systems there has been limited research effort related to the multi-echelon repair inventory systems. Even the published reports predominantly centre around military systems considering minimisation of system back-orders as the important and significant criterion, possibly due to its relevance to such systems. But in practice there are many public utilities having this system configuration for which it is necessary to provide the expected service at the lowest overall cost. Hence, in this study, minimisation of total system cost is considered to be the optimisation criterion. Further, minimum total cost has its significance to developing/underdeveloped countries due to social and economical commitments, besides being mission oriented and versatile in application. In this paper an integrated approach which facilitates interplays of various logistics decisions is attempted to achieve overall system effectiveness.

III AN INVENTORY MODEL FOR A TWO-LEVEL REPAIR SYSTEM AND ITS
     APPLICATIONS

The two-level repair inventory system considered consists of a central stockage and repair facility /central depot and workshop/ and a number of subordinate storage locations /sub-

depots/. The repairs are done only at the central workshop
location, while spares are stocked at both the first and the
second echelon locations. Here, the important inventory decisions are to determine the optimal number of spares to be
stocked at each sub-depot and central depot, in order to achieve
the desired system performance. As minimisation of total
system cost is considered to be the necessary criterion, a
total cost model is developed representing this two-level system.

The total system cost consists of the cost associated with
failure /cost of removing and replacing; and cost of normal and
emergency transportation/; the shortage cost /considering loss
of revenue, operational cost and social cost/ and the cost of
holding serviceable and failed items at sub-depot levels and
the cost of repair and the cost of holding serviceable and in-
process inventory at the central depot level. The total system
cost per day is represented as

$$
\sum_{j=1}^{N} [(C_F \sum_{D_j=0}^{n_j} D_j P_j) + (C_T d_{jo} \sum_{D_j=0}^{S_j} D_j P_j) + (C_T \cdot d_{jo} \cdot \alpha \sum_{D_j=S_j+1}^{n_j} D_j P_j)]
$$

$$
+ \sum_{j=1}^{N} [\sum_{D_j=0}^{n_j} P(D_j > S_j) (D_j - S_j)(L_1 + L_3) P((D_j - S_j) \leq S_o) +
$$

$$
P((D_j - S_j) > S_o)((D_j - S_j)(L_1 + L_3) + (D_j - S_j - S_o)(L_2)))] (B_c(1+P) - Q)
$$

$$
+ \sum_{j=1}^{N} [H_j(\sum_{A_j=0}^{n_j} \sum_{D_j=0}^{n_j} (D_j P_j - A_j P_j') + \sum_{E_j=0}^{n_j} \sum_{B_j=0}^{n_j} (S_j + B_j Q_j - E_j Q_j'))] + [\mu R_c]
$$

$$
+ [H_o(S_o + \mu - \sum_{Y=0}^{N_T} Y.P(Y)) + H_o (\sum_k \frac{\lambda}{\mu_k - \lambda})]
$$

where S_j and S_o are the decision variables, as S_j is the spare stock at sub-depot j /1 ... N/, S_o is the spare stock at central depot; D_j is the random demand at depot j with probability P_j; C_F, C_T, H_j, H_o and R_c are unit costs of replacement, transportation, holding at sub-depot j, holding at central depot and repair respectively; B_c, P, Q, α and d_{jo} are respectively backorder cost per day per bus, social cost factor, expenditure per day per bus, emergency transport factor and distance between sub-depot j and central depot; L_1, L_2 and L_3 are the components of total resupply time; μ and λ are expected output and input at central workshop per day respectively; and μ_k and λ_k are respectively the expected output and input per day at the k-th stage of the central workshop. The details of this model are given in /5/.

The repair inventory systems of engine of a large transport corporation operating more than 2000 buses in a major city in India having one central depot and 20 sub-depots is considered as an example. The optimal values of S_j and S_o are evaluated by finding the minimum total system cost. The results are given in Table 1.

This model is also used to investigate the impact of optimal location and the maintenance effectiveness of the repair facility on the spare stock and the system performance. In the system considered, the optimal location of the repair facility is determined using "Rectilinear distance location" problem. Suitable substitutions are made and the optimal inventory policy is identified as before. The results are shown in Table 2. Assuming that the throughput |tile /L_2/ is

600

linearly related to maintenance effectiveness and thus to the cost of repair, suitable evaluations are carried out to investigate the impact of maintenance effectiveness on the total system cost and spare stock.

IV   A SIMULATION MODEL FOR THE TWO-LEVEL SYSTEM

Since the purpose of this study is to investigate the impacts of total logistics, many realistic situations have to be taken into account. This will lead to computational complexity, if mathematical modelling is attempted. Hence simulation methodology is resorted to. Besides, the application of simulation is rarely found in the literature on multi-level repair systems.

A two-level simulation model is developed to represent the system described earlier. The verification and validation of the simulation model are done by comparing its output with that of analytical model, the outputs of various post-stabilised run lengths and various replications. The analysis of variance is used for comparing the replicated outputs and the results are shown in Table 3. This model is used to evaluate optimal inventory policies, the results of which are shown in Figure 1.

V   SIMULATION MODELS WITH CANNIBALIZATION AND TRANSHIPMENT

In complex repair inventory systems, failed parts are replaced by serviceable parts, the available quantity of which is limited not only by budgetary and volumetric constraints, but also by one's inability to forecast with certainty. This leads to disruption of operation of the system till a spare is avail-

able. Under such circumstances, cannibalization, the procedure
of interchanging parts within a generalised coherent structure
is advantageous so as to allocate the shortage to locations,
where it is least detrimental to system performance. The simulation model discussed in the preceding section is incorporated
with the aspects relevant to cannibalization and the optimal
inventory policy is evaluated. The results are shown in Figure 1.

Apart from the situations that call for cannibalization in
a hierarchical setup like multi-echelon repair inventory systems,
imbalance may arise because of the random nature of the system
variables, the stock at some locations may become insufficient
to protect against shortages, whereas other locations may be
overstocked. Under such circumstances it may be desirable to
appropriately redistribute stock among outlets and thereby the
imbalances can often be offset economically. This redistribution is termed as transhipment. The simulation model discussed
in the preceding section is incorporated with the aspects relevant to transhipment and the optimal inventory policy is
evaluated. The results are shown in Figure 1.

Since cannibalization and transhipment can be advantageous-
ly treated jointly, the simulation model is modified appropriately to make it amenable to handle cannibalization in conjuc-
tion with transhipment and the optimal policies are evaluated,
the results of which are shown in Figure 1.

To ascertain whether there is any significant variation
among the results of the above mentioned exercise and to assess
the interacting influence of various factors to help designing

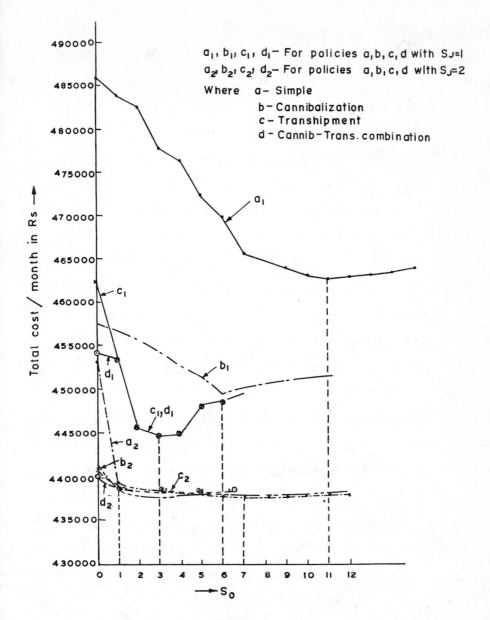

Figure 1   Results of simulation

the most suitable logistics systems, the above results were
subjected to Analysis of Variance. The results are shown in
Table 4.

VI   A THREE-ECHELON REPAIR INVENTORY MODEL

The preceding sections deal with various logistics decisions at strategic, tactical and operational levels, and the
impact of these aspects on the system spare stock and system
performance are investigated. In any multi-echelon inventory
systems, the number of echelons and the system configuration
play a strategic role. To consider this, the existing transport system is considered to be transformed to a three-level
system with one more level consisting of four regional depots
with five sub-depots under each. The regional depots carry out
the initial diagnosis on the failed items and as a result, the
failure is categorised as type I failure and type II failure.
Type I failure is attended to at the regional depot itself,
whereas type II failure is repaired at the central depot. A
mathematical model is developed to represent the total cost for
this system. As in the two-level system, the optimal policies
for spares at sub-depots, regional depots and central depot are
evaluated. The total costs of the three-level system and the
two-level system are compared and shown in Figure 2.

VII RESULTS AND DISCUSSION

From Table 1 it can be observed that the total system cost
per year attains the minimum level /Rs.4,394,257/ when S_j = 2
and S_c = 3. From Table 2, it can be observed that the total

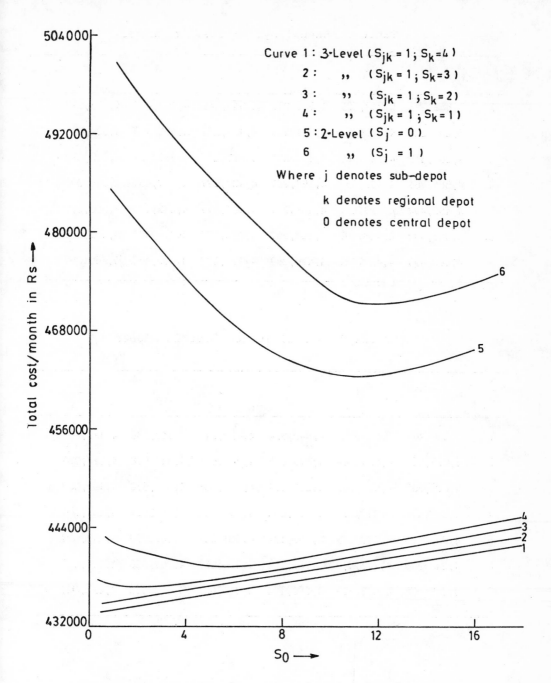

Figure 2   Comparison of 2-level and 3-level systems

Table 1. Annual System Cost in Rupees

S_o \ S_j	0	1	2	3	4	5
1	5,853,271	5,247,329	4,811.073	4,544,449	4,447,457	4,525,097
2	5,289,129	4,825,513	4,531,529	4,407,177	4,452,457	4,530,097
3	4,867,313	4,545,969	4,394,257	4,417,177	4,462,457	4,540,097
4	4,587,769	4,408,697	4,399,257	4,422,177	4,467,457	4,545,097
5	4,450,497	4,413,697	4,409,257	4,427,177	4,472,457	4,550,097
6	4,455,497	4,418,697	4,414,257	4,432,177	4,477,457	4,555,097
7	4,460,497	4,423,697	4,419,257	4,437,177	4,482,457	4,560,097

Table 2. Annual System Cost in Rupees

S_o \ S_j	0	1	2	3	4	5
1	5,560,407	5,024,979	4,643,524	4,416,044	4,342,538	4,423,007
2	5,027,635	4,626,649	4,379,639	4,286,601	4,347,538	4,428,007
3	4,629,305	4,362,762	4,250,194	4,291,601	4,352,538	4,433,007
4	4,365,419	4,233,319	4,255,194	4,296,601	4,357,538	4,438,007
5	4,235,975	4,238,319	4,260,194	4,301,601	4,362,538	4,443,007
6	4,240,975	4,243,319	4,265,194	4,306,601	4,367,538	4,448,007
7	4,245,975	4,248,319	4,270,194	4,311,601	4,372,538	4,453,007

Table 3. Three-way ANOVA for Validation

Source of variation	D.F	M.S.S $/10^{10}/$	Calculated F	Theoretical $F_{/1-\alpha/}$ $/m,n/$ 0.950	0.990	0.999
S_j	4	4.790	307.71	2.05	3.57	5.13
S_o	5	0.070	4.78	2.32	3.26	4.22
Replication	4	0.030	2.07	2.05	3.57	5.13
$S_j.S_o$ Int.	20	0.030	2.37	1.70	2.15	2.68
S_j.Rep.Int.	16	0.005	0.36	1.82	2.32	2.90
S_o.Rep.Int.	20	0.008	0.54	1.70	2.15	2.68
Error	80	0.015				
Total	149					

Table 4. Three-way ANOVA for Comparison of Policies

Source of variation	D.F	M.S.S $/10^{10}/$	Calculated F	Theoretical $F_{/1-\alpha/}$ $/m,n/$ 0.950	0.990	0.999
Policies	3	64.5	48.74	3.16	5.09	8.49
S_o	6	7.4	5.63	2.66	4.01	6.35
S_j	1	484.7	365.88	4.41	8.29	15.38
$S_j.S_o$ Int.	6	2.02	1.53	2.66	4.01	6.35
S_j.Policy Int.	3	75.6	57.12	3.16	5.09	8.49
S_o.Policy Int.	18	1.03	0.78	2.22	3.16	4.73
Error	18	13.1				
Total	55					

system cost is minimum /Rs.4,233,319/ when $S_j = 1$ and $S_o = 4$. This means that the optimum location offers a saving of Rs.160,938 per year by way of reduced total cost and a saving in inventory equivalent to 19 engines /where each engine costs about Rs.35,800/, indicating the impact of locating the repair facility at the optimal location. These savings have a recurring effect, since the decision involved is strategic.

From Table 1 it can be observed that the total annual system cost reaches its minimum level /Rs.4,394,257/ at $S_j = 2$ and $S_o = 3$ with the present level of expected throughput time /42 days/ whereas with the optimal level of 23 days, the minimum cost is at $S_j = 2$ and $S_o = 1$ /Rs.4,386,067/. A reduction of Rs.8,190 only is possible with a marginal reduction in inventory level. But with the expected throughput time kept at 24 days and shifting over to $S_j = 1$, the minimum cost occurs at $S_o = 2$ /Rs.4,400,607/. Although this involves an additional total cost of Rs.6,250 only, the reduction in inventory level is substantial /21 engines/. If the capital investment is constrained, a trade-off between maintenance resources and inventory level can be obtained, which will prove to be beneficial as manpower /which is cheaper in India/ can be increased to reduce spare stock level thus saving scarce capital investment. Such advantageous trade-offs can be investigated by such analyses.

Figure 1 shows the results relating to the simulation exercises, viz., simple cannibalization, transhipment and cannibalization-transhipment combinations. Since the results relating to these four policies exhibit appreciable variations

608

only with $S_j = 1$ and to some extent with $S_j = 2$, only these cases are shown in the figure. It can be seen that the policies of considering cannibalization and transhipment alone and in conjunction offer benefits only with $S_j = 1$, thus indicating the scope to keep less inventory in the system and at the same time reducing the total system cost. The results given in Table 4 statistically ascertain that the variation observed is not due to chance causes alone, but   to significant positive influence of these logistics decisions on the performance of the system, and thus indicate the effect of utilising the re-dundant resources.

Figure 2 compares the total system costs relating to the two-level and three-level systems. These curves indicate the dynamics of the trade-off among various costs of these two systems, thus revealing the merits of the proposed three-level system, in which the system effectiveness can be enhanced by way of reduced system shortages.

VIII CONCLUSION

In this paper a brief account of the research carried out to determine optimal policies in multi-echelon repair inventory system is given. From the results discussed it is evident that the concepts of integrated distribution management con-sidering the interplays of various logistics decisions can have synergic effect on the system performance and the spare stock.

REFERENCES

/1/ Aggarwal S.C. /1974/ A Review of Current Inventory
    Theory and its Applications. Int. Jour. of Prod.
    Res. 12/4/, 443.

/2/ Attila Chikán /1970/ Mathematical Models of Multi-Store
    Systems /in Hungarian/. SZIGMA 3/1/, 43.

/3/ Clark A.J. /1972/ An Informal Survey of Multi-echelon
    Inventory Theory. Nav. Res. Log. Quart. 19/4/, 621.

/4/ Hollier R.H. and Prem Vrat /1976/ A Review of Multi-
    echelon Inventory Control Research and Application.
    Tech. Report University of Birmingham.

/5/ Subash Babu A. and Prem Vrat /1978/ An Inventory Model
    for a Two-level Repair System. Jour. of Engg. Prodn.
    2/2/, 131.

Proc. First Int. Symp. on Inventories
Budapest, Hungary 1980

RESEARCH PORTFOLIO FOR INVENTORY MANAGEMENT AND PRODUCTION PLANNING SYSTEMS

HARVEY M. WAGNER

University of North Carolina at Chapel Hill, Chapel Hill, NC, USA

This paper discusses the current status of implementable inventory management systems from the perspective of what seem now to be the most critical issues needing better resolution. The focus is to identify the still troublesome analytic problems that exist despite the considerable advances in scientific theory and computer software that have occurred in the past two and a half decades and to suggest important knowledge gaps that need the attention of operations researchers.

This paper assumes throughout that an inventory replenishment system's design must reflect the inherent necessity to stock a large number of different kinds of items, easily several hundreds (taking account of different sizes, packages, brands, colors, grades, etc.) and quite often thousands. The design can be complex if it is essential to distinguish different usage environments, characteristics, and replenishment considerations for various items. The paper also assumes that there is an unavoidable uncertainty in specifying the amount of future demand (withdrawals and sales) of stocked items; the system must cope effectively with the fact that demand cannot be forecast with perfect accuracy. Part of the realized fluctuation in demand may be due to seasonal, promotional, or competitive factors. And, finally, the paper assumes that replenishment lead times are sufficiently long, and possibly of uncertain duration, so that safety stocks or buffers are essential in order to achieve a tolerable level of service.

1.   Diagnosing the Potential for Improvement

Consider an enterprise that questions whether there is anything substantial to be gained by replacing its current inventory management system with a new system. To ascertain whether such savings can be realized, the organization embarks on a phased study approach. The first phase assesses the improvement opportunities over the current system and compares them with the projected cost of developing, installing, and operating a new system.

Today, experienced practitioners perform the diagnostic phase with the help of standard techniques of statistical and economic analysis. The effort expended usually consists of looking at a sample of items selected from one or more stocking locations (frequently the selection is not randomly drawn) to assess how these items might have been better managed over, say, the past year or two. The results of this selective analysis must be extrapolated judgmentally to aggregate system measurements to provide rough estimates of overall potential improvements in service, economic contributions, inventory investment, transportation, and other stockage costs.

This initial diagnostic phase itself sorely needs analytic attention by operations researchers. The crux of the difficulties encountered in this phase is that the diagnostic team must produce estimates of future savings and service improvement _without_ actually designing and testing a new system (that effort is to be undertaken in the subsequent phases.)

Typically, inventory models now in the operations research literature assume that at least the parameters of the demand distribution, and often the distribution form itself, are known exactly. In reality, however, the parameters must be estimated from limited data, and the distribution form is usually unrecognizable from the data. Hence, the postulated expected cost function is probably a misspecification (if it is form dependent) and does not reflect an uncertainty adjustment that is due to parameter estimation. Further, the expected cost function usually is expressed in terms of the policy rule parameters, so that computing the optimum value of the function and its sensitivity to different input parameter levels requires solving first for the policy. Thus, the approach involves a two-step calculation, which need not be trivial to perform for a test set of items and their historical data, and is a cumbersome and indirect way to obtain the insights desired.

The analytic device needed is an approximative elementary model that calculates _actual_ system costs and service performance as functions of the annual projected demand level, a simple measure of its predictability (both the inherent variability and the further uncertainty due to having only limited historical information about this variability), as well as of the appropriate economic parameters and _target_ service levels.

2. Resolving Strategic Issues in System Design

When a diagnostic phase indicates that sizable benefits can come from an improved inventory management system, then in the second phase of the study, the organization must design the detailed procedures. Specifically, this task encompasses selecting replenishment algorithms and devising the necessary data processing approaches that prepare the inputs for the algorithms.

Several strategic decisions or assumptions are made in developing an inventory management system. These include which items are to be inventoried, the number and location of the storage sites, and the mode of transportation if items are fabricated at one location and stored elsewhere. The present state-of-the-art in dealing with such strategic issues is to handle them on an individual situation basis.

Multilevel and multilocation probabilistic models now in the operations research literature are only a start toward the needed understanding. Many assume a single item, make restrictive demand and cost postulates, and focus on computing a decision rule. These models typically do not derive an analytic cost expression that can directly provide the trade-offs among strategic alternatives. In order to assess these trade-offs, the analyst must compute the decision rules, which can be quite complicated, and possibly may have to simulate their impact (taking proper account of only the limited amount of historical demand data that are available for parameter estimation.)

It would be helpful to have operations research models that yield even approximate results indicative of the quantitative trade-offs of making

614

different strategic assumptions. Recent research in practical replenishment algorithms suggests that it is possible to devise analytic formulas that work very well under a wide variety of demand environments (in other words, the formulas are economically effective under many different demand settings;) Perhaps it also is possible to find widely useful analytic formulas that can predict the impact of strategic choices. Without such formulas, analysts rely on computer simulations. Although a computer simulation approach is capable of mirroring a highly complex reality, usually simulation is expensive and frequently gives rise to troublesome estimation issues. Perhaps a large portion of the results from a simulation could be obtained more easily from approximations that would require only a fraction of the development and computation expense.

3. Designing an Inventory Replenishment System

What is currently missing from the operations research literature is, for a wide variety of replenishment models, the inventory investment trade-off curve for different service measures (and the associated numerical transformation functions relating one service criterion to another). Some researchers have provided a few specific illustrations of trade-off (or exchange) curves. But even these do not show the trade-off between inventory and replenishment costs versus service when the salient parameters of the underlying demand distributions must be statistically estimated from limited historical information. More specifically, the published works that are meant to exhibit service from given levels of inventory investment and demand variability usually assume that the value expressing demand uncertainty in the replenishment rule, such as the standard deviation or mean absolute deviation of demand forecast error, is known and not statisically estimated. The expected value of service provided, however, can degrade substantially when the variability parameter must be approximated from past data, and there can be a significant observed variation around this expected value even when the measurement period is as long as a year.

Most operations research literature on inventory models is far removed from the data realities existing in actual applications. In particular, one rarely has enough historical data to recognize a parametric form for a demand distribution. State-of-the-art replenishment rules now are available that require as input only the demand mean and variance, presumably estimated from historical observations. But there are some serious technical considerations to be resolved when the statistical estimates of demand parameters are calculated: What is an appropriate procedure for possibly eliminating or transforming outliers (extemely large values) in a historical demand series? How should a "negative" demand be treated? How effective is it to estimate demand variability by use of a regression that is fitted to a set of historical observations (mean and variance pairs) for a sample of items? What are effective replenishment formulas when observed demand is mostly zero valued (for example, 40 weeks of no demand interspersed among 12 weeks of positive demand?) How often should the statistical estimates be updated? When is it warranted to infer that there has been a substantial change in the underlying demand structure, making the use of previous historical data inappropriate? What is

616

a sensible maximum for targeted service, given that the replenishment

formulas are based on statistical estimates with limited data?

As a final consideration, replenishment lead times usually vary with un-

certainty. Although it is possible to adapt many replenishment formulas to

handle the impact of lead-time uncertainty (usually the approach is to in-

flate the value of "variance of demand during lead time"), how to provide a

numerical estimate of lead-time variability is still an art.

4.   Forecasting System Performance

At the end of the initial design phase for the inventory management sys-

tem, the project team proceeds to the validation and testing phase. The ob-

jective is to predict the impact of implementing the system, that is, to forecast

what will happen to inventory levels, service, costs, and distribution

activities.

The crux of the problems is that, in actual situations, the limited amount

and relevance of historical data severly hamper making reliable forecasts of

basically volatile phenomena. Even if all the underlying probabilistic phe-

nomena can be described accurately, the variability in the random elements

preclude low-variance forecast errors for many system aggregates, especially

service. The further uncertainty that is introduced because the parameters

of the probabilistic phenomena must be estimated from limited historical data

adds greatly to the already high variability of the system's performance fore-

casting error distributions.

If the time series of historical demand is sufficiently long, say at least

three years, then the retrospective analysis can be initialized by using the

earlier years of data and simulated by using the more recent years. But

frequently in practice, long histories of demand are not available. If first

the replenishment policy parameters are computed using the limited available

history and then the policy is tested by a retrospective simulation using the

same demand values, the resulting service performance estimate for the sys-

tem typically will be greatly overstated. The paucity of historical data on

variable lead times exacerbates the problem further. Double use of historical

demand (in calculating policies and retrospective simulation tests) leads to

large estimation biases that do not wash out by taking a large sample of items

to provide the systemwide forecast of performance. Further, the historical

data inevitably reflect the influence of previous policies and consequently add

a subtle distortion that is difficult to quantify. Operations researchers have

made slow progress on this set of issues, and considerably more study is

needed.

5. Viewing the Logistics Function Broadly

Many logistics models focus on phenomena at the bottom levels of organiza-

tions. For example, the mathematical models derived over the past three

decades have dealt with replenishment of individual stock items, initial pro-

visioning of spare parts, sequencing of particular orders, overhaul of par-

ticular components, and so forth. A corollary is that these models have

concentrated on single types of logistics decisions (replenishment, procurement, maintenance, transportation) rather than on systems of decisions.

Thus, most operations research models dealing with logistics have not begun by attacking the questions that would be posed by the highest level of management. For example, when senior management is asked to approve a systems design effort to tighten inventory control, it wants an assessment of the possible share-of-market impact of having more or less inventory at each stocking location, which may be geographically removed from the company's customers. When a new product is to be introduced, top management may need to know the economic ramifications of providing for concomitant repair and service, including the costs of parts replenishment. In brief, senior managements typically seek a comprehensive economic analysis of the "big picture."

With rare exception, operations researchers have assumed, almost as an axiom, that to obtain answers to high-level management questions, one must build the analysis from the bottom up. Thus, to predict an inventory system's performance, the researcher has been inclined to add up the performance characteristics of the individual components. Regretably, this bottom-up presumption has not proved to be without severe limitations. One difficulty is the sheer effort involved in ascertaining and then "adding up" the component details. The analytic and data-processing difficulties that arise from starting at the bottom and aggregating up can be severe and can consume much of the analytic staff's time and energy.

It is becoming clearer that these top management issues ought to be modeled in their own right. The potential advantages include faster and more accurate results. Even more importantly, perhaps, starting at the top affords a better opportunity to focus on issues, assumptions, and evaluation criteria that are most relevant to senior management.

6. Conclusion

This paper has attempted to survey the status of inventory management systems from the perspective of critical issues that now need research attention. The research field of inventory management continues to offer stimulating challenges. Despite several decades of intense research effort and considerable success in the commercial application of previous research, many significant advances await exploration by inquiring scientists.

7. References

1. Clark, A.J. (1972): "An Informal Survey of Multi-Echelon Inventory Theory," Naval Research Logistics Quarterly 19, 621.

2. Ehrhardt, R. (1979): "The Power Approximation for Computing (s,S) Inventory Policies," Management Science 25, 777.

3. Gross, D. and R.J. Craig (1974): "A Comparison of Maximum Likelihood, Exponential Smoothing and Bayes Forecasting Procedures in Inventory Modelling," International Journal of Production Research 12, 607.

4. Hayes, R. (1969): "Statistical Estimation Problems in Inventory Control," Management Science 15, 686.

5. Herron, DP. (1978): "A Comparison of Techniques for Multi-Item Inventory Analysis," Production and Inventory Management 19, 103.

6. Hoadley, B. and D.P. Heyman (1977): "A Two-Echelon Inventory Model with Purchases, Dispositions, Shipments, Returns, and Transshipments," Naval Research Logistics Quarterly 24, 1.

7. Kaplan, A.J. (1976): "(R,Q) Inventory Problem with Unknown Mean Demand and Learning," Naval Research Logistics Quarterly 23, 687.

8. Kleinjnen, J. and P. Rens (1978): "IMPACT Revisited: A Critical Analysis of IBM's Inventory Package 'IMPACT'," Production and Inventory Management 19, 71.

9. MacCormick, A. (1978): "Predicting the Cost Performance of Inventory Control Systems by Retrospective Simulation," Naval Research Logistics Quarterly 25, 605.

10. Nahmias, S. (1978): "Inventory Models," in The Encyclopedia of Computer Science and Technology, Volume 9, J. Belzer, A. Holzman, and A. Kent (editors), Marcel Dekker, New York, New York.

11. Peterson, R. and E.A. Silver (1979): Decision Systems for Inventory Management and Production Planning, John Wiley, New York, New York.

12. Roberts, S. and D.C. Whybark (1974): "Adaptive Forecasting Techniques," International Journal of Production Research 12, 635.

13. Wagner, H.M. (1962): Statistical Management of Inventory Systems, John Wiley, New York, New York.

14. Wagner, H.M. (1980): "Research Portfolio for Inventory Management and Production Planing Systems," Operations Research 28.

Proc. First Int. Symp. on Inventories
Budapest, Hungary 1980

ON OPTIMAL INVENTORY CONTROL
WITH VARYING STOCHASTIC DEMANDS

KARL-HEINZ WALDMANN

College of Technology, Darmstadt, FRG

1. Introduction.

We consider a discrete review single product dynamic inventory model. In each period we will allow for a distribution of demand which is partially determined by the demand observed so far. The model will enable us to describe e.g. (1) inventory control under classical assumptions (independent demands, identically [arbitrarily] distributed in the infinite [finite] horizon case, (2) inventory control with seasonal and /or trend effects, (3) inventory control under uncertainty (i.i.d. demands depending on an unknown parameter).

The inventory model to be introduced may be described by the following (structured) sequential decision model in the sense of e.g. Hinderer /197o/, Schäl /1975/.

Let $S \times T$ be the state space, and let $D(s) \in A$ be the set of all admissible actions in state $(s,t) \in S \times T$. If one observes state (s,t) and picks action a, there is a cost $r(s,t,a)$ and transition occurs to state $(s^{\times} = g_1(a,Y_t)$, $t^{\times} = g_2(t,Y_t))$ according to the outcome of a random variable $Y_t \in X$ with distribution q_t depending on t.

Let $S = A = \mathbb{Z} := \{\ldots,-1,o,1,\ldots\}$ $[S = A = \mathbb{R} := (-\infty, +\infty)]$, $D(s) = \{a \in A, a \geq s\}$. Interpret $s_n[a_n]$ as the stock on hand prior to [after] placing an order at the beginning of period $n \in \mathbb{N} := \{1,2,\ldots\}$. An order placed is delivered instantaneously. We assume the stock on hand at the end of period n is $g_1(a_n,Y_{t_n}) \leq a_n$ with $g_1(\cdot,x)$ assumed to be nondecreasing for any $x \in X = D(o)$. Let T be a compact metric space. Interpret $t_n \in T$ as parameter underlying the distribution of demand in period n. We assume that $t_{n+1} = g_2(t_n, Y_{t_n})$ for period n+1 is determined by t_n and the demand observed in period n. We make use of Veinott's reduction to only fixed order costs from the beginning. Thus, let $k : T \to \mathbb{R}^+ : = \{x \in \mathbb{R}, x \geqq o\}$ denote the fixed order costs, and $G : A \times T \to \mathbb{R}$ the expected holding and shortage costs in order to define $r(s,t,a) = k(t)\delta(a-s) + G(a,t)$, where $\delta(o) = o$, $\delta(x) = 1$, $x > o$.

We will use the total cost criterion. We allow for a state-dependent discount factor $\beta(t) \in (o,1)$, $t \in T$. A decision rule $f \in F = \{f : S \times T \to A | f(s,t) \geqq s$, f Borel measurable} is thought of as a stationary policy specifying action $f(s,t)$ to be taken in state (s,t). We call f optimal if it is optimal with respect to the total cost criterion (e.g. Schäl /1975/).

We are interested in a natural extension of the well-known (s,S)-order-policy. A decision rule $f_{(z,Z)} \in F$ is called (z,Z)-order-policy, if there are Borel measurable functions $z, Z : T \to A$ with $z(t) \leqq Z(t)$, $t \in T$ and

$$f_{(z,Z)}(s,t) = \begin{cases} Z(t) & s < z(t) \\ \\ s & s \geqq z(t), \quad t \in T \end{cases}$$

In section 2, we will give sufficient conditions for the optimality of a (z,Z)-order-policy with

$$-\infty < \inf_{t \in T} \underline{z}(t) \leqq z(t) \leqq Z(t) \leqq \sup_{t \in T} \overline{Z}(t) < \infty$$

where the bounds $\underline{z}(t)$, $\overline{Z}(t)$ will result from assumptions (C1), (C2) below. Finally, in section 3, we will apply our general inventory model to the practical situations mentioned above.

2. Optimality of a (z,Z)-order-policy.

Remember that T is compact. Further, assume G, k, β, $g_1(\cdot,x)$, $x \in X$ to be continuous, g_1, g_2 to be Borel measurable, and $q(t,\cdot) : = q_t$, $t \in T$ to be a transition probability. Moreover, we state
(C1) (i)   there is an $\widehat{Z}(t) \in A$ with $G(\cdot,t)$ nonincreasing for $a \leqq \widehat{Z}(t)$ and
           nondecreasing for $a \geqq \widehat{Z}(t)$

(ii) $\lim_{a\to\pm\infty} G(a,t) > G(\hat{Z}(t),t)$, $t\epsilon T$

From (C1) and the continuity of G we easily infer the existence of $\underline{Z}(t)$, $\underline{\underline{Z}}(t)\epsilon A$, $t\epsilon T$ with $\underline{Z}(t) \stackrel{\leq}{=} \underline{\underline{Z}}(t)$ and $G(a,t) > G(\underline{Z}(t),t) = G(\underline{\underline{Z}}(t),t) < G(a',t)$ for all $a < \underline{Z}(t)$, $a' > \underline{\underline{Z}}(t)$. It follows as in Waldmann /1980/, Lemma 2.1 that $\underline{Z}_0 := \inf_{t\epsilon T} \underline{Z}(t)\epsilon\mathbb{R}$.

(C2) (i) $\lim_{a\to-\infty} G(a,t) > k(t) + G(\underline{Z}_0,t)$, $t\epsilon T$

(ii) $\lim_{a\to+\infty} G(a,t) > \beta(t)k(t) + G(\underline{\underline{Z}}(t),t)$, $t\epsilon T$

From (C2) and the continuity of G we infer (a) the existence of $\underline{z}(t)\epsilon A$, $\underline{z}(t) \stackrel{\leq}{=} \underline{Z}_0$ being the smallest one with $G(\underline{z}(t),t) \stackrel{\leq}{=} k(t) + G(\underline{Z}_0,t)$, $t\epsilon T$, and (b) the existence of $\bar{z}(t)\epsilon A$, $\bar{z}(t) \stackrel{\geq}{=} \underline{\underline{Z}}(t)$ being the largest one with $G(\bar{z}(t),t) \stackrel{\leq}{=} \beta(t)k(t) + G(\underline{\underline{Z}}(t),t)$, $t\epsilon T$. Note that $\underline{z}_0 := \inf_{t\epsilon T} \underline{z}(t)\epsilon A$, $\bar{z}_0 := \sup_{t\epsilon T} \bar{z}(t)\epsilon A$ (Waldmann /1980/, Lemma 2.1)

Finally, we have to introduce a concept of convexity. Following Schäl /1976/, let $\hat{k}\epsilon\mathbb{R}^+$, ζ an extended real number, $\hat{\phi} : S\to\mathbb{R}$ nondecreasing. Then $u : S\to\mathbb{R}$ is said to be $(\hat{k},\zeta)$-convex with respect to $\hat{\phi}$ (w.r.t.$\hat{\phi}$) if for $s_1 < s_2 < s_3 \epsilon S$, $s_2 \stackrel{\leq}{=} \zeta$

$$u(s_2) \stackrel{\leq}{=} u(s_1) + [\hat{k} + u(s_3) - u(s_1)](\hat{\phi}(s_2) - \hat{\phi}(s_1))/$$
$$(\hat{\phi}(s_3) - \hat{\phi}(s_1))$$

As usual we set $o/o = o$.

(C3) there are $\phi_t : S\to\mathbb{R}$, nondecreasing, such that
    (i) $G(\cdot,t)$ is $((1-\beta(t))k(t), \bar{Z}_0)$-convex w.r.t.$\phi_t$, $t\epsilon T$

    (ii) $\phi_{g_2(t,x)}(g_1(\cdot,x))$, $x\epsilon X$ is $(o,\bar{Z}_0)$-convex w.r.t.ϕ_t, $t\epsilon T$

(C4) $\int q_t(dx)k(g_2(t,x)) \stackrel{\leq}{=} k(t)$, $t\epsilon T$

If $G(\cdot,t)$, $t\epsilon T$ is convex (in the usual sense), then, by choosing ϕ_t, $t\epsilon T$ linear but not constant, (C3) is fulfilled. For additional remarks to the

concept of $(\hat{k},\zeta)$-convexity the reader is referred to Schäl /1976/, Waldmann /1980/.

Theorem 2.1.

Assume (C1) to (C4). Then there is an optimal (z,Z)-order-policy with

(i) $\underline{Z}_0 \lessgtr Z(t) \lessgtr \bar{Z}(t) \lessgtr \bar{Z}_0$

(ii) $\underline{z}_0 \lessgtr z(t) \lessgtr \underline{Z}(t)$, teT

The proof is a copy of Waldmann /1980/, theorem 4.1. There compactness of
T may be weakened in the following way.

Theorem 2.2.

Let T be a complete separable metric space only (not assumed to be compact),
let $\sup_{t \in T}\{\beta(t)\}<1$, $\quad \sup_{t \in T}\{k(t)\}<\infty$, $\quad \sup_{t \in T} \sup_{a \in A_0}\{|G(a,t)|\}<\infty$
for all compact sets $A_0 \in A$, and let (C1) to (C4) hold with $\underline{z}_0$, $\bar{Z}_0 \in A$. Then
there exists an optimal (z,Z)-order-policy with (i) and (ii) as in
theorem 2.1.

An optimal $(z.Z)$-order-policy may be computed by minimizing the right hand
side of the optimality equation of dynamic programming (e.g. Schäl /1975/,
theorem 5.3).

3. Applications.

Remember that g_1 describes the stock on hand at the end of a period. It
covers two well-known cases, the back Jog case, i.e. $g_1(a,x) = a-x$, and
the lost sales case, i.e. $g_1(a,x) = \max\{0,a-x\}$, $a \lessgtr 0$. In this section, we
will demonstrate applicability of our general model by adapting T to known
inventory models.

Example 3.1.

Let the demands X_1, X_2,... in periods 1,2,... be independent and identically distributed random variables. Then we may let T consist of one
element only, provided the costs and the discount factors are stationary.

Example 3.2.

Let the demands X_1,..., X_N in periods 1,...,N, where $N \in \mathbb{N}$, be independent

random variables with distributions $q_1,\ldots,q_N$. It is well known that a
finite stage dynamic program may be reduced to a stationary infinite stage
dynamic program by extending the state space S to S x {1,...,N} and by
defining the transition law suitably. Thus, let T = {1,...,N} ,
$g_2(t,\cdot)$ = min{t+1,N}, t∈T. Set $\beta(N)$ = o. If we suppose that the stock left
over N periods can be discarded with a cost V_o : S→$\mathbb{R}$, then we have to replace $G(\cdot,N)$ by $G(\cdot,N) + \beta(N)\int q_N(dx)V_o(g_1(\cdot,x))$ before setting discount
factor $\beta(N)$ equal to zero.

Example 3.3.
Let the demands X_1, $X_2,\ldots$ in periods 1,2,... be independent random
variables with distributions $\tilde{q}_1$, $\tilde{q}_2,\ldots$ underlying periodical fluctuations
of fixed length L∈$\mathbb{N}$, i.e. $\tilde{q}_{mL+1}$ = $\tilde{q}_1$, $1 \leq 1 \leq L$, m∈$\mathbb{N}_o$: = $\mathbb{N}$∪{o}. Then
we may choose T = {1,...,L}, $g_2(t,\cdot)$ = t + 1, $1 \leq t < L$, $g_2(L,\cdot)$ = 1, pro-
vided the costs and discount factors are stationary or underly the same
fluctuations.

Example 3.4.
Let the demands X_1, $X_2,\ldots$ be a homogenous Markov chain with state space
X = $\mathbb{N}_o$ and let the costs and discount factors be stationary. Then we may
choose T = X and $g_2(t,x)$ = x. The procedure may immediately be extended
to a m-dependent Markov chain with m > 1. For the special case of a first
order autoregressive demand process, optimality of a (z,Z)-order-policy
has been shown by Kalin /1979/.

Example 3.5.
Let the demands X_1, $X_2,\ldots$ in periods 1,2,... be independent and identically distributed random variables with distribution of demand $\tilde{q}_m$,
known up to an unknown parameter m of a compact metric space M. Let $\tilde{\beta}\in(o,1)$
denote the discount factor, $\tilde{k} \geq o$ the fixed order cost, and $\tilde{G}_m$: S→$\mathbb{R}$, m∈M
the expected holding and shortage costs. We will discuss three methods for
operating the uncertainty about m, (1) minimum constrast estimation of the
unknown parameter, (2) Bayes estimation of the unknown parameter, and (3)
Bayes adaptive control. For convenience, we will restrict attention to the
discrete demand case.

(1) minimum constrast estimation.
Following Pfanzagl /1969/, a family of functions h_m : X→$\mathbb{R}$, m∈M is called

a family of constrast functions, if

(i) $\sum_X q_{\widetilde{m}}(x)|h_m(x)| < \infty$, $\widetilde{m}$, $m \in M$

(ii) $\sum_X q_m(x)h_m(x) < \sum_X q_m(x)h_{\widetilde{m}}(x)$, m, $\widetilde{m} \in M$

We assume $m \mapsto h_m(x)$, $x \in X$ to be continuous. For $n \in \mathbb{N}$, a map $\varphi_n : X^n \to M$ is called minimum contrast estimate, if, for all $x_1, \ldots, x_n$, $\varphi_n(x_1, \ldots, x_n)$ minimizes
$$\frac{1}{n} \sum_{i=1}^{n} h_m(x_i).$$

Minimum constrast estimation reduces to maximum likelihood estimation by choosing $h_m(x) = -\ln \widetilde{q}_m(x)$, essentially. See Pfanzagl /1969/ for details. We may choose $T = \mathbb{N} \times X^{\mathbb{N}} = \mathbb{N} \times X \times X \ldots$, $g_2((n, x_1, x_2, \ldots), x) = (n+1, x_1, \ldots, x_n, x, x_{n+2}, \ldots)$, $q_{(n, x_1, x_2, \ldots)} = \widetilde{q}_{\varphi_n(x_1, \ldots, x_n)}$, $G(\cdot, (n, x_1, x_2, \ldots)) = \widetilde{G}_{\varphi_n(x_1, \ldots, x_n)}(\cdot)$, $\beta(t) = \widetilde{\beta}$, $k(t) = \widetilde{k}$, $t \in T$.

(2) Bayes estimation of the unknown parameter. Bayes procedures allow for the demands observed so far as well as a prior distribution on M. The estimation of the unknown parameter bases on a posterior distribution on M and a loss function suitably chosen. Therefore, T, $g_2, \ldots$ may be defined as in (1).

(3) Bayes adaptive control. For period n, the distribution of demand is given by $q_t(x) := \int t(dm)\widetilde{q}_m(x)$, $x \in X$, where t denotes the posterior distribution on M with respect to the demands $x_1, \ldots, x_{n-1}$ observed in periods $1, \ldots, n-1$. Moreover, the expected holding and shortage costs are given by $G(\cdot, t) := \int t(dm)\widetilde{G}_m(\cdot)$.

Therefore, T is given by the set of all probability measures on M. Each $t \in T$ describes the prior information about m, and $g_2(t, x)$, $x \in X$ the posterior information about m transformed according to the Bayesian formula. Note that T is compact and metrizable whenever M is compact and metrizable (cp. Parthasarathy /1967/, § II). For a more detailed description of the law of motion in a Bayesian decision model the reader is referred to Rieder /1975/, Van Hee /1978/, or applied to Bayesian inventory control, to Waldmann /1976, 1979/ and the literature cited there.

References

[1] Hinderer, K. (197o):   <u>Foundations of Non-stationary Dynamic Programming with Discrete Time Parameter,</u>
Springer-Verlag, Berlin/Heidelberg/New York

[2] Kalin, D. (1979):   Zur Optimalität von (z,Z) Strategien bei
Berücksichtigung von Bedarfstrends,
to appear in Mathematische Operationsforschung und Statistik

[2] Parthasarathy, K. R. (1967):<u>Probability measures on metric spaces,</u>
Academic Press, New York/London

[3] Pfanzagl, J. (1969):   On measurability and consistency of minimum
contrast estimates.
Metrika, 14, 249 - 272

[4] Rieder, U. (1975):   Bayesian dynamic programming.
Adv. Appl. Prob. 7, 33o - 348

[5] Schäl, M. (1975):   Conditions for Optimality in Dynamic Programming and for the Limit of n-Stage Optimal Policies to be Optimal.
Z. Wahrscheinlichkeitstheorie verw. Gebiete
32, 179 - 196

[6] Schäl, M. (1976):   On the optimality of (s,S)-policies in
dynamic inventory models with finite horizon
SIAM J. Appl. Math. 3o, 528 - 537

[7] Van Hee, K. M. (1978):   <u>Bayesian control of Markov chains,</u>
Mathematical centre tracts 95, Amsterdam

[8] Waldmann, K.-H. (1976):   Stationäre Bayessche Entscheidungsmodelle
mit Anwendungen in der Lagerhaltungstheorie,
Dissertation, TH Darmstadt

[9] Waldmann, K.-H. (1979):   Numerical aspects in Bayesian inventory
control,
Zeitschrift f. Operations Research 23, 49-6o

[1o] Waldmann, K.-H. (198o):   On the optimality of (z,Z)-order-policies
in adaptive inventory control,
Zeitschrift für Operations Research 24, 61-67

INDEX

Page numbers refer to the first page of the article in which the item appears.